THE MONTHLY EPIC

A HISTORY OF CANADIAN MAGAZINES

the MONTHLY EPIC

A HISTORY OF CANADIAN MAGAZINES
1789 - 1989

FRASER SUTHERLAND

Fitzhenry & Whiteside

The Monthly Epic

© 1989 Fitzhenry & Whiteside
195 Allstate Parkway
Markham, Ontario L3R 4T8

Editors: Beverly Sotolov-Anderson
          Frank English
Designer: Arne Roosman
Picture editor: Jane Affleck
Typesetter: Jay Tee Graphics Ltd.
Printed and bound by The Lakeside Press, U.S.A.

Canadian Cataloguing in Publication Data

Sutherland, Fraser
  The monthly epic: a history of
  Canadian magazines

Includes bibliographical references.
ISBN 0-88902-897-4

1. Canadian periodicals – History.
2. Periodicals, Publishing of – Canada
– History. I. Title.

PN4904.S87 1989   070.5'72'0971
C89-094798-8

ACKNOWLEDGEMENTS

I would like to thank the Ontario Arts Council for a grant that defrayed some of my research expenses. This book had its origins in a survey of literary magazines I did for *The Globe and Mail* in 1985, and thanks are due here to the *Globe's* book editor, Jack Kapica, and to its librarian, Amanda Valpy. I am also indebted to Dinah Hoyle, former executive director of the Canadian Periodical Publishers' Association, and the staffs of the following libraries: Pictou-Antigonish Regional Library, especially Fred Popowich; McLennan Library, McGill University; Robarts Library and Thomas Fisher Rare Book Library, University of Toronto; Metropolitan Toronto Central Library; the library of Ryerson Polytechnical Institute. Others who helped in various ways include: Robert McDougall, Ottawa; Adrian and Luci King-Edwards, Montreal; Roy MacLaren, Jack Batten, Marjorie Harris, Rachel and Allan Wyatt, as well as David and Lynn Warren, all of Toronto; and Doug Bennet of Mississauga.

I am responsible for all sins of conception, commission and omission, and expect, indeed hope, that my readers will remind me of them.

PERMISSIONS

TABLE OF CONTENTS

INTRODUCTION

PORTABLE RECEPTACLES

A magazine appeals to the miscellaneous imagination. No matter how specialized, the best magazines suggest the fullness and variety of life.

From the beginning, magazines were that way. Although the modern general magazine is considered to have its origin in 1731, when Edward Cave founded *Gentleman's Magazine*—''a Monthly Collection to store up, as in a Magazine, the most remarkable Pieces...''—its antecedents are much earlier, and indeed date from the invention of moveable type and the printing press.

If books and the earliest newspapers preceded magazines, the anthologizing sensibility that produced the sixteenth-century newsletters, chapbooks, pamphlets, almanacs and jestbooks (with their ''quick answeres,'' ''Merrie Tales'' and ''pleasant conceites'') later adapted itself to editing magazines. A similar instinct led seventeenth-century booksellers to annotate listings in their catalogues—ancestors of the periodicals calling themselves reviews.

As magazines distinguished themselves more sharply from books and newspapers, the editor and man of letters emerged, whose professional function was to bring, as Joseph Addison said, ''philosophy out of closets and libraries, schools and colleges, to dwell in clubs and assemblies, at tea tables and coffee houses.'' The magazine publishers, editors and writers became not merely mediators between academe and the emergent middle class, but merchants of information and entertainment. Once this professional class was in place, it needed only the industrial revolution—mechanical, chemical and electrical technologies—to make mass-circulation magazines possible.

Printing itself was both the parent and coeval of the industrial revolution. The use of moveable type and the printing press anticipated the division and specialization of labour. In turn, magazines, no less than books and newspapers, were transformed by the barrage of inventions in the nineteenth and twentieth centuries, at the same time as they were being rivaled and even dwarfed by competing media.

Yet, like print itself, magazines have proven to be a remarkably resilient and enduring medium. No sooner has each new medium—motion pictures, radio, television, computer networks—arrived than the death of print has been predicted. Yet each has been accompanied by a swarm of magazines. Printed magazines are still with us, and abundantly so, adapting where they can, in one guise or other surviving, even prospering.

The computer is one example of how print remains triumphant. Initially computers were supposed to offer a paperless, printless universe. The opposite is the case: with their printouts, computers generate *more* paper. In keeping computer users up to date, magazines are more vital. Apple Corporation, the big U.S. computer maker whose "icons" were seriously heralded as a means of superceding alphabetic characters, had financial troubles in early 1985. The company largely recovered by promoting the desktop publishing of, among other things, magazines. Computers have augmented, not abolished, print.

The influence of other media on magazines is pervasive: photography, films, TV and computers have made magazines more visually dramatic; photography, films, radio, TV and computers have shortened readers' attention span. But the influence also flows the other way, as attested by the numberless radio and TV programs that style themselves "magazines." Even situation comedies owe their formulas to the humorous short stories first written for magazines. Full-colour printing, photojournalistic formats, weekend supplements and sectional design changes in newspapers came directly from magazines, and magazine stylistics shaped and coloured newspaper feature writing.

Despite the haziness of its parameters, the magazine form has remained amazingly constant. Digests and newsmagazines were not invented respectively by DeWitt Wallace and Henry Luce, but can be discerned before the start of the eighteenth century. A Dr. Johnson come to life would be at home—though doubtless temporarily perplexed by the subject matter—scrutinizing a scholarly quarterly of today.

What, then, *is* a magazine? Although there is no precise or comprehensive definition—the *Canadian Encyclopedia*'s "paper-covered publications issued at regular intervals, at least 4 times a year" will not do—the maze of definitions that the *Oxford English Dictionary* supplies for the word in applications that have nothing to do with print suggest the printed magazine's essential qualities: it is a warehouse, depot, storehouse, or ship; an ammunition chamber for a repeating rifle; "a portable receptacle containing articles of value."

How does one measure a magazine's performance? Circulation, meaning how many copies reach people, is one measure, but a far from precise one. Readership is another: how many readers does each copy, lying around a barber shop or a living room, actually find? But these represent brute statistics. Another, more incalculable measurement is through a magazine's influence. This, in fact, may be the most important measure, because it means that the magazine is changing the world.

Depending on whether one is talking about location, readership, format, frequency, production, distribution, or contents, magazines come in a bewildering array of categories.

With much blurring and overlapping, magazines are situated midway between the book and the newspaper. The magazine's homage to the book is sometimes detectable in the arranging of issues in "volumes," and editors speak of magazines as "books," as in "back of the book." Librarians lump magazines, newspapers and annuals as "serials." By nature, an annual or even a quarterly is closer to being a book than a newspaper; the reverse is true of a weekly. But the typical and, in my view, ideal frequency for a magazine is once a month.

Magazines may be centred in a city, region, or nation. "Scholarly journals" appeal to the highly educated; "quality" magazines to the thoughtful; "mass" magazines to a broad social spectrum; "class" or "lifestyle" to a particular social group characterized by its peculiar mentality or pattern of leisure. For the literary minded, there are those small, irregular journals unhelpfully termed "little magazines." In varying degrees of specialization, magazines may align with their readers' gender, intellectual interest or educational level, social status or buying habits, business or profession or hobby, political, artistic or sexual inclination.

An interesting distinction may be made between "men's" and "women's" magazines. As evolved in the United States, men's magazines were dedicated to pursuits identified as distinctively male: military or outdoors adventure, hunting, fishing; then later to the excitement of *indoor* living: being a playboy. Women's magazines, though, have sought to touch all aspects of their audience's lives. For all their emphasis on feminine fashion and beauty, such magazines, treating women as more consonant and coherent human beings, have had much more general appeal.

Another, more specialized distinction may be made between literary and "little" magazines. A "little" magazine is usually literary, but a literary magazine is not always "little." To add to the confusion, both are small. Directed by one dynamic editor or a small group, the little magazine promotes an artistic style, idea or tendency. In the past its funding came not from a university or government arts council, but from a generous patron, or was painfully scraped from other private sources. Wherever published, little magazines have been forums for some of this century's most important literary art.

Magazines are usually divided into "consumer" and "trade." As the name implies, consumer magazines are directed to the ordinary buying public: the shopper who browses at a newsstand, the homemaker who checks his or her mailbox. Available by subscription or by single copy, they are distinct from the trade magazines that, through "controlled circulation," arrive free of charge at an office, factory or workplace and that depend entirely on advertisements to keep them in business.

Even this division is not so simple. Controlled circulation magazines delivered to selected households may resemble general consumer magazines. Indeed, the chosen method of distribution leads to further categories. Magazines may be sold on a newsstand or through subscriptions, arrive gratis, or be given away as a bonus or promotion for some other enterprise. Via an electronic network they may skid across a computer monitor and then be printed out on the consumers' office printer. They may come included with a newspaper or a society membership.

Physical appearance and style of presentation suggest other categories that change with each new technical innovation: for example, the "roto," much employed for newspaper supplements, was a product of the rotogravure printing process. A magazine may be a "pulp," printed on cheap newsprint, or a "glossy," whose coated paper can register a rainbow of colours. But a "slick" refers to the formulaic gloss of its *contents*. In format a magazine may be a self-explanatory "newsmagazine," or a "digest" that cannibalizes books and other magazines.

Whatever its form, the magazine has, or ought to have, a personality. It follows that a magazine has a life cycle, though it is tough to determine whether at any given point it is in its infancy, puberty, maturity or senility—or whether, to put it another way, it is in a stage of barbarism, civilization or decadence. But, as *Esquire*'s editor Harold Hayes said in 1969, "To land on the moon is to make news which transcends form: the faster the word gets out, the better. But once established, the fact moves from the simple to the complex, begging interpretation of a thousand varieties. A magazine's promise is the delivery, on a fixed schedule, of its own version of the world, its special attitude toward the reader."

The creation of a magazine is a complicated collective activity that resembles filmmaking or ballet as much as it does anything connected with cold print.

Keeping in mind that roles are often combined and that conflicts are traditionally endemic, a simple chart of a magazine's internal power structure and energy flow starts at the top (or bottom, depending on one's viewpoint) with the *owner* or *backer*, either a person or corporate entity, in any case the source of ongoing financing and the final repository of profit or loss. Next comes the *publisher*, who directs the magazine's overall policies, production, distribution, marketing, content, the hiring of key personnel. The *editor* selects and presents the magazine's visual and verbal content. The *artist*, loosely defined as the writer, photographer, or illustrator, supplies that content.

None of these people exists in a vacuum, and the magazine itself exists in a vortex of pressures and influences. Such external and interrelated forces continually affect the magazine's course. Through censorship or other restrictions on the flow of information, through control of taxes, customs tariffs and postal rates, through disposition of grants and subsidies, the *government* is a powerful influence on anything a magazine does.

Business, with its ebb and flow of supply and demand, impinges at many points: the cost of paper, ink and all the other raw and finished materials that go into producing the magazine and the level of wages, are all reflected in the prices charged by typesetters, printers and binders. And that's just the production. When it comes to distribution, discounts given to wholesale distributors and newsagents, and costs entailed in acquiring new subscriptions through advertising or direct-mail campaigns are reflected in the magazine's physical appearance.

One commercial force is important enough in modern magazine publishing to deserve a separate category. The magazine may depend heavily on *advertising*, which exists in a commercial and government vortex of its own. The ratio of ads to editorial matter decisively affects how the magazine looks. If the economy is down, the advertiser doesn't support the magazine; if the magazine continually offends what the advertiser considers its customer or clientele, again, the advertising is withheld.

Because the magazine communicates, the magazine's *readership* is an ongoing and pervasive force. All the people inside the magazine's structure, and the advertisers outside it, want the reader's full attention. But the flow is not one-way. Readers may telephone or write letters in protest or praise, organize boycotts or fund-raising campaigns, crowd or spurn the newsstand, take out or cancel a subscription. All these are ways of telling the magazine what it's doing right or wrong. So sensitive to the public's taste have many recent magazines become that few big changes occur without their being dictated or confirmed by a survey.

To cope with such external forces the magazine may set up other power structures and energy flows in cooperation—or sometimes rivalry—with the editorial process: accounting, circulation, advertising sales, market research. The potential for political and economic conflict both inside and outside the magazine is quite simply enormous. It's a wonder, in fact, that magazines ever get produced.

This is a history of Canadian magazines. As such, it is an account of the dreams or delusions writers, editors and entrepreneurs have had of creating thriving national consumer magazines.

My book gives an account of the first two hundred years of Canadian magazines. In doing so, I chart an endeavour that has grown from a single publication, the *Nova Scotia Magazine*—founded in 1789 and the first magazine to appear in what is now Canada—to an industry that in 1987, according to Statistics Canada, employed 10,000 persons, published 5,000 titles and spent more than $500 million on goods and services.

After the hesitant beginnings of magazine publication, Victorian journals, though they may have sought wide popularity, essentially found an audience which shared the view that periodicals should be edifying and morally improving. By the early twentieth century the prevailing tendency was away from such middle-class magazines and toward mass media, in the process diluting demands on the reader's time and energy and applauding, indeed reinforcing, popular taste. Then, in the rage for ever larger circulations, the mass, as it were, collapsed of its own weight. At the same time as magazines often became part of multimedia conglomerates, they became "targeted" to specific segments—city, lifestyle, business—of the overall audience. In a century, the pendulum had swung from class to mass and back again to class.

Apart from the fact that what we regard as chronology is more or less a convenient fiction, these developments were neither neat nor linear, and the start or stop of any given period is largely indefinite. What I call "The Era of Edification," beginning before Confederation, may have ended with the demise of the *University Magazine* in 1920, or with that of the *Canadian Magazine* (not to be confused with earlier magazines of the same name, or the later weekend supplement) in 1939. The mass magazine era—which I have broken down into "From Class to Mass" and "The Weight Collapses"—may have started when J.B. Maclean renamed his class magazine *Maclean's* in 1911, or with the inception of the *Star Weekly* about the same time. Its termination can be traced as late as 1980 with the death of *Today*, the last mass-circulation supplement. "The Uncommon Market" can be traced back to the 1960s, or to the start of such representative magazines as *Toronto Life* or *Harrowsmith*. But all these are only loose-fitting labels.

Besides the chronological movement, there was also a spatial one specifically tied to population growth. At first magazine publishing was centred in the Maritimes. Then it was Montreal's turn before the centre shifted westward to Toronto after the mid-nineteenth century. There, for good or ill, it took up seemingly permanent residence. In the Prairies and British Columbia—or for that matter in Newfoundland—magazines were never as important as newspapers, and indeed the only general-interest regional magazine to achieve national status, the *National Home Monthly*, in its early years Winnipeg's *Western Home Monthly*, ended up being edited in Toronto. Canadian magazine publishing has been much more centralized than was the case in the United States. When, in this book, a magazine's location has not been given, it should be assumed that it's Toronto.

The first task of anyone attempting a book of this scope is to draft a statute of limitations. Certainly a history that encompasses more than a hundred years and thousands of magazines cannot claim to be more

THE

NOVA-SCOTIA MAGAZINE

AND

COMPREHENSIVE REVIEW

OF

Literature, Politics and News.

BEING A COLLECTION OF THE MOST VALUABLE ARTICLES WHICH
APPEAR IN THE PERIODICAL PUBLICATIONS

OF

GREAT-BRITAIN, IRELAND AND AMERICA;

WITH

VARIOUS PIECES IN VERSE AND PROSE NEVER BEFORE PUBLISHED:

VOLUME II.

For JANUARY, FEBRUARY, MARCH, APRIL,
MAY, AND JUNE,

1790.

Lectorem delectando pariterque monendo.   Hor.
Scriptus et in tergo necdum finitus.   Juv.

HALIFAX:
PRINTED FOR THE EDITOR, BY JOHN HOWE
M.DCC.XC.

than a superficial survey. But the reader has a right to know the criteria by which I have chosen to emphasize some magazines at the expense or even exclusion of others.

Although there is sometimes a passing glance at others, I have dealt only with magazines published in English. To state the obvious fact that English is the majority language is not to deprecate the importance to their communities of periodicals published in, say, German, Yiddish or Ukrainian, much less those of French Canada.

The last is too important a topic to leave without a few brief comments. In one sense, Acadian or Québécois magazines are simply regional magazines with all the advantages and limitations of the category. In another sense, such magazines may express national aspirations in Quebec or, to a lesser extent, New Brunswick. Though different in degree and kind, and occurring at different times, such nationalism partly parallels that common to English Canada. If the English-Canadian nationalist has on occasion resisted Britain and the United States, the Quebec variety has at times resisted the cultural imperialism of Paris and the commercial opportunism of English Canada.

Yet in Quebec, magazines have had an advantage in possessing a more compact, homogeneous audience. If, at this writing, the titles of Quebec's leading-circulation magazines—*Sélection du Reader's Digest* and *Châtelaine*—mirror U.S. or English-Canadian ones, it is arguable if, for example, any magazine in the rest of the country has had the comparable social impact of the independentist *Parti pris* of Gérald Godin and Paul Chamberland in the 1960s, or the reformist *Cité libre* of Gérard Pelletier and Pierre Trudeau. And it is difficult to imagine an English comic or satirical magazine with a circulation of more than 70,000 like *Croc*.

Although *Quebec Magazine*, chronologically the second Canadian periodical, was bilingual, magazines in Canada have proceeded on separate linguistic tracks. The usual exceptions are those of national airlines, government departments, crown corporations and the odd cultural venture. Apart from the question of collective will, the demands on the magazine's space are prohibitive. But there are lots of examples in which magazines have been published in tandem, with or without overlapping content. The nineteenth century had its *Canadian Illustrated News* and *L'Opinion publique*, the twentieth century its *New World Illustrated* and *Nouveau Monde*, *Chatelaine* and *Châtelaine*, *Maclean's* and *Actualité*, formerly *le Magazine Maclean*.

To save reviewers trouble, I will list a few other omissions or diminutions. This is not primarily a history of the Canadian magazine industry in its narrowest economic sense, nor is it in the widest sense a history of Canada as viewed in the pages of magazines, though elements of both are here to provide a necessary context. Because I am using words not pictures to convey my message, the visual and tactile qualities of magazines, the contributions of art directors and artists, including photographers, are much more important than I have been able to show. In stock market parlance, I have underweighted technology. I am interested in the editorial content, not advertisements— except when the latter impinge on the character of the former.

For many fine writers, magazines have offered, in Val Clery's phrase, "a temporary limb of opportunity between the well-paid tyranny of daily newspapers and the ill-paid longueurs of literature." My emphasis, however, is on editors as the vital links between the writer and his or her public. I have tried to keep the recounting of office politics to a necessary minimum. Magazine politics is not *always* so vicious as that described in U.S. poet Kenneth Fearing's 1946 crime novel *The Big Clock*. In this story, a magazine's megalomaniacal proprietor is the murderer of his bisexual mistress, and one of his staff writers is given an assignment to find the missing witness, whom he knows to be himself.

Murderous or not, my biases will be everywhere apparent, though not, I hope, to the extent of evading or distorting relevant but uncomfortable facts. Although my own background is literary, I have only skimmed the surface of "little" or cultural magazines. As it happens, and unusually, these tend to be relatively well-documented elsewhere. I have merely touched on entire categories of magazines: the farm press (some of which, like the *Family Herald and Weekly Star*, had extraordinarily long lives); regional and city magazines; trade, union, government, corporate or professional organs (a few, like the Hudson's Bay Company's *The Beaver* or the *Imperial Oil Review*, have led a semi-autonomous existence, and sometimes have had worthy contents of general interest); religious or fraternal magazines; Canadian editions of U.S. magazines; student rags and scholarly quarterlies; specialized magazines in particular and controlled circulation ones in general; newspaper weekend supplements. Most of these categories deserve books of their own. None exist.

In the case of this book, the implied undervaluing of controlled circulation magazines and weekend supplements deserves explanation. Regardless of whether a magazine makes money, I believe that it is most prized when it costs the reader a sacrifice, however minor, and leads to a commitment of time and mental energy. However valuable a free magazine may be intrinsically—and at its best, *Quest*, for example, was valuable—only half the communication process is taking place when the reader stakes nothing more than an idle hour.

In the case of weekend supplements—the *Star Weekly*, *Weekend* and *The Canadian*—or other magazines that are included with the price of a newspaper, the situation is similar though not identical. Here the magazine is taken as part of a package, and its fortunes are tied to its parent's economics. However similar to magazines outside the newspaper package, the supplement lives a kind of half-life. Just as a magazine should make demands on its reader, so it should seem to the reader to be an independent and self-sufficient entity.

The titles I have emphasized, like *Maclean's* and *Saturday Night*, share most of the following characteristics: they endured (were published for at least 10 years); they made an impact on their audience and influenced their industry; they had general if not necessarily mass appeal; they were distinctive in some way; they tended to be monthlies; they aspired to be national.

Maclean's and *Saturday Night* cut across several of the chronological divisions I've set out, but I've also included separate chapters on several Victorian magazines, both to demonstrate the variety and vitality of the period and to banish any delusion that a vigorous Canadian magazine industry dates only from the 1976 passage of Bill C-58. This federal legislation disallowed income tax deduction of advertising in the U.S.-owned *Time* and (initially) *Reader's Digest*. I have also paid considerable attention to women's magazines, especially *Chatelaine*. Besides the fact that they seek their audience in more than half the adult Canadian population, they have also been among the most commercially successful of all magazines.

The magazines I have devoted most space to are those identified with particular persons, whether they were writers, editors, publishers or backers. One thinks of George Desbarats of the *Canadian Illustrated News*; J.W. Bengough of *Grip*; Edmund Sheppard, B.K. Sandwell and Robert Fulford of *Saturday Night*; Doris Anderson of *Chatelaine*; Ralph Allen of *Maclean's*. Some, like Goldwin Smith and J.B. Maclean, were associated with entire groups of magazines.

In the case of these persons, the perception was probably close to the reality. But it should be reiterated that producing a magazine is a collegial activity. As an aside, it's worth noting that titles on a magazine's masthead are notoriously unreliable guides to individual responsibilities and power structure, especially in the editorial sphere. An "associate editor," for example, is often code for staff writer, "contributing editor" a flattering term for free lancer, and much of the day-to-day power—assigning articles, directing traffic flow—may reside with the managing editor.

Having said that, it is possible to create a sociological profile of those who owned or published the largest Canadian magazines up to the present. There is a depressing uniformity to them. Like others in the corporate elite, they tended to be white male Protestants of Scottish, English or Irish extraction. If their families were not particularly affluent, they usually had useful friends. These men frequently attended private schools and university, especially the University of Toronto or McGill. Depending on the period, they belonged to the right clubs

(Empire, National, Canadian) and fraternal orders (Masons, the Orange Lodge) and in the nineteenth century were keen off-hours volunteers in the militia.

The editors were a more varied lot, though they, too, were always white and usually male. However, it is fair to say that women have been more prominent in editing magazines than has been the case for newspapers and books. The men or women were often Protestants, and some of them even the children of ministers. In the nineteenth century they were British immigrants or came from the Maritimes, Anglo-Quebec or Ontario. In the twentieth century they often gravitated to Toronto from the Prairies and British Columbia. Interestingly, many did not complete university or even high school.

Even among those who did not call themselves nationalists, the ideal of a national magazine, whether commercial or "quality," has been a constant in Canadian life since Confederation. Until recently, magazines have been the only national press Canada has had, an unsurprising fact for a country so farflung that, next to the Soviet Union, it is the largest on earth.

Though the style owes something to the famous prayer of St. Francis of Assisi, an elegant delineation of a national magazine's essential qualities was given by *Maclean's* editor W.A. Irwin in 1951 to the Royal Commission on National Development in the Arts, Letters and Sciences on behalf of the Periodical Press Association:

> By its very nature, the national magazine must be all that the name implies, else it withers.
>
> To live, it must reflect the larger vision.
>
> To serve its constituency, it must reveal the nation to itself, not only in its parts but as a unity.
>
> Of provincialism, or parochialism, it can have no part.
>
> Always it must maintain the open forum where opposing views can be aired and thus bring men to better understanding.
>
> Where there is strife, it must record the facts, the issues of the conflict; but always as the interpreter whose concern is the national interest—never as a partisan leader.
>
> Being above party, it must deal fairly with men of all parties; by so doing it brings to its readers the means to appraisal of current affairs unclouded by party bias.
>
> Being a means to self-criticism of the people it serves, it must speak bluntly of national misdemeanour.
>
> To be read it must be vital; which is to say it must make drama of the stuff of life.
>
> And since its field is the nation, it must perforce unfold the story of a nation's progress.

Which is why the national magazine is at once a means to a people's self-understanding and a dynamic national force.

Given that the magazine press became a national force, and that magazines like *Maclean's* and *Saturday Night* attained the status of national cultural institutions, it was bound to clash with the political, cultural and economic imperatives of its giant neighbour. With a population one-tenth that of the United States, three-quarters of whom live within 150 kilometres of the U.S. border, Canada has been blessed and cursed by the overwhelming proximity of American media. As the Report of the Senate Special Committee on the Mass Media (1971) puts it, "Geography has made us continentalists, whether we like it or not. Pride and history and the land have made us Canadians a people who, almost by definition, resist the cold logic of economics in favour of the warmer logic of the heart."

Admittedly, Canada has a special problem with the United States. Then again, the entire world has a special problem with the United States. It is militarily and culturally the most powerful nation on earth. Inevitably the dominance of its magazines on newsstands and subscription lists has been blamed for the demise of numerous Canadian publications, and given rise to much lamentation and more than one government enquiry.

The more strident free enterprisers have enquired why Canadian magazines have not attempted to capture the U.S. market. Actually, a few Canadian mass-circulation entrepreneurs *have* made headway elsewhere, but only by locating in another country and shrewdly deploying adopted formulas. The main exports have been personnel: from the earliest days Canada has sent a steady stream of writers, editors and publishing executives to Britain and the United States, and their contributions are worth a book by itself. To answer the original question, the reason Canadians usually have not sought to capture the U.S. market is that they have trouble enough capturing their own.

Yet this book is not intended to be another chord in a familiar dirge. If anything, its message is one of hope. Despite the fact that magazine publishing has always been a precarious business everywhere, a significant number of Canadian magazines has lasted more than a century. Even measured in mass circulation, all is not lopsided. At this writing, *Chatelaine*'s Canadian paid circulation is greater than that of the four leading U.S. women's magazines *combined*, and *Maclean's* outsells *Time* and *Newsweek* put together. If one went by relative populations and multiplied by ten the circulation of Canadian magazines to determine their U.S. equivalents, more than twenty would circulate at above a million copies.

This is the first comprehensive history of Canadian magazines. Until now there have merely been useful surveys like Paul Rutherford's *The Making of the Canadian Media*, anthologies, or scrapbooklike compilations. The only book to faintly resemble a history is Noel Barbour's *Those Amazing People: the Story of the Canadian Magazine Industry 1779-1967*, a former advertising man's posthumously published chronicle that, although a starting point, is haphazard and error-prone. Canadian magazines are practically unknown outside the country. In a recent *Encyclopedia Britannica*, some twenty words of the 15,000-word entry on magazines are devoted to Canada.

Suffice it to say there's a vacuum. In tracing the back files of magazines, I have sometimes felt like the bibliographer who wittily noted that "...*The Torch*, 'The Monthly all Canada Loves,' has been found in a fragmentary condition at the University of Saskatchewan only." When not identified in the text, my sources—books and magazine and newspaper articles—are listed in the bibliography. Not listed are such indispensable reference books as the *Canadian Who's Who*, the *Canadian Encyclopedia*, the *Dictionary of Canadian Biography* and their predecessors, as well as the successors and predecessors of the *Oxford Companion to Canadian History and Literature*. My researches have been handicapped by the lack of anything like an equivalent reference book on the personalities, events and institutions of the Canadian media, not merely about periodicals but newspapers, films, radio, television, computer networks and book publishers.

Edward Cave, the printer, publisher and editor of *Gentleman's Magazine* and the man who first used "magazine" in its present sense, styled himself "Sylvanus Urban." As a boy, Cave had been forced out of grammar school when the schoolmaster blamed him for robbing the master's hen roost. With meagre savings, Cave started his magazine and made it a great success. He first published parliamentary debates and later led in using original as opposed to reprinted contributions. Deceptively slow and sluggish, Cave rarely left his office. His friend and contributor Samuel Johnson said, "[Cave] never looked out of his window, but with a view to the *Gentleman's Magazine*." And another contemporary observed that "Upon the first approach of a stranger, his practice was to continue sitting, a posture in which he was ever to be found, and for a few minutes, to continue silent; if at any time he was inclined to begin the discourse, it was generally by putting a leaf of the Magazine, then in the press, in the hand of his visitor, and asking his opinion of it."

To magazine editors as obsessed as Edward Cave, and especially to good ones, this book is dedicated.

PART ONE

THE ERA OF EDIFICATION

In the era of Victoria and Edward, magazines were seen and saw themselves as instruments of moral and pedagogic improvement. Man was perfectible, and the periodicals he read would help perfect him. In the view of George Stewart, a magazine "is a great national university, diffused, without loss of effectiveness, throughout an entire nation."

At first the national status of magazines was doubtful. Writing in 1868, Henry James Morgan defended his listing of newspaper editors and writers in his *Bibliotheca Canadensis* by saying, "In our young country ...our principal newspapers may be considered as holding no unimportant position in Literature. We have not many periodicals of a purely literary kind; and the morning journal may be said to be as much a literary as it is a political organ.... Besides, the majority of our journalists have been men of superior education and literary culture, who have themselves written works and pamphlets. A very distinguished author has recently remarked 'that a hundred years hence the newspaper will be the only possible book.'"

In the short or even long term the distinguished author was proven wrong, but his prediction was not wildly unfounded. The nineteenth-century line between newspapers and magazines was blurred. Newspapers published much poetry and fiction, but usually left cartoons to magazines. Egerton Ryerson's *Christian Guardian*, the most important church paper before Confederation, resembled a magazine in some respects and was in fact the forerunner of the United Church's *New Outlook* and *Observer*. *Canadian Illustrated News* and *Grip* regarded themselves as weekly papers, and *Saturday Night* began as one.

Yet magazines, not books or newspapers, would emerge as the national medium. Magazines were advertised and reviewed as if they were books, and, for the writers of books, magazines were an indispensable bridge to their public. After or during a newspaper apprenticeship, most fiction writers began by contributing stories to magazines—for copyright reasons these were usually British or U.S.

magazines—and continued to produce short stories and serials while appearing between hard covers.

The causes for magazines' prominence were relatively simple. Newspapers, confined to cities and towns and often blindly partisan, could not present a judicious national overview. Books lacked the magazine's continuity, usually only presented one writer at a time and were beset by confused copyrights and unsatisfactory economies of scale. With its built-in advantages, a magazine could be all things to all Canadians.

"All" is used advisedly. The founders and editors of magazines were class-conscious, although the class consisted not of the aristocracy, but of those who, through diligence and intrinsic moral worth, proved themselves eligible for membership in an elite. The magazine's "mission," said George Stewart, "is to stimulate and afford expression to the higher thought and tastes of a people, to bring the country's best thought, under the most favourable circumstances and in the most attractive form, before the best classes of the country's readers—the classes upon whom the shaping of the political, social, intellectual and even industrial future of the nation most largely depend."

Stewart and his colleagues seemed to presuppose these natural leaders ensconced in armchairs, puffing pipes and nodding gravely or smiling gently in approval. For Stewart a good magazine is "reserved for the quietest half hours of comfortable leisure, when the mind is in the most receptive mood and most ready to respond to facts and arguments attractively and candidly presented, or to the quiet touches of beauty, humour, pathos that lighter literature furnishes...."

Ribaldry was not part of the lighter touch; even humour had its moral applications. Which is not to say that the Victorians were humorless. Besides *Grip*, their comic journals included *Punch in Canada*—founded in 1848 in Montreal, it was the first to run regular political cartoons—, *Diogenes, Grinchuckle, The Grumbler* and, in the Edwardian period, Knox McGee's *Moon*. Describing the struggle between the sacred and secular and how they might be reconciled was a constant in the higher-minded magazines, especially those published by the churches but also in the popular press. It was the age, after all, of *Origin of Species*, and the clergymen sometimes had to end in arguing that evolution itself was part of God's ongoing design. The relationship between science and theology was tirelessly examined and, only slightly less so, the gap between rich and poor. The latter was linked to the search for utopian panaceas like Henry George's Single Tax, and not just in J. W. Bengough's Single-minded *Grip*. As W. J. Rattray noted in *Belford's Monthly* in May 1878, "Whatever sins of omission or commission may be fairly laid to the charge of our age and generation, indifference to the momentous problems of human life and destiny is not one of them.... Men are far too seriously-minded in their search after truth...to treat the solemn questions which persistently obtrude themselves for solution on every age, with levity, scorn or a flippant superficiality."

In creating this edifying spectacle, the influence of the Scots Presbyterians, those relentless educators of themselves and others, cannot be overstated. With the merger of its sects in 1875, the Presbyterian church was until 1925 the largest Protestant denomination. Many if not most of the printers, publishers and editors were Scots and had all the characteristics of that enterprising, argumentative race. As Elizabeth Waterston has pointed out, Scotland created a battalion of literary exemplars: Robert Burns for lyric poets, Sir Walter Scott for historical romancers, Macaulay and Carlyle for the writers of "Great Man" and thesis history, Robert Louis Stevenson for those who wrote adventure stories for children, J. M. Barrie for those, like Ralph Connor and L. M. Montgomery, who limned regional idylls.

Literary taste tended to be conservative. Some editors like Graeme Mercer Adam deplored "the intellectual vivisection methods" of Henry James and W. D. Howells and "the loathsome realism and putridity" of Emile Zola and Anatole France. As Claude Bissell says in the *Literary History of Canada*, in poetry the Canadian critic and writer disliked "technical experimentation, the intellectual, any suggestion of the commonplace and the realistic." Desired "were elegance of diction, nobility of sentiment, and clarity and picturesqueness of observation."

Despite the bows made to poetry and fiction, what the editors took most seriously was intellectual debate. The great issues—the conflicting claims of science and religion, the overriding question of whether Canada would meld, even merge with the United States—were endlessly debated. In retrospect, free traders and protectionists, annexationists and imperialists all seem utopians. The free traders and annexationists imagined that a north-south flow would produce nothing but prosperity. The imperialists supposed not just that their country would have a magnificent future, but that it would become a partner or even leader in an ever more glorious British Empire.

One debate was about how magazines themselves would take form. The imperialist (and future knight) J. G. Bourinot, for many years the clerk of the House of Commons and a frequent contributor to periodicals, wrote that

> No doubt there is room in the Dominion for a magazine combining the features of 'Blackwood,' the 'Contemporary' and the 'Quarterly Review'; that is to say, poetry, fiction, criticism, reviews of topics of the day, and in fact, original literary effort of the higher order, which, though mostly ephemeral in its character, must have much influence for the time being on the culture and the education of the public mind... if such a venture is to succeed hereafter it must have behind it sufficient capital to engage the assistance of

the best Canadian writers, who now send their work to American and British periodicals. Such a magazine must be carefully edited, and not made the dumping-ground for the crude efforts of literary dabblers or for romantic gush and twaddle....

That Bourinot, an expert on constitutional history, could comment authoritatively on literary matters was typical. Victorians could comment authoritatively on *anything*. They were not narrow specialists, but took the world's mind and actions for their domain. Literature was not just poetry, fiction and *belles lettres*, but anything in which verbal analysis and narrative held sway. Limited as their aesthetic conceptions may have been, they did see humanity as a whole, and the best magazines they founded and wrote for had the same consonance and comprehensiveness.

Pre-Confederation Clusters

If the magazines prior to Confederation were usually short-lived, at least there were a lot of them. Solemnly conceived, desperately hopeful, they were pioneering and they knew it. The age of advertising had yet to arrive, and they relied on pitifully few subscribers. To a modern reader it is a confusing world of innumerable titular changes and contributors who were anonymous, pseudonymous or hidden behind initials. Colonial, these magazines heavily reprinted material from Britain and the United States, at the same time as they were tracing the faint outlines of a new culture.

Magazines in what is now Canada were not spontaneously generated by Confederation. If Confederation marked the birth of a big nation it also tolled the death of little ones. The eastern British North American colonies were, after all, embryonic independent nations, and ones whose periodicals aspired to serve self-contained publics.

The first magazine to appear in British North America was Halifax's *Nova Scotia Magazine and Comprehensive Review of Literature, Politics and News* (1789-92). It reached 200 subscribers—including judges, surgeons and the Bishop of Nova Scotia—and was printed on a wooden screw press by John Howe, father of the famous Joseph, who also sold it over the counter of his office (eighteenth- and nineteenth-century bookshops were often run in conjunction with a press and journal). Edited by the Reverend William Cochran, the magazine had some local content, though much of it was reprints. There then followed in the Maritimes such initiatives as the *Nova Scotia and New Brunswick or Historical, Literary, Theological and Miscellaneous Repository; Acadian Magazine and Literary Mirror; New Brunswick Religious and Literary Journal; The Pearl; Halifax Monthly Magazine;* and *Nova Scotia New Monthly Magazine*. Most had varying titles and were located in Halifax or Saint John. None lasted more than two years.

The most interesting of these, because of the people behind them, were *Mayflower, or Ladies Acadian Newspaper* (1851-2) and *Provincial, or Halifax Monthly* (1852-53). Mary Eliza Herbert, the nineteen-year-old daughter of an immigrant Irish blacking manufacturer, published *The Mayflower* as a thirty-two-page publication in May 1851, seeking readers in those wishing "to roam a while in the flowery fields of romance—to hold communion with the Muses." As the first female editor of a magazine in British North America, Herbert narrowly beat out Mary Jane Lawson *née* Katzmann. At twenty-four, Katzmann, the poetical daughter of a German and his New England wife, became the *Provincial*'s editor. Aiming for a wider audience—male as well as female—she drew more from regional writers than had Herbert and had higher cultural and social ambitions for her audience.

In Quebec the first magazine had been started in 1792, the bilingual *Quebec Magazine (Magasin de Québec; ou, Recueil utile et amusant de littérature, histoire, politique, etc., particulièrement adapté à l'usage de l'Amérique.* In its less than two years of life the Quebec City periodical was edited by Alexander Spark on the press of the Neilson family, prominent in Quebec printing for the next half-century or more.

In the Canadas, magazines trailed, doglike, the growth of population, though the potential audience was always small. In the 1840s, the market for a Toronto periodical might extend east to Montreal and south to New York State, but was mainly confined to the province's half-million widely dispersed inhabitants. The later distinctions among farm, church and literary magazines were smudged. Agricultural papers were the first family magazines, and the Anglican, Presbyterian and Methodist church journals often had literary content. Still, there were certain fast divisions between country and town. Those who aspired to gentility might turn to magazines with titles like the *Canadian Gem and Family Visitor*; the more practical-minded might opt for the *Canadian Agricultural Journal* (Montreal, 1848-68).

Whatever the magazine's tack, the power inherent in the press had come permanently, if at first precariously, to reside along the Great Lakes and the southern edge of the Laurentian Shield.

In Montreal, the foremost city, Samuel Hull Wilcocke ("Lewis Luke MacCulloh, Esquire") edited the iconoclastic *The Scribbler: A Series of Weekly Essays on Literary, Critical, Satirical, Moral, and Local Subjects, interspersed with pieces of Poetry* (1822-27), which shifted to nearby Rouses Point in Vermont after its first year. In Montreal, Nahum Mower printed the monthly *Canadian Magazine and Literary Repository* (1823-25), which amounted to four volumes of almost six hundred pages each, and David Chisholme, a Scot, edited the quarterly *Canadian Review and Literary and Historical Journal* (1824-26), which published "The Rising Village" by Oliver Goldsmith, grand-nephew of the playwright and novelist who had been Dr. Johnson's friend.

MONTREAL.

The publisher of the Literary Garland, *"A fragrant wreath, composed of native flowers, hoped that engravings of native scenes would also attract readers.*

In Upper Canada, where John Strachan attempted the *Christian Examiner* (1819-20), the first illustrated periodical was the *Canadian Literary Magazine* (1833). Published by George Gurnett in York (Toronto), each issue had an engraved portrait, "the first we believe," said the editor, "...ever engraved in Upper Canada—engraved too on Canadian stone, and from thence, by means of a Canadian press, transferred to Canadian paper."

Counting both Canadas, before 1850 there were magazines in Montreal, York, Kingston, Brockville, Cobourg and Hamilton. From a literary viewpoint, the most important was the *Literary Garland* (1838-51) in Montreal, published by John Lovell and edited by his brother-in-law John Gibson. Whichever literati the Canadas possessed were published in the *Garland*: John Richardson, Charles Sangster, Rosanna Leprohon, Anna Jameson, Catherine Parr Traill and her sister, Susanna Moodie. The Belleville wife of the former English officer and ne'er-do-well farmer Dunbar Moodie, Susanna even edited a magazine herself, rather pathetically entitled *Victoria Magazine: A Cheap Periodical for the Canadian People* (1847-48), and contributed serialized excerpts from novels, poems, even a song to the *Garland* (the first magazine to regularly publish musical scores). In its second year, it began to publish lithographs of landscapes, children and well-dressed citizens, with tissue-paper overlays to preserve the pictures for framing, though these expensive trappings were dropped in 1849 for reasons of economy.

The *Garland*'s mostly melodramatic fiction centred on lost and recovered children, nasty or nice aristocrats and faithless then repentant lovers. During its last years, the magazine was edited by two sisters, Mrs. Harriet Cheney and Mrs. E. L. Cushing, who had come from the United States with their mother, Hannah Webster Foster—all with reputations as novelists. The *Garland* died, said Mrs. Moodie, sounding what was to become a familiar refrain, because it was "utterly impossible" to combat the U.S. monthlies "got up in the first style, handsomely illustrated, and composed of the best articles, selected from European and American magazines" and "sold at such a low rate, that one or the other is to be found in almost every decent home in the province."

Apart from the short-lived *Barker's Canadian Magazine* (1846-47), whose Kingston founder, the surgeon Edward John Barker, had more success in starting his *Whig* daily newspaper, the only rival in literary range and substance to the *Garland* was the *Anglo-American Magazine* (1852-55), founded by Thomas Maclear. Its principal contributor was Robert Jackson McGeorge, a Scottish Episcopalian priest whom Bishop Strachan had placed in Streetsville (Mississauga). McGeorge, the "Solomon of Streetsville," also edited the *Church* (after 1852, the *Canadian Churchman*) and a weekly paper. He produced satirical columns like "The Chronicles of Dreepdaily" and "The Editor's Shanty" and contributed to virtually all the literary journals Upper Canada could boast.

With growing commerce, there was the rudimentary beginning of a business and professional press. For the learned, there was the *Canadian Journal: A Repertory of Industry, Science and Art*, founded in Toronto in 1852 by the geologist Henry Youle Hind under the auspices of the Canadian Institute (founded by Sandford Fleming and others in 1849), later the Royal Canadian Institute. In 1856, it broadened its scope to become the *Journal of Science, Literature, and History*. After suspending publication in 1879, the Institute issued annual *Proceedings*, an outlet for science writing until the century's end.

This scholarly journal's longevity was exceptional. But the mayfly-like existence of many periodicals in the century's first half is not the interesting fact. Rather, the source of interest is in the titles, in the competing popularity of *British* and *American* and *Canadian*. It was as if literate Canadians were trying to decide which nationality they had, and would have.

Technology and Communications

All through the nineteenth century, industrialism and technology continued to fragment human existence. But the same specialization and mass production were also improving the standard of living and making magazines feasible both as attractive artifacts and a national force.

When an anonymous author noted in the first issue of the *Canadian Monthly and National Review* in 1872 that "Whatever literary merit may have been possessed by the essays and lectures of twenty years ago, the manner in which they were embalmed for posterity, was sufficient of itself to repel all but the most curious readers. How folks managed to wade through those dreary pages of rugged typography, imprinted on smoky-brown paper, passes understanding," he was being not so much complacent as observant.

The physical appearance of magazines *had* improved and would continue to do so. A chain reaction of inventions gave the printer and editor new freedom. Even by Confederation, printing everywhere had rapidly changed. In quick succession, the electrotype and zincograph began to replace woodblock engraving as a means of reproducing illustrations. Paper was now made in Canada from wood pulp instead of from rags imported from England. The handworked wooden-screw printing presses, which until 1800 had changed little since Gutenberg, were now sophisticated machines made of metal and everywhere increasing in speed and capacity. If not omnipresent, cameras were now common. The dissemination of information was hastened by means as dramatic as the railway and telegraph, and as humble as the postage stamp.

After Confederation, Canadians participated in this exponential growth in speedier communications, with each big invention involving a series of concomitant smaller inventions. William Leggo's experiments in half-tone lithography helped make it possible to reproduce photographs accurately. By 1874, Alexander Graham Bell had perfected the telephone. The Intercolonial Railway connecting central Canada to the Maritimes was completed in 1876, and the first Canadian Pacific train reached Vancouver in 1885. Elsewhere, the first workable typewriter had been patented, and a pell-mell race was on to find a fast, flexible system of mechanical typesetting. In 1888, the year in which the first rotary press was used in Canada, George Eastman invented the first hand camera, the famous Kodak. The public showing of Edison's kinetoscope in 1894 (heralding motion pictures), trans-Atlantic wireless telegraphy in 1907...there seemed no end to the possibilities of human interchange.

Renowned for historical illustration, the omnipresent C.W. Jefferys did this fine drawing for "Stage Coaching in Ontario," in the August 1919 Canadian Magazine.

Illustrated Magazines

New technology, such as commercial photolithography, made the illustrated magazine feasible. The *Canadian Illustrated News* led the way, as did its brief successor, the *Dominion Illustrated*. Besides the *News*, the other magazine to use illustrations extensively was the *Canadian Farmer*, founded in 1864. The increased interest in Canadian art led to the establishment of the Ontario Society of Artists in 1872 and the Royal Canadian Academy of Arts in 1880, as well as to the first Ontario art periodical, *The Arion*. Art news was carried in even the most general magazine.

For the next two decades, magazines like the *Canadian Methodist Magazine*, the *Canadian Church Magazine* (1880-1898), *Massey's Illustrated* (1888-1895) and *Walsh's Magazine* (1895-96) were visually prominent, as was *Grip*. The Grip Company's *Canadian Pictorial and Illustrated War News* tracked the course of the second Riel Rebellion with special artists who accompanied the Northwest Expedition. Such artists, a common feature of the British and American press, anticipated the war artists and photojournalists who would be so conspicuous in the next century. Some of these magazines had church or corporate backing (the Massey-Harris farm machinery empire in the case of its namesake publication) and most drew on the new printing and engraving firms of Toronto. This was certainly true of the *Canadian Courier* (1906-20).

The *Courier*, at first a magazine, for a month in 1914 a daily and finally a weekend illustrated paper, sold for five cents like the *Saturday Evening Post*. Its editor, John A. Cooper, pioneered in the use of colour illustration, especially on the magazine's covers, using artists like Frederick Challener, Arthur Heming and C.W. Jefferys.

The artistic nationalism, fine design sense and stiff but scrupulous draftsmanship of Charles William Jefferys could be found everywhere

in late nineteenth-century and early twentieth-century Canadian magazines. He was, for example, art editor of *The Moon* and first art director of the *Star Weekly*. Indeed, the Torontonian, born in 1869 and best
known for his historical illustrations, was active until his death in 1951.

Next to the Family Bible

Since the family farm was the bulwark of the Canadian economy, it
followed that farm magazines were usually family magazines. Some,
like the *Maritime Farmer and Co-Operative Dairyman* of Sussex, New
Brunswick (1895-1961), would have great endurance. The Montreal-
based *Family Herald and Weekly Star* (1869-1968) became "Canada's
National Farm Journal." Published for a time in Boston as well as
Montreal, it built its circulation in the late 1880s and early 1890s, and
became reputed for its fiction. In the West was the *Free Press Prairie
Farmer*, founded in 1872. In 1965 it merged with the *Farmer's Advocate*,
founded 1866, to form the *Free Press Weekly Prairie Farmer's Advocate*.
Longest survivor of all was Winnipeg's *Country Guide* (1882—), which
in time came to absorb the *Grain Grower's Guide*, the *Nor'West Farmer*
and *Farm & Home*.

The church was another fulcrum of family life. Church magazines
were also family magazines, publishing short stories, biographical
sketches and travel articles. The most important and adult of these was
the *Methodist Magazine and Review* (1875-1906), which, under W. H.
Withrow (and with several titles), had Ryerson's zeal for social reform.
James Croil, the Glaswegian son of a West Indies merchant, was editor
of the *Presbyterian Record* in 1875 when four different journals were
merged and achieved a circulation of 46,000. The Nova Scotia-born
Reverend Ephraim Scott, a former shipyard worker, edited the *Presbyterian Record* from 1888, and founded the *Maritime Presbyterian* and
a weekend paper that began life as the *Children's Record* but was
renamed the *King's Own*. The *King's Own* was transferred to Toronto,
where it lasted well into the twentieth century. In 1896 the newspaperman and printer C. Blackett Robinson formed the Westminster Company, which founded *The Westminster* (1897-1920), at first a weekly
newspaper, then a monthly. It was to the *Westminster* that a Winnipeg
clergyman, the Reverend Charles Gordon (Ralph Connor), sent his novel
Black Rock to be serialized, thus beginning his career as a bestselling
author.

Matthew Arnold, who lectured in Canada in 1884, had a firm fix on
this home-and-family setting. In an essay written before his Canadian
tour, he reflected, "You know the conversation which reigns in thousands of middle-class families at this hour, about nunneries, teetotal-
ism, the confessional, eternal punishment, ritualism, disestablishment.
It goes wherever the class goes which is molded on the Puritan type
of life. In the long winter evenings of Toronto, Mr. Goldwin Smith has
had, probably, abundant evidence of it."

In undenominational contrast was the *Family Journal*, founded in 1882 in England but transplanted to Canada. Its pink woodcut-illustrated cover and unillustrated columns of close type would survive as a Victorian fossil far into the next century. A randomly selected quotation from a 1962 story, "If you want the truth, the girl I love and whom I want to marry, if she'll only have me, is you, your own dear self, Una," shows that little if anything had changed in the intervening ninety years.

Not even more intellectual magazines could ignore the family audience. The *Canadian Magazine* of 1871-72, not to be confused with the *Canadian Magazine* of 1893-1939, much less with the still later weekend newspaper supplement *The Canadian*, was edited by Robert Ridgway and published Mrs. Craik's novel *Hannah*. As A. H. U. Colquhoun put it, "The illustrations appear to have been drawn with a jackscrew, and one of them—a baby in its cradle—must have disturbed many a happy home."

Trading on Trade

Apart from papers for the Montreal and Toronto business communities, there were few specifically trade magazines until the 1880s, when several began, not only in those cities but in Winnipeg, the commercial centre of the New West. Especially significant for the future was J. B. Maclean's founding of the *Canadian Grocer*, the cornerstone for Maclean-Hunter and the start of a dynastic enterprise when William Southam bought a half-interest in the *Hamilton Spectator*. In the next century, Southam Inc. would encompass the largest Canadian newspaper chain, bookstores, a huge commercial printing business and many trade publications.

The Canadian Bankers' Association began its *Journal* in 1892; in 1893 Harold Gagnier founded the *Canadian Banker*, the first of Consolidated Press's holdings in trade magazines; and seven years later *Industrial Canada* became the mouthpiece of the Canadian Manufacturers' Association. The professions had their journals, as well, the most important of which were Dr. Wallace Seccombe's *Oral Health*, origin of Seccombe House, a publisher of trade and professional journals, and the *Dominion Medical Journal*, renamed the *Canada Lancet*. The latter was purchased in 1870 by Dr. John Fulton and edited by him for the rest of his life.

The union press may have had its start in the *Trades Journal* (1880) of Springhill, Nova Scotia. All the fraternal organizations—Free Masons, Odd Fellows and the like—all had their arcanely insular journals.

Nests of Journalists

Sometimes editors of magazines came packaged in families. Archibald MacMurchy, principal of the Toronto Grammar School and editor of the *Canadian Educational Monthly*, sired Marjorie (feminist, author, future wife of Sir John Willison and literary editor of her husband's paper, the *News*) and Dr. Helen (founder of the *Canadian Nurse* and author of influential early twentieth-century reports on infant mortality and the mentally handicapped. She was sometimes called "the Feeble-minded MacMurchy," to distinguish her from her sister).

Even more extraordinary was the Roberts clan of New Brunswick, starting with the children of Canon and Mrs. George Goodridge Roberts. Brought up in a rectory, their so-called Nest of Singing Birds, they included poet-novelist Charles G. D. Roberts, editor of the *Week*; his brother Theodore Goodridge, editor of *Newfoundland Magazine* and the *Kit-bag* (1902-03), as well as the short-lived Maritimes literary magazine *Acadie*; William Carman, for many years editor of the *Literary Digest* in the United States; and author Elizabeth Goodridge MacDonald. Nearby were born their poet cousins, Barry Stratton and Bliss Carman. Nor did the talent end with this generation: Charles's son Lloyd, Elizabeth's son Cuthbert and grandson Goodridge MacDonald and Theodore's daughter Dorothy Roberts Leisner were all writers; and Goodridge Roberts, Theodore's son, was a notable painter. In one way or another, all figured in magazines well into the twentieth century.

Magazine Hinterlands

Although the balance had decisively shifted to Montreal and Toronto, there was some magazine publishing in other places. In the Maritimes, activity was centred in New Brunswick. In Saint John, the weekly *Humorist* (1864-65) was outhumoured by the *True Humorist* (1864-79), patriotically renamed in 1867 the *New Dominion and True Humorist* and edited by George W. Day, a persistent launcher of newspapers and periodicals. Saint John was the publishing centre. There was *Stewart's Literary Quarterly*, the *Maritime Monthly* (1873-75) and *Gripsack* (1888-1902), renamed the *International* in 1901, and at first a general magazine but in its last year dedicated to strengthening ties between Canadians and Americans.

There was also *New Brunswick Magazine* (1898-99 and 1904-06). Its most notable editor was William Kirby Reynolds, who had also published *Gripsack*. Modelling his publication on the *New Brunswick Magazine*, David Russell Jack—incidentally the Spanish vice-consul in Saint John—founded *Acadiensis* (1901—). It was suspended in 1909 but was later revived as a quarterly devoted to the biography, genealogy and history of the region. The *Atlantic Advocate* (1910—) began life as the *Busy East* and was based in Saint John, then Moncton and finally Sackville. The shortest lived and probably unique magazine was *Neith* (1903-04), a monthly edited by Abraham B. Walker, a black lawyer and author (*The Negro Problem, or The Philosophy of Race Development from a Canadian Standpoint*). *Neith*, Walker said hopefully, "is not a Negro magazine, but a Canadian magazine, out for fair play to all, and will discuss the Negro, not because the Editor is himself a Negro, but because the Negro is downtrodden, a Canadian, and Canadian people, black and white, believe in fair play for all.''

In the sister provinces there were the *Nova Scotia Illustrated* (1895) and *Prince Edward Island Magazine* (1889-1905). And in St. John's, in the British colony of Newfoundland, the short-lived *Newfoundland Magazine* (1901-03) was begun. Also founded in 1901 was the much more enduring *Newfoundland Quarterly*, incorporating *Aspects* of the Newfoundland Historical Society. In 1966 it was superseded by the *New Newfoundland Quarterly*.

The New West also had its magazines, such as *The Manitoban* (1891-93) and *British Columbia Home Magazine* (1907-15). A few of these regional magazines, like the *New Dominion and True Humorist*, had broader ambitions. In Vancouver, *Canada West Magazine* (1907-18), which featured "Little Sermons to Young Men," often by railway tycoons, was renamed *Canada Monthly* to become a putative national magazine.

Neighbourly Relations

Given the proximity of the United States, it was inevitable that periodicals from the richer, more populous country would flood Canada. Equally predictable was the Canadian reaction. Most readers wished all possible access to escapist fiction. For an intellectual and artistic minority, whether or not they were publishers, Canadian culture was like air: it was difficult to breathe the pure, clean northern breezes if one was inundated with southern gas. It was also nearly impossible to make money.

As usual, governments dithered in the matter of taxation and postal rates, taking away with one hand what they gave with the other. In 1880, second-class mail was introduced to allow favoured mailing rates for Canadian magazines, though there was as yet no coast-to-coast carrier for them. For some, John A. Macdonald's National Policy was no protectionist blessing. In his trade journal, *Books and Notions*, the young John Bayne Maclean protested that although news dealers had to order foreign-published periodicals in bulk and pay duty on them, in turn charging the customer more, these same magazines were admitted duty-free when mailed directly from the United States.

In 1900, the second-class postal rate was cut from four cents to one cent a pound, in order, said Sir Wilfrid Laurier, to "foster a national consciousness." National consciousness had grown. In 1874 there had been forty-one monthlies of all sorts in Canada and other lands under the Crown. By 1900 there were 202. But now there was a new problem. Printed papers from the United States were untaxed, but there was a twenty-five percent tax on plain paper. According to A. H. U. Colquhoun, the Ontario Deputy Minister of Education, writing in the *Canadian Magazine* (1903), "Canadian paper-makers, printers, binders, engravers and publishers are losing business of a million dollars a year. On periodicals and newspapers imported in bulk there should be a duty equal to the duty on the unprinted pages. The raw material should not be taxed more than the finished product." In 1906 the Post Office refused second-class mailing privileges to fifty-seven U.S. periodicals on the grounds that they were rated as third class at home. Then, upon the protests of Canadian readers, it restored them two years later. So it would go, generation after generation.

There was no tax or surcharge on employment. Canadian editors were able to flow across borders with enviable ease. Charles G. D. Roberts, editor of *The Week*, worked in New York for many years; his brother Theodore Goodridge Roberts was a war correspondent in the Spanish-American War. Aged thirty-one, Robert Barr moved permanently to England in 1881 to co-found the comic magazine *The Idler* with Jerome K. Jerome. The Quebec-born Palmer Cox created the famous Brownies for the U.S. children's magazine *St. Nicholas*; E. W. Thomson was on staff at another notable U.S. magazine, the *Youth's Companion*; the humourist Peter MacArthur, who had contributed cartoon ideas to *Puck* and *Grip*, worked in New York between 1890 and 1908, where he edited *Truth* magazine, and in London, where he regularly contributed to *Punch*.

A Magazine Named Goldwin Smith

No picture of nineteenth-century Canadian journalism would be complete without the guardian-angel presence of Goldwin Smith hovering above or among the clouds of cerebral debate. Tall, thin, dark and bald, looking perennially overworked but not without a certain grim humour, he was omnipresent.

Born in Reading, England, in 1823, Smith was a doctor's son who attended Eton and made a brilliant career at Oxford. He was called to the bar, but instead returned to his alma mater, where he helped bring about many reforms in what was still essentially a medieval institution. Always an advocate for meritocracy, Smith also worked as private tutor on such unpromising material as the Prince of Wales. A Royal Commissioner, pamphleteer and conductor of a public row with Ruskin, he became a vigorous abolitionist during the U.S. Civil War, authoring *Does the Bible Sanction American Slavery*. After 1866, when his deranged father committed suicide, Smith withdrew from Oxford—and England. He took the chair in English and constitutional history at Cornell, a new, nonsectarian, middle-class university, numbering among his colleagues Louis Agassiz and James Russell Lowell. After an extended visit to Toronto, where he had several relatives, he settled there in 1871. Although he would remain fond of Cornell, leaving to it the bulk of his estate, he had become disillusioned with U.S. politics.

This patron of lost or losing causes wasted no time in Toronto in enlisting himself in the public-spirited and intellectual corps. He contributed

Although opposed to factions, Goldwin Smith used several periodicals as his political soapboxes. In September 1875, J.W. Bengough drew him sitting on The Nation. The *Canadian Monthly and National Review is near at hand — or foot.*

CANADIAN POLITICS: A PICTURE FOR THE "PARTIES"

to newspapers and loaned money to John Ross Robertson to help him found the *Evening Telegram*. Though he declined when the planners of the *Canadian Monthly and National Review* offered the editorship to him, he contributed copiously to it. Besides essays, both signed and unsigned, he produced a few pieces as "A Bystander," which would become his adoptive persona.

Smith was only starting. By 1874 he was made senator of the University of Toronto, was a member of the Council of Public Instruction, representing the province's public school teachers, had joined the Canadian National Association and was first president of the National Club. He was a grand catch for the nationalists. After late 1874 he wrote as many as three leaders a week for more than a year to *The Nation* (1874-76), a weekly paper that had begun that spring as the organ of the Canada First movement. Smith corresponded with E. L. Godkin, editor of the U.S. *Nation*, telling him that "Our main object is to look at all public questions not from the party but from the national point of view."

Born at a meeting in an Ottawa hotel room in the spring of 1868, Canada First was a small group of idealistic patriots like Charles Mair and William Foster who possessed vague but emphatic political views. The young men, as historian P. B. Waite says, had "little to hold them together but a rather callow, English-Protestant nationalism." By the time Smith and Edward Blake, the Liberal party's eloquent but unstable leader-in-waiting, got interested in it, some original members had withdrawn or become disaffected, to be replaced by young Toronto lawyers like Thomas Moss, a colleague of Foster on Erastus Wiman's

humour magazine *The Grumbler*. For a brief, heady period the group
thought it was gaining political momentum after Blake gave a passion-
ately nationalistic speech in Aurora in October 1874. Smith helped to
back Blake's newspaper, *The Liberal*, which ceased publishing within
a year. Canada First waned, its nonpartisan ambitions "choked," as
Waite says, "with constitutional projects, the imperial connection,
proportional representation, reform of the Senate."

For Smith, 1875's most significant personal event was his September
marriage to money in the person of Harriet Dixon, a Bostonian heiress
and widow of Henry Boulton of "The Grange," a fine Loyalist residence with ten acres of grounds that had once been a place of rendez-
vous for the Family Compact. Given Smith's publishing expenses and
hospitable habits it was fortunate that the Widow Boulton had a lot
of resources—house and money.

To fellow journalists, Smith, said W. S. Wallace, had to give "repeated
lessons on respecting the anonymity of the press and the courtesies
of public discussion; and with the public generally, he made himself
unpopular by the expression of his views, wholly academic though they
were, as to the political destiny of Canada." Perhaps that was the
difficulty. To the partisans of his time, bystanding was a synonym for
grandstanding. When George Brown snorted in *The Globe*, "Mr. Goldwin Smith more than hints of his ambition to become a martyr. He may
save himself the trouble, and make up his mind to be regarded as only
a nuisance," J. W. Bengough came to his defence in *Grip* with verses
called "The 'Globe,' 'Mail' and 'Nation'":

> If true, your truth shall more appear
>   By giving reasons, plainly told,
> Than screaming 'traitor!' for a year,
>   Or shouting 'liar!' till you're old.

Yet the abuse smarted, and in February 1876 Smith resigned from
The Nation and temporarily withdrew from the pillory. Canada First
was in trouble. The Canadian National Association had ceased existence after the defection of its hero, Edward Blake, and internal disputes over whether it should become a third political party. So
opinionated a man as Smith could not keep silent. In 1879 "A
Bystander" was once again back in *Canadian Monthly and National
Review*. Not only that, but Smith founded and almost entirely alone
wrote *The Bystander*, an independent publication with several metamor-
phoses: as a monthly whose motto was "Not Party, But the People,"
from January 1880 to June 1881; as a quarterly from January through
October 1883; and then again as a monthly from October 1889 to September 1890.

Between the second and third series of *The Bystander*, a new Toronto
publication, *The Week*, was launched in December 1883. Here was

another outlet for the omnipresent Smith. "A Bystander" was to be found digressing in the section "Current Events and Opinions" for more than a year, and longer still anonymously.

He dominated the weekly from the start, proclaiming, says Claude Bissell, "independence in politics and on the right and indeed the duty to criticize freely; a concern with the national scene but, at the same time, a due regard for what was happening in the United States and in Europe. *The Week* liked to think that both in conception and by achievement it could take its place beside the great literary periodicals of the day." Certainly it revered George Eliot and Matthew Arnold, authors much admired elsewhere in the Victorian world. Attractively printed by Blackett Robinson, *The Week* had writers who included Montreal poet, essayist and literary critic John Reade; William Douw Lighthall, patron of letters, writer and anthologist; and Ottawans William Dawson LeSueur and Archibald Lampman, who like LeSueur worked for the Post Office Department. Agnes Maude Machar of Kingston, "Fidelis," wrote novels, poetry and *belles lettres* ; Louisa Murray wrote romances and protofeminist commentary.

A. R. M. Lower succinctly summarizes the many stances *The Week* assumed:

> What *The Week* was against—and it was against most things—would give us a fair idea of where the centre of social opinion rested.... It was against "hot and strong" religion, which included the evangelists Moody and Sankey and particularly those incomprehensible, lower-middle-class hot gospellers then just getting under way, the Salvation Army. It was against French ultramontanism and Protestant bigotry, the Quebec theocracy and the Bible in the schools. It was against Sabbatarianism pushed to an extreme, but it was also against secularism and militant free-thinkers, though it admitted their right to be militant. It was against French-Canadian religious *naïveté* and separate schools in Ontario but not against either of them with the ferocity of the Orange Order and the late George Brown. It was against democracy in education and the abandonment of standards because of democracy. It was for...a bilingual country. It was against racialism. It was against imperial federation. It was against prohibition and for temperance. *The Week* was clearly a middle-of-the-road liberal and intellectual periodical. The Canada of the eighteen-eighties afforded no hospitable niche for the civilized person who is all for maintenance repairs but finds that the world does not need turning upside down.

Eminently civilized but vehement, Smith did not cease polemics after *The Week* ended. He appeared in the *Canadian Magazine* from 1893, and in August 1896 "A Bystander" began a weekly commentary in the *Weekly Sun*, a paper for Ontario farmers, which he continued up until his death in 1910.

Smith produced a quasi-epitaph for his literary or publishing activities in a letter to *The Week* in August 1894:

> In the field of periodical literature, what chance can our Canadian publishers have against an American magazine with a circulation of a hundred and fifty thousand, and a splendour of illustration such as only a profuse expenditure can support? The idea that Canadian patriotism will give preference to the native product is not borne out by my experience.

Consistent in his own lights, retrospectively Smith appears a study in contradictions. At first he allied himself with nationalists and in 1881, after a press banquet held in his honour, was hailed by the July *Canadian Monthly and National Review* as having "inspired and directed" the magazine's aim and efforts "to build up...a patriotic feeling in the Dominion, and to encourage a literature—indigenous in character and honest and pure in spirit." Yet he came to advocate commercial union, indeed outright annexation by the United States—though not the U.S. subjection of the Philippines. A convinced anti-imperialist and opponent of the Boer War, he campaigned against Home Rule for Ireland. Although he had signed John Stuart Mill's petition for women's suffrage, he came to oppose not only this cause, but that of co-education. No socialist, he could say that "the grossly ignorant and the totally irresponsible, instead of being metaphysically entitled to the suffrage, are morally and politically entitled to be exempted from the exercise of the power which they could only use to wreck the commonwealth." A rationalist nibbling at the edges of agnosticism, he regularly attended church. The magazines he assisted, like *The Week* and *Canadian Monthly and National Review*, encouraged Canadian literature, yet he could say that "No such thing as a literature in the local sense exists or is likely ever to exist." At the end, in his *Reminiscences*, he lapsed into self-pity: "My Oxford dreams of literary achievement never were or could be fulfilled in Canada." The historian Harcourt Brown summarized his career: he was "in the broader sense not a thinker; he was not even a critic. He was a man of principle gifted with a vitriolic pen which produced by some automatic device the answer to every problem." He was "a journalist, less well endowed than Morley, less colourful than Carlyle, less intelligent than he thought."

University Men

After generalist magazines like the *Canadian Monthly* and *The Week* declined and fell, universities only partly picked up the slack. The first attempt was by Queen's with its *Quarterly* (1893–), founded by George

G.M. Grant — Presbyterian divine, liberal educator — spoke for Queen's University, and founded its Quarterly.

Munro Grant, one of the great men of Victorian Canada and one of its busiest controversialists.

Grant, "Geordie" in his youth, was born in 1835 in Albion Mines, Nova Scotia, in a part of the province—Pictou County—that produced an indefinite series of distinguished men. An ordained Presbyterian preacher, in the summer of 1872 he accompanied his friend and parishioner Sandford Fleming, the famed deviser of Standard Time and surveyor, along the route of the proposed transcontinental railway, producing his popular account, *Ocean to Ocean*. Named principal of Queen's University in 1877, he fought to keep it from being moved from Kingston and assimilated into the University of Toronto.

Grant was a staunch imperialist who applied Christian ethics to any political or social situation. Such convictions led him to oppose prohibition and discriminatory legislation against Orientals and to hope for a time when all the Christian churches might be united. In his shadow, the *Queen's Quarterly* vowed to be nonpartisan and nonsectarian. To that end, it was founded as a stock company, never profitable but owned after a fashion by Grant, Fleming and members of the staff. Most of the early contributors were Queen's men, like the scientist N. F. Dupuis, who in 1895 wrote that "the rise of the Bicycle and its influence in human affairs...can be equalled only by the modern applications of electricity."

Besides Grant, the most important contributors to the magazine were the English professor and dean of arts James Cappon and the philosopher John Watson. Cappon, like Grant an imperialist, often wrote in 1906 of the "literature of exposure," the muckraking into civic corruption and corporate graft found in U.S. magazines. Scots-born John Watson was the first Canadian philosopher to achieve an international reputation. A speculative idealist, he also contributed to many other magazines. Grant himself, later succeeded by Cappon and O. D. Skelton, wrote the much quoted "Current Events" column on Canadian and international affairs. Although the *Quarterly* ran few book reviews (indeed the Queen's library possessed no novels), verse was published, including, in 1898, Frederick George Scott's first work.

After Grant's death in 1902, the *Quarterly* was reorganized under a consulting committee composed of professors inside and outside Queen's. With such nebulous direction, it began a decline in substance that would last until the late 1920s.

The *University Magazine* (1901-20) was a more consistent and livelier journal than the *Quarterly*, at least when Sir Andrew Macphail controlled it. Moreover, it represents that rarity in Canadian journalism, a magazine of intelligent conservatism.

Of Scottish ancestry, John Andrew Macphail was born in 1864 on the family farm at Orwell, Prince Edward Island. He was given a Church of Scotland upbringing from his sympathetic, sceptical mother and his father, a teacher who became an inspector of schools and superintendent of the hospital for the insane in Charlottetown. After becoming bored with teaching grammar school, Macphail took a medical degree at McGill, earning twice as much by free-lance writing as he had as a teacher. Following a round-the-world trip, he completed his medical studies in London and returned to Montreal in 1892. Ten years later his life was dislocated by the death of his wife, who left him with two children.

A large, gloomy, red-bearded man who had lost the sight of one eye, Macphail practised medicine and taught it at McGill, editing the *Montreal Medical Journal* and founding, then editing the *Canadian Medical Association Journal*. He was a *habitué* of the Pen and Pencil Club, whose members included Stephen Leacock and John McCrae, the future author of "In Flanders Fields," and painters like William Brymner, Maurice Cullen and Robert Harris. Just as Leacock returned to Orillia each summer, Macphail would return to Prince Edward Island. In 1907 he interrupted this private, professional life to take over the semiannual *McGill University Magazine*, a moribund alumni journal. With "McGill" deleted from its title, it was to be directed by an editorial board from the universities of McGill, Toronto and Dalhousie—Dalhousie's Archibald MacMechan was to be a frequent contributor.

From the beginning, the magazine was entirely Macphail's. "An editor is merely a man who knows his right hand from his left, good from evil, having the honesty of a kitchen cook who will not spoil his confection by favour for a friend. Fear of a foe is not a temptation, since editors are too harmless to have any," Macphail was to say. "The purpose of the University Magazine is to express an educated opinion upon questions immediately concerning Canada; and to treat freely in a literary way all matters which have to do with politics, industry, philosophy, science, and art." Goldwin Smith, a very different kind of thinker, might have applauded Macphail's statement that it is "only a bystander who can direct a game or win a battle."

Most issues of the magazine had at least one piece by Macphail, often two. And they were generally the best in the number, despite such illustrious contributors as Rudyard Kipling—like Macphail an imperialist who loved men of action—and Arthur Balfour. Although Macphail published fellow imperialists like G. M. Wrong, Maurice Hutton, Castell Hopkins and George Grant's son William Parkin Grant, he also admitted to his pages feminists, the socialist J. S. Woodsworth and the agrarian protest leader William Good. He called himself "the last Conservative," yet at times his stands and standards were assailed in newspaper reviews and letters by Tories—and by feminists, assorted professors, pro-Americans and Liberals.

To his friend Leacock, Macphail's mind "was as a shadowed pond with shifting shades but no ripples." He had a gift for aphorisms: "Private waste in peace has taken the place of public waste in war"; "Canada will be loyal to England so long as England is loyal to herself"; "Quebec believes in education, Ontario believes in schools"; Montreal "was coming to be the worst governed community in America through an alliance between the worst elements of the French and the worst elements among the Jews. The English did not care. Any one could govern as long as they grew rich."

Although Macphail later translated Louis Hémon's *Maria Chapdelaine* and wrote a memoir entitled *The Master's Wife*, poetry and fiction were subsidiary in the magazine to, for example, a discussion of, during 1907 and 1908, British international treaties as they affected Canada. But in October 1907 an intelligent article by J. W. A. Hickson noted that "Even those who witness Ibsen's plays with distaste or weariness will probably return to the accustomed theatrical diet with a keen consciousness of its artificialities." And Macphail also launched the career of the poet Marjorie Pickthall. Although the magazine was not illustrated, it had dignified layout and large, readable type.

When World War I started, Macphail joined the medical corps in Europe, leaving a committee that included Leacock and the Principal, Sir William Peterson, in charge. The magazine, which had been faltering financially, recovered somewhat, but suffered editorially from Macphail's absence. From abroad, Macphail contributed what remains one of the best short pieces of Canadian prose, "An Ambulance at Rest." Straightforward, sturdy, but subtly nuanced, it tells of the field ambulance's "rest" in August 1915, a short billet between battles in the Ypres salient: "In the Canadian Corps there is a saying that the life of a soldier is a long Newfoundland rest, which means that one stops work and begins again. A Field Ambulance never rests, unless it be by accident."

Such an accident, in the Flanders village of Boolezele, occurs, a kind of miracle. "In the little room that fronts a street a table was spread. There were peas from the garden, an omelette from the clean kitchen, coffee clear as a trickle from a Highland peat bed, milk hot—yet free from scum—little breads of white flour, and butter made whilst the food was preparing." Macphail concludes quietly, beautifully, by saying that in the morning "We took the road, southward by Watten, and as if the portent were not complete, a rainbow raised its arch in the western sky. 'A rainbow in the morning is the sailor's warning,' the sergeant said. And it fell out as the sergeant foretold."

When Macphail returned from the war, knighted for his services but in ill health, the magazine ran aground. It had never made money, and McGill's partners had given only halfhearted support in subscriptions and financial aid. The highwater mark for subscriptions was 1912, when there were 5,300; by 1918 there were only 400.

Macphail himself continually made good the magazine's deficits and, in fact, sank more than $3,000 into it. In fiscal matters as in everything else, Macphail was incorruptible. Not only did he insist on paying contributors—almost unheard of for a university journal—but he refunded subscription money when the magazine expired.

The editor distrusted mass democracy and believed that when city dwellers "come to a full comprehension of the futility of the machines and the factory, they will learn to apply their labour to the thing itself and not to the making of machines which yet leave the thing undone." Macphail oddly anticipated the small-is-beautiful and back-to-the-land movements that would come half a century later. But the impression that remains strongest is of a character essentially decent, even noble.

The End of Class

By the war's end, magazines like Smith's or Macphail's were almost invisible, their last feeble, by then anachronistic representative was probably Sir John Willison's monthly *Willison's Magazine* (1925-29), "A National Magazine Devoted to the Discussion of Public Affairs [in] Canada and the Empire." Upon Willison's death in 1928 it passed briefly through the hands of W. Eric Harris in Sarnia, Ontario, "as devoted a Canadian as he is an ardent Imperialist." The ancient, name-dropping note was sounded in the June 1929 issue: "Any magazine which can, in one issue, carry articles by both The Hon. Rodolphe Lemieux, KC, MP, FRSC, and The Hon. Raoul Dandurand PC may count itself fortunate. The article on Edward Blake by The Speaker of the House of Commons is the first of three which he has written for *Willison's*, the other two of which will appear in succeeding issues." It was like old, very old times.

Even before World War I, mass mentality was altering the nature of magazines. T.G. Marquis complained in 1913 that "Latterly Canadian magazines have been in lighter vein, aiming to please rather than to instruct. Caught by the spirit of the time, publishers now devote more of their attention to the pictorial than to the literary side of their publications. In a commercial age, too, business and finance occupy more attention, and many of the leading periodicals give more space to the literature of the dollar than to anything else."

Stephen Leacock, comic writer and political economist, was equally bleak, writing in 1910, "Today we are overridden in the specialties, each in his own department of learning, with his tags, and label, and his pigeon-hole category of proper names, precluding all discussion by ordinary people.... The broad field of human wisdom has been cut into a multitude of little professorial rabbit warrens." For him, history was "dwindling into fact lore and is becoming the science of the almanac; economics is being buried alive in statistics and is degenerating into the science of the census; literature is stifled by philology, and is little better than the science of the lexicographers."

The sharp division between myopic specialists and mass homogenizers had become the norm. Class was giving way to crass.

"SHALL WE GATHER
AT THE RIVER?"

THE *NEW DOMINION MONTHLY*

A four-year-old went to church on the Sabbath, and when he got home his grandmother asked him what the minister had said. "Don't know," said he, "he didn't speak to me." A good many people might answer in the same way."
— joke (with moral) in the *New Dominion Monthly*, 1 August 1867

That those who gathered by the Ottawa River on the first Dominion Day had something to sing about, loud if not so clear, was indisputable. A straggling northern nation of less than four million souls had been ordained by imperial edict, and optimistically proclaimed to stretch from sea to sea. No matter that the nation resembled more polygamy of convenience than divinely sanctioned marriage, or that it had been scared into wedlock by the recently ended ordeal by gunfire of the U.S. Civil War and by the Fenian raids. Forgotten for the moment was the fact that two partners, Nova Scotia and New Brunswick, had been dragged, kicking and scheming, into union with such unlikely bedfellows as the French Catholics of Canada East and the British Protestants of Canada West. Incompatibilities abounded. Even the new capital paired shrieking sawmills with the granite buttresses of a pseudo-Gothic parliament building.

Notwithstanding, nuptials must be celebrated.

That same year, 120 miles downstream on the *île riverain* of Montreal—the Canadian capital in everything except politics—others mingled to sing joyful praises:

Shall we gather at the river
The beautiful, the beautiful river
Shall we gather at the river
That flows by the Throne of God.

So went the words, accompanied by music, to the hymn printed in the inaugural issue of the *New Dominion Monthly*, the first magazine to be published in the fledgling state and one fittingly compounded of patriotic fervour and relentless self-improvement. Did not an eloquent Father of Confederation, Thomas D'Arcy McGee, that year orate that the "forces of a nation" consisted of the "moral, mental and physical"? Railways were needed, the implication went, but also something to read during the train journey, matter edifying and entertaining. And what better than what the *New Dominion* called itself: "a high-class literary magazine"?

"Literary" should not be interpreted too narrowly. The *New Dominion* sought a general and national audience, albeit one confined to the middle class. Hence the first number's unsigned editorial bragged of the new nation's global ranking as a hewer of wood and drawer of water, and "for fisheries, when Newfoundland joins us, we shall probably be first." And it included snippets from British and U.S. publications: "Something about Jellyfish," from the *American Naturalist*, historical reminiscences ("Montreal in the Olden Times"—"olden" being a scant fifty-one years earlier), and recipes (snow pudding, currant jelly). An anonymous poem, "What are Woman's Rights," however its title might seem to suggest feminism to come, assigned traditional obligations:

> The right to wake when others sleep;
> The right to watch, the right to weep;
> The right to comfort in distress;
> The right to gather, the right to bless;
> The right the widow's heart to cheer;
> The right to dry the orphan's tear;
> The right to feed and clothe the poor;
> The right to teach them to endure;
> The right, when other friends have flown
> And left the sufferer alone,
> To kneel that dying couch beside
> And meekly put to Him who died;
> The right a happy home to make
> In any clime for Jesus' sake:
> Rights such as these are all we crave
> Until the last—a peaceful grave.

To this sacrificial proclamation the editor piously appended, "It is to be hoped that men are not excluded from these rights."

The righteous Scot who founded the *New Dominion*, among many other enterprises, was one John Dougall, who, aged eighteen, had immigrated to Montreal from the weaving town of Paisley. With his brother James, another restless entrepreneur (and later a founder of Windsor, Ontario), he sold textiles on commission. In more than the goods he sold was Dougall dry. Having switched from the Presbyterians to the more impassioned Congregationalists, he plunged—if that is the word—into evangelical word and deed, writing an *Essay on the nature of wine and strong drink mentioned in the Scriptures* and forcefully editing the *Canadian Temperance Advocate*. Nor was such temperance activity the work of a crank. Half the 12,000 arrests made in Montreal yearly were for drunkenness.

Besides inveighing against drink, Dougall took to platform and pulpit on behalf of the French Canadian Missionary Society, an organization haplessly devoted to converting the Roman Catholics of Quebec. Meanwhile, he had become involved in banking, bookselling and publishing, capping these transactions by marrying Elizabeth Redpath of the Montreal English-speaking upper class. In 1846 he embarked on his biggest, most successful venture, the weekly (later daily) Montreal *Witness*, an aggressive penny newspaper of Manichean tendencies: with the light embodied in commercial free trade and the protected sanctity of the Lord's Day, and the dark generally to be found in Papism—whether French or Irish hardly mattered.

By 1867, John Dougall's son John Redpath Dougall (one of nine children) was helping to direct the Montreal enterprises. Although the Dougalls had their share of business failures, the father triumphed in Manhattan. There he launched the New York *Witness*, a flourishing twin of the Montreal newspaper in format, tone and frequency. Whether the elder or the younger Dougall most influenced the *New Dominion* is uncertain, but one suspects the latter, since, by 1871, the elder was busy witnessing in New York.

In any event, the tendencies the Dougalls personified in the daily press took a milder, more ecumenical form in the monthly. Indeed, the Dougall dynasty became progressively less sectarian: "Miss Dougall," the author of a poem the *New Dominion* published, was likely John Redpath's adolescent sister Lily, later to be a religious writer and author of intellectual but melodramatic novels like *What Necessity Knows* (1893). Lily Dougall's home at Cutt's End, Cumnor, near Oxford, England, became a centre for tolerant Christians who held that "there can be no real opposition between true religion and true science or true art."

But this was far in the future. The rabble of the 1840s may have required strong words in the *Witness* to move its emotions, but in 1867 sweet reason was more suitable to the *New Dominion*'s middle-class audience, those who aspired to tireless industry, intellectual prowess and moral rectitude. Although John Dougall was deeply suspicious of Roman Catholicism's racial tendencies in Quebec, the magazine published such bicultural figures as the convent-educated poet and novelist Rosanna Leprohon née Mullins (1829-79). She had married Jean-Lucien Leprohon, of an old French-Canadian family, a much-honoured physician who had founded an early medical journal, *La Lancette canadienne*.

The New Dominion Monthly *revered Thomas D'Arcy McGee, whose simian face adorned its May 1868 issue.*

The mother of thirteen children, Leprohon was read widely by both French and English.

Of Romanism and liquor, the former was plainly the lesser evil. The January 1868 issue of the *New Dominion* featured Thomas D'Arcy McGee's "Father Theobold Mathew and His Works," which the magazine averred was a "very spirited sketch of one of the greatest of history's moral leaders." McGee had taken a pledge of abstinence administered by Mathew, although—this the *New Dominion* did not add—it was to be oft broken. As a youngster, McGee had been an eloquent speaker at temperance tea parties in Wexford, then flirted with the anti-British Young Ireland movement, fleeing Ireland disguised as a priest. A boozing companion of John A. Macdonald ("Look here, McGee, this Cabinet can't afford two drunkards and I'm not quitting"), McGee had suffered a decline in his political career by 1868. His paean to Father Mathew was one way of going public with his new resolutions, quoting from a Mathew biographer thus: "There is no possible safety for those liable to excesses, and unable to resist temptation, save in total abstinence...there is no fear that the lesson will not be applied, or that Providence will not inspire, or even raise up, those who will put it into practice as Father Mathew did, for the sake of religion, humanity, and country."

McGee jettisoned the wine and liquor in his cellar and began attending church regularly. Three months after his piece was published, this lovably ugly man, irregular in habits and magnificent in oratory, a scourge of the Fenians, was shot dead on the doorstep of his Ottawa

In its quest for general readers, the New Dominion Monthly *even embraced women's fashions.*

FASHIONS FOR OCTOBER.

boarding house. Besides the 80,000 who thronged McGee's Montreal funeral, the *New Dominion* was not least among those who lamented him in print.

In death or life, McGee was not the only public figure to be honoured in the magazine. Many numbers bore frontispiece engravings of worthies like the renowned naturalist Louis Agassiz and George Brown, proprietor of the Toronto *Globe* and Macdonald's detested ally in the English-Canadian aspects of nation making. With each engraving came a biographical note, and the one for Sir Hugh Allan, leader of the syndicate that was building the Canadian Pacific Railway, is, in retrospect, deliciously ironic. The September 1871 issue told readers: "Disinterested goodness will receive its reward where it looks for it; but we learn the lesson from the life of Mr. Allan, that he who develops and concentrates the powers that are within him cannot fail to serve his people while he improves his own position...." Later some would claim that Macdonald sought to be served when he sent his notorious telegram to Allan: "IMMEDIATE. PRIVATE. I MUST HAVE ANOTHER TEN THOUSAND." The Canadian Pacific scandal brought about the downfall of Macdonald's regime.

But more interesting than the magazine's homage to the mighty was its intimate yet public relationship with humble contributors. From the start, the magazine endeavoured to develop the talents of Canadian writers. Each Canadian contribution was tagged "Original," to distinguish it from reprinted excerpts. In the January 1868 issue, the editor thanked and listed the authors of thirty-seven articles and pieces that had appeared till then, and the writers of forty-two others were told: "Though there are many and varied excellences in the greater part of them, we cannot, for various reasons, make room for them." As in an ongoing writers' workshop, tips were supplied: "The manuscript should be handwritten only on one side of the paper, and in distinct and legible a hand as may be. It should always have the writer's name and address at the beginning or end...." The editors invited articles of "an interesting kind" on the arrival, settlement and dispersal of the Acadians and Huguenots, on the Duke of Richmond's and Lord Selkirk's attempts to settle respectively the St. Clair and Red River countries, on the Highland Clearances and their effect on Canada, and on United Empire Loyalists and the pioneers of Glengarry County.

Even more startling was the *New Dominion*'s later habit of printing *personalized* rejection slips. To one "Aural Mead" it noted: "Your subject is not of sufficient interest. Try again." To "Ethel": "We regret that your contributions will not suit." To "Aspirans": "'The Little Drummer' is accepted. The rest are not quite so good, and we have no room for them." To "M.S.R., Shannonville": "Rather too diffuse. We want condensation and sustained interest." Even artists were not exempted from the pedagogic note:

> We have to thank the artist, Mr. Henry Sandham, for the engraving which forms the frontispiece of the present number.... Mr. Sandham is his own woodcutter; and, although but an amateur, is fast learning to do justice to his own spirited designs.

That frontispiece, "February in Canada," showed a bare-handed woodsman hacking at a tree and knee-deep in snow. Its rustic and romantic atmosphere lacked only a hungry wolf.

Romance did not imply sex. Any readers who might have hoped that "Early Recollections" by Nell Gwynn in the December 1878 issue would be an account of royal romps by Charles II's mistress were treated to yet another specimen of pioneering fortitude. Poetry was represented by, among numerous poetasters, abler figures like Charles Heavysege, whose turgid "Jezebel. A Poem in Three Cantos" appeared in January 1868. Fiction seldom advanced beyond the sentimental and moralistic, as evidenced in the work of "Alicia," the "authoress" of "Willing Heads and Willing Hands."

Yet the *New Dominion* kept pace to some extent with the scientific spirit that was shaking some of the revered verities. A book review took approving note of an experiment in "public health and infant education" in a school called a kindergarten: "...observers of its effects say that it has a marked tendency to prevent hysteria among girls." In the

January 1874 issue, W. H. Withrow's "Physical Training" animadverted on a similar topic:

> Girls are too generally kept at tight pressure during the whole educational course, and are turned out at its close finished young ladies with an exquisite French accent, brilliant piano execution, a deathly pallor, and all the fashionable infirmities of fine-ladydom, and are doomed to invalidism for life.

That same year Withrow, an Ontario clergyman and sometime novelist of missionary life, became editor of the *Canadian Methodist Magazine*. The astringent reformist tone of his essay, so different from that of "Woman's Rights," clearly indicates how far the magazine had moved with the times.

Toward the end of its twelve-year life, the *New Dominion* had become a typographically cleaner, better organized magazine that broadened its appeal with articles on pets ("If we keep a canary, of course we want it always to be healthy and happy"), sections for "Young Folks" and the fashion-conscious (September 1870: "The fashion plate is omitted this month, as it is too late for summer styles, and fall fashions are not yet out"); besides regular columns on chess and checkers. But on the commercial side, the *New Dominion* was not moving fast enough.

At first the prospects were "cheering." In its initial year it was able to report that "although we printed 6,000 of each of the first three numbers of the *New Dominion Monthly*, we are already out of the October and November numbers, and we have only about 700 of the November number on hand." To widen the fold, the magazine offered bundles of subscriptions that included other Dougall publications: the *Canadian Messenger*, a thriving semimonthly temperance paper that, like the *Northern Messenger*, would be a kitchen and front-parlour staple in rural and small-town Canada well into the next century; and the daily, weekly and semiweekly *Witness*. It also enticed subscribers with bonus packets of mixed tulip bulbs. A dire warning about spurious advertising salesmen was given: would-be canvassers might be authenticated by "a satisfactory letter of introduction from the Minister or Postmaster of his locality."

Although at one point the *New Dominion* claimed to be printing 9,000 copies, the circulation dropped to about 3,500 by 1875. In the January 1879 issue a farewell note gave several reasons for the magazine's demise: economic hard times, of course, but also the decisions to pay contributors, expand the number of pages and improve the technical quality. The most suggestive reason, though, concerned the magazine's relationship with the parent *Witness*:

> The reading matter which first appeared in the magazine was afterwards inserted in the WITNESS. It was only by this means that the magazine could be sold at the very low price

asked for it, one dollar a year; but at the same time the field of WITNESS readers, a very large and important constituency, was cut off from it.

This error was very soon seen and remedied. But irretrievable damage had already been done.

Amid this candour, one significant factor was ignored. Perhaps because the Dougalls relied so much on circulation for the financial base of their newspapers and exercised a censorial hand on advertisements they deemed immoral or distasteful, the sale of ads was neglected in the magazine. Yet advertisements were already becoming increasingly vital for the survival of magazines everywhere. Only the last issue had name-brand advertising: the back cover extolled the virtues of Colman's Mustard, Symington's Pea Flour and Rowntree's Rock Cocoa.

In any case, the farewell note rather pathetically promised that "at some future time, when a fitting opportunity again arrives, the publisher may pick up the tangled threads of the unfinished coil and locking them together, profiting by the experience so dearly gained, bring to a successful conclusion the efforts they have already made."

This was not to be. As the *New Dominion*'s stylistically efflorescent chess correspondent, J. G. Ascher, might have remarked in a different context, any attempt to start a magazine is "Very hazardous, involving loss of pawn immediately with very little equivalence of position."

Elsewhere in the final number, the Dougalls consciously returned to their Scottish roots. The frontispiece, with coloured tartan backdrop and tissue overlay, was of the Marquess of Argyll and Lorne, the poesy-minded Governor General of Canada. There were engravings of Scottish castles and the music and words to "The Campbells Are Coming": (*allegro marcato*) "The Campbells are comin', O-ho, O-ho!"

The Dougalls were going.

THE *CANADIAN ILLUSTRATED NEWS*

"...he had a great deal of the inventor in him, something of the artist, and very little of the businessman."
— Peter Desbarats on his great-grandfather

An unlikely revolutionary was born in Quebec City in 1838, scant months before the dawning of the daguerreotype. The son and grandson of the King's and Queen's printer, George Edward Desbarats, Jr. was only a year old when his mother, *née* Henriette Dionne, died, and three years old when his father remarried, this time to an English-speaking wife. This bilingual, bicultural pattern would mark the boy's life. At age seven, George Edward was sent to Holy Cross College in Massachusetts to be educated by the Jesuits. After a lonely five years, he was enrolled in Montreal's Collège Ste. Marie under French-speaking Jesuits. All this training in literature, philosophy and rhetoric might have seemed better preparation for the law studies he took up at the Université de Laval than for his father's business, but it was in the latter that he became active after he returned from a European tour. Perhaps it was in the blood. A family of Desbarats in the French Pyrenees, from which the Quebec branch derived in some undetermined way, had been printers for more than a century.

From 1841 to 1864, George's father, George Pascal, was the Queen's printer, based mainly in Toronto. In the capital-designate he built a huge printing plant that rivaled John Lovell's, then the largest in British North America. The Desbarats firm published a literary periodical, *le Foyer Canadien, Recueil Littéraire et Historique* (1863-66), whose contributors became a potent force in developing Quebec literature. George Edward knew these men intimately. In 1860 this literary lawyer cum printer married Lucianne Bossé, daughter of a Quebec City lawyer who later became a judge and a senator. In the first eight years of what was to be a happy but disaster-prone marriage, Lucianne gave birth to six children.

After his father's death, Desbarats moved to Ottawa to become the dominion's first Queen's Printer, a civil servant with sizeable commercial commitments in Montreal. If this was to create conflicts, genuine misfortune soon followed. D'Arcy McGee was shot down outside the boarding house that Desbarats owned near his printing plant. (Desbarats erected a commemorative plaque.) Then came the night of 20 January 1869. Desbarats was hosting a superb costume ball, arranged as a surprise for his devoted wife, when he was called away. His printing plant was burning. The fire not only destroyed the building, only partly insured, but also $100,000 of stock, including the plates and sheets of a lavish six-volume *Oeuvres de Champlain*. Within a year Desbarats had resigned his appointment and sold his stone mansion to Sandford Fleming. Henceforward he would rise or fall in Montreal.

In Montreal, or possibly Quebec City, Desbarats met William Augustus Leggo. A restless inventor and entrepreneur, Leggo was a German immigrant to Quebec City whose three brothers were engravers and whose father had trained in Munich under Johann Aloys Senefelder, the perfecter of lithography. For centuries, illustrations had been printed from carved wooden blocks fitted into the letterpress. Senefelder took his impressions from a stone (later a metal plate was used for photolithography). The lithographer drew on the stone with greasy chalk, then dampened it. When he rolled a greasy ink over it, his drawing absorbed the ink. Paper placed on the stone and run through the press soaked up the inked portions, creating the lithographic print.

If lithography was a cheaper, faster and more reliable method of furnishing illustrations for books and papers, photography had even greater potential. The challenge was to find a way to reproduce photos on the printed page. Like many others, Leggo experimented with what had become a commonly accepted idea: a photographic negative that was a cross-ruled screen on which myriad tiny dots varied in intensity so as to produce shadings. In effect this was the modern half-tone.

Throughout most of the 1860s, the Leggos were engravers in Quebec City, and William Augustus was busy patenting and promoting many techniques of line- and photo-engraving, like the "leggotype" and the "granulated photograph." The most significant was the leggotype, patented in 1865.

By 1869, Leggo and Company had moved to Montreal and were making satisfactory experimental half-tones. There, the conjunction of Desbarats and Leggo produced dramatic results. On 30 October 1869, the cover of the first issue of the revived *Canadian Illustrated News* carried a reproduction of William Notman's photographic portrait of H.R.H. Prince Arthur on the occasion of the Prince's visit to Montreal. Scooping its mentors and rivals in America and Europe—the *Illustrated London News, le Monde Illustré* and *Harper's Weekly*—the *Canadian Illustrated News* had come up with the first photographic half-tones to appear

in the history of journalism. As the prospectus circumspectly put it:
"The imagination is so closely linked to the perceptive faculties, that
the speediest and surest way of reaching the mind and impressing
thereon facts and objects, is to lay them vividly before the eye...."

The revolution in human perception brought about by the invention
of photography in the late 1830s had spread with astonishing speed.

Soon after Louis Daguerre in France and William Talbot in England were able to fix unique images on metal or paper, there were about forty photographers in Quebec and Montreal. By 1865, there were more than 360 in British North America.

Though photography was booming, pre-Confederation illustrated magazines constituted a pinched and pallid scene. Admittedly these were early days. The world's first illustrated weekend paper, the *Illustrated London News*, had only been founded in 1842, although soon followed by many others, notably *Harper's Weekly* in 1857. The patently derivative comic paper *Punch in Canada*, founded in 1849 by an eighteen-year-old Montrealer, was the first to publish cartoons regularly. In the 1840s, John Lovell had tipped a few steel engravings into his *Literary Garland* as an enticement to subscribers. From 1858 to 1860, Samuel McLaughlin, an Irish watchmaker, later a photographer, printed and published the *Photographic Portfolio: A Monthly View of Canadian Scenes and Scenery*. And in 1862 an unstable Scottish immigrant named Alexander Somerville started the *Canadian Illustrated News*.

Somerville, who had once received 100 lashes as a punishment for publishing a letter revealing reformist tendencies among his fellow soldiers, had been a ploughman, sawyer, quarryman and hack journalist. Together with six children—his wife died shortly after the family's arrival—he fetched up in Hamilton in what was then Canada West.

Somerville's *Canadian Illustrated News* (1862-64) promised at least five engravings in each issue and employed a few artists, besides the occasional Hamilton or Toronto photographer supplying prints to be engraved. Apart from the *Canadian Farmer*, it was the first magazine to illustrate its pages extensively. Despite the promises, Somerville's undoubted energy and a florid masthead, the magazine did not survive longer than fifteen months. When the last of three owners shifted it to Toronto, Somerville remained behind. This particular *Canadian Illustrated News* succumbed, its proprietors pathetically noted, after "a succession of difficulties never encountered by any journal in Canada —never probably by any in the world."

Poised in Montreal for *his* journalistic leap of faith, George Desbarats benefitted from the technical improvements in printing that were going on everywhere, and forthrightly said so in his prospectus, promising that each issue of *Canadian Illustrated News* would have a leading article on the pressing questions of the day, that it would be "High-toned and thoroughly independent," and be "a complete repertory of current events, and a record of the feelings and ideas of the times."

He vowed weekly publication, sixteen large folio pages (most papers then consisted of four pages of dense type), "heavy tinted paper specially manufactured for the purpose" from the Buntin works in Valleyfield, Quebec, and a minimum of seven pages "handsomely illustrated by the beautiful and wonderful process of leggotype, which being in result the transformation of a photograph into a relief engraving by purely chemical appliances, ensures accuracy as well as beauty of effect."

Not only that, but subscribers occasionally would be "presented with a large engraving, on fine extra heavy paper, worthy of being framed as a decoration to the library. This print will sometimes be coloured, and will itself be worth a year's subscription."

And in the issue of 30 October 1869, there on the front page, almost living proof of the paper's virtuosity, was H.R.H. Prince Arthur. Inside was a splendidly executed line drawing of the Prince's reception in Montreal, drawings of the famous sculler Ned Hanlan and John A. Macdonald, and the *News*'s weekly ration of disasters, discoveries and expeditions.

Making sure his public knew of the riches to come, Desbarats had 6,000 sample copies mailed. News agents would receive a "most liberal discount," contributions "will be thankfully received and carefully considered, and if accepted and published, will be liberally paid for." He set the highest advertising rate in Canada up to that time, although he promised it would not increase until the circulation reached 10,000. Obviously Desbarats was confident it would.

No public event is more efficacious to a picture magazine than a good war. It was fortunate for the *News* that there was no shortage of them in the 1870s. The Canadian expansion westward that led to Louis Riel's seizure of Fort Garry and the establishment of his provisional government—the issue of 30 April 1870 carried his proclamation—the dispatch of Canadian troops to Red River and the Métis leader's flight were all reported in the *News*. On 18 June the *News* dispatched "a special artist" to the Huntingdon border to observe a Fenian raid. The result was a vivid sketch entitled "Stampede of the Fenians through Trout River Village." The great European event was the Franco-Prussian War of 1870-71, which the *News* covered by raiding the pages of British and continental magazines.

Although the half-tone was a dramatic innovation, the *News* was also, as A. F. Moritz has noted, next to *Picturesque Canada* (1882) "the single most important publication in the history of wood-engraved illustrations in Canada. It was, in fact, more wholly a Canadian enterprise than the book and over the course of its history published many more pictures though they are generally of a lower artistic and technical standard."

Lots of itinerant engravers and illustrators drifted through Montreal, and the *News* employed most of them. Some would figure in the history of Canadian art: William Armstrong, an Irishman who visited the Rockies in 1877 as part of Sandford Fleming's survey; the New Brunswick-born sea and ship painter Edward John Russell; Frederic

CANADIAN ILLUSTRATED NEWS

Vol. I.—No. 25

MONTREAL, SATURDAY, APRIL 23, 1870.

[SINGLE COPIES, TEN CENTS.
[$4 PER YEAR IN ADVANCE.

When Louis Riel's Métis executed Thomas Scott on 4 March 1870 it was a natural, if gruesome, cover subject for the Canadian Illustrated News.

Marlatt Bell-Smith; John Henry Walker, who designed mastheads for many Montreal publications; C. W. Jefferys; William Cruikshank, the nephew of Dickens's great illustrator (the issue of 18 June 1870 carried a leggotyped portrait of the novelist). Many of these artists had their *News* work appear in *Canadian Illustrated Portfolio and Dominion Guide*, a short-lived yearly directory that Desbarats founded in 1872, and several were represented in *Picturesque Canada*.

The most important *News* artist was the superb cartoonist Henri Julien. Julien's father had been a printer for Desbarats, and Henri was sixteen when he entered the business about 1868, working there until

1874, when he accompanied the first sortie of the Royal Northwest Mounted Police to crush the Prairie liquor traffic. Julien's *tour de force* for the *News* probably came on 18 January of that year with a magnificent two-page spread entitled "The Unspecific Scandal": "An Original, Poetical, Critical, and likely to be Historical Extravaganza performed by Her Majesty's Servants at the Great Dominion Theatre, Ottawa." In it the "Genius of Canada" advises his readership, "don't be too hard on Sir John." After a spell back at the firm, Julien was hired by Hugh Graham for the *Montreal Star*, where he worked himself to death (in 1908) as head of the art department, or possibly at home—he had eighteen children.

The fare that Desbarats placed before his readers in his first year served up fiction as life and life as fiction. Rosanna Leprohon's final full-length novel, *Ada Dunsmore*, appeared in the *News* and was followed by several other stories. Her fiction, as a commentator has said, was "filled with tearful partings, broken engagements, timely and untimely deaths, chance meetings, and happy reconciliations...." Ideal for the *News*, it would seem, for the magazine offered prizes for the best Canadian historical romances. Like Desbarats, she mediated between two cultures.

Desbarats, who had been president of the St. Jean Baptiste Society, admired the monarchy, any monarchy. There were two-page spreads on the Empress Eugenie's visit to Corsica and Prince Arthur's visit to the Provincial Exhibition in London, not to mention his reception in Montreal. The marriage of Princess Louise to the Marquess of Lorne, future governor general of Canada, was fulsomely covered on 22 March 1871. The monarch even invaded the "Science and Art" column. The issue of 18 June 1870 noted that "The Queen has expressed her intention to give a prize of 1,000 f. (£40) for the best fan painted or sculptured by a female artist under twenty-five years of age, and exhibited next year. The competition will be international."

The big news was the Riel uprising, and there was a long series on the Northwest Territory. At this point, few items were signed, but the visual material was often credited. A "Group of Indians at a Lacrosse Tournament" in the 9 October issue was from a photograph by "Indlis"—of a better quality than the cover, as it happened; the long-running—more than 300 parts—"Canadian Portrait Gallery" (Honourable George Brown on 30 April 1870) and "Distinguished Members of the House of Commons," engraved from Notman photographs. A fine engraving of Lady Lisgar from a Notman photo combined old and new techniques: the engraver's cross-hatching at the bottom of the sketch and minute dots at the top. On 24 December 1870, an extra supplement, "a second sketch, or full-size supplement, by way of distinguishing our Christmas No.," included a full-page sketch of "Santa Claus at Work."

Always expansion-minded, Desbarats began a second paper, *l'Opinion publique*, in January 1870, which used illustrations from the *News* but had a separate corps of editors and contributors. He followed it with an export version for Franco-Americans, *l'Étendard publique*. A year later he started the Dominion Telegraph Institute, a school for telegraphers, and strung a private line between his office and printing plant. In May that year he acquired a weekly magazine of fiction serials called *The Hearthstone*, replacing it in late December 1872 with a similar publication called *The Favourite*. The same year he began a bi-annual directory, the *Dominion Guide*, the monthly *Canadian Patent Office Record and Mechanics' Magazine* and the *Canada Medical and Surgical Journal*. But these were picayune enterprises compared with Desbarats's audacious plans for New York.

This would be what a prospectus called the *New York Daily Illustrated*, an eight-page, 30,000-circulation newspaper. It was to be published by the Union Art Publishing Company and capitalized at $500,000, with half the stock allotted to Desbarats and Leggo "as a consideration for surrender of their various patents." The balance would be sold to New York and Montreal investors.

Somewhere along the tortuous route to creating the *New York Daily Graphic* (1873-80), which Frank Luther Mott has called "the world's first illustrated daily newspaper as well as the first to print half-tone photographs," Desbarats and Leggo, who had moved to New York at the end of 1872, lost control of their enterprise.

In other ways, Desbarats's fortunes were declining. His youngest son, John Robert Alexander, died in 1873 at the age of five. (A last child, Charles Henry Hullett, arrived the following year and eventually took over the family firm.) Overextended and caught by a Canada-wide depression, Desbarats had to auction off his father's magnificent home, and the next year he declared bankruptcy; the *News* of 7 March said that plans to form a new company had been thwarted by "undue pressure in certain quarters." Pluckily he promised that "Should he be enabled to regain possession of the business, he is confident that its present efficient state, and its powers of production, may enable him in time, and with industry and perseverance, not only to recuperate, but to reimburse those whom his failure may temporarily affect."

In 1874 the magazine's publisher—and all the other periodicals and patents—became the Burland-Desbarats Lithographing Company. "The Company proposes to build a magnificent structure in a conspicuous and convenient locality in the City, where the business can be permanently established on a footing second to none of its kind in America." A few months later the *News* reported that "since the assumption of the business by the new Company, our advertising and subscription patronage has largely increased...." At first a director, Desbarats left the joint stock company two years later, and his name disappeared from the masthead in 1879.

While Desbarats was facing adversities, the *News* was carrying on its coverage of politics, war and leisure pursuits with three columns of dense type and increasingly detailed illustrations. Science, too, had its innings. An article in the editorial section on 29 March 1874 entitled "Primitive Conscience" quoted a writer for *Popular Science Monthly* who denied that deaf mutes had consciences. "We wonder whether there is any truth in this," the *News* said, "and would like to have thereon the views of our local specialists. Dr. Palmer of the Brockville Asylum and Dr. Widd of the Montreal Deaf-Mute Institution might throw some light upon this extremely curious and interesting question."

The issue of 4 April was typical. The cover showed Prime Minister Alexander Mackenzie and reported the Speech from the Throne. A regular feature, "Experiences of a 'Commercial Traveller' By 'One of Them,'" was datelined Owen Sound, under the signature "Wayfarer." There were extracts from other magazines, a full-page illustration of the English Ministry, of "The Sorrowful Master" and "Easter Morning," of "St. Petersburg—The Procession of the Church of St. Isaac after the Easter Service" and scenes of German emigrants in steerage from Liverpool to Quebec. There regularly appeared verbose notes about "Our Illustrations," sections such as "Oddities," "Scraps" and "News of the Week," and serialized novels.

As if to signify both the leisure of the affluent and the industrial revolution in full tilt, the cover for 24 June 1874 shows a moonlight steamer excursion on the St. Lawrence. Strolling on deck are men in open coats, vests and straw boaters, cigar in hand, their women with parasols and flounced dresses. Overhead the funnels belch clouds of billowing black smoke.

Five years later the formula was intact. There were still long series, such as "The Cities and Towns of Canada," with inset portraits of worthies, principal industries and notable houses, and tiny jokes: "The best illustrated paper out—a banknote." This appeared in the 18 January 1879 issue. Ironically enough, considering his fiscal record, Desbarats later become president of the Canada Bank Note Company.

Interest in the consciences of deaf mutes had yielded to questions about the state of the Montreal water supply. On 10 September 1889 there was a full-page enquiry entitled "City Water Under Microscope," said to be "a variable admixture of FOOD, DRINK, DIRT, and DISEASE!" by J. Baker Edwards, the secretary of the Montreal Microscopic Club. He urged the use of household filters to screen out the wriggling horrors depicted in the candid drawings. Although "No. 1, Paramecium, and Rotifera, No. 7, are lively scavengers with enormous appetites like the polyps" and "may be dried up again and again, and like very Rip Van Winkles, come to life again after a long snooze and are as busy as ever," readers were doubtless relieved to find that

H. CHINEE: Why you sendee me offee? A.D.C.: Because you can't or won't "assimilate" with us. HEATHEN CHINEE: What is datee? A.D.C.: You won't drink whiskey, and talk politics and vote like us.

Ostensibly scurrilous, the Canadian Illustrated News's *1879 cartoon depicting the "Heathen Chinese" was actually a dig at the xenophobic Amor de Cosmos.*

"They are probably digested in the acid juices of the stomach."

If the *News* always espoused the onward and upward progress of the middle class, its political attitudes changed somewhat after Desbarats's departure. It urged on 27 November 1880, in reaction to the French-Canadian nationalism of the 1880s, that English be taught as the main subject in schools "because by the end of this century this country will be essentially English." On the other hand, it could imply a measure of tolerance, as in the 26 April 1879 cartoon of Amor de Cosmos, the MP for Victoria, British Columbia, and self-styled "Lover of the Universe." The cartoon showed de Cosmos, who had introduced a bill discriminating against the Chinese, pushing away "The Heathen Chinee in British Columbia."

Apart from its visual emphasis (there were now more front-page cartoons), the *News* had come to resemble its fellow journals in Ontario, and began to use many of the same people as contributors. On 14 June 1879, it boasted that as part of a number of improvements, it would now be occasionally employing such distinguished writers for the "Literary Department" as J. G. Bourinot and W. D. LeSueur in Ottawa, Nicholas Flood Davin and Charles Lindsay in Toronto, George Stewart and James M. LeMoine in Quebec. On the face of it, the most unusual contributor may have been Count de Premio Real, Spanish consul in Quebec. But the most conspicuous summer feature was that renewable resource, royalty in all shapes and proxies, in this case the vice-

A printing dynasty. Shortly before his death in 1883, George Desbarats posed with his family. Beside the seated Desbarats, right, are two future owners of the business: William, standing, and Charles Hullett, at his father's feet.

regal visits to Kingston, Quebec and Toronto. The Zulus supplied the war of the year, and the significant sporting event was Ned Hanlan's world championship sculling.

The *News* lost a valued contributor that year. On 20 September, No. 316 of the "Canadian Portrait Gallery" series concerned George Tolley, literary editor of the *Montreal Evening Star*, who had drowned near Brockville. The *News* had assigned Tolley "to visit the principal towns, cities and manufacturing districts of the Dominion for the purpose of illustrating their principal features and writing accounts of their resources." Thus engaged the previous two years, Tolley had most recently dealt with Brockville. He was, said the *News*, a "universal favourite."

Not so the *News*, which called itself "the only illustrated paper and the only purely literary weekly in the Dominion." It ceased on 28 December 1883 "for the simple reason" that it was "not remunerative." Blaming tardy subscribers for some of its troubles, the editorialist stated that "it is quite possible that Canada has not yet obtained a sufficient population to enable the successful publication of an illustrated weekly journal to be made...." As an inducement to subscribers to pay up, it offered "a beautiful OIL PORTRAIT of SIR JOHN A. MACDONALD in 16 colours, Size 18 x 24. FREE."

Although the *News* was extinct, neither Desbarats nor his family was done with magazine publishing. In 1885, he started the *Dominion Illustrated News*, also called the *Dominion Illustrated Monthly*. It was glossy as opposed to the *Canadian Illustrated*'s newsprint and incorporated many of the technical advances made since 1869, including the now perfected half-tones. Certainly it had many links with its predecessor: Jean Lesperance was an editor, as he had been with the *News*, and its contributors included Charles G. D. Roberts, who had also had poems published in the earlier publication. In one respect, at least, the magazine was differently conceived: this time Desbarats had fellow investors, among them, Donald Smith, president of the Canadian Pacific Railway; Andrew Allan, a shipowner; and Sir Sandford Fleming. Notwithstanding this support, the magazine only lasted until 1895.

Desbarats died in 1893. A Notman photo taken shortly before his death at the age of fifty-four shows the paterfamilias with his mostly grown-up children. With his dimpled chin and sensitive mouth he is a handsome man. He is staring steadily away from the camera.

Beside him is his wife, Lucienne, and to her right their daughter Cecile and son Édouard Stanislaus. Standing behind their parents are Lucienne and William. Seated at his father's feet is Charles. It was a remarkable family. Cecile became the Mother Superior of Sacred Heart convents in Montreal and in the United States; Édouard, the president of the important Desbarats Advertising Agency; Lucienne, Lady de Blanquière of Bath, England. William became president of the Desbarats Printing Company, one of Canada's largest, and Charles his successor. Charles's grandson David William was president of the company in 1969 when he died at thirty-three years of age. But it was David's elder brother Peter who harked back to the family tradition. A reporter, television commentator and dean of journalism at the University of Western Ontario, Peter, as if in homage to his Victorian forbear, affected sideburns after they had ceased to be fashionable and founded a short-lived Montreal magazine with the apt title *Parallel*.

But what of the editor of the first *Canadian Illustrated News*? While his venture was in the process of collapsing after its move from Hamilton to Toronto, Alexander Somerville remained behind to report on the Fenian raids across the Niagara and Lake Erie frontiers. Having been promised cash from Thomas D'Arcy McGee to write an immigrant's handbook, Somerville left for Ottawa, where he learned that his sponsor had been murdered. Thence he went to Montreal and, from 1869 to 1872, he wrote for the second *Canadian Illustrated News* as part of his scatter-shot career.

From 1873 until 1875, Somerville edited the *Church Herald* in Toronto until it merged with an American church paper, when he was reduced to being a "Canadian Editorial Correspondent." In the words of the *Dictionary of Canadian Biography*, "By the 1870s Somerville was elderly, mountainous (he weighed 300 pounds) and eccentric. Books and clippings from the British newspapers, to which he wrote weekly letters, filled his rooms at the City Hotel and later at a York St. boarding-house. He moved finally into a wood-shed, living on cold porridge flavoured with bits of raw onion; from 1880 to 1885 he apparently wrote 5,000 pages of memoirs which have never been found."

But some of Somerville's words did survive, and were equally as relevant to George Desbarats's enterprise as to his own: "Description fails, however graphic, terse, minute, to convey to the mind a correct, or lasting impression. For this reason there always has been, and is, a strong desire to substitute sight for sound, the real for the imaginary. To meet this want, to portray objects as they are, or were, to present to the eye a lifelike representation, is the aim of an Illustrated Paper."

THE *CANADIAN MONTHLY AND NATIONAL REVIEW*

When sobersided literary men gather, the subject of magazines inevitably arises, especially when few exist. Such was the case in the Canada of the early 1870s. To Toronto in 1871 had come the learned controversialist Goldwin Smith, his money and prestige like twin shafts for any available cart of scholarship, literature and commentary. But what beast of burden to pull it?

For this, Smith and other like-minded citizens turned to one of several indefatigable Scots in the vicinity, Graeme Mercer Adam. Born in Scotland in the town of Loanhead—an eerie presentiment of his future fiscal entanglements—Adam had come to Toronto as a young man to manage a retail book business. In 1863 he strengthened his connections with the Canadian literati by marrying Jane, the daughter of John Gibson, editor of the *Literary Garland.* He then took over the business in partnership with James Rollo and published and reviewed for the *British American Magazine*. This journal, "devoted to Literature, Science and Art," lasted all of one year. He dissolved the firm in 1866 and, a keen militia man, helped to beat back a Fenian raid. In 1867, together with John Horace Stevenson, he started another firm: Adam, Stevenson and Company, booksellers, agents, jobbers and publishers. Adam published, edited and wrote almost every word in a trade quarterly called the *Canada Bookseller & Miscellany*, the country's first genuine book-trade journal, which his company put out until 1872.

This zealot in the cause of Canadian publishing was thus an ideal candidate to fulfil the idealistic ambitions of The Canada First Movement. Yet, though the cover of the first issue in January 1872 had three entwined maple leaves, the journal was no propagandist organ of a political movement. Its introductory note asserted that "the utmost latitude will be allowed to contributors in the expression of opinion, as well as in the choice of subjects; but the Magazine is not open to party politics or to party theology [sic]; nor will anything be admitted which can give just offence to any portion of the community." More positively, the magazine's chief aim would be "to deal with Canadian questions and to call forth Canadian talent.... Having a rational object in view, the managers of the Magazine will sincerely endeavour to preserve, in all its departments, a tone beneficial to the national character and worthy of the nation."

The tone and balance of that first issue would be consistent throughout the magazine's lifetime. There was a long article on the 1871 Treaty of Washington and several poems, including Charles Sangster's "The Mocking-Bird" and John Reade's "Paolo and Francesca." Art and the natural world were reflected in "Marguerite Kneller: Artist and Woman" by Louisa Murray and "Man's Place in Nature" by H. Alleyne Nicholson. "An Historical Night in the Old Parliament" from eight years earlier was counterweighted by the foreign and contemporary: "The Cavalry Charges at Sedan—The Autumn Manoeuvres—The Moral They Convey" by the hard-riding Lieutenant-Colonel George T. Denison, Jr. and "The End of Bohemia," a clumsily translated essay on the "part played by Literature and Journalism in the recent Events in France" from the *Revue des Deux Mondes*. Stated the article: "It will be recognized in future to guard against idealizing under the charming names of fancy, of independent life and freedom" those "disorders in morals and brains" that led to the "getting up of revolutions."

The *Monthly* would not be getting up revolutions. Along with shorter "Literary Notes" in small type, there was a long review of a book on Americanisms and a densely detailed survey of religious works. "In attempting to take a general view of contemporary literature, we naturally give precedence to works bearing upon the subject of Religion." For the next ten years unsensational short stories or serialized fiction would follow, as well as such columns or departments as "Current Events"—including United States, Britain and Europe; "Science and Nature," "Current Literature"—often deriving from those British heavyweights *The Fortnightly* and *The Contemporary*; "Fine Arts," "Music and the Drama"—local coverage; "Down the Table"—in effect letters-to-the-editor; and "Literary Notices." During the magazine's first year it reviewed at length four biographies, six books on language and literature, five histories, five books on religion and ethics, a reprint of Susanna Moodie's *Roughing It in the Bush* and a few novels and travel books.

With its format jelled, the *Monthly* went about chronicling the country's intellectual progress. To some degree this paralleled the peregrinations of Goldwin Smith's mind. Having declined the editorship of the magazine, Smith was to be a frequent contributor anonymously, pseudonymously and under his own name. In February 1872, the "Bystander" discussed the recent fall of the Sandfield Macdonald government in Ontario. Soon he was explicating "The Women's Rights

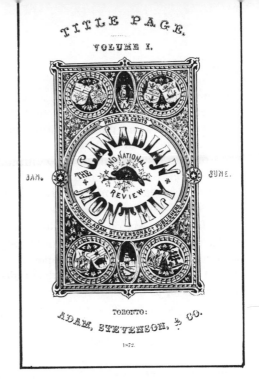

The beaver and owl in an heraldic title page for early volumes of the Canadian Monthly and National Review *symbolized industry and wisdom.*

Movement"—"Woman may be man's helpmate, or she may be his competitor: both she cannot be;" federal and provincial politics; and "The Oneida Community and American Socialism." From December, with the start of the "Current Events" column, Smith figured mainly as an anonymous commentator.

Smith was far from the only commentator or proponent of causes. In March and July, Thomas White, Jr. wrote two proposals for encouraging immigration. An anonymous piece, "Juvenile Pauper Immigration," in September 1877, also favoured an influx of immigrants. The *Monthly's* authors opposed ultramontist tendencies in Quebec's Roman Catholic Church, applauded Gladstone and derided Disraeli, espoused university amalgamation in Ontario, supported, then were disillusioned by Edward Blake and were hopeful about Laurier, and dismissive—here Smith either spoke directly or by proxy—of John A. Macdonald's protectionist National Policy.

At first the auspices were hopeful. In July 1873, the *Monthly* proudly observed that the start of its second volume "will be taken, we trust, as proof that the *Canadian Monthly* is not destined to share the fate of those short-lived predecessors, the recollection of whose brief existence has been one of the chief obstacles to the progress of the present enterprise." There were other points of pride:

> We note with pleasure the appearance among our contributors of members of both political parties. It shows that our profession of neutrality is felt to be sincere, and that the magazine is regarded as a suitable place for the impartial discussion of questions relating to the broad interests of our

common country. To keep it so will be our earnest endeavour. We can truly say that those who guide it are entirely free from party connotations and party bias, and that whether their cause be right or wrong, it can be dictated by no motive but regard for the common good. The national need of an organ devoted not to a party but to Canada is apparent already, and is likely to become more apparent still.

The following March, as if to deny any undue influence on his part, Smith, in "Current Events," would call the magazine "the organ of nothing but perfect freedom of speech, and it will do its best to guard against any attempt to muzzle discussion or set among us a narrow tyranny of opinion."

Smith was right. The pages of the *Monthly* were open to anti-nationalists like Jehu Mathews of Toronto, whose review article, "Political Future of Canada" in July 1875, provoked no less than three replies by Canada Firsters and his own counter-rebuttal. That same year Charles Mair was extolling "The New Canada: Its Natural Features and Climate" in a series, and another one had George Grant recalling the late, great Joseph Howe. The July issue had an intriguing counterpoint in its titles: a fiction serial called "Medicine and Matrimony" and an article called "Alcohol and Medical Science."

Certainly moral and political preaching was not confined to non-fiction. In January 1873, Agnes Maule Machar's fiction first appeared. The Machar novels serialized in the *Monthly*, such as *For King and Country* and *Lost and Won*, promoted her many viewpoints, as did her essays and poetry. The tiny, elfin-faced "Fidelis" was the daughter of the second principal of Queen's University, a feminist who wrote an article entitled "The New Ideal of Womanhood" in June 1879. She was an admirer of Henry George's Single Tax doctrine, a promoter of wilderness parks, a crusader against the use of birds' plumage in ladies' hats and an open-minded Presbyterian whose views often coincided with those of George Grant, another frequent contributor to the *Monthly*, except regarding the availability of liquor—she was a fervent Prohibitionist.

While Machar was making her debut, all was not well with Adam and the *Monthly*. Adam's publishing firm was caught by the 1873 depression and the next three years were devoted to coping with fiscal emergencies. Adam merged the *Canadian Bookseller* with the *Monthly*. But his publishing firm (the retail bookselling business had been sold earlier) went bankrupt after incurring massive debts.

Adam now had to fall back on the resources of his wife's family. John Lovell, publisher of the *Literary Garland*, which had been edited by Adam's father-in-law, launched into the United States. He set up, and later expanded a printing plant in Rouses Point, Vermont, which was managed by his son John Wurtele. The family moved there and the junior Lovell's sister Sarah married Frank L. Wesson of the Massachusetts gunmakers. Thus it was that Adam went to New York to form the firm of Lovell, Adam, Wesson & Company. Although not a conspicuous success, the company was the beginning of what would become a massive book-publishing enterprise, the United States Publishing Company.

Under uncertain leadership and with shaky finances, the *Monthly* carried on. The January 1877 issue led off with the fiction of "Juliet," by Mrs. H. Lovet Cameron: "'Ernestine,' said Mrs. Blair to that talented damsel, during the course of the same day that Colonel Fleming had as suddenly left Sotherne Court. 'Ernestine, you are looking very pale.'" Also included was an instalment of the series "Swift and the Women Who Loved Him," ably compiled by Louisa Murray, an active free lancer who like "Fidelis" had Kingston connections and emphasized Christian ethics. Born on the Isle of Wight to a military family on both sides, Murray had first appeared in the *Literary Garland*.

While the *Monthly* was struggling, *Belford's Monthly Magazine*, "A Magazine of Literature and the Arts," was begun by Charles Belford in 1877. Belford was an Irish Protestant who had come to Canada from County Cork twenty years earlier with his brothers Alexander and Robert. Charles had been a trained draughtsman, but in Canada he became a newspaperman, an ardent Tory on the *Leader*, published by his great-uncle James Beaty, and edited the *Mail*. In 1876 the Belford brothers started as publishers, and taking advantage of the loophole-strewn Copyright Act of 1875, specialized in pirating American best-sellers like those of Mark Twain. (In this they were in common company: the Americans were pirating the British and dumping their reprints in Canada.)

When the same firm publishes books and magazines there are sure to be conflicts of interest. Certainly *Belford's* seemed to soft-pedal any adverse criticism of current literature. In any case, *Belford's* aims were less elevated than the *Monthly's*: it had more illustrations—an illustrated insert for Christmas—and employed artists like Henry Sandham and the rising lithographic firm of Rolph, Smith & Company. Its fiction tilted more toward the lowest common denominator, as in George Stewart's "How Three Little Midgets spent Christmas Eve."

Stewart, whom the Belfords brought to Toronto, was to play a brief, troubled but important role in the history of the *Monthly*. Born in New York but schooled in London (Ontario) and Toronto, Stewart was something of a prodigy. At the age of seventeen he had founded the *Stamp Collector's Monthly Gazette* and edited it for two years in Saint John, New Brunswick, before beginning *Stewart's Literary Quarterly* in 1867. In its five years of life this reputable magazine drew contributors from Newfoundland to British Columbia. Brought to Toronto, Stewart took charge of a merger: *Belford's* and the *Canadian Monthly and National Review* were now combined as *Rose-Belford's Canadian Monthly and National Review.*

The "Rose" in *Rose-Belford's* came from George Maclean Rose, a Scottish immigrant, Orangeman, Unitarian temperance advocate and active Liberal, who also belonged to a printing family. In 1879 he formed the Rose-Belford Publishing Company with Robert and Alexander Belford, after an exhausted Charles had withdrawn from the firm. A year later the Belfords left the company and set up shop in Chicago, leaving only a branch in Toronto. Alexander married the daughter of Andrew McNally of Rand McNally and Company, and Robert went to New York and later, like the swallows, to Capistrano, where he raised olives and walnuts. Rose's business—all his four sons were active in it—was the cornerstone of the well-known printing firm of Hunter, Rose.

No doubt nonplussed with these hectic business transformations, Stewart added more illustrations to what was still essentially the *Canadian Monthly.* Because Canadian engravings were so expensive, he ended up buying cuts that already had appeared in *Harper's, Scribner's* and *Lippincott's*—hardly an act of Canadian nationalism, or in general good magazine practice. He also bought *The Haunted Hotel, a Mystery of Modern Venice* and *Fallen Leaves* from Wilkie Collins for profitable North American serial and book publication rights. About one of his characters in *Fallen Leaves,* Collins wrote Stewart to say that "perhaps, some of the nice people with nasty ideas, on your side of the ocean, may raise objection.... I believe Simple Sally will be the most lovable personage in the story. But, we have (as Mr. Carlyle reckons it) thirty millions of fools in Great Britain and Ireland and (who knows?) some of them *may* have emigrated."

Another of Stewart's contributors was W. J. Rattray, who reviewed books and filled in for Goldwin Smith in "Current Events." Said Stewart, he "wrote a very small, fine hand, on little squares of paper, and he never kept the printers waiting for copy." John Reade was often present, as was the U.S. consul in Toronto, William C. Howells, William Dean's father. "Fidelis" did a series on the Buddha and his relation to Buddhism and Christianity, and T. R. Browning a two-part essay on "Communism," writing that "...man proceeds from communism to individualism."

Stewart remained with the magazine only about a year. The Belfords had arranged for him to write a subscription-published book called *Canada under the Administration of Lord Dufferin,* but when he asked to be paid he was told it was part of his magazine duties. He promptly took the Belfords to court for damages but lost on a technicality, whereupon he quit to become editor of the *Quebec Chronicle.* His successor was Graeme Mercer Adam *redivivus.*

Adam returned to Toronto in 1879 and, as was his custom, started a magazine, the *Canadian Educational Monthly* (1879-84). The next year he became literary assistant to Goldwin Smith and manager of Smith's *Bystander*. Adam's recent experiences in the United States and Smith's influence were to powerfully affect his life, but initially his opinions were by no means identical to the older man's.

The September 1879 issue of what was now *Rose-Belford's* contained "A Few Words About Iron"—the magazine's titular style was always straightforward and sometimes unintentionally punning: a September 1875 example was "Relics of Loyalty, or Scraps from the Catacombs: Being Remains of the Coffin Family." The September 1879 issue also carried an unsigned piece about the northern lakes and Winnipegosis country, "one of the most inaccessible regions of the North-West," and Smith's "The Prospect of a Moral Interregnum," a somewhat sceptical piece about organized religion. This provoked an answer by "G.A.M.," possibly a slightly disguised Graeme Mercer Adam: "I believe there is no other power than the doctrine of the Cross wherewith to meet the danger of a moral interregnum...."

The conflict between sacred and secular, transcendent and immanent, divine and materialistic, were issues of absorbing interest for the *Monthly* before and after its renaming, as they were for most educated Victorians. In "Science and Materialism," W. D. LeSueur said in January 1877 that "The prodigious development of natural science" was "the cardinal fact of the nineteenth century." The ensuing possibility of a new ethical code and its definition was the subject of an extended *Canadian Monthly* debate in 1875—five articles in all—between LeSueur, writing as "Laon," and the broad-minded theologian George M. Grant. LeSueur, who much admired the great French critic Charles Augustin Sainte-Beuve, worked for the Post Office from 1870 until his death in 1902. In articles like "Old and New in Canada" (January 1875) LeSueur questioned scientific, political and historical orthodoxy. Almost every aspect of Christian practice and belief, materialism and spirituality, had a hearing in the magazine, whether taken up by Smith, Grant, LeSueur, Murray, Machar—for example, her May 1875 "Prayer for Daily Bread"—William Dawson of McGill, John Watson of Queen's.

What also preoccupied the *Monthly* might be summed up in the title of an essay J.G. Bourinot wrote for it, "The Intellectual Development of Canada." To that end, the magazine published at least a quorum of creative prose and poetry. The young Sara Jeanette Duncan's first published prose work, "Diogenes on Bric-à-Brac," appeared in June 1880; in September the aspiring Brantford writer published the lyric "It Might Have Been," and more work followed. Poetry was viewed as an expression of the highest morality. In reviews, as R. L. McDougall says, "almost everything is taken seriously." Reviewers especially favoured George Eliot and Thomas Hardy. In any case, three-quarters of the books reviewed were works of scholarship or intellectual polemic.

If in 1876 the winning entry in its essay contest, Thomas Davison's "Mechanic's Institutes and the Best Means of Improving Them," said that "It is an unfortunate fact that the public taste inclines to 'fiction,'" the magazine encouraged new Canadian literature. Sometimes oppressively so. In January 1881, a reviewer—few of the reviews were signed— noted that the magazine "has endeavoured, in reviewing the yearly harvest of native literary work, to abstain from the sin of puffing mediocre literature merely because it is Canadian." Yet, as McDougall has pointed out:

> although obvious literary monstrosities are rejected customarily (some slip by beneath an uncritical eye), they are rejected in the mildest possible terms . . . With respect to the numerous displays of what it plainly takes to be mediocrity, the *Monthly* can usually seize upon sufficient indications of merit to enable it to take refuge in vague laudatory comment or to settle comfortably for limited objectives. Time and time again a sort of galvanic happy cry is raised over the progress currently being made by Canadian literature, only to echo away into uncritical silence.

Silence, uncritical *and* critical, was soon to be the *Monthly*'s fate: 1882 was the *Monthly*'s last year. Departing entirely from illustrations—possibly too expensive at this point—but including a young people's section, the magazine's contents were otherwise much as usual. In the January issue, for example: "The True Basis of Legislative Prohibition" by George W. Hodgson asked, "Does the evil directly resulting to the whole community from the liquor traffic outweigh any possible good coming from it?" The author thought it did. And there was Rose E. Clarke's surprisingly sympathetic "A Peep at Convent Life and Education." Then in June came bitter words: the magazine would be suspended. "The experiment of establishing and maintaining a periodical of such pretensions as THE CANADIAN MONTHLY in our inchoate state as a nation, and in the face of the active and ever-increasing competition of English and American serial publications, it will be readily admitted, was a hazardous and courageous one." The magazine had never been profitable; it had always cost a lot to run.

> To reproach the public for its want of appreciation, we need hardly say, is no wish of either publishers or conductor. The public has its preferences, and has a right to them, and if it gives little heed to native projects in higher literature, or finds more attraction in those that have their source abroad, Canadian publishers must accept the situation and await the development of a national spirit more favorable to culture and intellectual advancement. Till we reach the self-containedness and self-dependence which it is hoped the

country will one day attain, Canadian literary enterprise will have little to encourage it. Those who have aided, and are aiding, the approach of a better time for Canadian letters, if we accept Dr. Johnson's dictum that "the chief glory of a people arises from its authors," deserve the thanks of every true friend of Canada. They must be largely supplemented, however, and receive more encouragement from the press and from our public men, before they can hope to infect the people with that ardent interest in intellectual growth which is the true mark of national greatness and the best quickener of national life. Without the stimulus of patriotism all enterprises of a purely literary character must languish, and Canadian talent be drafted off to more remunerative spheres.

The farewell ended on a note of querulousness and self-pity.

In the midst of the present political excitements, few, it may be will heed, or concern themselves with this announcement; but a day, we hope, will come when "the political game" will not absorb every thought of the nation and when litera- ture will hold up its head in honour. Till then the higher thought of the country must find such channels of utterance as public caprice or indifference graciously open to it, and Monthly Reviews must uncomplainingly suffer eclipse.

Appropriately, the long poem in this issue was "The Last Tourna- ment" from Tennyson's *Idylls of the King*.

So it had come to this. The sentiment that W. E. LeSueur had expressed in January 1879 about the Canada First movement, that "It was the revolt of educated and thoughtful men against the inanity and worse than inanity of what was offered to them as political discussion," might have equally applied to the *Canadian Monthly*. As Roy Daniells elegantly summarizes in the *Literary History of Canada:*

The desire to preserve, justify, and substantiate national unity imparts to these volumes an extraordinary unity of topic and tone. Criticism is constructive; love of country is everything from deep affection for the terrain itself to patriotic pride over memories of Lundy's Lane; the very book reviews shine like stars in a moral firmament. A world is created, its centre in the Canadian home, its middle distance the loved land- scape of Canada, its protecting wall the circle of British insti- tutions, associations, and loyalties. Across this welcome breastwork the United States, now neither menacing nor necessarily hostile, is to be viewed, and more exciting because less familiar, the great outposts of the civilization of continental Europe—France, Italy, Germany, and behind

these the splendours of ancient Greece and Rome. It is a
world as centripetal as that of Sherlock Holmes and as little
liable to be shaken by eruptions of evil.

The Canadian Monthly had been more than shaken, it had been
sunk—not by evil, but by the failure of manifestly good intentions. Writing to George T. Denison in 1882, Charles Mair termed Canadians "literary eunuchs" and said he was "filled with shame & contempt & regret
when I think that I am a Canadian."

In his own way Adam, the probable author of the magazine's last
words, was to know failure, too. In 1883, he compiled a schoolbook
series, the Royal Canadian Readers, and the next year he and John
Lovell fruitlessly planned a prestigious series of reprinted Canadian
books. While this was going on, Adam's politics began to change. Adam
had favoured Canadian publishers reprinting foreign books as a means
of securing a sound financial foundation; Smith was opposed to it. Adam
was a Canadian nationalist; Smith an annexationist. But now he sided
with Smith, becoming secretary of the Reciprocal Trade Movement and
an ally of the writer and editor Erastus Wiman, who had once been
an economic nationalist but became a U.S. citizen in 1897. After Adam
remarried in 1891—his first wife had died in 1884—he went to the
United States, where he worked for Lovell, then as a hack compiler
of encyclopedias, textbooks, guidebooks, scenic books and trifling works
like *Sandow's System of Physical Training*. He then edited a magazine
with the quintessentially American title of *Self-Culture*. Many of his last
years were spent in Akron, Ohio.

He died in New York.

BENGOUGH'S *GRIP*

Not a riverboat gambler but the caricaturist J.W. Bengough, seen here in a self-portrait.

...I enrolled myself under the auspices of the Ontario Society of Artists. If I had only appreciated the advantage of persevering through the dry and irksome early stages of the course, I should no doubt have had reason to be thankful ever after, but patient plodding was not to my taste, and the copying of the placid countenances of Greek deities in plaster castes [sic] proved too much for me before the end of the first term. I foolishly preferred to 'study from life.'

—J. W. Bengough in "Reminiscences of a Chalk-Talker"

J. W. Bengough's happily pugnacious mastiff's face suggests a man devoted to many causes, lustily pursued. As angry as Bengough may sometimes have been, cheerfulness kept breaking through.

Certainly he had all the vices and virtues of the autodidact. Born in Toronto in 1851 to evangelical Presbyterian Scots and Irish parents, he attended grammar schools in Whitby, and was, he said many years later, "much given to the lead-pencil." It was sometimes said that he was frequently thrashed for caricaturing his headmaster. In any event school was not his natural milieu. Instead he quickened to the great cartoonist Thomas Nast in *Harper's Weekly*, and his assault on the New York civic corruption of Boss Tweed and his Tammany Ring. Interestingly, Bengough came to agree with criticism that Nast was an imperfect draughtsman—the very censure that would be applied to his own work. Far more important was Nast's "moral force, in many cases great and terrible." In tribute Bengough sent Nast a pencil drawing of him encircled by the Tammany Ring, heads bowed in obeisance.

While sharpening his pencil on local notables, Bengough became a printer's devil on the *Whitby Gazette*. When Prussia declared war on France, the *Gazette* decided to pace the battles by publishing a four-page daily war bulletin. The only difficulty was that the editor sometimes lacked enough overseas copy, and Bengough was required to provide such filler as a serial memorably entitled "The Murderer's Scalp, or the Shrieking Ghost of the Bloody Den."

In search of scalps, or perhaps shrieking ghosts, Bengough arrived in Toronto about 1871, becoming a city reporter on *The Globe*, then edited by Gordon Brown under the eye of his better known brother, George. At this point there were no cartoons in *The Globe*, or in any other North American daily. Having declined to persevere with his studies at the Ontario Society of Artists, Bengough did a caricature of Senator James Beaty, owner of a conservative rag, *The Leader*. When Sam Beaty, James's nephew and the paper's business manager, chanced to see it, he had it lithographed at nearby Rolph Brothers and a copy sent to Bengough. For a twenty-three-year-old unfamiliar with lithography it was a revelation: "the ease and accuracy with which the reproduction was done struck me with amazement; but further, it gave me an idea. Why not start a weekly comic paper with lithographed cartoons?"

Why not, indeed? The moustachioed young man had little money, but he got backing from A. S. Irving, manager of the Toronto News Company. *Grip* he called after the namesake raven in Dickens's novel *Barnaby Rudge*. In his first issue, 24 May 1873, the editor reflected that

Though the raven race have no enviable reputation, being traditionally stigmatised as bearers of ill-omen only, there is no reader but likes *GRIP*'s company, for he is in all points an exceptional bird: there is, for instance, such a wholesome contrast between his glad and frequent *"Never Say Die!"* and the dismal, *"Nevermore"* of his dusky mate in literature—the

despairing croaker that perched upon Mr. *EDGAR POE*'s bust
of PALLAS; and according to the latest account,

> Still is sitting, still is
> sitting
> there.

Although Irving was initially listed as publisher and proprietor, many
others—some of them pseudonymous—wandered across his masthead.
But Bengough was plainly in charge of the show, and would remain
so until roughly two years before the magazine's demise, his emblem
a raven with a quill in its beak, his masthead or cover-page motto: "The
gravest Beast is the Ass; the gravest Bird is the Owl;/The gravest Fish
is the Oyster; the gravest Man is the Fool."

The pink-paper cover crowded with business-card-sized advertisements, the four pages inside with soft-pencil drawings—none of these
achieved immediate success. But help was on the way, and from the
Prime Minister who would become his favourite subject. John A. Macdonald's distress would be Bengough's glee. "There was no great public
furor over the initial number," Bengough recalled, "and it is hard to
say what might have been the outcome of the venture had it not been
for the sudden occurrence of a great political sensation which is now
known in history as the 'Pacific Scandal.' The whole country was at
once aflame with interest and excitement, and an absorbing theme [was]
adapted to keep *Grip* going for many issues...." The Pacific Scandal led
to what was probably Bengough's most famous cartoon. Confronted
by a stonily accusatory Alexander Mackenzie, Macdonald blandly
retorts: "I admit I took the money and bribed the electors with it. Is
there anything wrong about *that*?"

By 12 July 1873 the editor was able to boast that he was offering

> a larger quantity of original matter than in any previous one,
> and we are now making arrangements, which when com-
> pleted will make 'Grip' a thoroughly enjoyably [sic] little
> sheet....Like Artemus Ward, our politics agree with those of
> any person with whom we come in contact; neither fearing,
> nor currying favour, we intend to use the lash of ridicule in
> whatever direction abuses call for it.
>
> In this spirit we hope our numerous friends will peruse our
> paper, and if the laugh should be against their political stand-
> point on some occasions, recollect that their risible faculties
> will have an opportunity of being exercised at their oppo-
> nents on others. Having had our croak, we now withdraw to
> give place to matter more appropriate to our pages.

Among the appropriate matter on 25 October 1873 was some sport
connected with the recently founded *Canadian Monthly*. When the

Monthly's anonymous "Current Events" column was attributed to Goldwin Smith, Bengough published fictitious notes "for the guidance of guessers":

> *Government House, Ottawa*
> DEAR GRIP: I am instructed by the Right Hon. the Premier
> to say in advance that in the matter of the 'Current Events'
> arts, his hands are clean. The rumour that he is the writer
> the Govt deny *in toto*.
> Yours, etc.,
> J. A. M.—D—LD.
>   per _____ , *Private Secretary*

The 12 July masthead page had included "Newly Coined Words" neatly keyed to the Pacific Scandal: "JONATIATE—To wriggle, prevaricate, recriminate, procrastinate." "ALLANISE—To scheme, to subsidise, to affidavitise." Elsewhere in the issue, a full-page cartoon concerned the forthcoming October meeting of Parliament. A sickly John A. rests in bed, while nearby Miss Canada confers with the doctors, made up of such Liberal rivals as Alexander Mackenzie and George Brown:

> Miss Canada (*anxiously*)—"DOCTORS, HOW DO YOU FIND
> THE POOR DEAR PREMIER?"
> Dr.B—n (*for the M.D.'s*)—"MADAM, WE'VE JUST HAD A
> CONSULTATION; THE SYMPTOMS ARE HOPEFUL—WE
> BELIEVE HE CAN'T SURVIVE OCTOBER!"

This was certainly topical enough—and prescient, since the Conservative government was defeated.

In the same month a full-page cartoon demonstrated another ongoing preoccupation. Entitled "The Eclipse of Human Rights," "With a View of the Sign-Board as It Will Be After the Dark Shadow of Landlordism Has Passed Off," it shows intersecting globes. One is "As a Just Creator meant it to be" with a signboard: "NOTICE. THE LAND, LIKE THE AIR AND THE WATER, IS FOR THE EQUAL USE OF ALL MANKIND." The other is labelled "The Human Invention of Injustice." The only words not scratched out on the board are "NOTICE. THE LAND is for the use of LANDLORDS."

Nor was the message signposted enough. Sketched in is a worker with upraised shovel who shouts, "With the Land free from the Clutch of Monopoly I defy Poverty!"; a new globe proclaiming, "NOTICE. LANDLORDS MUST HEREAFTER PAY ALL RENTS FROM LAND TO THE PUBLIC TILL. LAND CANNOT BE PRIVATE PROPERTY"; and a tax collector helpfully explaining to a labourer, "You simply pay a single tax on the value of the land you hold—no Tariff taxes—no taxes on your Industry."

A hint of Bengough's own business practices was evidenced the same year with a note on the masthead: "When Contributors require payment for their productions, the amount expected must be marked on the MS. All articles will be considered as gratuitous unless so marked." Entertainer he may have been, but he was also a resourceful entrepreneur. Both these functions were combined in the "Chalk-Talks" that he began on 20 March 1874 with "Pleasantries of Public Life," and that he would continue for the next forty-seven years, including tours in the United States, Britain and the Antipodes. For his debut he commissioned a script from W. J. Rattray, who had done work for *The Grumbler*, an earlier Toronto comic paper. As he would later recall of that night in the Music Hall, he was attired not in "the regulation full-dress" but "in all the glory of a brown velvet sackcoat....I found myself in the presence of a 'large and fashionable audience.' My mechanical equipment consisted of a tripod easel furnished with a supply of white newsprint paper, and a quantity of black conté crayons not much thicker than slate pencils. In addition I had my manuscript—'mine' since I had paid for it!—which I had fairly mastered."

Somehow he kept *Grip* going while he chalk-talked his way across the continent, counting on an amazingly dependable postal system to keep his work flowing to Toronto—in the case of his first Pacific Coast tour he supplied an illustrated page in the form of an autographic diary. Only once did the mails let him down, and at the last minute he was forced to redo his work back at the office. A previously drawn-up list of local celebrities and a quick eye enabled him to produce rapid-fire crowd-pleasing sketches. In Ingersoll, Ontario, "I had the celebrated [for his badness] poet [James] McIntyre on my list. I pictured him in the act of reading one of his matchless odes to an Ingersoll-made cheese, and the acclamations of the throng inspired him to rise in his place and treat us to a brilliant impromptu:

I am thankful to Bengough
For the way he has taken me off.

If a cartoonist had taken off Bengough himself, he might have found some contradictions between word and deed. Bengough may have said that LAND CANNOT BE PRIVATE PROPERTY, but the cover for 2 February 1879 advertised houses, orchards and farms available from the firm of Bengough and Musson, "Next to Post Office;" pens and penholders at the Grip Office; "Cheap Books" at Bengough Brothers, "One door west of Post Office;" and a stock of printing types at the Grip Job Department. The same cover also featured a fantastic scene of flying, hopping and perching humans, birds—including the inevitable raven—frogs and other creatures interwoven with a rustic logo that overlooked mock-heraldic vignettes.

Bengough's life was complicated. His brothers George and Thomas were also in the business; a younger brother, William, in his own right became a well-known magazine illustrator. Founded in 1882 with Thomas a director, the Grip Printing and Publishing Company was capitalized at the substantial sum of $50,000, and had until 1886 an able manager in S. J. Moore. Moore, who later helped support the *Canadian* and the *Canadian Courier*, invented the Paragon flipover-carbon salesbook and started a company that would become the world's largest manufacturer of business forms.

One of Bengough's ventures in 1885 was the one-shot *Bengough's Illustrated Monthly*. Its February issue described itself as

> a newspaper illustrating the principal events interesting to the public, has a free circulation of 5,000 copies, distributed proportionately among the advertisers, who re-distribute it as a souvenir to their patrons, and, unlike other periodicals, the entire circulation is confined to Toronto. All the advertisements are pictorial, and every advertiser is entitled to a picture of anything he may desire, printed together with his reading matter, thus making an advertisement interesting in itself, and ensuring its complete perusal. Being the only illustrated newspaper in Canada, and to be had free, it will be an irresistible attraction to the public.

Though the public resisted this attraction, Grip Printing and Publishing issued not just Bengough cartoon collections—*The Decline and Fall of Keewatin*, subtitled *The Free-Trade Redskins; The Grip-Sack; A Caricature History of Canadian Politics*—but educational periodicals and serious books of politics and history by Alexander Mackenzie, George M. Grant and Arnold Haultain. After 1893 it was principally an engraving business, changing its name in 1901 to Grip Limited, a forerunner of the company later called Bomac Batten. However radical Bengough was, he was patently no Communist.

Five years after *Grip*'s inception the little comic weekly had cleaner type, sharper lines and thicker paper. Single-page cartoons were now loose in the magazine, hence suitable for framing. By the end of 1878 *Grip* even included a hand-tinted, two-colour extravaganza called "Christmas Among the Politicians." By 1883, prosperity was even more apparent in the statistics Bengough provided in the 12 May issue: "Our attention is called to the figures given in *Rowell's Newspaper Directory* representing the circulation of GRIP as 2,000 weekly. We beg to state that this estimate was furnished to Rowell two years ago, since which time our weekly circulation has increased to between 7,000 and 10,000 and the paper is perused by fully 50,000 readers every week."

By 1883, *Grip* had its principal features in place in a magazine that had expanded from four to ten pages and would eventually reach fourteen, excluding cover. They included "Cartoon Comments," elaborating on the "Leading Cartoon," now bound into the magazine; a section

Twinned with his favourite subject, John A. Macdonald, Bengough sometimes misfired with his prophecies. Perched on the easel in this 1878 cartoon is Grip, the eponymous raven of his magazine.

O, OUR PROPHETIC SOUL!
(See last week's Cartoon.)
JOHN A.—"I DON'T KNOW, BUT IT SEEMS TO ME, THIS PICTURE OF YOURS, MY PROPHETIC FRIEND, NEEDS A LITTLE 'READJUSTMENT,' DON'T IT, HEY?"

of short items called "Croaks"; "Our leading article"—"Supplied each week to GRIP," said the issue of 4 August, "by a Syndicate of Grit and Tory editors"; and "Our First Person Singular." All were vehicles for Bengough's opinions. These were offered with a freedom inconceivable under later libel laws, as in this choice item from 1 September: "Sir Charles Tupper's fame has been well earned, and it ill becomes his own countrymen to aid and abet foreign slanders in seeking to diminish his glory as the boldest corruptionist of modern times."

As always, the line drawings, cartoons and caricatures in advertisements remarkably harmonized with the rest of the magazine, because, after all, Bengough drew them, too. Loving pseudonyms, he even invented a distinct style for one of his alter egos, "L. Coté." As Bengough recalled it:

> *Grip* had scarcely any artistic contributions apart from my own. The cartoons which appeared for a time dealing with current political issues in the Province of Quebec and signed L. Coté were not an exception to the rule. When the first of the series appeared I remember that a connoisseur of art, high up in the city schools, happened to come into the office. He was looking through the current number on the counter, and when he came to the Coté cartoon he gave a delighted start and became immensely interested. "L. Coté," he cried, "Who is he? Where did you come across the chap? That fellow can draw; no offence, you know, but really you ought to model yourself on his style." Of course I felt gratified; so much so that I couldn't refrain from telling the visitor in

strict confidence that I had done the work myself, purposely adopting a slashing "French" style of handling.

Whatever guise Bengough assumed, the sale of *Grip* was a welcome event every Saturday. Along with tackling monopolies, in particular the Canadian Pacific Railway, he exploited the Second Riel Rebellion, publishing in 1885 four numbers of the *Canadian Pictorial & Illustrated War News*.

Bengough, though dominant, was not alone in his endeavours. Peter MacArthur, the son of a homesteader who became a well-known columnist for the *Globe*, began his career writing jokes for *Grip*. Sam Hunter, a fine cartoonist, was also a regular contributor. In *Grip's* first year, one "Jimuel Briggs"—known elsewhere as "Jimuel Briggs, D.B., of Coboconk University"—was listed as the editor, perhaps only for a single issue. This was a pseudonym for Phillips Thompson, an atheist who later became a theosophist, a reporter for the *Telegram*, the *Globe*, the *Mail* and a copious writer of skits, sketches and satirical poems. He was also married to two sisters, though not—it must be noted—at the same time. In 1874 and 1890 he founded the short-lived radical weeklies *The National* and *Labour Advocate* and, as a convinced socialist and sometime political candidate, wrote a column for the weekly *Palladium of Labor*. He is described in the *Grip* of 11 December 1880 as having "a high forehead, Roman nose, and straight sandy whiskers, a tall, thin, ungainly figure...a genial, jovial gentleman."

There were other, less well-known characters in *Grip's* portmanteau, one who figured on the production side—*Grip* had gone from lithography to wood engraving to zinc etching. As Bengough remembered it:

Sometime in the late eighties there walked into the office one day a quaint figure of a Scotsman, who announced that he had a method of etching on zinc by which he could make an autographic reproduction of a drawing which could be printed along with the type, thus combining the advantages of lithography and wood-engravings while being cheaper than either. This was William Stewart, who accordingly settled down in the *Grip* establishment and impressed his personality upon all connected therewith. He was deeply immersed in the mysteries of his new art—I think he claimed it as his own discovery, which I now regard as doubtful, though he was unquestionably the pioneer of zinc-etching in Toronto—but he was rarely too preoccupied to be ready and willing to discuss the fine points of theology with any "foeman worthy of his steel." On such occasions he supported the position of the agnostics with an absorption which not only endangered the orthodoxy of his opponent but the successful outcome of the batch of cartoons on the sheet of zinc he had at the moment

This time unwittingly prophetic, on 30 May 1891 Bengough had the Liberal politician, Richard Cartwright, show an ominous painting to John A. Macdonald. A few days later Macdonald was dead.

in the acid bath, which he was meanwhile rocking to and fro like a cradle. Poor old Stewart! He was a kindly soul with all his queerness...his sublime indifference to appearance in the fit and style of his clothes. He remained with *Grip* long enough to see the art of photo-engraving develop in the city to a degree which quite superseded his crude methods, and at length he drifted out of the establishment as quietly as he had drifted in.

The year 1891 was to be momentous for Bengough, for he lost a favourite target. On 30 May he had published a cartoon of Sir John A. Macdonald leaning on cane, viewing a painting, "A Nocturne in Black, Entitled "The Future of Canada." The picture was entirely black. Six days later Macdonald was dead.

Bengough commemorated the event rather conventionally with a cartoon of a riderless horse and a commentary whose mangled type either mirrored Bengough's grief or Macdonald's mischievous ghost:

THE EMPTY SADDLE—The great chief of the Conservative party has gone the way [sic] all flesh, and although he is succeeded, he can have no successor. The face and form which for many years ha e ended [sic: broken misaligned type] thes e pages v [sic] have parted for ever. It is a satisfaction to feel, as we do, that although few numbers of GRIP have appeared without "John A." being depicted in some shape, we have never treated him with less than justice. This he was not slow to admit himself on the occasion of the only interview we ever had with him, and which took place in Ottawa a few years ago. "GRIP has been conducted most fairly and impartially so far," said he. "I hope you will never let it get into the control of either party."[Bengough later recalled that "The quality in the great leader which impressed me most during those few minutes was his air of shrinking bashfulness!" Little wonder.] It was not the least of Sir John's gifts as a public man (from GRIP's standpoint) that he had a face supremely good for caricature purposes. In that respect, as well as in others, we may say with *Hamlet*, "We ne'er shall look upon his like again." This journal, however, like Her Majesty's Government, *must* be carried on. May he rest in peace.

As if to atone for the many times he had made merry with the Old Chieftain's bulbous nose and indolent form, Bengough also added a black-bordered poem:

DEAD! Dead! And now before
The threshold of bereaved Earnscliffe stand
In spirit, all who dwell within our land
   From shore to shore!
Bengough concluded:
He was no harsh, self-righteous Pharisee —
The tender Christ compassioned such as he,
   And took their part.

   As to his Statesman-fame,
Let History calm his wondrous record read,
And write the Truth, and give him honest meed
   Of praise or blame!

Ever the entrepreneur, Bengough ran an ad on 22 August for the *Life of Sir John A. Macdonald*, written by the dead statesman's nephew, Colonel J. P. MacPherson. Grip Printing and Publishing Company was the publisher's agent. Commercial considerations aside, Bengough, or at least *Grip*, seemed a bit lost without its perennial target.

The tone was strained on 2 January 1892 when, along with announcing a humour competition, an editorial stated:

...we have braved the storms of eighteen years and six months—a long, long life as journals go. Yes, we're growing old, reckoning by the watch. Still, as the Fool i' the Forest remarked, we take no note of time. We keep our youth and our vigor unabated. Judge for yourself, O gentle one! Is not this, the first number of Vol. XXXVIII, as spry and chipper and jokey, and withal as full of sound sense as was No.1 of Vol.I?

It wasn't. In July 1892, Phillips Thompson became editor and a year later the Grip Company suspended publication. In 1894, Bengough returned as proprietor. "The public did not feel disposed to do without their GRIP, and ever since have kept up a pathetic clamor for his re-establishment. In compliance with this general demand, the Old Bird has been revived under the guidance of his founder, and having risen from his ashes under the auspices of the Phoenix Publishing Co., hopes to go on an indefinitely long career of usefulness...."

As it happened, the issues became progressively thinner, with little editorial content other than the cartoons—a decline soon leading to death.

Bengough was not a great artist, but he had a quality many better draughtsmen lacked: his lines lived. He was also fortunate in having so marvelous a subject in the long-serving prime minister, a combination of cartoonist-and-victim not equalled in Canadian journalism until the late 1950s with Duncan Macpherson and John Diefenbaker. As a cartoonist he had many capable successors, but as an editor of a Canadian humorous magazine, none with his versatility and talent. After *Grip* ceased, Bengough cartooned for the *Globe* and *Montreal Star*, and continued as a touring chalk-talker up until his death in 1923, even branching into movie making as part of an anti-smoking campaign. He left an indirect aesthetic legacy, too. As an engraving house and design firm, Grip Limited in the 1900s and 1910s employed designers and illustrators who, like the painters Tom Thomson, Franklin Carmichael, Arthur Lismer, F.H. Varley and A.J. Casson, would change the course of Canadian art.

Perpetual critic that he was, what did Bengough believe in? He believed in Dickens. He fervently believed in Henry George's Single Tax on the value of unimproved land. He believed in total abstinence from liquor and tobacco and opposed vivisection. From the early 1880s, he believed in women's suffrage and in their professional advancement. He believed in the Liberals more than in the Conservatives and in the late 1880s in a short-lived Third Party led by a Methodist, Dr. Alexander Sutherland. He believed in keeping streetcars idle on Sunday so the working man could have a day of worship or at least of rest. He believed in the efficacy of political action, in patriotism, and, though in 1896 he declined a federal nomination on the Prohibitionist ticket, he did become a Toronto alderman. At first he believed in the protective tariff, but a decade later he ardently espoused free trade, though certainly not annexation. He believed in a Canadian republic with elections determined by proportional representation, in a strictly separated church and state, and in a unilingual country speaking English, of course.

Mostly, he believed in himself.

A COWBOY'S
SATURDAY NIGHT

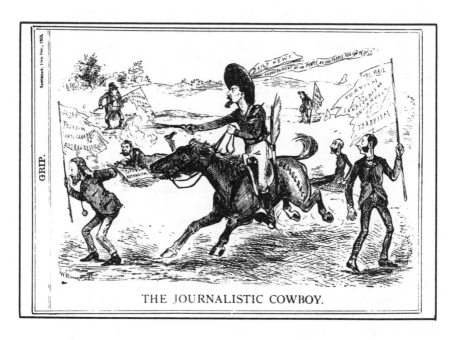

THE JOURNALISTIC COWBOY.

In mid-December 1883, a full-page cartoon in *Grip* depicted a moustachioed, goateed gentleman hard-riding a steed branded "Democracy." In his holster is a giant quill and he is firing a six-gun at various dismayed pedestrians whose banners identify them as "Globe Fogyism, Anti-Canadaism, Retrogression," "Telegram Nothingism," "Irish Canadian Toryism," "The Mail Toryism, Landlordism, Snobrule, Toadyism," "World Neither Fish Nor Fowl." The cartoon's title was THE JOURNALISTIC COWBOY. The cowboy was Edmund Ernest Sheppard, his rag or nag the recently founded *News*.

Sheppard was born in 1855 near St. Thomas, Ontario. His mother died when he was an infant and his father, an emigrant Englishman, was a preacher in the Christian Church, Disciples of Christ. Founded in Kentucky, the aim of the Disciples of Christ was to reduce Christianity to a few articles of belief to which all could subscribe, with the inevitable consequence that yet another sect was created. One of twelve children, Sheppard attended country schools in Elgin County and, briefly, the college from which his father had graduated, Bethany in West Virginia.

Whether the Disciples atmosphere or the medical course he was taking bored him is unknown, but at nineteen he headed for the southwestern United States, where he became a cowboy and stagecoach driver. From his four years there he took his persona, his pen-name "Don" and his startling tastes in footwear, haberdashery and hygiene. A contemporary recalled his "top-boots of fine Spanish leather; outdoors he wore a tall plug hat, indoors a slouch hat; he continually chewed tobacco, and was proud of his range and the accuracy of his aim."

In 1878, Sheppard returned to Canada and in quick succession worked for the *London Advertiser, Standard* and *Free Press*, the Toledo (U.S.) *Commercial*, the St. Thomas *Journal* and *Toronto Mail*, and became editor and later proprietor, of the *News*. With its pink paper much favoured by little boys for making kites, its rampant sensationalism and "Peek-a-Boo" gossip column, its championing of an elective Senate, in fact the election of every office down to dogcatcher, the *News* under Sheppard was the most talked-about newspaper of its day. But Sheppard's stance had risks. When a Sheppard underling claimed that the 65th Rifles of Montreal, a largely French-Canadian unit, had been slackers in suppressing the Riel Rebellion of 1885, all its officers sued. For two years Sheppard alternately dodged warrants and fought in court to have the actions tried in Toronto. Surrendering, Sheppard went to Montreal and paid a fine, also undertaking not to engage in daily journalism. The latter was the least of his problems: the litigation costs had ruined his newspaper. He sold it.

But while he was absent from Toronto, a second venture recouped his prestige if not his fortune. It was *Toronto Saturday Night*. In its salutation, the Sheppard Publishing Company derided a predecessor and predicted a bright future for itself:

> While newspapers have multiplied in Toronto and throughout the whole of Canada there is no competitor to contest the field with *Saturday Night*. The *Canadian Illustrated News*, published some years ago in Montreal, failed because of its lack of excellence, but we feel confident that a really good pictorial paper cannot but succeed if its scope is wide enough to meet the tastes of the general public. In order to enlarge our constituency, *Saturday Night* will not only present illustrations as its leading feature, but will supply departments of social and family reading which cannot fail to amuse and instruct.

The fledgling publication would not be "a political paper," though it would have "remarks to make about politics and politicians, and in a breezy yet thoughtful way will point out the follies and foibles of those who assume so much and do so little." Departments would embrace society doings, music, drama, commerce and sport. Nor would students be neglected, "as it is the aim of the editor of their department to make it really representative of their best ambitions, amusements and even hilarities, thoroughly remembering that we were boys once ourselves."

Doubtless mindful of the *News*'s recent adversities, *Saturday Night* did not intend

> to speak evil of anyone, and the publishers and editors desire
> that nothing shall appear in these columns which will
> alienate a friend or cause either anger or pain. To be good-
> natured will be the chief aim of this journal, now and then
> perhaps pointing out or smiling at the weaknesses which
> mark the human race, but avoiding always anything that is
> scurrilous or improper. The journey of life is naturally over
> many rough places, and those are not friends of society who
> add to the ruggedness of the road or increase the disquiet and
> turmoil, which, under the best circumstances, cloud so much
> of heaven's brightness and obscure so constantly the sunshine
> of good fellowship and neighbourly kindness.

Although concentrating on literature, *Saturday Night* "will be essentially a paper of to-day, dealing with current topics, and should not be looked upon in any sense as simply 'a storypaper,' though novels, illustrated sketches and stories will form one of its many features."

Although Sheppard was soon to dominate the paper, those soothing words, and indeed the idea of the paper itself, were probably those of Walter Cameron Nichol, who in 1887 was a twenty-one-year-old writer of verse and skits for the *Toronto News*. The son of a Queen's Counsel, he had founded a small journal on cycling as a boy and at the age of twelve had gone to work in a law office before reporting for the *Hamilton Spectator* and then the *News*. He swayed the *News*'s advertising manager, W. E. Caiger, to the idea of the weekend paper, but both had to wait until their chief raised the money and moved the enterprise into a corner of the Grand Opera House on Adelaide Street, enlisting such $500 subscribers to the Sheppard Publishing Company as the opera house manager, a Baptist Church organist and a type founder. The little staff sat up all night folding sheets for the first issue, as they would do for some time to come.

If this was the hidden reality of the enterprise, *Saturday Night* was determined to maintain an opulent outer show. The editorial offices were well-appointed and the visitor's chair well-padded, and on the wall of the business office hung a sumptuous gold-framed painting by

Guercino entitled "The Seven Ages of Man", apt parable for a magazine as well as a man. All was to be decorum, even the advertisements,
which would "be limited in space, and will be clean. No quacks or
'before taking' and 'after taking' illustrations will ever appear in its
columns, as the public to which we appeal are doubtless tired of having all the ills of life and the symptoms of every disease that flesh is
heir to continually paraded before them."

Although *Saturday Night* was by no means a woman's paper, it paid
much more attention to what was still called "the fairer sex" than most
of its contemporaries. The principal illustration depicted a pert house-
maid in cap and apron carrying a tray laden with a copy of *Saturday
Night* and captioned "Your Paper, Ma'am." The lead item concerned
the current city mayoralty contest. Page 2 was dedicated to social notes
from Toronto and environs, Page 3 to music—the articles were written
by E. W. Schuch, a choirmaster, conductor of light operas and music
critic for the *Globe* who signed himself "Metronome"—in this case the
first of a long series of illustrated articles on Toronto choristers called
"Singers of Sacred Song." Nichol handled drama, and there were such
departments as "Hints for Housekeepers," "Notes for Women,"
"Fashion Gossip," "Advertising as a Fine Art," "Skating and Curling,"
"Arts and Artists," "The Officer's Mess" (military news), "Chat from
'Varsity'" and "Notes About Horses." A third of the twelve-page first
issue was given over to fiction, including the first instalment of *Widower
Jones*, Sheppard's novel of rural Ontario. His first novel, which bore
the deadly title of *Dolly: the Little Widder Up to Felders*, had been published the previous year.

This Toronto publication of leisure and the light touch proved to be
an instant success in the tightly knit little city of 125,000. Priced at five
cents, the issue of 3 December 1887 sold out its 9,500 copies, reaching
an average of 10,000 within the first year, a plateau that would remain
constant for two decades.

With the second issue, "Don" took the stage with the words "I was
in church last Sunday night trying to hear a good sermon." This was
to be the first of many sermon reviews by Sheppard, a focus not so
startling as it might appear in retrospect. Sermons are, after all, a literary form of long standing. Though hardly common, sermon criticism
in Canada can be traced back to 1825 and the *Colonial Advocate* of William Lyon Mackenzie. In *Saturday Night*, preachers were portrayed in
images as well as prose with the illustrations of Duncan McKellar, who
was also a versifier and who became assistant editor.

Others joined the fledgling publication. The first articles of the famed
newspaperwoman "Kit" Coleman, the Irish-reared friend of Sarah Bernhardt, appeared in the magazine. From 1891 the Chatham, Ontario-born
"Lady Gay" (Grace Sandys, later Denison) covered society. Jean Graham, like Lady Gay, became a long-time staff writer. Hector

Charlesworth's first contribution was a prize poem entitled "The Prisoned Streamlet" at Christmas 1890, and he often sent in other verses, sometimes signed "Touchstone." Having obtained the approval of Charlesworth's father—the versifier was still a teenager—Sheppard took him on staff from March 1891 until 1892.

"Amaryllis" (Agnes Scott), described with such verve in Sandra Gwyn's *The Private Capital*, reported on the Ottawa social round from 1897 until July 1902. Telling of the auction of Sir John A. Macdonald's effects, she noted: "There was a framed photograph of a young Canadian woman, a violinist, little more than a girl in the picture—it was bought for twenty-five cents by someone who knew her, not for the frame."

Until 1900, Valance Patriarche, who began writing for the magazine as a young girl, worked there and later wrote an engaging account of her free-lance adventures:

> Every weekend saw me experiencing like anything . . . . . . The
> account of enthusiastic participation in a Methodist revival
> was considered to be in bad taste, coming from one carefully
> nurtured in the more astringent atmosphere of the Church of
> England, and a story of thwarted attempts to be an active
> performer in a mass baptism and get myself immersed in the
> tank of a Baptist Tabernacle was voted vulgar in the extreme;
> upon another occasion there was cold ostracism after an
> interview had been obtained with an amateur flea-trainer
> who had his pets badly under control. In spite of this lack of
> sympathy, [from her family] however, the pursuit of life went
> on and life largely consisted of the things SATURDAY
> NIGHT might see fit to publish.

But "Don"'s causeries were the paper's centre. He scorned the prudish Toronto matrons who spurned the St. Andrew's Ball because it was rumoured that the "Jersey Lily," the theatrical beauty, Lily Langtry, would attend. He chastised Goldwin Smith for accusing Edward Blake of "taking the wages of iniquity" in agreeing to represent the CPR before the Privy Council. Penning, or rather dictating—"I have an instantaneous mind"—these animadversions, Sheppard worked out of a sanctum behind a large outer room.

Here Sheppard functioned as business manager—and not coincidentally established a series called "Advertising as a Fine Art" before the end of 1887, wrote the front-page commentary "Around Town," special pieces and the weekly 4,000 words of *Widower Jones*. On the side he ran, with the help of Kate Westlake, a former reporter and proofreader on rural weeklies, an inoffensive "kitchen fiction" paper called the *Fireside Weekly*. He set up departments celebrating the seasonal cycle of sports, a Poet's corner, the occasional "Railway Chatter" and

"The Brotherhoods," which dealt with fraternal societies—Sheppard was active in several.

He was resourceful. Lest he be caught short of illustrations, he squirreled away a large stock of used electrotypes of wood engravings, whose Germanic-sentimental tenor may be inferred from titles like "The Lion's Bride." When these were too big to fit the front page he simply ran them sideways in the inside. But he also used local talents like J. W. Bengough, the cartoonist Sam Hunter, and William Wallace, a staff artist who later went to London to found the Carlton Group of commercial illustrators.

Sheppard did not monopolize commentary. The editorial pages included an anonymously attributed department called "Here and There" and a half-page in the centre of the paper dealing with public issues, such as the importance of reading Canadian books. He always had a keen eye for newcomers. To the young job applicant who later became Lady Willison he advised: "First, insist upon being paid for whatever work of yours is published. Don't let an editor tell you that it is honour enough to have your work published in his paper without being paid for. Second, never refuse a job even if you don't like the kind of work. You will find it easier to get work you do like if you are already in a position. Third, don't try to explain every detail in the lives of your characters. Leave something to the imagination."

All was not helpfulness on the staff. Sheppard feuded with Nichol and Caiger, who, believing that Sheppard was usurping what after all had been their idea, departed in 1888 to commence a rival weekly called *Life*. Within six months Sheppard was able to exact a neat revenge by writing: "The name of *Life* has been changed to *Death*." This proved to be not altogether a bad thing for Nichol. Before the decade was out he had left for the goldfields of the Kootenays, en route to acquiring the *Victoria Province*, directorships in insurance, trust and mining companies, and the lieutenant-governorship of British Columbia.

The same year Nichol left *Saturday Night*, the magazine published the first of its special Christmas issues, this particular one featuring one of Sheppard's finds—the Mohawk princess Pauline Johnston. By the 1890s, the glossy Christmas issues had lithographed colour covers and folded colour supplements. Inside was more contemporary, less sentimental visual content, with black-and-white sketches or half-tone reproductions of paintings, usually by members of the Royal Canadian Academy of Art, Ontario Society of Artists or the Art Students' League. The text of poems was embellished and unified with borders and figures, and advertisements, too, were often elaborate. For premiums, Sheppard offered a huge number of premium reproductions, such as a mezzotint of Robert Harris's "Fathers of Confederation." Christmas issues were especially prone to Madonnas, one of whom caused the editor less trouble than amused diversion around 1895.

When a woman in the southern United States claimed that the lithograph represented her and demanded heavy damages, the editor, says Hector Charlesworth, wrote her

> courteously and with meticulous observance of politeness that his ownership of the picture was perfect, and that the lady would be up against the necessity of proving several things: e.g., actual relation of woman and child, proof of motherhood, name of child and where now residing, whether the photographic process expressed the actual relationship; mere production of a child by a photographic process conveys no background for damages through trespass to maternal sensibilities....

There were no more claims.

While *Saturday Night*'s looks were being improved, Sheppard continued his novel-writing career. *Widower Jones*, like *Dolly*, was an example of generic backwoods humour, but *A Bad Man's Sweetheart*, published in 1889, focused on big bad Toronto. He was also writing stories, and one of the 1888 issues included "The Adventures of a Dollar Bill." The dollar bill's exploits began in the hands of a store clerk and many hands later ended up in a gambler's pocket where it was pierced by the bullet that killed him.

Sixty-five years later, Hugh Garner hilariously encapsulated *Saturday Night*'s taste in fiction when he recounted the plot of a serial called "Sally Nettlefold's Lovers":

> A three-column illustration bears the caption "Amos sprang forward and caught her in his arms, kissing her lovely surprised face rapturously." This probably sent a whole generation of servant girls into a tizzy and set the matrons' bosoms to heaving like the Bay of Biscay. The accompanying picture, however, only shows Amos (who looks all of seventy-five, and this before male hormones were dreamed of) making the initial grab at our own Little Nell, and not kissing her at all. She seems to have placed her bustle in the way, and Amos has probably reconsidered dalliance with a dame hiding herself behind the thorny name of Nettlefold.

Sheppard's political career in province and city had more than a passing resemblance to his dollar bill. The year the paper was founded, he'd been the unsuccessful candidate for Toronto West; in 1890 he was beaten in Haldimand; and in 1893 he failed to become mayor. Ideologically he was spattered across the map. Generally labelled an Independent Conservative, he had belonged to the Knights of Labour. But he also supported Laurier, who in 1897 gave him a reward by sending him on a trade mission to Central and South America.

The editor now entangled himself in the fortunes of the *Toronto Evening Star*. In 1887, he had begun using the work—signed "Frances Burton Clare" and later "Clip Carew" of Elmina Elliott, a young Oakville woman whom he liked so much he brought her to Toronto to be his society editor. She later became Sara Jeanette Duncan's successor as a columnist on the *Globe*'s women's page under the name "Madge Merton." In 1892, she married an ambitious young editor named Joe Atkinson, whose publishing progress would also cross that of *Saturday Night* at many points.

In 1895, Sheppard ostensibly bought the *Star*, which had been started three years earlier by a group of Toronto printers who had been locked out of the *News* after they had battled the newspaper's introduction of mechanical typesetters. Financially beset, the paper was bought in 1893 by the school textbook publisher W. J. Gage, who used it to promote Toryism and campaign against the Sunday use of streetcars. Gage in turn sold the paper to Sheppard.

He, however, was only the front man. The only public clue to this Machiavellian state of affairs was the change in the masthead a month after Sheppard appeared on this scene: he was now called president, not proprietor. The real purchaser was Frederic B. Nicholls, the Tory president of Canadian General Electric and founding publisher of the Canadian Manufacturers' Association magazine, *Canadian Manufacturer*. With his holdings in utilities and streetcar companies, Nicholls naturally favoured Sunday streetcars, but required Sheppard's convenient façade. During his less than two years' stay Sheppard was merely a salaried figurehead, though one endowed with managerial power. For example, he moved the *Star*'s printing equipment to the *Saturday Night* building on Adelaide Street where, for the next nine years, *The Star* was printed and, for most of that time, even edited.

After Sheppard left, so did many of the staff, disgusted with Nicholls's blatantly commercial manoeuvres. In late 1899, their Tory boss sold the ailing *Star* to a group of Laurier lovers, who hired Joseph Atkinson to run it.

Sheppard had been a bad man's sweetheart. Nor was it the end of his commercial wheelings and dealings during the nineties. He made an abortive attempt in 1893 to start a Winnipeg version of *Saturday Night*. Then, too, there had always been his somewhat ambiguous way with advertisers. The first issue of the magazine had promised decorous ads and that those of the before-and-after variety would be spurned, but an ad in the 31 July 1897 issue, virtually indistinguishable from editorial matter, was headlined "Better Than Gold" and read: "A Nova Scotia lady says, 'I consider Dr. Williams' Pink Pills a Priceless Boon to Suffering Humanity.'" Sheppard wrote the series "Advertising as a Fine Art" as a lure to space buyers, and even went so far as to contract with the Grand Trunk Railway to "not unfairly or unjustly criti-

cize'' that company. When John Ross Robertson of the *Telegram* assailed the magazine for the practice, Sheppard's front-page editorial retorted, ''Why should anybody object to that? It is not a newspaper's business to unfairly or unjustly criticize anybody.'' *Saturday Night* was, as a January 1897 issue had it, ''a Twelve-page, handsomely illustrated paper, published weekly, and devoted to its readers.'' Especially if they bought ads.

A decade after its founding, the magazine's principal departments included ''The Drama''; ''Sporting Comment''—one column signed ''The Umpire'' dealt with the feats of the Parkdale Cricket Club; Lady Gay's ''Between You and Me''; a correspondence column conducted by a graphologist; ''Social and Personal''—*Saturday Night* devoted a vast amount of verbiage to weddings; ''Studio and Gallery''; ''Society at the Capital'' by ''Amaryllis's successor ''Pera''; and ''Music.'' Although later readers have remarked on *Saturday Night's* bigotry, it seems, if anything, more tolerant than its contemporaries. A highly complimentary favourable 20 February cover story in 1897 was devoted to Madame M. Sissieretta Jones, ''The Black Patti,'' and the favour was repeated on 30 October.

Poems, of course, included some from Florence H. Randal, the poet Dorothy Livesay's mother. There were framed portraits of civic worthies on the cover, more half-tones—a mass photo of British Association for the Advancement of Science at the Royal Canadian Yacht Club and reports on the Klondike gold rush, whose U.S. ruffians should assuredly be curbed by the Mounted Police. In July the magazine snorted that "We are invited to believe...that it is quite easy to dig up one thousand dollars to the pan. If we allow eight pans to the shovel, we have eight thousand dollars for each shovelful of earth, and if you are a good spade hand...you could dig ten spadefuls in a minute, or in other words, you could make $4,800,000 in an hour. Why not run up to the Klondike for half a day?"

Apart from its predictable campaign in favour of Sunday streetcars, the paper's most notable cause that year was its support of the Retail Merchants' Association against a dangerous new phenomenon, the department store. A worried headline on 27 February asked, "Is the Department Store a Legitimate Enterprise? Is the Development of such an Institution a good thing for the City of Toronto and the Province of Ontario?" On the same page was a large mock ad for "Ketchem, Skinem & Cookem's Mammoth Department Store." On 31 July the magazine said of the Eaton Company: "It is not necessary for me to give some recital of the shams practised by this or other department stores."

The author of the gigantic articles on the demonic department stores was "Mack," the pseudonym of Joseph T. Clark. A small man with yellow hair, glittering blue eyes and an oversized head, Clark was born in Flesherton, Ontario in 1866. At the age of thirteen he was apprenticed to the printing works of the *Grey County News*, and, before he was twenty, became a journeyman printer at newspapers across Canada and the United States. Meanwhile, his sister Mabel and brother James became newspaper editors. When the *Pickering News* was sold, James bought it and the two brothers ran it. Finding this unprofitable, Clark got newspaper work in Toronto, where he was soon spotted by Sheppard. When Sheppard went south on his Laurier patronage mission he hired Clark to write "Front Page" editorials—Clark reputedly coined the famous boast "the twentieth century belongs to Canada"—naming him assistant editor. He also helped out on the *Star*, and left when Sheppard did.

As Clark's son Greg recalled it many years later, *Saturday Night* worked out of

tiled, tangled offices with much frosted glass and a sublime smell of ink rising from the basement, and, on certain days, a rumble that was and is a music like the Ride of the Valkyries to those who write, there was an elevator that went up six floors.

And from the sixth floor you walked up one, and there you were. In a kind of glass-roofed photographer's studio. Only it was my father's office.

Few of the millions of words Greg Clark wrote for the *Star Weekly*, the *Montreal Standard* and *Weekend* match the loving snapshots of his father he did for *Saturday Night* many years later. Here is the Sheppard-Clark relationship as seen through the eyes of a small boy:

A handsome door half open. A white-whiskered hatted Mr. Sheppard, just going out. A hollow weak voice, slightly querulous.

"Joe, come on over to McCaffery's?"

"I can't. I've got to take the lad here, taking him home."

"Pah," said Mr. Sheppard.

"Pah to you, Mr. Sheppard!"

Of Sheppard, Joseph Clark would say: "He had about as handy a vocabulary as it is possible for a man to pick out of the English language after sorting it all over. He had a way of standing a proposition on its head to see what concealments would fall out of its pockets, that was often attended with great success. When he got after anybody, there was fun for the spectators and a fresh hide nailed on the barn door to dry."

Here is another filial look at Clark-the-editor:

Into the wintry bright skylight room plunges an extraordinary figure. He is raggled and taggled and unshaven and in agony. He shivers and trembles and grits his teeth.

"Joe," he gasps, "a quarter. Just a quarter."

"The kid," warns my father, with eyes sideways at me sitting very lively.

"Oh, ho, ho," says this grotesque battered man, looking at me, in agony. "Sorry, sorry. Joe, a quarter, this once, a quarter. Just to finish it. I'm just over it."

My father is fishing in his pocket, his mouth tightened up, a sullen expression on his generally laughing face.

"Here," he mutters.

"Oh, ho, Joe," sobs the bizarre creature, all movement, all shakes, all hands pawing mouth, all body swaying over the desk. "Joe, I'll...really I'll...."

"All right, all right," says my father, coming around the desk and escorting the queer man to the door and all-righting him right down the stairs.

My father comes back into the vivid room and stands looking back at the doorway with a look so sullen, so soft, so tender, and so guilty that it is the miniature I took of him with me to the war and used to take out and look at it in the night, in the trenches. Then he turned and looked at me.

"That," he says, "is a great poet."

It was The Khan.

The Khan was Robert K. Kernighan, best known for his fervently patriotic "The Men of the Northern Zone."

Joseph Clark left the magazine when one of Joseph Atkinson's first managerial acts was to pluck him for the *Star*'s editorial staff. But he was not done with *Saturday Night*.

Worn out by fecklessly running for office, catering to advertisers and nailing hides to doors, Sheppard sold *Saturday Night* in 1906 and went to California. Just as obsessed as any of his contemporaries with religion and science, he wrote a book entitled *The Thinking Universe* and converted to Christian Science.

In retrospect, E. E. Sheppard seems less a coherent human being than a bundle of attitudes and opinions. A Canadian nationalist in many of his public pronouncements, he often resembled a typical cantankerous American opinionator. He wished the separation of Britain and Canada and urged the adoption of a Canadian flag and the end to church exemptions from taxes. An Orangeman, he disagreed with his fellows in everything but religion. He was past grand master of the sovereign great priory of the Knights Templar of Canada. He professed to hate

Yankees, French Canadians, monarchists and Catholics. He was, in fact, half crank, half sycophant.

The new owner of *Saturday Night* was Harold Gagnier, a man of Louisiana-French ancestry whose family had been active in the tobacco trade. Gagnier had a string of trade journals; now he had to contend with a magazine whose circulation had stagnated since 1887 when, over the same period, the Toronto population had doubled. Gagnier hired Clark as editor and Frederick Paul, an old friend who was city editor of the *Montreal Star*, to handle the financial pages. These were to be increasingly important.

Paul became editor of the twenty-page "wholesome paper for healthy people." Clark returned to the *Star*, where he founded, at Atkinson's behest, the *Star Weekly*. Now thirty-six pages and in three sections— "The Front Page" of political and social commentary, women's, and financial—*Saturday Night* increased its staff, its cover price (from five to ten cents) and its advertising rates. A book page was added, as well as the new departments "Motorists and Motoring" and "City and Country Homes." There was comparatively little fiction.

Once again, but this time to greater effect, *Saturday Night* pledged advertising probity. Clark's first editorial announced: "We decline to accept at any price the class of advertisements that were condemned in the first issue of the paper nineteen years ago....Get-rich-quick men, Shylock moneylenders, palmists...and secret cure people...are not allowed to annoy the readers of this paper with announcements that offend the intelligent and trap the inexperienced." And Paul greatly increased the financial coverage in keeping with the mining (Cobalt silver), railways construction and stock market booms that were then underway in Ontario. With its coated stock and reduced newspaper-trim size, Toronto *Saturday Night* was well on the way to becoming, not a city paper, but a national magazine. Many years later the magazine would claim that by 1907 its success had inspired imitators in Vancouver (*Saturday Sunset*), Winnipeg (*Saturday Post*), Detroit and Johnstown, Pennsylvania.

Although Paul's mother came from an old Quebec family, his father was an Alsatian who had settled in Saratoga, New York, where he ran a newspaper. Paul, who had been a reservist in the Spanish-American War and once owned a newspaper in the mining town of Hazelton, Pennsylvania, began raking the Toronto financial muck in 1910.

Lady Gay was still around, and the columns now extended to "The Investor" and "Automobile Topics." There was a "London Letter," "Notes from New York" and, *mirabile dictu*, numerous ads for the Eaton Company: "In the one vocabulary of Business the one word most pregnant with meaning is V-a-l-u-e."

Gagnier was giving value for money, at least to his well-fed audience. In early 1910, Hector Charlesworth had rejoined the magazine and was put in charge of the extensive picture services and music, theatrical and art criticism. But, like everyone else, he was also helping to expose fraud; as he recalled it, paddy wagons used to raid bucket shop promoters shortly after *Saturday Night* appeared. In 1911, Fred C. Pickwell, who had worked on prairie newspapers, was dispatched to Winnipeg to harvest Western rogues. In all this derring-do, *Saturday Night* was not deterred by numerous, though unsuccessful libel suits. In 1912, the magazine announced that, besides its offices in New York, Chicago, Montreal, Toronto and Winnipeg, it had opened one in London. By 1917 there were such financial columns as "Gold & Dross," "Concerning Insurance" and "In a Bird's Eye View."

Elsewhere in the paper, the fiction often came from H. Franklin Gadsby, the St. Catharines,Ontario-born former editor of *Collier's* Canadian edition. Socializing was found "At Four O'Clock," in "Hearsay and Happenings" and in a column called "My Lady's Dressing Table"—"Though winter is a rash and quarrelsome old chap, miladi [*sic*], ensconced in all the privacy of her boudoir and with all the weapons of the Dressing Table at hand, has no need to fear his blustering onslaughts."

During the war, *Saturday Night* was perfervidly patriotic, indeed jingoistic, running caricatures depicting the Kaiser, Robertson Davies has noted, as a "cringing, evil German emperor, wearing a helmet with a spike, with extraordinary upturned moustaches and a sneer that would chill the blood of a crocodile." Reports of a sort came from the front: Bonnycastle Dale, a gunner in the Canadian Field Artillery in France, "is sending some wonderful accounts home of wildlife close to the lines." The lead piece in the Women's Section of 3 February 1917, "Relic Hunting at the Coast," was a surprisingly sympathetic account of the Kwakiutl of British Columbia.

From Montreal, Paul had brought with him such colleagues as the young Peter Donovan, who became familiar to *Saturday Night* readers as "P.O.'D.," and women's editor Constance Marston. Donovan's deftly comic pieces were later collected in books like *Over 'Ere and Back Home.* His light touch is shown in a 24 November 1917 column entitled "The Gentle Plagiarist," with a woodcutlike illustration of a man pasting items into a scrapbook. "P.O.'D." remarked that:

Not long ago we published a very pretty and timely little poem called "The Old Canoe." It was contributed by one Eric A. Darling of Sault Ste. Marie presumably as his own. No doubt the reader remembers it. The first stanza ran as follows:

My seams gape wide, so I'm tossed aside
To rot on a lonely shore,
While the leaves and mould like a shroud enfold,

> For the last of my trails are o'er;
> But I float in dreams on Northland streams
> That never again I'll see,
> As I lie on the marge of the old portage
> With grief for company

As soon as the paper was off the press, the editor of the
Women's Section came in with a copy of it in her hand, and
said that she certainly had seen that poem somewhere
before....Enter the scrapbook! A gentleman in St. Mary's,
Ontario, wrote in to say that he had a copy of the poem in
his homemade anthology. He had clipped it years before from
"The Youth's Companion" or "The Literary Digest," where it
was attributed to George T. Marsh in "Scribner's Magazine."
In fact the gentleman in St. Mary's sent us the clipping, and
there was the original poem, credited to Scribner's, and with
Mr. Marsh's name as the author.

The next step was to write Eric A. Darling and ask him to
explain this singular coincidence. The managerial note
pointed out that SATURDAY NIGHT had no objection to
republishing good verse, as long as the little formality was
observed of putting the real author's name on it.

Darling wrote back to say "I have been writing for all manner of publications for some twelve years using different names at different
times....I do not recollect that 'George T. Marsh,' but that is quite possible in the chaos of the years." P.O.' D. comments:

> Very pretty phrase, that "chaos of the years!" And inciden-
> tally, what light it throws on the career of the busy man of
> letters to find a gentleman who has written so much and
> used so many names that he can't even recall them....He
> even states in his letter that he has sold the same poem to
> another Canadian publication, where it will appear
> shortly...."It is remarkable to me, amusing, how certain
> beings hover unceasingly, like unto vultures, over the literary
> trail, ready to pounce upon the traveller thereon with pirati-
> cal accusations." Then Mr. Darling is led into a long recital of
> the great number of publications he writes for.

Since Darling had mentioned that Donn Byrne was a pen name he
used for work in the *Saturday Evening Post*, *Saturday Night* wrote the
Post. On being told that Donn Byrne was not a pen name, and that his
address was Larchmont, New York, the magazine then wrote Byrne,
who promptly replied, "It's awfully decent to call my attention to this
little compliment of this man Darling's. I hope for his own health's sake

he remains in the fastnesses of Sault Ste. Marie, as I have a bigger reputation in certain quarters as an amateur boxer than as a professional writer.''

After the war, *Saturday Night* had to endure the cancellation of thousands of subscriptions because it had opposed Prohibition. As Charlesworth recalled, he and Paul believed that although restricted liquor traffic in wartime might be necessary, ''such temporary expedients should not become permanent restrictions on public liberty.'' The magazine nonetheless remained a modest commercial success.

In 1920, four years before Edmund Ernest Sheppard's death in San Diego, Harold Gagnier happened to be in California and looked up the old cowboy. When Sheppard asked how *Saturday Night* was prospering, Gagnier showed him a balance sheet with a satisfying bottom-line. Raging, Sheppard threw the upstart out.

Less than fifty years old, Gagnier himself died in 1922; Paul died in 1926, aged sixty. Managerially, *Saturday Night* entered a period of divisiveness and, editorially, an interregnum.

THE TRANSITIONAL
CANADIAN

*The wit and humour, the eloquence and the thought were of an exceedingly
high order, and, taken as a whole, were never equalled at any other gathering in Canada.*
—report on the *Canadian Magazine* banquet held 17 February 1897

That banquet must have been an edifying spectacle. As reported in the
Canadian Magazine of March 1897—in contrast to the three-month lead
time of late twentieth-century magazines this Victorian publication was
exceedingly quick off the mark—"The unanimous verdict of all who
attended was that the gathering was the finest of its kind that they witnessed."

Catered by Henry Webb, "the Delmonico of Toronto," the dinner
was chaired by the Honourable Thomas Ballantyne, the former speaker
of the Ontario Legislative Assembly. The "vice-chair" was occupied
by Mr. Barlow Cumberland and the *Canadian Magazine*'s editor, Mr.
John A. Cooper—though presumably not sitting on the same seat.
Although the Honourable J. C. Patterson, a former minister of militia
and at the time Lieutenant-Governor of Manitoba and president of the
Canadian Magazine, was unable to attend because his province's legislature had been summoned for the next day, and numerous letters of
regret were read, doubtless adding to the wit and humour, there
remained no shortage of distinguished guests.

Among them were Dr. George Stewart, editor of the *Quebec Chronicle*; Professor James Mavor; Alexander Muir, author of the unofficial
national anthem, "The Maple Leaf Forever"; Mr. J. S. Willison. In all,
seventy-one persons attended. "The speaking commenced at nine-
thirty, and it was an hour past midnight when the last speaker concluded." And the toasts! Toasts were offered to "the Queen," "the
Dominion," "Our Educational Institutions," "Canadian Art," "Our
Poets," "Our Prose Writers." Proposing or responding were the hard-
riding police magistrate Colonel George T. Denison, Jr. and Dr. W. H.

Drummond of Montreal. And Mr. J. G. Bourinot. Euterpe, the muse of lyric verse, was honoured by the reading of poems by Mr. Archibald Lampman and Mr. Charles G. D. Roberts. Nor was the founder of the feast neglected. Among several newspapers recording the event, the *Globe* reported that: "The part played by 'The Canadian Magazine' in the furtherance of literature in Canada was warmly praised by the speakers."

Small wonder, for they were praising themselves.

The *Canadian Magazine of Politics, Science, Art and Literature* came into being four years earlier. Its officers represented a redoubtable cross section of the Liberal establishment. President of the Ontario Publishing Company was Patterson, vice-president Ballantyne, and its directors, drawn from Toronto, Stratford and Collingwood, and listed with full scholarly credentials, included such worthies as John Ferguson, MA, MD, PhD; J. Gordon Mowat, DLS; and T. H. Best, the business manager, who, though lacking academic degrees or honorifics, was the most indispensible of all and in many ways the most representative. Born in Port Hope in 1848 of Irish parents, Thomas Henry Best was manager of a large department store in Collingwood. A lifelong Liberal and staunch Presbyterian, he was a businessman who pursued advertisers and priced the new publication at a stiff twenty-five cents a copy.

The *Canadian Magazine*'s first editor was J. Gordon Mowat, sometimes known as "Moses Oates," the name he had used once as an unreliable meteorologist. An experienced journalist, he had already helped set up D. K. Mason's short-lived *Lake Magazine* in July 1892. Issuing from 23 Manning Arcade, King Street, and printed by Hunter, Rose, the March 1893 number announced that it was intended "to fill, in some measure, for Canada, the purpose served in Great Britain and the United States by the great Reviews of these countries." The magazine would cultivate "Canadian patriotism and Canadian interests...endeavouring to aid in the consolidation of the Dominion on a basis of national self-respect and a mutual regard for the rights of the great elements which make up the population of Canada." The announcement then hummed a tune much reiterated in Canadian magazine history. "To those who recognize how much Canada has hitherto been dependent for magazine literature on foreign countries, and how unfavourable such dependence is to the growth of healthy national sentiment in our homes, our appeal, we believe, will not be in vain."

Yet this first issue seemed more civic than national. Its frontispiece was a photograph by "Bruce" of a mist-shrouded ravine, "Early Morning in Rosedale, Toronto." The leading article was "The Manitoba Public School Law" by D'Alton McCarthy, QC, MP, the Dublin-born hero of the Orange order and scourge of all who would extend the French language beyond Quebec. Elsewhere in the issue was "Conduct and Manner," a sermon disguised as an essay, by Professor William Clarke,

DCL, FRSC, and Principal Grant's "Anti-National Features of the National Policy." In substance and in the worthiness of their authors, these articles might easily have appeared in the *Canadian Monthly and National Review*. However, there were indications that this magazine would be more populist in tenor.

William J. Fox's "In the Shadow of the Arctic," complete with drawings, was a readable account of an 1884 expedition to seek a shorter route for Northwest wheat to Europe via Hudson Bay. Aboard the first steamer to enter the Bay, Fox was pleased to report that Churchill, Manitoba, had a revenue of $100,000 a year from porpoise oil. Duller, despite its subject matter, was John Home Cameron's illustrated "Glimpses of the 'Quartier-Latin'"—"you are forced to recognize that France has still an extraordinary vitality, and...you pray she may long live to hold her proud place in the civilization of the world." One could turn from the mild satire of "The Regenerators" by "Uncle Thomas" to "An Open Window and What Came of It" by William T. James, a sentimental tale of a mother losing a child on a train—easy to do: all that's needed is to retrieve a cap that's flown out the window when the train stops; inevitably, the train moves on—only to be reunited with him when the little chap becomes a man.

Although it was patterned after such "quality" U.S. magazines as *Scribner's, Harper's* and the *Atlantic Monthly* and sold at the same price of twenty-five cents, the *Canadian Magazine* was plainly having a little trouble deciding whether it wanted to be a solid literary journal or a popular, even mass-circulation magazine. The tension was epitomized in two poems, the alliterative "The Birds' Lullaby" by the Mohawk princess Pauline Johnson—"we drowse to your dreamy whispering"—and M. P. Morse's classically minded "An Imitation of Horace."

Even if issues might run to more than 150 pages, of which fifty to sixty might be advertising, the magazine was no economic bonanza. At this stage at least, contributors were paid badly, the advertising blocked in the usual fore-and-aft fashion and the layout a stately two columns.

Visually, the magazine relied on members of the Royal Canadian Academy, the Ontario Society of Artists and the Toronto Art Students' League—in December 1894, notebook sketches are from the last—and people like F. M. Bell-Smith, F. H. Brigden, A. H. Heming, and C. M. Manly. Heming specialized in the Canadian wild west and animals; Bell-Smith and Manly in Toronto itself; Brigden in historical and costume depiction.

In 1897 another artistically like-minded periodical merged with the *Canadian Magazine*. This was *Massey's Illustrated*, which had evolved from *Massey's Magazine*, founded fifteen years previously. Backed by the Massey-Harris farm machinery company, the ten-cent magazine had been the first to publish the work of amateur photography clubs

The work of the Art Students' League enlivened the pages of the Canadian Magazine, *as in these sketches by one of its members, John Kelly, Jr.*

and one of the first four-colour half-tones in a magazine, "Lights of a City," made from a Bell-Smith painting. In its attempt, starting in 1896, to become a popular magazine, *Massey's* had begun bravely, but soon foundered, announcing in its June 1897 issue: "*The Canadian* and *Massey's Magazine*s have demonstrated that it is possible to produce a magazine, the work of Canadian *littérateurs* and artists that will compare favourably with the magazines of any other country. If this has been done while the two journals were entirely independent, how much more can be accomplished when the field is left entirely to one—that one comprising all that is best in the two."

John A. Cooper was now editor. Like his brother Ernest—later a London, England, industrialist who was knighted—he was a bookseller's son who had worked for J. B. Maclean's trade papers in the early 1890s. In the June 1897 issue of the *Canadian Magazine*, Cooper's "Current Thoughts" column protested that "Canadian book publishers are highly protected, but Canadian magazines are apparently beyond the care or concern of the Government of this country." Announcing the merger, he stated that although both his and *Massey's* magazines "have been successful because strongly supported by Canadian advertisers and Canadian readers," "the field for magazines in Canada is exceedingly limited," and hence "one strong and purely Canadian magazine is desirable."

Though by now the *Canadian Magazine* carried many more, albeit muddy photos and had much superior paper, combinatorial visual improvements were not immediately obvious. As for the text, Cooper's contributors were often politicians—prominent attorneys general and the like. It being 1897, there was much Jubilee Victoriana, including in June a round-up survey, "The Queen's Reign: Its Most Striking Characteristic and Most Beneficent Act." The most striking response was Arthur Conan Doyle's: "I am often sent conundrums of this sort, and I never remember answering one before. Since you make a point of it, however, I send my opinion for what it is worth—which is, that chloroform is the most beneficent invention of Her Majesty's Reign."

June also offered "A Canadian Negro V.C." by D. V. Warner. After beginning well—"It will, no doubt, be interesting to many Canadians at this time, to those of us, especially, who have a more or less pronounced 'race prejudice,' to know that a Negro native of this Dominion [a Nova Scotian named William Hall] won a Victoria Cross during the Indian Mutiny, within a few years after the institution of this order"—it then blotted out the tolerant effect by adding, "His parents were extremely poor; and the boy, showing more independence than is usually found among young coloured men in this country, shipped before the mast in 1844...."

Eighteen ninety-seven was also marked by a series of sketches of provincial premiers since Confederation and, in September, an article by Walt Whitman's friend Richard Maurice Bucke, "Shakespeare or Bacon," stating "The proof (partly from a just discovered anagram) that the real Author of the so-called 'Shakespeare' drama was Francis Bacon." In December this brought forth Goldwin Smith's rebuttal that "Mrs. Delia Bacon, who originated this fancy...thought the plays too good to be written by anyone but a Bacon."

Perhaps the most characteristic example of the magazine's ideology came at the exact turn of the century, when Cooper's "Editorial Comments" in December 1899 asserted that, during the wars in South Africa and the Philippines, it was "difficult to write of 'Peace on earth, good-will toward men' when both branches of the Anglo-Saxon people are engaged in subduing inferior races." Yet such necessary wars in aid of "progressive civilization" would yield to peace "when the Boer and Filipino have been made to realize that the Anglo-Saxon race never errs, that it makes war only for the benefits of humanity."

In the next few years there was at least some worry that the Mother Country was letting the side down. Along with much interest in the career of Joseph Chamberlain, there was praise in December 1903 of Kipling's famous poem "The Five Nations" and the section called "The Islanders":

Then ye returned to your trinkets; then ye
    contented your souls
With the flanneled foot at the wicket or
    the muddied oafs at the goals.

THE CAPTURED COW-MOOSE
DRAWN BY WILLIAM BEATTY FROM PHOTOGRAPHS

*As it published
more photographs,
the* Canadian
Magazine *pro-
vided such
delights as this
"Captured Cow-
Moose" June 1903.*

Also in 1903, the
Canadian
Magazine *showed
John Craig Eaton
in his "Electric
Runabout".*

It was a tidy little Toronto world in which the many private schools—Royal Victoria College, Trinity College School, Westbourne, St. Monica's—advertised their status as training ground for the very sort of people who would contribute to the magazine, John A. Cooper on "People and Affairs" and the Scottish-born anti-imperialist, John A. Ewan on "Current Events Abroad." From 1892 until the end of his life, Ewan worked on the Liberal *Globe*, along with men like John Willison and S. T. ("Sam") Wood, another *Canadian* contributor.

Most of the articles were illustrated, and often with photos. The lead item in June 1903 was "Capturing a Moose Alive" by Frank Carrel of the *Quebec Telegraph*. Its photos bore wonderful captions: "A Moose-Yard at Montmorency Falls Park, Near Quebec—animals are the property of Holt, Renfrew & Co."; "A Moose Hunt—Serving a Cup of Hot Bovril." In August the following was run: "The Photography of Birds' Nests" by O. J. Stevenson and "Automobiles in Canada" by A. Grant Brown: "It is almost certain that the automobile will be a feature of our civilization for many years to come." Included in the Brown piece were photos of gentlemen in open-air vehicles, such as "Mr. J. C. Eaton in His Electric Runabout." Another populist touch was evident in the choice of fiction: Robert Buckley's "In the Secret Service," published in April 1902 "Episode X—Trifling with Russian Secret Police."

Shakespeare could always be relied on to merge the popular and scholarly, and in 1902 to 1903 there was an extensive series on the Bard's use of birds, insects, flowers and the Bible. History was a further compromise: in 1903 the War of 1812 was recapitulated in many instalments.

In 1906, the *Canadian Magazine* gained a new and less narrow-minded editor after Cooper left to edit the *Canadian Courier*. (He later raised a battalion in World War I, and was a Borden appointee to the Canadian Bureau of Information in New York, as well as the overseer of the motion picture industry in Canada.) Newton McTavish had been a reporter and editor on the *Globe* and a frequent contributor to magazines in Canada, the United States and Britain. One of the founders of the Arts and Letters Club, he would twice become president of the Canadian Authors' Association. His connections in the art and literary worlds were many: he was on the executive of the Toronto Art Gallery and from 1923 was a trustee of the National Gallery; among his friends he numbered poets like Bliss Carman, Duncan Campbell Scott and E. J. Pratt, politicians like Mackenzie King and painters like James Wilson Morrice. He collected paintings and first editions.

In many ways, McTavish was a transitional figure. With his spectacles on a ribbon, he looked, like Sir Charles G. D. Roberts, the very picture of the studious yet sensitive late Victorian; and his collection of short pieces, *Thrown In*, presents gently amused recollections of Ontario village life and a Methodist upbringing—others appeared in the *Canadian Magazine* under the heading "Thrown Out." But for his day he was aesthetically forward-looking, and his daughter Maxine married the cartoonist Richard Taylor, who became a fixture on the *New Yorker*, that Manhattan emblem of a new, more sophisticated generation.

In 1907, however, the *Canadian Magazine* had basically the same format as 1893, though with added subheadings. A new section, "What Others Are Laughing At," reprinted jokes. The editor's notes, termed "The Front Window," appeared at the back. The photo essay was exemplified in March 1908 by Clifford H. Easton's "Northern Types." It included "The Missionary," "A Voluntary Exile"—"Many a time has it been the lot of the young man to tramp hundreds of miles to Chimo in search of relief for friends and relatives starving in the interior camps"—"Primitive Man," "An Old Body of the Silent Place," and the "Nascaupees of Labrador."

McTavish at least spruced up graphic components. He ran decorative vignettes by Arthur Lismer and J. E. H. MacDonald, and reproduced etchings or illustrations by Clarence Gagnon and J. W. Beatty in sympathy with the new trends in nationalistic landscape painting. After Morrice praised Maurice Cullen in a letter, McTavish wrote appreciatively about Cullen in April 1912 in an article entitled "A Painter of the Snows," denying that Canada was "a country naturally unsuitable for the development of the art of painting." Morrice himself did not fare so well himself in the magazine's pages: the colouristic subtleties of his own paintings and those of others were reproduced in murky black-and-white.

McTavish ventured forth in other ways. An example of alert urban reportage appeared in November 1909 in "The Drama of the 'Ward'" by Augustus Bridle, the associate editor of the *Canadian Courier* and the *Star*'s music and drama critic. Bridle discussed how Jews and Italians took turns in dominating a fast-changing Toronto neighbourhood.

The writing tended to be brisker, the points of view less stultified, as in March 1910, when Mrs. Fred A. Hodgson in "Bull-fighting in Mexico" remarked that "Despite what moralists say to the contrary, there is an attraction not wholly demoralising attached to the bull-fight...." The principal departments now were "Current Events," Jean Graham's "At Five O'Clock" whose drawing-heading showed three ladies taking tea; (*Saturday Night* had a similar department called "At Four O'Clock"); "The Way of Letters"—book news; "What Others Are Laughing At" and McTavish's own "Within the Sanctum."

McTavish not only edited, but wrote a great deal for the magazine, and did so throughout the war years. By 1914, the magazine had colour covers. Katherine Hale (Amelia Beers Warnock, the Galt-born versifier who also was an editor on the *Canadian Century*) was a steady contributor, as was the poet Isabel Ecclestone Mackay. Nor were they confined to the "Woman's Sphere" department, which had been edited by, among others, the accomplished journalist Emily McCausland ("Sama"). McCausland, an MPP's widow who was active in the National Council of Women. In November 1918, the writer-photographer team of Victoria Hayward and Edith S. Watson, whose work would be featured into the 1920s, presented "Foreign Women Who Work for Canada" and spoke of Galicians, Ruthenians—generic labels for most eastern Europeans—Mennonites and Russians who formed "one of the most important human working-forces of the prairies, the garden-land of Canada." Hayward was "struck by the ease with which the women labour, by the absence of all apparent effort in accomplishing the heaviest manual labour."

November 1918 offered A. H. U. Colquhoun's "solemn warning against a premature and disastrous peace." It occurred that month any way. A year later the magazine was presenting Canadian war pictures by such artist-servicemen as Wyndham Lewis and Frederic Varley. True to the magazine's Liberal predilections, Sir John Willison's dreary *Reminiscences Political and Personal* was serialized in twelve issues, leavened by the fact that from three to six short stories appeared in each issue.

When it came to literary topics, the attempt to combine the popular with the solemn sometimes was strained. In December 1919, J. D. Logan, author of *Comedy and Humour of the Bible*, pronounced Saint Matthew "the 'Boswell' of Christ'" in his article "Christ as Poet" and concluded, "Be ye, therefore, perfect, as poets, even as Christ the poet, was perfect." Yet in the same issue one of the most important and most overlooked documents in the history of the Canadian modernist poetry movement appeared, Arthur Phelps's "Bobcaygeon: A Sketch of A Little Town." Despite its diffidence—"It will be noted that the word 'sketch' does not necessarily carry the idea of poetry or verse, or even free verse"—it is a gently cadenced, tremendously evocative word picture—illustrated with an air photo of Bobcaygeon, a lakeside town in the Kawarthas—with subtle metaphysical undertones.

> In summer
> The electric lights
> Gleam in the hurrying waters of the river;
> Like the stars
> They hit the water,
> And the splash remains.
> Strange, the splashes of light remaining at one place
> On the hurrying river!
> Until midnight,
> When only the stars
> Make the splashes,
> And the town and the stars and the river
> Are quiet
> But most quiet the bridges.

One has only to look at L. M. Montgomery's "The Gate of Dream" in the same issue to see that Phelps's poem was not only unconventional, but much superior:

> I seek a little garden gate
>   That will swing wide to me —
> Haply beneath a sunset-cloud,
>   Or moonrise wizardry,
> Or in some winking vale of noon
> And shadow I may find it soon.

By the 1920s the typeface for headings was in mock-rustic style. The rigid departments disappeared in 1922-23 but returned the next year, including "Investment and Progress," "Travel," and "The Seven Lamps"—the pictorial and performing arts. Optimism came to the forefront: a November 1923 lead article, "The New Diplomacy," predicted that "With a British League of Nations with the League of Nations, with perfected machinery for world conferences in the open, with all the cards on the table, peace will forever be secured and the world made safe for democracy." And the cover price was still twenty-five cents a copy. But drastic changes in format, price and relationship to audience were about to occur.

First the size: a larger, floppier format. According to the editor's "Our New Dress" in July 1924, only four of the magazine's 15,000 readers objected: "things must move with the times, and this seems to be the time of the larger, flatter magazine." Readers were reassured that the magazine would continue to be "made in Canada by Canadians, whose artists are Canadian, whose whole outlook is Canadian. So that, after all, the question of size is not so all-important."

The larger size, and the coated stock that went with it, made the presentation of colour art more practical, and the Canadian landscapes that were the *Canadian Magazine's* stock in trade were shown to advantage on the cover throughout the 1920s, as were the cover designs done by Grace Judge. By mid-decade, the covers had the art deco look prevalent on newsstands everywhere.

The magazine now had a new, more personal way of addressing the reader. In August 1924 it asked: "Why the reduced price?" and answered for itself: "As it used to be, many persons of a literary or artistic turn were prevented from subscribing by the mere fact that in order to do so it was necessary to write out a cheque, or procure a post-office or express money order. Now, however, all who find these details irksome can easily put a two-dollar bank bill into an envelope. The percentage of losses in the mails is almost nil, so that with confidence anyone may subscribe in this convenient way."

These changes were "by no means final," the magazine warned or promised: "at the present rate of increase, by the time these words are read in the magazine, the number of subscribers will have increased ten per cent more than it was at the time the changes were made. The increase, naturally, is from new subscribers, but it is an interesting fact that the average percentage of renewals by subscriptions to THE CANADIAN MAGAZINE has been more than seventy-five. Very few magazines can show a record equal to that." It also added that "It is not possible to keep in touch with Canada's literature and artistic progress and development unless one takes the Magazine regularly."

But the biggest change of all came in 1926, when it was announced that the *Canadian Magazine* would be published by Canadian Magazines Limited, in effect by Hugh C. MacLean Publications, owner of a chain of trade and technical journals which had acquired the magazine from the venerable Ontario Publishing Company.

By now most of the oldtimers were gone: by 1922 the seventy-four-year-old T. H. Best had withdrawn from the company, and his own firm, the T. H. Best Printing Co., founded in 1911, was concentrating on book printing and binding. The editor was Joseph Lister Rutledge, who had started out as a reporter on the *London Advertiser* and worked for J. B. Maclean. Hugh C. MacLean promised that "the general policy of the magazine in respect to the development of Canadian resources and Canadian ideals will be even more pronounced under the new direction...."

If that was possible.

In its quest to be a mass-market family magazine, some things, like xenophobia, did not change during the 1920s. In October 1924 Charles Lugrin Shaw in "Canada's Oriental Problem" approved of Australian and New Zealand curbs on immigration and noted that "Leaving aside the smaller issues, British Columbia's demand is for absolute control and rigorous regulation of Oriental land tenure, making it impossible for Orientals to gain absolute ownership; and for a sane, well-controlled immigration policy that will forever abolish the possibility of Oriental domination of the province's industries." This, after the author had observed that the fruit and vegetables the Chinese, Japanese and Indians sold were cheaper and better, and the work force harder working and more reliable.

The magazine was paying more attention to business and Canada's place in the international sphere—a 1925 series was "Canadian Contributions to World Progress"—but also increasing its compliment of fiction, some of it by the familiar Theodore Goodridge Roberts and Frank Oliver Call, but also popular British fiction by John Galsworthy and "Sapper." The complicated relations between the sexes, that staple of women's or family magazines, became more common as a subject, as in July 1926 with Mimi Jordan's "Are Men or Women More Selfish?." On a similar theme, Muriel Wrinch wrote on "Modern Eve," who "has the qualities of her defects...she may insist upon decorating the walls with futurist pictures of weird design, but she is a better companion than ever she has been before."

Plainly the *Canadian Magazine* was trying to have it both ways. In February 1927 it introduced Margaret Pennell, its new women's editor, as "one of Canada's most successful business women" who "yet has retained and developed in herself and in her work all the charms of viewpoint and domestic feeling that are sometimes considered old fashioned today." As Mary Vipond has noted of other *Canadian Magazine* articles in the twenties, "Much emphasis was placed on the vase of flowers which a woman executive placed on her immaculate desk, and on the paintings and mirrors she hung on her office walls. Even more stress was placed on how 'serene,' 'womanly' and innocent she was able to remain despite her career."

The *Canadian Magazine* juggled stereotypes in a photo feature, "The World's Most Painted Pretty Girl" and "The Emancipation of Household Slaves," by W. R. Carr, "Ph.D." in June 1926. However tinted, there would be much more emphasis on women's activities. Women appeared on the cover more often, a "Director of the Department of Women's Interests" (Florence N. Webb) was appointed; a series of articles "designed to dramatize this business of 'home finance'" was run; a regular section "Of Special Interest to Women" dealt with food, fashion and decorating—this alongside the questions-and-answers of "Major Monk's Motors." Presumably of interest to both sexes were

"New York Graphology" and "The Fine Art of Bridge."

Despite its patriotic avowals, the magazine now most resembled the *Saturday Evening Post*, and ran such *Post*like series as "Dear Hank"— "Letters from Hiram Hogson of Hogson's Corners, Iowa, to his Son-in-Law in Canada." In January 1930 the contributor's notes for Mary Lowrey Ross credited her work for the *Post* and the *Ladies Home Journal*, not for *Saturday Night*. A favorite fiction author was Norman Reilly Raine, a Canadian and *Post* contributor who had made good in Hollywood.

Certainly, fiction became a strong, or at least often played card; an issue had as many as twelve stories among the ads for Pepsodent, Dodge cars and Kotex. The poet Ron Everson, then making a living out of pulp fiction, contributed such genre pieces as his April 1930 story entitled "The Shooting of Lalagage"—northwoods adventure—and in November "This Amazing World"—"A Tale of Two Innocents Abroad." There were stories by Morley Callaghan, Will R. Bird and frequently Nellie de Bertrand Lugrin (Mrs. Charles Shaw, who was born in Fredericton and lived in the Yukon before residing in Victoria), such as "Timber Wolves"—"Another story of those young giants of Thanes from the St. John River Colony who came to try their mettle against the frozen bitterness of the Yukon Trail of '98.") As many as six of the *Canadian Magazine*'s stories would turn up in Edward O'Brien's well-known annual anthology.

In January 1933 an editor, Jean Ritchie Anderson, led off with a fib. "It is one hundred years or more since the first *Canadian Magazine* was published. To be exact, in the summer of 1823, the press of Nahum Mowrer of Montreal, himself one of Canada's pioneer printers, issued the *Canadian Magazine and Literary Repository*"—a claim as spurious as the *Saturday Evening Post*'s boast that it had been founded by Benjamin Franklin.

Five years later the *Canadian* was still repeating the lie of its ancient ancestry. John Atkins, vice president and general manager, said that the magazine "has been published since 1823." Equally dubious—or ambiguous—was the boast that the magazine was "first with 120,000 families." The rest of the pronouncement seemed to strive for how often it could intelligibly use the word *Canadian*: "Its aim will be to lead in interpreting Canada to those good citizens who are consciously Canadian; it will endeavour to be a medium of inspiration, information and entertainment to the most progressive and most constructive group of people in Canada.

There was, in 1938, "a sound fundamental reason for CANADIAN MAGAZINE, a reason that springs from the imperative need for Canadian publications that do not ape in a smaller field what publications outside Canada are doing in a larger field." The magazine did not

pretend to serve the social register, or the ultra-smart, nor yet the gypsy-minded class of people who wander over the literary earth seeking super-sensations. We have no intention of serving these groups. Beyond that, we have no intention of wasting effort upon any group of people who have no fundamental conception of life or of Canadian ideals and purposes.

Rather we see as our definite field a wide group of substantial people, who are not swayed by every wind of fortune. They are people with families, and an active desire to give these families the largest measure of opportunity. They are people with open minds, who still have convictions and a respect for those things that lead to better citizenship. They are people who are interested in seeing Canada become a world example and a world force, for the sake of their children and their children's children.

The magazine promised "many changes, many improvements, many enlargements of the services we are offering. But we will make no change in the audience we have elected to serve or in the policy that looks to a better and more united Canada."

The page size was now larger, a photogravure section was added, contributors had photographs to go with their biographical notes. The reader was informed in February that Commander Andrew D. MacLean, the company's vice president and Hugh MacLean's son would soon go "on a discovery trip...armed with pen and camera." Although educated in part at the Royal Naval College in Greenwich —he served in World War I and became a naval commander—Andrew Dyas Maclean had worked for several of his father's business publications and a weekly illustrated tabloid, the *News Mirror*, and was even R.B. Bennett's private secretary for a short time in 1932.

There were articles on Canadian affairs by Peter Stursberg and on foreign ones by Willson Woodside. Fiction was the familiar tried and untrue. The events of the late 1930s were rapidly catching up with the magazine. A May 1938 editorial, "Don't Be a Fascist Fool," concerned a group called the Canadian Nationalist Party in Toronto and Montreal:

...in Canada there is no left (Communism) or right (Fascism) except as it exists in the disordered minds of a few who have failed to constructively exercise their rights.

Let the young forget the black shirt and make it a sweat shirt instead—the wholesome, healthful life of Canadian sport.

The popular front the magazine presented was cracking. In August the *Canadian Magazine* announced that next month it would take "the most dramatic forward step in all its long history. The smaller size...has been made popular by many of the outstanding American publications."

There will be no change in the policy that *The Canadian* has been following, of creating a publication that is strictly Canadian in its viewpoint and ideals. But there will be a material enlargement of the services we have been giving, and many innovations that we feel confident our readers will appreciate.

Although the text was broken more by headings and the layout was more inventive, there were no significant new departments. Fiction was no longer serialized but came complete in each issue. The quality of fiction was epitomized by Todd Downing's "Night Over Mexico": "a strange night of mystery and romance under the ominous pall of brooding Mexican skies."

In October, T. B. Costain appeared for the second time on the subject of good neighbourly Canada-U.S. relations and early the next year Jean-Charles Harvey reminded "all Canadians how woefully lacking in mutual understanding are even the two main sections of the Canadian people." M. Z. R. Frank's "The Jew Within Our Gates" observed that "The dread of anti-Semitism and persecution is a very important element of Jewish life both individually and collectively" and that "The Canadian Jewish Congress owes its existence almost entirely to the accession of Hitler to power and to the spread of anti-Jewish propaganda by Hitler's agents and sympathizers." Woodside and Graham McInnes continued to contribute regularly. "Lights! Camera! Action!" recounted the month's movies, the photographs were green-tinted and up to twenty pages of the back sections were printed on newsprint.

Then, abruptly, with a month's gap in publication, came the April issue. There were no editors listed, just the familiar tiresome lie on the cover and in the grim sentences of Hugh MacLean's valedictory. "The CANADIAN MAGAZINE was founded in 1823, and was published intermittently until 1893, and with regularity and continued improved service to its readers since that date."

Claiming that the magazine's circulation had risen from 9,600 in 1926 to more than 137,000 in 1938, thanks to more than $500,000 in investment, MacLean said that even a further loan from the magazine's parent company—actually a loan from Hugh's brother John Bayne—did not help. He blamed "unfair legislation, mounting costs and dumping of great quantities of foreign magazines," adding that

Since 1926 CANADIAN MAGAZINE has paid out to the Dominion Government $135,000 in postage alone. Millions of copies of foreign periodicals are carried in Canadian mails without paying Canadian postage. Although foreign periodicals enter Canada absolutely free of duties or taxes, the cost of materials and advertising in Canadian magazines is increased by duties and taxes not imposed upon their foreign competitors. Almost everything that the Canadian publishers

They had just started on the hors d'œuvre when a waiter stepped up to the girl and whispered a few words in her ear.

Even in its last gasp attempting to be all things to all people, the Canadian Magazine *luridly illustrated the romantic adventure of John Portas's "Road to Kalgan".*

In its April 1939 final issue, the Canadian Magazine *headlined the humble legal status of Quebec women.*

Where Women Are Children
by Walter Turner

"Quebec classes its married women as minors. They may not vote, and in a democracy, who does not vote, does not count".

require is taxed. Foreign competitors contribute nothing in duties or taxes.

The suspension of CANADIAN MAGAZINE throws many persons out of employment. It reduces the revenue of Canadian writers and artists, and those who gain their livelihood through the manufacture of engravings, paper and ink, and in actually producing the magazine, will suffer the not inconsiderable loss of a quarter of a million dollars annually.

Readers could choose to have their unexpired subscriptions filled by the *National Home Monthly, Chatelaine, Maclean's, Canadian Home Journal* or *Saturday Night.* The April issue had an Indian maid on the cover, a piece about the fight for women's status in Quebec and John Portas's

"Road to Kalgan": "Chance brought them together, the girl, just a youngster too young to be mixed up in this game of blood and war. Farley was different, danger was his element—and running rifles through Siberia to China, just a supercargo's job! But even Farley found dangers multiplied strangely with the presence of the girl." In "Mister Editor," the letters-to-the-editor department, a fan from Yoakum, Texas, wrote to say that he read the magazine "cover to cover."

The *Canadian Magazine* was no more. Hugh C. MacLean undoubtedly felt safer in the Muskoka Lakes district north of Toronto, where he operated steamers and hotels. There was to be a false start in 1962. The *Toronto Star* quoted Andrew D. MacLean, who had resigned as chairman of the Southam-MacLean Publishing Company, as saying he might revive the magazine, which would be printed on the presses of his weekly *Muskoka News* at Gravenhurst. But nothing came of the proposed revival.

The magazine's history can be traced through its physical dimensions. First the large octavo of the "quality" periodical: 16 cm x 23.5 cm. Then in 1924, the bigger 22.5 cm x 29.5 cm. In 1930, the 27 cm x 34.5 cm. Finally, in September 1938, a reversion to roughly its 1924 size. The increase in size had coincided with a massive circulation drive and, not coincidentally, with the quest for U.S. advertising. (Electrotypes for advertisements could be imported duty-free.)

At the same time as it crowed its Canadianism, the magazine became in form more Americanlike. Nor did advertisers respond to this faking: by January 1939 there were merely seventeen pages of advertising, of which only one was a quadricolour. In trying to be both a modern mass-circulation family magazine and something like its chauvinistic former self, the *Canadian Magazine* failed at both. But its record was also in some ways the story of the Canadian magazine industry up to this point. The era of edification had ended.

PART TWO

FROM CLASS TO MASS

The notion that magazines should cater not to an intelligent elite, or a group defined by farm, church or home, but to the literate or semi-literate majority instead, did not come suddenly to Canada. But it did come later than was the case in the United States. To effect economies in production and distribution, magazines require a sizeable population base, and a largely urban one. Only in 1921 did more than half of all Canadians live in towns and cities.

The tremendous growth in U.S. advertising that inevitably followed widespread industrialization alerted Canadian publishers that there was a lot of money to be made. The first Canadian advertising agency, Anson McKim, was set up in 1889; others followed to promote the emerging name brands and department stores. But, though there might be national advertising, there was a dearth of nationally distributed media.

What tantalized Colonel J. B. Maclean, Joseph Atkinson and others, was the possibility of a large national audience that might bring the success their U.S. rivals had won south of the border. At the same time, the very size of the U.S. magazine industry was the Canadians' most conspicuous threat. What consumer magazines and weekend supplements attempted to do was wed U.S. form with Canadian content, sometimes resulting in U.S. form *and* content.

Newspapers, like the *Toronto Star* with its *Star Weekly* or the *Montreal Star* with its *Standard*, had a built-in circulation base from which to launch relatively small, localized weekend alternatives to the U.S. magazines. But Canadian magazine conglomerates were puny compared to the colossi across the border and relied on trade magazine profits to keep them afloat. Among these were the J. B. Maclean (*Maclean's, Chatelaine, Canadian Homes and Gardens, Mayfair*) and Hugh C. MacLean (the *Canadian Magazine*) companies, and Consolidated Press (*Saturday Night, The Farmer* and *Canadian Home Journal*). Some publishers, like J. J. Harpell and Seccombe House, just stayed with trade journals.

They had reason to do so. American consumer magazines outsold Canadian ones at the rate of roughly four to one.

Inevitably the federal government, with its power over tariffs and postal rates, got calls to intervene. Unfortunately for the Canadians, the government raised second-class postal rates in June 1920, effectively ending the low rates their magazines had received compared to their U.S. competitors. Mackenzie King did throw a sop to them in 1926 in the form of the Advisory Board on Tariff and Taxation. It was to this body in Ottawa that Maclean and other industry representatives, especially those in the new Magazine Publishers Association (MPA), trudged back and forth for the rest of the decade.

The magazine men at first wanted a duty imposed on imported magazines, though Maclean, for example, would have gladly settled for a situation in which Canadians would not have to suffer taxes and duties from which Americans were free. One argument was that Canadian publishers paid taxes on the paper, ink, engravings and artwork they had to import. The Americans, with a home market of 110 million, could simply dump surplus copies on Canadian doorsteps and saturate the Canadian market with U.S. advertising.

A November 1924 *Saturday Night* editorial summed up the scene:

...six out of every seven magazines read in Canada come from the United States. Twenty-five of the best known of these magazines and periodicals have a total circulation in Canada of nearly 600,000 copies per issue, or a grand total of upward of twelve million copies per annum. [The best-sellers were the *Ladies Home Journal, Saturday Evening Post, Pictorial Review* and *McCall's Magazine* in that order.] And these figures take no account of dozens of other U.S. publications of the cheap magazine type sold throughout the country....The Government must get behind the product to the extent of giving publishers some degree of protection against the dumping process which is now going on and which over a space of ten years has increased the sale of United States periodicals in the Canadian market by upward of three hundred per cent.

In lobbying, publishers were backed by a catch-all coalition that included old-line imperialists and new-style nationalists, as well as local industries most affected by the U.S. influx: the Imperial Order of Daughters of the Empire; the National Council of Women; the Association of Canadian Clubs; the Canadian Authors' Association; the Ontario Chamber of Commerce; the pulp and paper industry; and unions. Such varied interests at times resembled more polymorphous perversity than marital bliss.

Although the magazines had a parliamentary ally in H. C. Hocken of Toronto, a former newspaper editor and a Unionist, later a Conservative MP, there was effective opposition from the two main wholesale distributors, represented by R. J. Deachman. Deachman, a former journalist, argued that the MPA represented only eleven out of more than 1,500 publications in Canada, moreover those from urban Ontario. He pointed out that Canadian exports generally were growing, as was, for that matter, the Canadian national consciousness.

After failing to get U.S. advertising taxed or a duty imposed on imports—the Liberals wanted free trade votes in the West, and Canadians *liked* low-cost American magazines—the Canadian publishers opted for a tax-break on the U.S.-made materials they used and promptly lost their allies among photo-engravers and makers of pulp and paper.

King, who had dabbled in journalism himself, was unsympathetic. In 1926, with an uncharacteristic lack of oiliness, he wrote that good Liberal, Newton MacTavish, "So long as Canadian periodicals are used as media for helping to embarrass and destroy the Government of the day, it is not a surprise to me that their owners find it difficult to enlist the sympathies of the Administration...."

Nonetheless, a 1926-27 postal amendment slightly reduced postal rates for Canadian magazines, and the Board reclassified some fiction magazines like *Argosy* and *Real Romances* as liable to duty. In 1927 the MPA claimed that Canada was globally unique in that it "combined the lack of any copyright or tariff protection with propinquity to a giant neighbour of the same language." Finally, the 1928 budget gave the Canadian publishers a bigger concession: an eighty per cent drawback on customs duties on some magazine paper stock and other printing materials.

This was effective. Within a year both the import of paper and the circulation of Canadian magazines increased. But the big commercial gain occurred when the Tories returned to power in 1930. After September 1931, U.S. magazines with contents of more than twenty percent advertising were taxed on a per-copy basis; fiction, feature and comic magazines were charged per pound. At once there was a steep decline in the circulation of American magazines here, to the direct benefit of the five leading Canadian magazines.

Some resourceful Americans simply set up subsidiaries *inside* Canada: by 1932, shipping their lithographic plates across the border duty-free, forty-seven of them published Canadian-circulation press runs for magazines ranging from *Ballyhoo* to *Ranchland Love Story*. Ironically, this helped the printing branches of Southam and J. B. Maclean.

In the seesaw of federal political power that marked the twenties and thirties, the Liberals were back in power in late 1935. Under a three-year Canada-U.S. Trade Agreement, the United States demanded that its magazines be given free entry. King wiped out the tariff.

On the separate issue of giving Canadian publishers a tax break, King equivocated. In 1936 he gave a fifty percent drawback on duty on the paper used by magazines and lifted the duty on printing plates. The next year the drawback on paper was increased to seventy-five percent, the sales tax on paper, ink and editorial illustration removed, and presses could be imported duty-free if unavailable in Canada.

The net effect of these moves was that the U.S. subsidiaries, no longer facing a tariff, scuttled back across the border. Cosy in their own homes, the American magazines had more than tripled their 1935 circulations by 1938. As Mary Vipond puts it, "Within a period of five years, Canadian government policy had managed first to create and then to break the custom of publishing foreign magazines in Canada, without having much effect on the circulation of foreign periodicals in the country."

For the magazine industry, the most significant events of the next few years were not legislative acts, but the setting up of three formidable U.S. magazines on Canadian soil.

Liberty, which called itself "Canada's Largest Weekly Magazine," had been organized as a Canadian company in 1932. It had minimal Canadian content—a mere editorial page signed by its Hamilton-born associate editor, Wilbur Philpott. Typically fifty-four pages, it was the archetypal populist magazine, inspiring intellectuals' mirth by its habit of ending articles with statistics about "reading time"—"5 minutes 35 seconds"—plainly a magazine for people in a hurry. So opposed was it to the declaration of war that a Canadian reading *it* alone would not have discovered World War II had broken out until the issue of 14 October 1939.

More significant over the long term was the arrival of *Time* and *Reader's Digest*. Young giants in the United States, they were founded within a year of each other: *Reader's Digest* in 1922, *Time* in 1923. Canadians already knew them both well. The *Ottawa Journal* noted on 3 September 1929 that, though *Time* was "bright, readable, acute," in a recent story about Canada, "It would be hard to crowd more ignorance and misinformation into any equal number of words."

In 1943 both *Time*, initially printed in Chicago, and *Reader's Digest* set up shop in Montreal; a compelling reason was that they could thus obtain a Canadian paper ration, rather than dip into U.S. stock. With a Canadian circulation of 41,700, *Time* kept its content practically identical to its U.S. parent, though after 1944 it ran the two-page feature "Canada at War." The first Canadian correspondent arrived in 1944, and the next year space devoted to Canada was increased to three pages. An advertising office was opened in 1946: four years later, Canadian circulation was more than 120,000. Although Time International of Canada was incorporated in 1952, its final editing then, as later, was done in New York. At first just printed in Canada, *Reader's Digest* produced a separate Canadian edition in 1947, and a French version, *Sélection du Reader's Digest*, in 1948. Although Canadian editions of U.S. magazines were nothing new, *these* newcomers were by far the most ambitious and energetic yet. With imaginative sales campaigns and increasing circulation breadth, *Time* and *Reader's Digest* were soon devouring sizeable chunks of the advertising market.

The purely financial question of how much Canadian magazines suffered competitive disadvantage in their own country was complicated, some would say muddied, by an array of moral, aesthetic and cultural considerations.

Some, for example, curiously contended that Canada was cleaner, purer, more unsullied than its neighbour, and that the country needed protection against immoral bacilli. In August 1922, *Saturday Night*, raging against the popularity of "pornographic" magazines like the just born *True Confessions*, squalled that *True Confession's* Minneapolis publisher, W. H. Fawcett, was "unabashed in his declaration that he intends to publish the dirtiest material that he can lay his hands on." He even had "the audacity to claim a moral intention by asserting that knowledge of the fouler things of life may help some young people to avoid such error." According to *Saturday Night*, "if our laws against indecency are worth the paper they are written on it should be excluded from the mails, the newsstands and the railway trains."

The following month, the magazine was pleased to report that Customs and Excise had banned *True Confessions*. "A customs embargo is a much more effective way of meeting the tide of pornographic magazines than could be provided by any system of local censorship, and it is to be hoped that the machinery of the department will be invoked to check future attempts to flood Canada with filth." In 1925 the National Council of Women persuaded the government to ban such magazines as *Droll Stories, Breezy Stories, Saucy Stories* and *Telling Tales.* Some clever publishers counteracted this by the simple expedient of changing titles.

Along with its more sensible economic arguments, the MPA also got into the act, claiming before the Tariff Board that the largest-circulation U.S. magazines were "cheaply printed on cheap paper, and devoted almost entirely to fiction that is sensational, suggestive and generally as demoralizing [sic] as the publishers dare make them...." Canadian publishers suffered from a "moral handicap," said the *Canadian Magazine's* spokesman, since they would never "stoop to profit by the publication of such literature."

The appeal to prudery worked. In 1927, such wholly-fiction magazines as *Argosy* and *True Detective* were denied entry, with no noticeable effect on the moral standards of impressionable youth. These bannings and seizures were often temporary, and almost always ineffectual. In April 1938, *Life* was banned for carrying a four-page section photos on "The Birth of a Boy." In 1940, the federal revenue minister banned *True Confessions* yet again, along with other pulps like *Front Page Detective* and the nudist *Health and Efficiency*. But by the year's end, *all* comic books and pulps had been restricted under the War Exchange Conservation Act.

The war brought a new focus of moral concern, only this time it was patriotism. In 1939, the government banned Arnold Gingrich's magazine *Ken* after protests about a cartoon it ran making fun of George VI. Then in 1940, B. K. Sandwell attacked the *Saturday Evening Post* in *Saturday Night* for its "anti-British tendencies": "That the Canadian Government would be amply justified in using its authority to ban the entry into Canada of a number of anti-British periodicals from the United States, we have not the slightest doubt."

Though Sandwell preferred a voluntary boycott, he certainly would have concurred with the MPA's brief, which stated that magazines made it possible

> ...to build up a strong Canadian literature, a matter of first importance to Canadian unity, the preservation of Canadian tradition and ideals, and the development of a national consciousness....There is the particular danger of the people of the western provinces feeling that they are more or less cut off from eastern Canada, and we maintain that the establishment of magazines and periodicals with national circulation will do much to bring the extreme West, particularly, in closer touch and sympathy with eastern Canada.

The government was certainly interested in national unity—of a kind, anyway. Parliament passed a War Measures Act making it unlawful to speak or publish any opinion likely to hamper the prosecution of the war. Economic controls tightened, too. In 1942 the Wartime Prices and Trade Board ordered that no person could sell or buy in Canada any newspaper, magazine or periodical at a higher price than that charged or paid for between 15 September and 11 October 1941.

Once the war was over, the debate about the banes and benefits of U.S. magazines resumed. According to Frank Underhill in the August 1951 *Canadian Forum*, "If *Maclean's Magazine* achieved its ambition, and American competitors were shut out from its constituency, it would continue to be what it is now, only more so, i.e., a second-rate *Saturday Evening Post* or *Collier's*. It is mass-consumption and the North American continental environment which produce these phenomena, not some sinister influences in the United States."

Family and Furrow

During the first half of the twentieth century the old farm-and-family magazines ploughed their familiar furrow. Largest was the *Free Press Weekly Farmer*, the weekly edition of the *Winnipeg Free Press*, which had almost a 150,000 circulation by 1931, and the *Family Herald* with 217,000. The latter, "Canada's National Farm Journal," included, in addition to family fiction, short farm and general news reports—9 October 1935: "Antelopes have caused considerable damage to grain and alfalfa fields in southeastern Alta. this past season. Herds of from 100 to 500 have been roving the fields causing extensive damage to the maturing crops in the Wildhorse district." So beloved was the *Herald* in some homes that one woman—the mother of the economist and historian Harold Innis—named (more or less) her son after it.

J. B. Maclean started *Farmer's Magazine* (1910-21,) which had extensive scientific and political coverage, illustrated fiction and a women's section. It succumbed, the colonel petulantly protested, because "farmers just will not support their own magazine. They are suspicious of advertising in general, and even more so to the normal businesslike messages addressed chiefly to them by the agricultural suppliers." The Ontario field was left to Consolidated Press's *Farmer*, later confusingly called *Farmer's Magazine*. At its peak it claimed a circulation of 100,000.

In the West, the *Grain Growers' Guide* (1908-28,) whose longest-serving notable editor was George F. Chipman, had crusaded for temperance, educational reform, the co-operative movement and the Progressive Party, merged into the *Country Guide* (1908—), which eventually absorbed the *Nor'West Farmer* (1882-1936) and took over publication of *Cattlemen* (1938—), a quarterly that went monthly in 1944.

The real growth area for the family market was among newspaper supplements. In Montreal, the *Standard* (1905-51) had been founded by George Murray and later purchased by Hugh Graham, Lord Atholstan. It sold mainly in Quebec and the Maritimes and, at its height, reached a circulation of 300,000. More formidable was the *Star Weekly* (1905–73), due to the cunning of the *Toronto Star's* editor (later owner) Joseph E. Atkinson, who, some said, took his middle initial from his wife's name and was known to the irreverent as "Holy Joe" or "Whispering Joe."

Atkinson put Joseph Clark in charge. Clark wanted something like an unpretentious English weekly and brought in Harry Jakeway from *Saturday Night* to be his editor. The first issue had no comics and only coarse-screen half-tones, and seemed little competition for the rival *Sunday World*. By the year's end, the circulation was up and J. H. Cranston had succeeded Clark. But it was only after World War I and the addition of many new reporters that the *Star* won the battle with the *World*, taking it over in November 1924. The *Star Weekly* stressed entertainment, not education: comics, light fiction, colour.

Among the new staff hired after the war was Joseph Clark's son Gregory, who had dropped out of the University of Toronto and whose columns became illustrated by a twenty-year-old Jimmy Frise. This was the start of a partnership that would last thirty-eight years. Clark also became buddies with some part- or full-time staff writers, such as Morley Callaghan, who wrote his first column at the age of eighteen, and Ernest Hemingway, whose short, unhappy life at the *Star* ended in late 1923.

The "G.C." who speculated about
skirts for men was the Star Weekly's
Greg Clark. Jimmy Frise was his cartoonist partner.

Harry Hindmarsh, Hemingway's old enemy and Joseph Atkinson's son-in-law, wanted all reins in his gauleiter's fist. By 1928 he was managing editor of both the daily and the weekly, and demoted Cranston until he resigned. In effect editing the weekly himself until his death in 1956, he added westerns, mysteries and sports stories. The *Star Weekly*'s circulation nearly doubled in Hindmarsh's first five years.

In 1938, the *Star Weekly* dropped *Toronto* from its title, and the next year, during the Royal Tour, the *Star Weekly* sold 300,000 copies of one issue, 70,000 more than the normal run. By the end of 1940 it was selling almost 60,000 copies on newsstands in the United States. The 1940 Energy Conservation Act, which excluded all imported comics not "bona fide supplements used with newspapers," was a huge boon to the *Star Weekly*. The circulation shot up so fast that, when the government rationed paper, the weekly had to drop its U.S. print-run and its news section. By 1949 its circulation was more than 905,000 copies—almost all of them sold on newsstands.

Meanwhile, two of the paper's most reliable crowd pleasers had quit. While Greg Clark was in Europe in 1944 his son Murray, an army lieutenant, was killed in action. After visiting his son's grave, Clark met delays trying to get an RCAF plane home to see his wife, who had had a nervous breakdown. Clark blamed the *Star*, which might easily have arranged transportation, for the delay, and resented its tactlessness in running his humorous columns while he mourned. Frise, too, had grievances, and in 1946 the pair bolted to the *Montreal Standard*, soon to become *Weekend*.

National Initiatives and the *New World*

Maclean's was merely one attempt to create a national magazine in the first half of the twentieth century. As early as 1908, Max Aitken, later Lord Beaverbrook, had flirted with magazine publishing with his Montreal-based *Canadian Century*, a costly date that lasted a mere two years. When he left to make his political and journalistic fortune in Britain in 1910, he turned the *Century* over to a group promoting a Canadian tariff-protection policy. The magazine failed a few years later. An attempt to beat the *Reader's Digest* at its own game was mounted by the *Magazine Digest*. Founded in Montreal in 1930, it moved to the United States in 1948 and became an organ of several small ultra-conservative groups.

Aitken was not the only tycoon to embark on a magazine. In 1940 the wealthy brewer E. P. Taylor started the *Life*-like picture magazine *New World Illustrated* (1940-48,) and its French counterpart, *Nouveau Monde*. Since beer and liquor advertising were banned in Ontario, Taylor took advantage of *New World*'s Montreal location to run ads for his brands of beer.

Edited by J. K. ("Jake") Thomas, *New World* was a zestful publication that soon had 100,000 readers. "We have got away," the editors reported in February, "from the old idea of Canada as a land covered eternally with snow, and populated by beavers." Instead,

> We have lived with Canadian airmen....We have shown with what zest the Canadians play. Our writers and photographers have swum in the Pacific and fished for lobster in the Atlantic in the long lazy days of summer [sic]....NEW WORLD has been into the plants and offices of Canadian industries....We have gone into the laboratories of Canada....We have knelt in prayer with priests in a Canadian monastery, and told the story of their austere lives of sacrifice and devotion to our own people.
> [ellipses supplied]

The same issue had equally stirring words about its publisher:

> Not the new world but the North Atlantic made NEW WORLD's publisher a figure in the news last month. As Joint Director General of Munitions Production for Canada, EDWARD PLUNKETT TAYLOR was on his way to England with Munitions Minister C.D. Howe when the liner *Western Prince* was torpedoed. After the ordeal at sea, Mr. Howe's party, reduced by the death of financial adviser Gordon Scott, arrived in London, and Mr. Taylor reported that they were

getting down to business on the theme of spurring Canadian aid to Britain.

The sports editor, later associate editor, was Morley Callaghan, and Graham McInnes looked after art. *New World*'s main assets were the pictures that accompanied stories: "Toronto Gets a Night Club"(January 1942): "Stand-out of one week was Ana Pastora, talented Spanish dancer from New York, here doing her exotic Moorish dance. Formerly a concert dancer, Ana finds night clubs offer better income." In March 1944, there was "Russian Breakthrough: Radio Pictures of Fighting on Eastern Front." Seven years after *Life* did it, *New World* showed a baby being born, and even headlined it "Life's Most Vital Half Hour." Women, whom the war had drawn into the industrial work force as never before, dominated its pages.

Often there was a discreet show of leg or breast, as in April 1945's photo feature about "secrets of sleep." An attractive blonde in a nightie takes a batch of nonfiction to bed rather than "too-exciting a book." The same issue had a poll that might equally have induced slumber in the lady. Among the questions asked was "How Can We Have Better Unity?" Maurice Duplessis, Quebec premier, provided *his* answer when he addressed the Chemical Institute of Canada: "I suggest that the initials of your Institute in future also stand for the slogan 'Canadian Inter-Provincial Cooperation.'"

Small Starts

In the provinces, regional magazines straggled along. The *Atlantic Advocate*, having absorbed *Busy East* in 1910, subtitled itself *The Maritime Provinces, Alive and Distinctive*. On the west coast *British Columbia Magazine* (1911-27) existed under various names.

With organizational backing, a few special interest magazines made starts: the Alpine Club of Canada's surprisingly readable *Canadian Alpine Journal* (1907—); the Ontario Motor League's *Canadian Motorist* (1914—, later named *Leisureways*); the Hudson's Bay Company's *The Beaver* (1921—), at first a company organ, but later a respected magazine of Canadian, especially northern, social history. In Montreal, the monthly *Canadian Business* (1929—) appeared, sponsored by the Chamber of Commerce, and in Ottawa the newly founded Geographical Society's *Canadian Geographical Journal* (1929,—later *Canadian Geographic*) was first edited by the polymath and librarian Lawrence J. Burpee.

Among church or religious magazines was the socially aware *New Outlook* (succeeding the *Christian Guardian* in 1925, succeeded by the *United Church Observer* in 1939), whose editor, the Reverend William Black Creighton, supported the Fellowship for a Christian Social Order. Father of the conservative historian Donald Creighton, William Black Creighton was accused of turning the magazine into a "red propaganda

sheet." More typical was the old faithful *Northern Messenger*, still owned by the Dougalls, which advised its prospective writers, "Publication is religious in tone. Smoking must not be practised by characters in stories; no drinking, gambling, etc. There must be nothing which could possibly contaminate youth."

In a period that included—in its widest definition—two world wars and a global economic depression, some publications of levity, escapism, or recreation actually got started, a few of which definitely *aimed* to contaminate youth.

One example was *The Goblin* (1921-30), which adopted the North American fad for college humour: flappers, hip flasks and the like (a local source of umbrage was the Ontario Temperance Act, whose baleful decade of life began in 1917). Initially an undergraduate Toronto paper launched by four college students, at the peak of its popularity it achieved a national circulation of 47,000—selling more copies on newsstands than any contemporary Canadian magazine. Edited by a committee, the magazine featured sketches, vignettes, cartoons and satires, and such humorous goblins as Stephen Leacock, Greg Clark, Merrill Denison and Peter MacArthur, with art by Jimmy Frise and Richard Taylor—who would often draw as many as eight sketches an issue, all in different styles. Several of *The Goblin*'s principals, among them Joseph E. McDougall, James A. Cowan, Keith Crombie and E.B. Haslow, went on to have successful careers in advertising and public relations—Haslow, in fact, pioneered in writing that blend of advertising and editorial copy called "advertorials." *The Goblin* spent its last year of life in Montreal. Though not primarily a humour magazine,

Alvah Beatty's *Montrealer* (1924-70), a pale approximation of the *New Yorker*, was another symptom of the jazz age.

Humour was one strength of *Wings,* the Second World War air force magazine from Ottawa that gave early experience to Sergeant Eric Nicol, one of the distinctive postwar writers of comedy. When pulp magazines—detective, science fiction, fantasy, "weird"—were banned from entering Canada during the war, a few local versions sprang up to feed starved Canadian fans. William B. Forbes, a *New World* editor, started the initially successful but short-lived *Factual Detective Stories* and *Actual Detective Stories*. After the war Forbes formed a well-known photo journalism team with Ronny Jaques and Kenneth Johnstone. In Parry Sound, Ontario, Leslie A. Crouch started his "fanzine" *Light,* devoted to fantasy art and literature. A more full-fledged fantasy magazine was *Uncanny Tales* (1940-43), which published original work. Many more magazines contented themselves with reprinting British and U.S. material.

Nationalist Forums

The 1920s was one of those periods when nationalism, always an undercurrent in Canadian life, made waves. The First World War, besides demonstrating Canadians' valour, also revealed their uniqueness.

In another time, the old intellectual-class magazines might have expressed this nationalism, and other concerns of mind and soul, but by now such journals had almost vanished. The old ideal had to be pursued, as Robert McDougall says, through magazines like the *Dalhousie Review* (1921—) ("What we have in mind is the need of that public concerned about the things of the intellect and the spirit, which desires to be addressed on problems of general import and in a style that can be generally understood") and the *University of Toronto Quarterly* (1931—), whose first editorial spoke of a scholarly review "amusing because it was reminiscent of all the nine Muses, and instructive because it was concerned with serious topics competently treated."

Despite their tiny circulations these quarterlies made a literary impact: *Dalhousie Review*, found and edited for twenty-six years by the philosopher Herbert Leslie Stewart in Halifax; *Queen's Quarterly*, which in 1928 had revamped its format, begun paying an editor in chief and enlivened its contents, eventually published poetry and fiction; and in 1936 the *University of Toronto Quarterly* created its influential annual survey, "Letters in Canada."

But if universities upheld the old generalist tradition, some agents of specialization were keyed to professional interests. The quarterly *Canadian Historical Review* (1920—), with W. S. Wallace as editor, succeeded *Review of Historical Publications relating to Canada* and in 1922 became the official outlet of the newly founded Canadian Historical Association. Likewise published by the University of Toronto Press, the *Canadian Journal of Economics and Political Science*, founded by the Canadian Political Science Association in 1935, eventually was split (in 1967) into the *Canadian Journal of Economics* and the *Canadian Journal of Political Science*. The same was true in science. The *Canadian Journal of Research*, founded by the National Research Council in 1929, was divided into specialist journals.

Among literary journals, the *Canadian Bookman* (1919—), "A Quarterly devoted to Literature, the Library and the Printed Book," later "A Monthly Devoted to Literature and the Creative Arts," was initially edited by B. K. Sandwell and affiliated with the Canadian Authors' Association. At first a large quarto with up to ninety pages an issue, the *Bookman* shrank with unprofitability to virtually leaflet size and even failed to appear sometimes in 1937. In spring 1938, a renovated *Canadian Bookman* appeared under the management of a company headed by Lorne Pierce and directed "exclusively to the book reader," but closed in 1939, though its title was echoed from 1943 in that of the Canadian Authors' Association's *Canadian Author and Bookman*. The CAA's *Canadian Poetry Magazine* (1936-68) published good new work during Earle Birney's brief turbulent term as editor from 1946 to 1948, during which he warred with the "stuffed owls" of the association.

Other arts were served by magazines like Montreal's *Canadian Stage, Screen and Studio* (1936-37) and the more substantial *Canadian Review of Music and Other Arts* (1941-47). Edited by Christopher Wood with the assistance of Godfrey Ridout and first titled *Canadian Music*, it contained news as well as criticism. After 1943, it was owned and edited by Louis de B. Corriveau, who sank much of his own money into the enterprise and steadily made it more of an art magazine.

Some general magazines of art and commentary, like the *Canadian Nation*, in one way or another were linked to the past. The *Nation*, published irregularly during the 1920s, was edited by D. M. LeBourdais and Graham Spry, the Canadian Club's national secretary. (The Canadian Club had been set up by a group of businessmen in Hamilton, Ontario, in 1892.) Donat Marc LeBourdais, whose varied career included spells as a telegrapher in the Yukon, sawmill operator, insurance salesman and oil company promoter, was a constant contributor to many magazines and editor of *Mental Health*—coincidentally, he was later defeated as a CCF candidate to the Ontario Legislature and the House of Commons.

The authentically new nationalism of the 1920s was one function of the debunking spirit that prevailed after the war. After the war's carnage, and the horrendous influenza epidemic that followed it, human beings had quite enough reminders of death to do them for some time. They wanted to *live*, and part of living was to reject the past. All the old institutions and ideas of status, the ideal of chivalry itself, were eminently mockable.

As F. W. Watt has pointed out, one manifestation of this spirit was the *Canadian Forum* (1920—), which had evolved from a small, drab, deceptively titled University of Toronto publication called *The Rebel* (1917-20). No magazine that included the xenophobic classicist Maurice Hutton as a contributor could be *too* rebellious. As the *Forum's* editorial said of *The Rebel*: its "rebellion still in progress was against the conventions, not against society. Their excursions into politics were neither numerous nor protracted. It was in the field of arts and letters that they flaunted their banners...." *The Rebel's* motto, "They that reverence too much old times, are but a scorn to the new." would be more convincingly carried into this new "permanent monthly journal of opinion." It would not be part of some old economic-protectionist "Made in Canada" movement. "Real independence is not the product of tariffs and treaties. It is a spiritual thing...."

This nationalism had little to do with that of the CAA. Of the CAA's promotion of "Canadian Authors' Week," Barker Fairley sardonically noted in December 1921: "The problem of Christmas presents has been somewhat lightened. More than that, we now know by heart the names of all the Canadian authors and run over the list in bed at night before dropping off to sleep, with the result that we awake next morning purged of pity and fear, and see things more clearly than we did a few days ago." Less jocularly, he added, "We all recognize the several rights of publisher, author, and critic but we are apprehensive when we see them indiscriminately mingled...."

This cultural nationalism relied on artists like Fairley, A. Y. Jackson and J. E. H. MacDonald, all of whom had contributed articles to *The Rebel*. An old pro, C. W. Jefferys, who'd done caricatures for *the Rebel*, designed the *Forum's* cover, and another veteran of *The Rebel*, Fairley, was to become literary editor. Such painters and engravers as F. H. Varley, Lawren Harris, Frank Carmichael, A. J. Casson, David Milne, Thoreau MacDonald (J. E. H.'s son) and poets like E. J. Pratt, F. R. Scott and Dorothy Livesay frequently contributed. The painters were often pen men: J. E. H. MacDonald, for example, wrote reviews and verse. From 1920 to 1951, the *Forum* ran almost 400 original illustrations. Thoreau MacDonald, who also did layout and page decorations, alone made 150 pen and brush drawings. After 1926, new artists came forward: Bertram Brooker, Paraskeva Clark, Pegi Nichol and Jack Shadbolt.

From the start—the first subscription list numbered thirty-five names—the *Forum* drew on a University of Toronto talent pool. During its early years its cover, masthead and table of contents in fact resembled that of an academic publication. Of early importance were Peter Sandiford and the novelist and newspaperman Fred Jacob, though Jacob died by the end of the decade. In April of 1927, a generous English book publisher, J. M. Dent, backed the perpetually penurious maga-

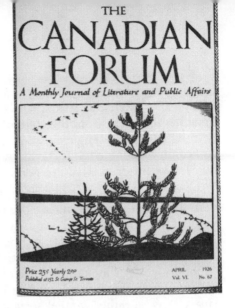

THE
CANADIAN
FORUM

A Monthly Journal of Literature and Public Affairs

Price 25¢ Yearly 2⁰⁰
Published at 152 St George St Toronto

APRIL   1926
Vol. VI   No. 67

The Group of
Seven and their
followers often
adorned the
Canadian Forum,
*as in this April
1926 cover by
J.E.H. Mac-
donald's son
Thoreau.*

zine. When Dent's could no longer afford it, the *Forum* was taken over in 1934 by a group of young Liberals under Steven Cartwright, and then in 1936 by the League for Social Reconstruction, a social democratic organization in the British Fabian Society mould. In keeping with this alliance, the *Forum* envisioned a Canada that was neutralist and social democratic: capitalism was mostly evil, imperialism wholly so.

Although still promoting what it perceived as distinctive in Canadian painting, poetry and theatre, and adding new writers like A. M. Klein— himself the editor during the thirties of *The Judean*, the monthly of Canadian Youth Judea and the *Canadian Jewish Chronicle*, Earle Birney, Ralph Gustafson and Anne Marriott, as well as such versatile literary critics as W. E. Collin and E. K. Brown, both of whom wrote for the *University of Toronto Quarterly*'s "Letters in Canada", the magazine became more stridently political. The 1931 crackdown on Communists ordered by Prime Minister R. B. Bennett, and the ensuing raids, arrests and deportations, offered an excellent target, as would the War Measures Act in the 1940s. In 1941 the *Forum* rallied to the defence of the iconoclastic historian Frank Underhill, whose "O Canada" column in 1929-32 had been one of the magazine's liveliest features. Writing in February, Carlton McNaught said, "The recent attempt by members of the governing body of the University of Toronto to frighten one of its professors into resigning by the threat of impending dismissal again leads one to ask what notion prevails in such quarters about the university's function in a democracy."

In its vigorous social critiques, the *Forum* was greatly aided by F. R. Scott, a poet and McGill law professor. Scott, the poet and critic A. J. M. Smith—another frequent *Forum* contributor—and Leon Edel had founded the *McGill Fortnightly Review* (1925-26). Although since overvalued as a precursor of modernist poetry in Canada—after all, Arthur Stringer had used *vers libre* in his 1914 collection *Open Water*—the

Review was a stimulating literary journal. Scott and Edel also founded the *Canadian Mercury* (1928-29), which urged "the emancipation of Canadian literature from the state of amiable mediocrity and insipidity in which it now languishes." A monthly of literature and opinion (contributors included S. I. Hayakawa, later famous as a semanticist), the *Mercury* merged with the *Forum*.

The 1920s was a decade of parties; the 1930s, of Parties. At least five were formed in Canada during the decade. If the *Forum* tended leftward, it was too mild for some who started magazines during the Depression. *Masses* (1932-34), published by the Progressive Arts Club of Canada, was much more stridently Marxist. *New Frontier* (1936-37), "A monthly magazine of literature and social criticism," regarded the CCF, in which the *Forum* had such hope, and its "professorial braintrusters" as "a rather genteel sprig clipped from the suburban hedge of British Fabianism."

New Frontier might have been talking about the *Forum*: such key contributors as Scott, Graham Spry, Underhill, Eugene Forsey and King Gordon had all attended Oxford and absorbed the social democratic lessons of R. H. Tawney. Writing for *New Frontier* were Dorothy Livesay (also an editor), Leon Edel and Mary Quayle Innis. Many writers overlapped in these magazines: a founding editor of *New Frontiers* was J. F. White, who had also helped to start the *Forum*; still another was the *Canadian Nation*'s Graham Spry, an enthusiast of publicly owned broadcasting. A special issue on Spain in December included W. A. Deacon's comment "we should cut clear of the Empire and the whole continent of Europe." Like the *Forum* and *Masses*, the magazine often ran Depression short stories revolving around the causes and consequences of unemployment. Though it had a short life, it was revived by Margaret Fairley in 1952 as a quarterly on culture and the arts, and included work by Milton Acorn and George Ryga. It ceased publication in 1957.

In this decade of extreme alignments, *Canadian Comment* (1932-38) was in the centre, or mildly leftist. Subtitled *On This Changing World*, its editorial board included E. J. Pratt, the sportscaster Foster Hewitt, Arthur Lowe, Wallace Seccombe, the economist A. F. W. Plumptre, and Nicholas Ignatieff.

The *Forum* represented the variegated left: Earle Birney, a Trotskyite, became literary editor in 1936, but editors and contributors included such active members of the League for Social Reconstruction and of the CCF as Forsey, Gordon ("Ralph Connor"'s son), Underhill, Scott and Spry. But there were also University of Toronto classical scholars like Louis Mackay, George Grube and Eric Havelock. This talented crew, Birney recalled, "sat around Eleanor Godfrey's dining room table, making up the dummy far into the night." Apart from supplying poems as fillers, Birney obtained essays from Sherwood Anderson and begged fiction from Hugh Garner and Morley Callaghan. They had fun.

"L.A.M." (Louis MacKay), who specialized in political lampoons, unfavorably reviewed "John Smalacombe"'s poetry chapbook *Viper's Bugloss*. Smalacombe hotly responded with a letter and a poem to rebut the allegation "that I do not know a sibilant from a snake in the grass." Both writers were Louis MacKay.

Oppressed by the war it had so vigorously opposed, the *Forum* lost some of its energy. When the League for Social Reconstruction disbanded, the board and editors that the League had appointed carried on until the war's end. At this point, important contributors like Underhill began to shift away from Canadian nationalism towards continentalism and the Liberal Party.

Although the *Forum* remained important as a literary outlet—given the scant number of magazines, it could not fail to be—its role as a home for new talent yielded to other magazines. In the February 1939 issue, "Dust Patterns After Revolution" by "David Andrade" appeared. "Andrade" was a pseudonym for Patrick Anderson, whose "Poem on Canada" was the longest ever run by the *Forum*. He would found *Preview*, one of the Montreal little magazines to emerge in the 1940s. Although their writers often also appeared in the *Forum*, such magazines would be the new spear carriers of literary expression.

In its first three decades, the *Forum* was never quite as daring or irreverent as it liked to think. Sometimes it was downright earnest. In October 1927 a piece of social realist fiction appeared, Jean Burton's "Phyllus." Its protagonist, a hairdresser, is seduced and commits suicide. "Phyllus," whose most salacious line was "Jake's hand moved about her breasts," aroused indignant letters. In response, the *Forum* sounded like the *Canadian Monthly and National Review*: "Is it really in the interests of morality that this inhibition should be continued? And if we agree that ignorance and innocence are not synonymous, is not fiction a valid medium for the purpose of enlightenment?" Much more effective was Hugh Garner's "Toronto Cabbagetown," his first published prose, in June 1936. Speaking of the ghetto's housing, he said: "They are five-or-six room houses, and are supposedly easy to heat. That is why the landlords refrain from the expense of providing a furnace to heat them."

Many of those who wrote for the *Forum* were far from being permanent outsiders. In fact, their ideas and actions helped shape Canadian society in the next three decades. In such fashion does a new establishment supplant the old.

J. B. Maclean

The growth of mass magazines in Canada, and of the corporate structures to support them, begins in the first decade of the twentieth century and is epitomized in one bullet-headed little man by the name of John Bayne Maclean.

*The hard-headed
J.B. Maclean,
looking genial.*

*About to begin a
hard-working day
is Maclean-
Hunter's indispen-
sable treasurer
and first female
employee, Priscilla
Forbes.*

Born on Boxing Day 1862, he was a child of the manse in West Puslinch, Upper Canada. The elder of two brothers, Maclean had a journalist uncle in the Reverend James Cameron, editor during the 1870s
of the Presbyterian *Canada Christian Monthly*. In this frugal, pious,
industrious scene Maclean was educated in Owen Sound, Durham and
Toronto. He made a common nineteenth century station-stop: teaching in country schools. Already he was busily involving himself in the
militia, at first with the 31st Greys of Owen Sound, later with the 10th
Royal Grenadiers in Toronto. Maclean's civilian career centred on journalism.

In 1882, two years after a family friend, George Brown of *The Globe*,
was assassinated, Maclean began reporting for the *Toronto World*, a two-
year-old toddler of a morning newspaper that was outspoken editorially but fiscally ill-nourished. Of necessity, Maclean free-lanced for
financial papers, switched for a few weeks to the *Globe*, then moved
to the Tory-mouthpiece, the *Daily Mail*. Although he was promoted,
he resigned in 1887. At first his idea was to start a livestock trade paper,
but then he decided on something a little farther down the food chain.
With $2,000 derived from a few shrewd investments and smaller sums
from friends, he started the *Canadian Grocer*, a magazine whose name
had previously graced a pickle company's house organ.

Taking an office in his printer's building, he put out the magazine's sixteen-page first issue on 23 September, "Published weekly in the interests of the grocery, produce, provision, liquor and confectionery trades." It was the first weekly Canadian trade paper, and, once established, the subscriptions piled up. With its woodcuts and decorative masthead created by Fred Brigden of the well-known engraving firm, this substantial publication had an editorial stance that combined boosterism with an attack on the then current proposals for commercial union with the United States.

Maclean was plainly onto a good thing, and lost no time in promoting himself and his enterprises. For one thing he was a great joiner: he belonged to the Swiss Club, Imperial Federation League, Gaelic Society, the Fencing Club, Ontario Rifle Association, Toronto Canoe Club, the St. John's Ambulance Brigade and the Canadian Red Cross. In tandem with magazine publishing, he became commercial-financial editor of the *Empire*, remaining three years, then secretary of the Canadian Packers' Association for five years.

On New Year's Day 1888, his six-years-younger brother, Hugh, gave up his job in a print shop and came to work for him—the start of a sixty-year relationship marked by intermittent fondness and consistent bickering. A keen militiaman, Hugh married the daughter of Jack's friend T. W. Dyas. The brothers were distinctly different. More routinized, a detail man, Hugh was also more prone to such get-rich-schemes as mining stock promotions. Gruff and direct, where Jack was silky, lacking his brother's ostensible detachment, Hugh was sometimes left to do such dirty work as firings.

Another help to J. B. Maclean was his first woman employee, Priscilla Forbes, an office manager/office girl who would remain with the company for more than fifty years. In the early days, she would sometimes put her savings into the cash box so that urgent expenses could be met.

Soon Maclean was expanding. In 1888 he took over an impoverished trade paper called *Books and Notions*, later called *Bookseller and Stationer*, which had been founded four years earlier to cater to the book, stationery, fancy goods, music and wallpaper trades, and *Hardware and Metal Merchant*, later named *Hardware Merchandising*, which bore J. W. Bengough's Byzantine cover design.

Prosperous and on the move to new quarters on Wellington Street, Maclean formed a joint stock company with himself as president and his brother as secretary-treasurer. *Dry Goods Review* came out in 1891, its trade "the only one in Canada which has hitherto not had a journal of its own." Like the others, it would have a long life. The Macleans used good stock, not the common newsprint; they printed advertising rate cards and stuck to the rates; and unusually for the time, they let advertisers provide new copy for each issue without fresh typesetting

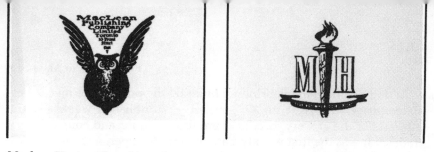

Maclean-Hunter often changed its name — and logo. Maclean Publishing was a "We never sleep" owl, M-H a "Fear not when doing right" torch.

charges. They paid their bills; they specialized. All these practices helped ensure an enduring success.

The *Canadian Printer and Publisher* appeared in May 1892, but Maclean was not content merely to add one trade journal after another to his pile. T. W. Dyas, then circulation manager for the *Mail*, decided to combine the popularity of art with the new process of photoengraving by offering a premium, special supplements of "masterpieces," to new subscribers. Maclean took this idea under his arm in 1893 and ran to New York with it. With Dyas he launched the *Art Weekly*, whose pages reproduced paintings in black and white that bore such evocative titles as *Rutting Stag* and *Gathering Dandelions*. Each weekly issue was shipped in bulk to contracting newspapers, who then resold the supplements to their readers cheaply, but with the rider that a coupon had to be clipped from one of the paper's current issues.

Although initially profitable—art reproduction giveaways were a hardy perennial of the promotion business—this venture was in the nature of a gimmick linked to a fad, and Maclean got out when trade began to decline. A more lasting effect of his New York sojourn came from meeting publishing magnates, such as Frank A. Munsey, the gloomy, ruthless former Maine farmboy who had parlayed $40 in cash and a few manuscripts into *Argosy* (publisher of Horatio Alger) and the hugely successful monthly *Munsey's Magazine*. Another was the extroverted Irishman, S. S. (Sam) McClure, who in 1893 had founded *McClure's Magazine*, *Munsey's* great competitor in the dime-magazine field. *McClure's* paid hugely for the work of Arthur Conan Doyle, H. Rider Haggard, Rudyard Kipling and James M. Barrie. McClure also ran exposes like Ida M. Tarbell's series on the Standard Oil Company. The examples of both men were not lost on Maclean.

Munsey, founder of the first ten-cent mass magazine, gave his younger Canadian colleague stock market tips. The pair remained friends even after they competed for the affections of Anna Denison Slade, the Bostonian who became Maclean's wife.

After Maclean returned from New York he went to Montreal, involving himself in the *Canadian Military Gazette*. Meanwhile Hugh had hit an exceedingly rough patch. His wife Bessie had died young, as had one of their two children. The survivor, Andrew, was only three years old when, in 1899, J. B. Maclean bought Hugh's interest in the company for $50,000, while cancelling a $23,000 stock market debt owed the company. Hugh then started a new firm, the Hugh C. MacLean Company.

Although an active publisher of trade magazines—he absorbed the Mortimer weekly trade journals in 1903—and occasional rival of his brother, Hugh only strayed into the consumer area when his company acquired the *Canadian Magazine* in 1926, an expensive adventure that had ended, despite Jack's cash injection, with the magazine's demise in 1939. Much later Southam acquired the MacLean firm, now owned by Andrew, and after a transitional period, changed its name to Southam Business Publications.

Until the 1930s Jack's firm was known as the J. B. McLean Company. Eventually he lower-cased the "L" in Maclean, and his firm then became Maclean-Hunter. Later the hyphen was dropped, too (after 1980). However he spelled his name, Maclean was busy. He transformed the *Military Gazette* into the *Military Gazette and Gentleman's Magazine* in 1900 and then sold it to a group headed by Lieutenant-Colonel Andrew Thompson in 1906. He had, after all, already started a bona fide consumer magazine, the *Busy Man's*, the immediate forbear of *Maclean's*. All boded well for the future, especially since Mrs. Maclean had presented him in February 1903 with what was to be their only child, the heir apparent, Hector Fitzroy Maclean. As if to put aside his old guise as glamorous militia man and certify his new role as paterfamilias, he sold his regimental uniform of lieutenant-colonel, Duke of York's Hussars, complete with frogged tunic, white-cockaded busby and spurred boots.

Down at the Front Street offices, key personnel were in place. Among the thirty or so employees was J. Meredith McKim. In charge of advertising for all trade papers, McKim would later move to London, England, as Maclean's representative. H. Victor Tyrell, a detail man hired as a compositor in 1898, was soon expediting advertising and smoothing press schedules; he later became general manager and vice-president. In 1903 the twenty-two-year-old Horace Talmadge Hunter was hired to sell ads for *Hardware & Metal Merchant*; he had already put himself through university selling space for the weekly *Presbyterian*. A cautious but determined man, Hunter oversaw advertising and increasingly made policy. He would become the company's vice-president by 1911 and link his name with Maclean's in the corporate title. All was hard work and prudence, with placards proclaiming: TURN OUT THE LIGHTS WHEN NOT IN USE and DON'T WASTE PAPER.

Gifted people at home, gifted people in the field. The company had offices in Montreal, Vancouver, New York and Winnipeg. Out west Maclean relied for trade paper reportage on E. Cora Hind, an Ontario woman who had moved to Winnipeg in 1882 to become the first public stenographer and typist west of the Great Lakes. As an expert on the crucial grain harvests, she became internationally celebrated as a reporter.

Maclean was obviously well-served. But it's worth taking a last short look at the new father and founder of what was to become a multimedia empire. A snob—"you will be interested to know that Mrs. Maclean is related to the king of Portugal"—inveterate people-collector and name-dropper, he loved dogs and every night dressed for dinner. He had simple but fussy tastes. Prone to Scottish ancestor worship, toward the end of his life he paid to restore the clapboard manse where he was born near Puslinch Lake and arranged with Hugh to provide an endowment for its perpetual care. Parsimonious with paper, he was quick to pick up restaurant tabs. With high cheekbones and piercing eyes, his face had a vaguely Oriental aspect, belied by its rosy skin. Crafty, unsmiling, self-contained, he was by no means lazy, though he did relish his leisure. When he could, he absented himself for five months of the year in Palm Springs and other places, directing homeward a warm front of memos. Floyd Chalmers tells us that, even in his sixties, he "wrote thousands of words a week, all by hand in his neat, minuscule script, and his secretary, Miss Ethel Dove, impersonally copied the sheets and gathered up—for permanent filing—the dozens of scraps of paper on which his preliminary notes had been scribbled at the desk, in the garden, in the bath or in bed."

Although many employees quit over his constant picayune carping criticisms, his greatest management skill was probably in hiring the right people for the right jobs. To a few of these he could be generous. While Hunter fought a two-year bout with tuberculosis, Maclean kept his job for him.

Although politically he could not be conveniently pegged—he was not opposed to organized labour as such, spoke out against the Canadian Manufacturers' Association and opposed the empire building of Sir Adam Beck, the chairman of the Ontario Hydro-Electric Commission—he was a man of many likes and dislikes. According to his biographer, "He distrusted intellectuals," especially Rhodes Scholars, "university professors, British politicians, Baptists, heavy drinkers, teetotalers, international bankers, paper manufacturers and Winston Churchill. He held to the conviction that most missionaries were sent abroad to spread subversion," with the exception of Scots, "especially if they were Presbyterians." He respected municipal politicians, school board politicians and civil servants, except those who handled postal rates or tariffs. "The Colonel's steady favourites among the human race were Mrs. Winston Churchill, French Canadians and Scots...plus Jews, Roman Catholics, Presbyterians, United Empire Loyalists, most of European royalty, almost all the people of the U.S.A. and a sizeable group of their leading captains of industry."

Having survived the Toronto waterfront fire of 1904, Maclean's company appealed to Canadian captains of industry by founding *Canadian Machinery and Manufacturing News* in 1905, which urged the adoption of the metric system. More significantly, it started the weekly *Financial Post* in 1907. By the outbreak of the First World War he had added more trade papers, flirted with buying the *Mail and Empire* daily newspaper, become president of the Canadian Press Association, which then included magazines, and opened new offices at 481 University Avenue. There Maclean treated himself to an office with imported Tudor-period panelling and a framed quotation from Munsey: "You cannot get out of a man what God Almighty did not put in him. You have to suit the man to the job and not the job to the man." He also bought a new home, located a hundred yards from the site of Sir Henry Pellatt's folly, Casa Loma, then being constructed. In October 1910 he began *Farmer's Magazine*, and often wrote its signed editorials.

After the war ended, Maclean arranged to share his firm with Hunter and Tyrrell. Now was added someone whom Robert Fulford would later call "a man of great simplicity who hoped to be thought complex." In any event he made a great impact on the company. The career of Floyd Chalmers follows some of the lines of a fairy tale and the Horatio Alger legend: an impoverished childhood, orphanhood—his mother died when he was seven; a cruel stepmother—the paternal grandmother who then looked after him; then a steady rise "through sheer application to high principles and hard work"—not to mention surrogate adoption by a rich man, one John Bayne Maclean.

Born in upstate New York, Chalmers was raised in Orillia where a schoolmate was Leslie Frost, a future premier of Ontario. (As it happened, his father did a column on maintaining saws and knives for *Barrel and Box*, a U.S. trade journal that, for sentimental reasons, Floyd Chalmers later brought into the Maclean fold.) While in high school in Toronto he free-lanced for the *Star Weekly*, among other papers, then reported for the *News* and the *World*. An omen of his future corporate as well as journalistic success occurred while he was overseas with a tank battalion. In 1918, he edited a weekly paper in England called the *Khaki Varsity* and a daily newssheet called the *Tank Tatler*. He took "pictures of my comrades going about their training. I had the snaps developed at a penny each in Bournemouth and sold them for twopence apiece to soldiers to send photographs of themselves home. In this manner, I earned a profit of five or six pounds every week, a princely sum."

In 1919, Chalmers joined the *Financial Post*. At the *Post*, Chalmers, a competent writer and scrupulous reporter, reported, sold advertising and married Jean Boxall, another *Post* employee. In 1923 when the Montreal editor and advertising salesman of the *Post* quit, claiming they were overworked, he was sent to replace them both. By 1925 the tall, gruff and rumpled Chalmers had become editor of the *Post* and four trade papers, then their manager, increasing the *Post*'s circulation from 8,000 to 21,000 in four years. He was also becoming something of a pet with the Macleans.

By this time, the Colonel had survived several crises in his personal life. He had outlasted an attack of typhoid; Mrs. Maclean, stricken with polio in 1910, was now confined to a wheelchair. Saddest of all in 1919 they had lost their only child, who had died suddenly from an intestinal problem while still in his teens. It was natural that the lonely Maclean would look on Chalmers almost as a son, to the point where, shortly before Christmas 1932, when the Colonel decided to take a Caribbean cruise he invited Chalmers—but not Chalmers's family—to join him. Chalmers' wife, Jean, ever the loyal corporate wife, "settled the matter by telling Colonel Maclean that of course I would go with him."

While Chalmers was rapidly climbing the ladder, there were many changes within the company. In 1920, Maclean sold thirty percent of the company's common shares and ten percent to Tyrrell. In 1921, the *Farmer's Magazine* succumbed. Although *Farmer's* had been ploughed under, the company bought the one-year-old *Canadian Homes and Gardens* in 1925, and in 1927—the year the colonel acquired his custom-built Rolls-Royce—it initiated *Mayfair. Chatelaine* followed in 1928.

Hunter, the remote delegator, became president in 1933, and Maclean became chairman of the board. In 1934 Chalmers was named manager—Maclean code for publisher—of the *Post*, but was not named to the company's board of directors. Though disappointed, he declined other job offers, and in fact kept buying shares. Chalmers's family would eventually hold twenty-two per cent of the stock. By the end of 1939, Maclean's company had twenty-eight publications, including five in the United States and England.

In 1941, Chalmers traveled to Britain via Lisbon with the British MP and *Maclean's* columnist Beverley Baxter. In London he was operating out of a couple of small rooms the company retained after giving up their larger space off Trafalgar Square to the Canadian army. Chalmers reported for the *Post* and *Maclean's* in an effort, lasting throughout the war, to get his magazines' public behind the war loans. Lending such company staff members as Byrne Hope Sanders and Ken Wilson to the Wartime Prices and Trade Board, he also advanced the idea that every periodical in Canada would promote a common theme—the Union Jack—to coincide with a Victory Loan drive, thus blanketing the newsstands.

Named vice-president in 1942, Chalmers shunted Napier Moore to the post of editorial director, leaving *Maclean's* effectively in the hands of Arthur Irwin. Chalmers also sorted out personal conflicts between Moore and Roy Perry, *Chatelaine*'s capable manager—confusingly, *Chatelaine*'s editor had been responsible to Moore, and *Mayfair* and

Canadian Homes and Gardens were under Dick Huestis. He raised salaries and set up an internal training program.

In May 1945, Victor Tyrrell died, and since the heir apparent, Hunter's son Donald, was overseas, the question arose as to who would be number three after Maclean and Hunter. After some infighting, Chalmers moved into Tyrrell's office. Every day, Tyrrell used to read the number of advertising lines sold up to the previous night in each of the company's five leading publications; Chalmers favoured a more decentralized mode, setting up a system of brief monthly reports from each publication. He rehired returning vets and pressed his contention that "fewer mistakes are made by pushing young people ahead too fast than by holding them back too long." In 1945, the company had thirty-three publications; in 1947, it built a $2.3-million plant on the northern edge of the city, overseen by Donald Hunter.

When Maclean died in 1950, he left an estate of just over one million dollars, his Toronto residence and the Crieff manse going to his nephew Andrew. Only a tiny minority share in the company was part of the estate. Control had long since passed to Hunter, and, besides Chalmers's shares, smaller bits of ownership belonged to Maclean employees ranging from executives to secretaries.

Subliminally the company had acquired a culture, mentality and character of its own that were a product not just of Maclean but of those who worked for him. It was a slow-moving but determined concern, relying not on debt-financing but on reinvested profits. Maclean had never paid himself much salary or expenses, relying on shrewd investments to maintain his standard of living. Neither were profits dispensed to the public: the first grudging dividends had been issued in 1927. The company, though not in general its consumer division, had been consistently profitable. Avid to acquire trade papers, it was much more cautious in taking on or starting consumer magazines.

Often the company was right to do so. When in 1921 Maclean was offered a surviving remnant of his old friend McClure's empire, *McClure's Magazine*, then still selling 350,000 copies a year, he turned it down—the magazine ended in 1924. But once the company embarked on a project it tended to stick with it, and by 1950 its four chief magazines—*Macleans, Chatelaine, Canadian Homes and Gardens*, and *Mayfair*—grossed more than $4 million in advertising. This tenacious attitude would well serve *Maclean's Magazine*, to name only one publication, in the coming years, just as the acquisition of the Toronto radio station CKEY would point the company in a new direction. The Maclean company was the harbinger of both mass and multimedia.

MACLEAN'S
A MAGAZINE FOR BUSY MEN

Near the end of 1894, John Bayne Maclean, just back from New York, further irritated his irascible brother and business partner, Hugh, by moving to Montreal. There he began to interest himself in the *Canadian Military Gazette*.

Inspired by the clangorously patriotic coverage of the 1885 Riel Rebellion, a Northwest veteran had started the magazine when he returned to Ottawa, frailly conducting it until its sale in 1893 to a pair of Montreal regimental officers. They were E. J. Chambers, a young major and former Northwest correspondent who then wrote for the *Star*, and Edward Desbarats, another militia officer who was advertising manager for the Maclean brothers in Montreal and later founded an early and important advertising agency.

After two years, they sold it to Maclean, who had been talked into it by militia well-wishers. Maclean initiated what he would later call "the paper's aggressive, perhaps offensive, but always fair, constructive policies." He would also bear "the political and social punishments that followed." By early 1896 the fortnightly had improved its looks and begun a series of exposés, even scooping the nation by revealing that a militia force would be sent to fight in the Boer War. It carried much-reprinted eyewitness reports from the front, sent by Major F. S. Dixon, cunningly published under a pen name.

Military enthusiast that he was, Maclean had broader ambitions—to publish a more general magazine. He started what Floyd Chalmers called "a gossipy-chatter weekly," the *Metropolitan*, subtitled *Montreal Life*, and persisted with it until about 1900. Like the *Metropolitan*, the *Gazette* had never been profitable, but the same year Maclean renamed it the *Military Gazette and Gentleman's Magazine*, and began running departments like "Masculine Modes" (of fashion) and the occasional book and theatre review.

Maclean was experimenting. He thought of starting a women's magazine, and even had a chance to buy into the Crowell Company, the American publisher of the hugely successful *Farm and Fireside* and *Women's Home Companion*. Instead, Maclean stuck with what he knew best, acquiring the house organ of a Toronto advertising agency that,

after five years as *Business: the Business Man's Magazine*, boasted a circulation one-hundredth that of the *Companion*.

In October 1905, the first issue appeared as the *Business Magazine*, 14 cm x 21 cm, 144 pages, twenty cents a copy, two dollars a year. At first it was a digest, whose contents were culled and sometimes condensed by Maclean or his editor, W. Arnot Craick, from magazines in America and Britain. As Chalmers explains, "the Colonel paid nothing....If they gave him permission to reprint, he would credit the piece to its original vehicle, and also publicize their regular issue by listing major article titles as featured therein. To publications at home or abroad, this seemed a fair offer...." It was a more innocent time.

The start was not without its little hitches. The editor noted that "Owing to the confusion consequent upon the publication of this first number of THE BUSINESS MAGAZINE, under new management, a few mistakes have been made. In some copies, the folios will be found to be a little out from page 72 onward. Readers will kindly overlook this small error."

They did so. Subscriptions poured in, and the November issue featured the first original article, Augustus Bridle's success story of Senator George Fulford of Brockville, Ontario, patenter of "Pink Pills for Pale People." Bridle, a prolific contributor, would publish a collection of his biographical sketches in 1916 as *Sons of Canada*.

At the start of 1906, Maclean was still having a little trouble with titles, not to mention volume numbering. In December's "Inside with

MACLEAN'S MAGAZINE

Grabbing
Legislation at Ottawa

Heroism and Exploration
in Canada
By J. B. Tyrrell

MARCH

MACLEAN PUBLISHING COMPANY·LIMITED
MONTREAL · TORONTO · WINNIPEG

the Publishers,'' he announced he was changing the title to the *Busy Man's Magazine*. Maclean's preoccupation with titles even extended to contents listings: ''mere titles convey but little meaning and give only a doubtful idea of what the article is about. We have accordingly gone a little further and, after the title of the more important articles, have put their contents, so to speak, into a little nutshell. A reader can thus go over the list of articles, pick out those that appeal to him, and purchase the magazine in which they appear.'' Then in February 1906, having skipped the previous month, the magazine announced that ''The present issue is in reality the January issue, although we have labeled it February.''

Eventually the magazine sorted itself out. Until 1911, the enlarged ''Cream of the World's Magazines Reproduced for Busy People'' continued with its fairly new title. Hitherto most of the Canadian features were written by staff, among them George Van Blaricom, who used several pen names along with his own—which itself sounded like a pseudonym—and by the quiet Craick, who, tired of the Colonel's prying, resigned in 1910 and began to edit the Canadian Manufacturers' Association magazine *Industrial Canada*, though he would continue to contribute such pieces as ''The Romance of the Taschereau Family.''

Although it claimed to embrace all ages and classes, *Busy Man's* cover suggested more propertied interests: there were pillars top, left and right, framing some worthy's portrait. In 1906, Maclean sold the *Gentleman's Magazine* and put his money—by 1909 the magazine actually had a budget to pay contributors—and prestige behind his Toronto venture.

So why not call it *Maclean's*? The magazine, renamed in March 1911, was typically 150 pages, not counting the cover and an astounding 115 pages of heavily illustrated advertising at the front and rear: "When writing advertisers kindly mention Maclean's Magazine"; "Say you saw the advertisement in Maclean's magazine"; "It is to your advantage to mention Maclean's Magazine." It measured 23.5 cm x 16.5 cm. The fiction, such as Robert Service's "The Trail of '98," still came from other journals. There were reviews, departments called "Politics and the World" and "After Office Hours," as well as cópious photographs. There were articles by "experts" like H. H. Mortimer, whose August 1911 article "Why the Jew is Healthier than the Christian" explained that "The Jew of the present day, blindly following the Mosaic Law of his forefathers in the squalid, overcrowded ward, is safer from sickness than the wealthy Christian or [sic] aristocratic ancestry to whom the very thoughts of such an environment suggests disease."

The magazine was not so commendatory about blacks. In October, Britton B. Cooke's "The Black Canadian" was breathtakingly bigoted. Photos of southern U.S. blacks—"A Spinster and Her Cabin," "The Nigger Quarter"—bore such captions as: "The lady smokes. This is no serious objection, but there is a general air of neglect about the place and nonchalance about the evident proprietress that is not reassuring when this person is looked upon in the light of a possible Canadian Mother. A few dollars, a little encouragement and this person might, under some circumstances, be led to trek northward and, as some colored man's wife, become the mistress of Canadian acres, and to some small extent, Canadian destiny."

The article was able to sanctimoniously note that "One would hesitate to suggest that any legislation be enacted which might be interpreted as narrow-minded, or harsh, or a mere outcropping of racial prejudice," while adding that "The colored man is nine out of ten unsuited to the development of the highest sort of citizenship in Canada...and, if he is assimilated, he must leave a tinge of the colored blend [sic] in the *Ultimate* Canadian Race—a race that should be bred from the best 'stock' that can be found in the world."

Without Craick and Van Blaricom, Maclean edited and rewrote—he was himself a windy and disorganized writer—and even had the nerve to expand an anecdote about Sir Charles Tupper by another knight, William Van Horne. Maclean wrote the annoyed author: "In the case of the magazines, which are read at leisure, we have found from long experience that the average reader likes the small talk, and it was with small talk your article was padded." Van Horne wrote back: "I am not a little amused at the idea that a magazine article must be padded out to certain proportions. I know that this is the prevailing idea with magazines, but isn't that the reason why they are nearly all so dishwatery?"

Dishwatery or not, the May 1913 issue had a total circulation of more than 25,000 and comprised 272 pages, 150 of which were advertising. The prosperity was reflected in the attractive cover art in colour after 1914, like Lawren Harris's pencil sketch "Sunday on a Skyscraper" in November 1911 and F. S. Coburn's work, which was used throughout 1914.

An enamoured couple in a horse and sleigh ushered in the 1914 Maclean's. *Cupid appears frozen to a runner.*

In January 1914, the magazine had a new size, 21.5 cm × 29 cm, and by October a new editor. Born in Brantford, Ontario, in 1885, Thomas Bertram Costain had written four rejected novels by the time he was seventeen. After a small-town newspaper career, he toiled for several of Maclean's trade journals. He shaped a more consistent, visually appealing magazine: the illustrations were larger and the ads distributed among the editorial copy rather than bunched at the front and back. Sworn to uphold Maclean's Canadianism, Costain made even greater use of C. W. Jefferys, Arthur Heming and the embryonic Group of Seven, and there were short stories by Arthur Stringer, Alan Sullivan and Sir Gilbert Parker. He even printed the twenty-three-year-old Beverley Baxter. Writers like Stephen Leacock, H. G. Wells and Jack London could now get as much as $100 an article. Another contributor was Hugh Eayrs, the future Macmillan publisher, who was then an editor of the Maclean company's trade magazine *Men's Wear*. A quiet, unflustered man with a luxuriant head of hair, Costain wrote fiction for the magazine, and his wife, Ida Spragge, contributed verse.

During the war, Maclean rallied behind his pal Sam Hughes, the rambunctious and controversial federal Minister of Militia and Defense.

In January 1915, *Maclean's* published Robson Black's profile, "General-The-Honourable-Sam," and in the same issue a spy fiction piece in which the detectives were Prime Minister Sir Robert Borden and his "Minister of Militia." As Chalmers says, "The unsolved mystery is how the Colonel escaped a libel writ, for the nasty, highly ingenious spy of the plot turned out to be none other than the military secretary to the Ministry of Militia!"

The next issue featured another spy thriller, "How the Canadian Armada Was Saved." This time the gallant minister was right there in name and illustration, ready to be accosted in the Château Frontenac restaurant by "a fascinating woman," one "Madame de Tourneauville." The beauty tells him about an impending German Zeppelin raid on Canadian ships bearing a contingent overseas. Thanks to Hughes's quick action, the soldiers were saved. Hughes finds his informant and tells her that he will personally tell Lord Kitchener "what we, and the Empire, have to thank you for." The story ends: "And he did."

According to Chalmers, when the press asked Hughes if the events had actually happened, he said, "Yes! Every word was true except for one minor error. There wasn't one woman; there were three!"

In February 1918, Maclean criticized the conduct of the war and British political interference with the generals under Costain's headline "Why We Are Losing the War," which caused the editor to be chided by the chief censor, who had been charged to enforce the order-in-council forbidding the press "to print, publish, or publicly express any adverse or unfavorable statement, report or opinion concerning the action of Canada, the United Kingdom of Great Britain and Ireland or any Allied Nation in prosecuting the war."

As if to make amends, the January 1919 cover showed David Lloyd George, the British wartime leader. By now the magazine was 26.5 cm x 34 cm. The year brought a series by Vilhjalmur Stefansson on "Solving the Problem of the Arctic" and Edith M. Chapman's series "On Choosing a Girl's Vocation." (It was now plausible that women *could* have a vocation other than wife and mother.) There was fiction by the Baroness Orczy and by W. A. Fraser, whose "reputation was first built as a writer of stories of wild animal life, but his 'Thorobreds' establishes him in the eyes of the public as the master of horse-racing stories." In October, the cover boasted that more than 70,000 copies were being printed. Inside, the magazine made the momentous announcement that from 1 February 1920 *Maclean's* would be published twice a month. "The ultimate aim is to develop *MACLEAN'S* into a Canadian national weekly. If the progress that has been made for the past two years can be maintained, it will not be long before this high ambition will have been attained." It would take, in fact, only fifty-six years.

Always defensively minded, Maclean had Bolsheviks on the brain. In June 1919, both *Maclean's* and the *Financial Post* carried his signed

Screened by "Canada's Industrial Unrest," a Bolshevik sniper takes aim at "Canadian Life" in a 1919 Maclean's.

article, "Why Did We Let Trotsky, Bolshevist Leader, Go?" Trotsky had been interned briefly in Nova Scotia—and the next issue had "Planning Soviet Rule in Canada: Tracing to the Centre of the Web," including a photo of "Sauteri Nuorteva, the German who is inspiring and directing from New York the labour troubles in Canada"—such as campus unrest and the recent Winnipeg general strike. In September, "Klondyke Boyle: [Joe Boyle] the Canadian Who Saved Roumania and Bullied the Bolsheviks" was portrayed. Carrying his anti-Bolshevik campaign into the early 1920s, Maclean went so far as to give confidential reports to the McGill principal and former commander of Canadian troops in France, Sir Arthur Currie, ("Colonel Birdlime" in John Glassco's *Memoirs of Montparnasse*) about the backgrounds of speakers coming to address his students.

Although Maclean's convictions were sincere enough, there is no doubt he had an eye for a headline and the good it would do his magazine.

In 1920, Costain was hired away by the *Saturday Evening Post* at double the salary Maclean was paying him; after a thriving career there, he became in middle age a best-selling author of historical romances. *Maclean's* new editor was Costain's assistant, J. Vernon Mackenzie, who called himself "Mac" in his contents-page column. The thirty-seven-year-old Mackenzie, a one-time hand on a trans-Atlantic cattle boat, had been a much-traveled newspaperman who had recently been Canadian trade commissioner in Scotland. Chalmers claimed that Mackenzie, whose associate editor was Joseph Lister Rutledge, had "little perceptive, analytical capacity; he was a bluff, hearty individual who reinforced his strength hour by hour with a chew of candy or gum from the top drawer of his desk." He didn't spend all his time at his desk: four months of the year he traveled across Canada, drumming up talent for the magazine.

At first it was uncertain whether *Maclean's* in the person of Thomas B. Costain had gone to the *Saturday Evening Post* or whether the *Saturday Evening Post* had come to *Maclean's*, for the covers of 1921 were very much in the *Post's* humorous mode. The fiction, too, was *Post* style: in the 15 April issue there was Frank L. Packard's "Nigger, Stop that Fight!" and, oddly enough, an Archie P. McKichnie prizefight story. The Canadian story of that fortnight was the formation of the Canadian Authors' Association, then termed a "Union." The regular departments included "Business & Investments," "Wit, Wisdom and Whimsicality," "Women and Their Work" and a long-running column of jokes culled from other magazines called "Maybe Adam Laughed at These."

Later in the year, the magazine was caught by the Toronto printers' strike and had to combine the four issues of July and August into two. But by September it was back on track. On 15 September, Harold D. Crew's "The Pictorial That Died" concerned the demise of the Canadian National Pictorial, a two-year-old, government-funded weekly newsreel that had been shown in up to 200 theatres, and "Canada's First 'Persian Lamb' Ranch." The illustrations in 1921 were often by C. W. Jefferys, the fiction by the likes of G. K. Chesterton.

That year, *Maclean's* published a flattering piece about Winston Churchill by the British general, Sir Ian Hamilton, who also proposed to Maclean an article about Belted Guernseys, which he was raising in Scotland. These, he told Maclean, "would milk copiously and cut up well in the Hudson's Bay territory." There was another kind of cutup. Hugh Eayrs, now of Macmillan, had commissioned Augustus Bridle to write a series of brief biographies called *Masques of Ottawa* under the pseudonym "Domino." Bought by *Maclean's* as a serial under the byline "The Make-up Man," it became the subject of complaints from high Ottawans. Then Maclean was startled to find a section on "Colonel J. B. Maclean," in which he learned that he "has for the whole of this century so far been engaged in odd jobs of plumbing in the house called Canada." He was also a man whose "head comes to a peculiar apex without a dome" and whose "smiles are probably sub-conscious, or reserved for rare occasions when, if I were a confederate of his, I should expect something either portentous or villainous." Maclean ordered the series dropped and retained the offending chapter. It did not appear in the book.

Maclean would also turn down a 1924 novel by "Gilbert Knox" (the Ottawa writer Madge Macbeth) in which Arthur Meighen, the former prime minister, could be identified in one of the characters. Decreed the colonel,

> We must on no account publish matter that would hurt any person's feelings for the sake of creating a sensation. It is only when the interests of the country are involved that we

should hurt anyone's feelings... When a publication is fighting its way for public recognition, it would be justified in a policy of sound, accurate sensationalism. We have got beyond that stage.

Indeed, Maclean seemed ready to placate any section of the community, with the exception of blacks and Communists. This was evident in 1923 after Mackenzie teamed with the British publisher Hodder & Stoughton to sponsor a $2,500 competition for an original Canadian novel. The winner was Gordon Hill Grahame's *The Bond Triumphant*, which was split into five sections and sent to be illustrated by Jefferys. In this tame historical romance about French Canada in 1661, Bishop Laval was portrayed as a bigot. When the 1 July issue appeared, there was an outcry from French and English Catholics, and considerable kerfluffle over an illustration depicting the hero, Étienne, sitting on a bench with his arm around a girl in a nun's habit, although in the text the girl was a volunteer, not a religious sister. Though not offended himself, the Colonel ordered the galleys withdrawn. This created an anomalous 15 July issue that listed the book in the table of contents— in a section printed prior to his decision—but had the chapter replaced with a short story by Archibald McKichnie.

With the 15 August issue came the statement "The story was taken entirely on the judgment of, and awarded first prize by, a committee of literary experts outside our organization. It is absolutely contrary to the principles and policies upon which *Maclean's Magazine* has been built up to publish partisan material which would hurt any reputable body of citizens in the Dominion." The final sentence summed up: "A Canadian magazine, the contents of which will be welcomed cordially in every real Canadian home, regardless of religion or race; and will further the development of goodwill and understanding through the interpretation of the sections and divisions of our people, each to the other, for the purpose of building up Canadian nationhood." The violently Orange *Toronto Telegram* bought the book's serial rights.

An amusing picture of the 1920s *Maclean's* appears in Earle Birney's memoirs. In the summer of 1924 the young Birney joined a New Westminster, British Columbia, crew selling the magazine door to door to help boost the magazine's circulation above the 80,000 range. "The central idea we had to get over was that *Maclean's* was both Canada's National Magazine and a journal of 'international' articles and stories." The total Canadian content in the 1 April issue was a cover photograph of a Rockies lake by the Banff photographer Byron Harmon and an article by a Canadian veteran who had re-visited Vimy Ridge. Most of the space was occupied by tawdry U.S. fiction—"an E. Phillips Oppenheim serial, a Norman Reilly Raine short story set in some city with 'the faint, sickly smell of the Orient,' and another by an equally slick writer of mindless romances, Beatrice Redpath—'Always Twenty: the vivid story of a girl who didn't grow up.' '' The "international articles" consisted of digests of pieces published in British or American journals months previously. The 15 April issue "had an ersatz *Saturday Evening Post* cover of a tiny toddler holding a giant Easter egg. Both issues lacked any Canadian fiction or anybody's verse, but they did carry special subscription offers: Send in a $3 sub and get *Maclean's* for a year plus an A. S. M. Hutchinson novel or Ralph Connor's 'latest masterpiece,' *The Gaspards of Pincroft*. Send in three subscriptions and get TWO Hutchinsons." Birney gave up the job to become a housepainter.

The 1920s *Maclean's* featured a long-running series entitled "The Bride's Club," advising women on married life, as part of its gradual awareness of women's new economic importance. In 1925 and 1926 Dorothy Bowman Barker contributed pieces with titles like "Vera Learns How to Keep a Husband" (1 June 1926) and "Vera's Pickle Problem Promptly Capitalized as Canning Exchange "(15 January 1925). As Mary Vipond has noted, what was "especially interesting about this series was its encouragement to women to band together to help one another survive as housewives." The feminist Anne Anderson Perry, in "Is Women's Suffrage a Fizzle," in the 1 February 1928 issue, noted that "We are, in fact, very confused in our minds between old ideals of shrinking, dependent femininity, and the more modern conception of woman as an independent entity with a destiny of her own, both political and economic."

In the 1920s, for the first time more Canadians than not lived in cities. Maclean's Lou Skuce drew farmers golfing in the 1 September 1926 issue.

The outlook became dark indeed, when two agriculturists were discovered tentatively taking up golf.

Mackenzie resigned in 1926 and became dean of the School of Journalism at the University of Washington. He was succeeded by H. Napier Moore. Born in Newcastle-upon-Tyne, Moore came to Victoria, British Columbia, in 1912. He was a reporter there and in New York, where he served as the *Montreal Star*'s correspondent. A small, dapper, talkative man with a protruding lower lip, he had contributed to the magazine since 1922. Impatient and sometimes sarcastic, he would at times seem to be more concerned about rising in the Maclean-Hunter hierarchy than leaving his mark on *Maclean's*. To some, Moore was a far from infallible editor. In 1928, for example, he rejected the gifted historical novelist Thomas Raddall's early story "Tit for Tat." It was snapped up by *Blackwood's Magazine* in Britain, and was the beginning of a long relationship between the Nova Scotian writer and the British magazine. In November 1939, Raddall learned to his fury that without his knowledge a self-appointed agent had resold his stories—including "Tit for Tat"—to Napier Moore. Having forgotten he'd contemptuously rejected it, he "was now impressed by its publication in a world-famous magazine." It was to be the first of many Raddall stories *Maclean's* reprinted from *Blackwood's*.

In fairness to Moore, it should be added that the magazine *had* published Raddall's first short story in the 28 January 1938 issue though it did change a line about a barometer dropping "like a gull's dung." *Maclean's* barometer just dropped. By late 1946, the magazine had run more than nineteen of his tales, more than by any other writer.

On 1 July 1928, in "The Truth About the War," the magazine first used the man who would be its 1930s headliner. George Drew was the kind of man J. B. Maclean most admired, a Communist-hating small-

town Ontarian, a stalwart imperialist. Moreover, he was a photogenically handsome man very much on the make. Drew came from Guelph, not far from Crieff manse, was wounded in wartime France, then studied for the bar while rising to become a militia lieutenant-colonel. Elected mayor of Guelph in 1925, the youngest in Canada, he became Master of the Ontario Supreme Court. His 1928 piece attacked a recent contention in the *Saturday Evening Post* that the British war effort had been lackluster. *Maclean's* ran the *Post* author's counter-reply and, on 1 November, another blast by Drew. It was all good copy. By now Drew was chairman of the Ontario Securities Commission. After he left the post, he became Maclean's personal lawyer.

In August 1931, Drew's exposé on Sir Basil Zaharoff and other armament makers, "Salesman of Death," was translated into thirty languages as a League of Nations pamphlet. Sometimes, though, Drew's articles got trampled by history. He thought that, although Hitler was preparing for war, he could be held in check if Britain and the Empire assured him "access to supplies of certain raw materials in exchange for finished goods which Germany can make so well." On 1 September 1939, Drew's "Canada's Armament Mystery"—researched with Napier Moore—created a national furor when Drew described how the well-connected industrialist James E. Hahn had landed a lucrative contract to make Bren guns without the trouble of competing with others. The piece led to reforms on the awarding of contracts, creation of the Defence Purchasing Board and later C. D. Howe's Department of Munitions and Supply. Drew went on to become Ontario Premier and federal leader of the Conservatives.

Apart from Drew's exposés, the magazine remained rutted with its 1920s array of departments, as well as a crossword puzzle and at the back a chatty "In the Editor's Confidence"—later "In the Editor's Corner." "Women and their Work" had become, or returned to, "Women and the Home." The hoary "Review of Reviews" and "Maybe Adam Laughed at These" were still present.

And in the early 1930s the magazine was still as virulently racist as ever: A. R. M. Lower's "Can Canada Do Without the Immigrant?" (it could, Lower thought) on 1 June 1930 was mild and intellectually justifiable. Not so L. M. Ffrench Blytagh's [sic] "British Columbia's Racial Problem," which appeared in the same issue: noting that young girls and boys of different races were becoming "dangerously familiar," it urged an "absolute prohibition of mixed marriages" since "The Eurasian product of such unions would oust the white man from all secondary occupations...." By 1937, possibly through the influence of the associate editor, W. A. Irwin, the tone had changed. An April piece, "The Oriental Wants to Vote" by Charles Lugrin Shaw, was relatively fair-minded for a change: "British Columbians are eager to share the benefits of cheap Asiatic labour but are unwilling to recognize the brown man's social and political equality." Perhaps it was the Orientals' allegedly high birthrate that led to W. B. Hurd's 1 September 1937 article "Decline of the Anglo-Saxon Canadian": "Unless current trends change, Canadians of Anglo-Saxon descent will number less than 40 per cent of the Dominion's total population within the next 35 years." This was implicitly thought to be A Bad Thing.

There were crowd-pleasers, such as a competition for the best holiday snapshots—nearly 6,000 were sent in—and "A large number of prints have been retained for use in future issues"—as well as a series on "Leaders of Business," "Honour Schools" and "Great Coronation Dramas." By the decade's end, "In the Editor's Confidence" had moved to the front, there were many more cartoons, department headings were less coy and Beverley Baxter had a "London Letter." In 1937, Max Braithwaite sold his first magazine piece to *Maclean's*. Norman Reilly Raine, a Canadian friend of Moore who had created the immensely popular "Tugboat Annie" series for the *Saturday Evening Post*, co-won an Oscar for his screenplay *The Life of Emile Zola* and also worked on the script of *Mutiny on the Bounty*, was still a great favourite in the fiction section.

Naturally, in the late 1930s, the magazine was dominated by rumblings of war in Europe. "The Defence Problem" ("Maclean's publishes this series in order that the various schools of thought may be clearly defined. The opinions given are not necessarily subscribed to by the magazine itself.") included Frank H. Underhill's "Keep Canada Out of the War," whose subheading was "Overseas War Would Destroy Unity."

Another issue in early 1937 carried a letter from J. E. Doerr of Winnipeg, indignant at an earlier piece about some Canadian boys who had stayed at a Hitler Youth Camp. The boys, A. B. Hodgetts's piece stated, "came chiefly from private schools and were accustomed to luxury," hence they sniffed at breakfasts of "dried-out rolls, jam and undrinkable coffee." The point, said Doerr, was that "The German Authorities are apparently resolved that each citizen of tomorrow will and must know a little more of the problems and viewpoints of every other citizen than he has been able to imbibe heretofore, and our friend would have found that this is the *raison d'être* of these youth camps, in addition, of course, to producing healthy bodies and sound minds to fit them for whatever part they may have to play either in peace or war."

It would be war. Had the subject worn a different uniform, Hitler might have approved of the 1 May 1941 cover of a Canadian armed force bugler, "A natural colour photograph taken for *Maclean's* by Karsh." *Maclean's* was now fifty-two pages, and the covers tended to be photographic, not, say, a painting by A. J. Casson. Inside was a pictorial section featuring the work of new young photographers like Ronny Jaques; the comic items were now copious and variously labeled

MACLEAN'S
CANADA'S NATIONAL MAGAZINE
JUNE 15, 1945 • TEN CENTS

THIS ISSUE: **THEY ARE RETURNING — by E. J. PRATT**

"Humor," "Wit and Wisdom" and "Parade." A special department called "War Oddities" paid two dollars for each entry: "Soldiers in a London suburb are buying up all available supplies of colorless nail polish because, when applied to the brass on their uniforms, it keeps the metal clean for a fortnight." The 1 August pictorial was "Women in Uniform." One of the captions read: "Young woman who wants to serve Canada—slim, fair, steady eyes, capable, eager to learn." On 15 September a special air-force issue included "Men Take Wing" by Flight Sergeant Norman F. Drolet, the RCAF news photographer.

On 1 November, the magazine ran Beverley Baxter's diary of a 5000-mile cross-Canada trip in which the London correspondent gave twenty-eight morale-boosting speeches across Canada. The magazine's circulation rose sharply to almost 250,000; *Maclean's* sent a special free edition to Canadian forces overseas. The *Toronto Star*'s much fired reporter, Gordon Sinclair, also boosted morale by writing effective as-told-to pieces "by" Canadian servicemen, beginning with 1 October 1943's "I Bombed Berlin." In all, Sinclair would write fifteen stories of various kinds for *Maclean*'s before 1945. But these were exceptionally colourful. With its propaganda and grainy photographs—typical of drab wartime—the first half of the decade was not *Maclean's* at its best, but then again the same was true of most magazines.

Most welcome was Robert Marks's 1 March 1945 portrait of Richard Taylor, the Toronto cartoonist who had done cartoons for *Maclean's* in 1930 and gone on to be a *New Yorker* regular. "Just how," I asked him, "do you achieve the distinctive bulbous-eyed blankness which is the hallmark of all Taylor-made figures."

Taylor replied, "After I've had my inspiration, it is simply a matter of adding haphazard conversation, the faces of friends and relatives, and a little morbid curiosity. Further, I am convinced that long after the events of the present are remembered, my art will be forgotten."

On 15 June, V-E Day, the cover by Franklin Arbuckle—a frequently used artist who married Franz Johnston's daughter—showed an infantry man with duffle bag over one shoulder opening a door. That issue also included E. J. Pratt's poem, "They Are Returning":

> They shall come back to build in lofty rhyme,
> Out of Laurentian rock and Norman lime,
> Memorial towers Canadian
> Across a continental span;

Six weeks earlier, Napier Moore spoke of the "return of Managing Editor W. A. Irwin, who has been touring England and the fronts in Holland and Belgium, arranging for coverage of future developments...."

In Canada those developments would include a rejuvenated *Maclean*'s.

WOMEN'S MAGAZINES
NUMBERING THE HEARTHS

It was only a matter of time before magazine publishers twigged to the fact that although women were limited in their earning capacity, they had a great deal of leeway over the spending of disposable income. This was, in fact, a mass audience with power of the purse. Except for *Maclean's* and the weekend supplements, it was women's magazines that best exploited the potential of mass appeal. Through research services for advertisers and readership surveys they grew alert to changing trends and tendencies; through escapist fiction and consumer bureaus they bonded their pecuniary interests with their readers' fantasies and workaday preoccupations.

Of course, there had been earlier magazines directed to women, focussing on what was regarded as women's proper sphere: the home. But if, in the early twentieth century, a woman's place was still in the home, the sphere was certainly expanding. As Mary Vipond says,

> The new occupations connected with writing which developed at the end of the nineteenth century offered excellent opportunities for women. As journalists, novelists, librarians and archivists they did not have to struggle to enter professional schools or contend with such a well-established male hierarchy. Writing as a career could be combined with marriage, for one could work part-time or at home. Women writers publicized the enterprise and inventiveness of other women who were pioneers in new occupations or who started their own businesses.

Besides the effect of such economic inroads—even in the 1920s there was a magazine called *Business Woman*—there was also a new readership in those women who wanted more flexible patterns of human relationships, including sexual and biological freedom. Tentatively at first, women's magazines gradually tapped this audience, too, because it was in their nature to aim to be all things to all women. For one thing, the smaller market in Canada at this point meant that women's magazines could not specialize in a particular social status or age group.

Whether extended political rights for women was simply a function of democracy itself or part of a gender revolution can be debated; the fact was that no magazine could ignore the reality. In the late nineteenth century, numerous women's organizations were formed. However conservative their membership and aims, such groups as the Young Women's Christian Association, the National Council of Women, the Victorian Order of Nurses and the Women's Institute showed that women could unite into cohesive and powerful political units.

As it happened, one person who helped women acquire direct political power as opposed to the hand-that-rocks-the-cradle type was a frequent contributor to magazines of all kinds. Her career and opinions also epitomized the social and psychological struggles women then underwent, and the accommodations they made.

Emily Murphy ("Janey Canuck") was born Emily Ferguson near Cookstown, Ontario, in 1868. Of Irish, Tory, Orange Lodge stock—two Members of Parliament and two Supreme Court judges were in her family, and three of her brothers became barristers—Emily attended Bishop Strachan School in Toronto. At nineteen she married a young Anglican priest named Arthur Murphy. They spent several years in western Ontario, raising three daughters as they moved from one parish to another. The Reverend Murphy became a mission preacher in Huron Diocese and then in southern England. In 1900, they settled in Toronto, where Emily became an active journalist, the next year publishing *Janey Canuck Abroad*, a book of travel sketches. Her family then met a sequence of disasters. Both senior Murphys successively contracted typhoid fever, and the British missionary society ran out of money before Arthur recovered, leaving the family hard-pressed financially. Worst of all, the youngest daughter died of diphtheria.

Making a new start, the Murphys moved to Manitoba, where Arthur became a timber merchant. Then in 1907 they moved to Edmonton, leaving behind them in Swan River a community skating rink donated by Arthur and a new hospital built from funds raised in a campaign led by Emily. In Alberta, Emily accompanied her husband on business trips—land deals and coal-mining operations—and published three more books of sketches. Constantly campaigning for women's legal rights, in 1916 she was named the first woman in the British Empire to occupy the post of police magistrate.

Women gained the right to vote federally and to stand for election in 1921: Agnes Macphail was elected as an independent. Murphy had often been mentioned as a suitable candidate for senator; but was she, as a woman, eligible? It seemed that the British North America Act did not regard women as "persons" legally, at least not according to the Canadian Supreme Court. But in 1929, Murphy and four other Alberta women won a British Privy Council decision overruling the highest Canadian court. Women were indeed persons.

Janey Canuck's impact was not confined to women's issues. A series of articles she published as "Judge Murphy" in *Maclean's*, and expanded into her book *The Black Candle* (1922), exposed the drug trade and led to stringent laws regulating narcotics.

Gluyas Williams pokes fun at Good Housekeeping *here, but he might have had* Canadian Home Journal *equally in mind.*

As politically advanced as she might be, Murphy did not look favourably upon some tendencies of the 1920s, a decade in which the birth rate fell and the rate of divorce rose. In a May 1928 *Chatelaine* article on "Companionate Marriage," she said that "Industrious sinners are always sensitive to words and, in this instance, we find them coining a new one. As applied to marriage, the word 'trial' has a repulsive aspect—even a nefarious one; little wonder its upholders have manufactured the term 'companionate.'" For women to live with men outside marriage, she said, was "little more than the common coquetry of cats."

But socio-sexual innovation was only one of the questions women grappled with in their magazines. For the middle class, the prospect of actual careers entailed inevitable conflicts with wifehood and maternity. This in turn led to many articles attempting to reconcile, resolve, or balance traditional domestic arrangements with the demands of a workplace some distance down the street. Sometimes it was concluded that "Only a Super-Woman Can Juggle Both a Family and a Career" (Virginia Coyne Knight in the July 1928 *Chatelaine*). Simultaneously women's magazines talked up scientific efficiency, "home economics," as if to show that with superior management all might be accomplished. Love and work, love and fame, love and money—all might accrue to the woman, provided she did the right things. (Or provided, a later generation might add, that she was permitted to do so.) Even the triple-barreled names of editors and contributors seemed to suggest stretched identities—single/married, homemaker/careerist.

Whether women's magazines led or followed their audiences is a moot sociological point. Certainly there was often a discrepancy between magazine content and statistical facts, as shown in Susannah Foster's study of women's image in two Canadian mass magazines, one of them *Chatelaine*.

Analysing fiction and profiles in the four decades after 1930, Foster discovered that, although fictional heroines lived more or less where the general population did, most of them were single women in their twenties, and of British or Nordic ancestry: "Over one-third of these women received a marriage proposal in the stories." Once married, they did not usually work outside the home. A little more than half the fictional heroines were housewives; the next largest category— professionals, managers, proprietors—constituted a mere 13.6 percent. (If they did get jobs, they tended to be high status.) This was all very different from the sociological facts. As Foster says, "most of the increase in female labour force actually has been due to increased participation of *married* women."

Since for many years home and hearth were identified with women, it was natural that the first modern women's magazine should be called the *Canadian Home Journal* (1905-59). Edited for many years by Jean Graham, it began as the twenty-two-page *Home Journal* with the motto *"Pro Domo et Patria."* It contained recipes, dress patterns, behavioural advice and short stories, what would be in fact the core of most women's magazines. The founder was James Acton, who, among other trade magazines, owned a shoe and leather goods journal; indeed, the first issue's advertising relied heavily on footwear. Within two years the magazine had doubled its size and subscription rate, and was acquired by its advertising manager, Bill Rooke. In June 1910, it added *Canadian* to its title, and two years later was bought by Harold Gagnier's Consolidated Press. By 1925 it had a circulation of just more than 68,000. In 1928 Graham worried, "What about the husband in all this clamour for a career? Is he a poor thing without any rights at all?...He must feel rather desolate when he returns, tired, from a busy office, to find that his wage-earning wife is still downtown, absorbed by office cares. Surely a man's pride must suffer injury when his wife turns wage-earner, too, and his home becomes merely a lodging-house."

By the 1930s, the magazine was edited by Catherine Wilma, later Tait, who would run it until the late 1940s. To an extent, the early *Home Journal* shared the muckraking spirit of its times: it refused quack-medicine advertisements, urged school medical inspections and the pasteurization of milk. It also campaigned for a ban of wedding ceremonies in shop windows.

Editorially, *Everywoman's World* (1914-22) was not much different from *Canadian Home Journal*. But it was the first magazine to make heavy use of premiums, contests and saturation canvassing, and built

*What could be
more domestic
than a birdbath?*
Canadian Homes
and Gardens's
May 1926 cover.

its circulation from 50,000 in 1914 to a 1917-high of 100,000, the largest then achieved by a Canadian magazine. Among its features was a column on poultry-keeping, not quite so anomalous as it sounds: for many women, the egg money was the only independent income they had. The magazine ceased publication after its purchaser, Harpell Brothers, the Garden City, Quebec, publisher of the women's magazine *La Canadienne*, gave up consumer magazines to concentrate on its trade papers.

A magazine that aimed higher on the social scale and tried to cut across gender was *Canadian Homes and Gardens* (1924-62). Founded by Senator Rupert Davies, the proprietor of the *British Whig* newspaper in Kingston and the novelist Robertson Davies's father, the magazine had a cover design by J. E. H. MacDonald. Its opening editorial noted that, "Several United States magazines which deal with the home and the garden come into Canada in a limited circle, but they deal almost exclusively with the expensive homes of America's rich, and are of little help in this country." Limited to 5,000 paid-up subscribers in advance, sample copies and a newspaper and direct mail campaign aiming for "an exclusive clientele," the magazine asserted that "The future is in the hands of our friends." Rather it was in the hands of J. B. Maclean, who bought it in 1925.

If this venture into exclusivity was not enough, Maclean's firm began *Mayfair* in 1927. It was intended to "interpret the life and interests of Canadians in their most gracious moods." The magazine, which took its name from the "West End neighbourhood adjoining Belgravia east of Hyde Park", would each month "present the pageant of Drama, Fashion, Literature, Art, Society and Sport as it touches or amuses our own people across the Dominion." With discreet gossip, photo features on costume balls and royalty, horsy brides and lissome horses, show rings and badminton courts, *Mayfair* sought the upper and, it was hoped, heavily spending end of the market, and at first succeeded, growing to 150-page issues within two years.

Life is a carnival. At least, Mayfair *hoped so in this illustration for its May 1927 contents page.*

The editor of both *Canadian Homes and Gardens* and *Mayfair* for many years was J. Herbert Hodgins, who came to the jobs from a trade magazine and then *Maclean's*. He wrote under the pseudonym "York," but to his boss, J. B. Maclean, his name was mud when he ran pictures of the gardens in Victor Tyrrell's new country estate. To the dismay of the socially ambitious Tyrrell, the company's vice-president, Maclean dictated that "no publicity of the personal kind should ever be used in either *Canadian Homes* or *Mayfair*." Hodgins's captions were re-written. When the Colonel saw a *Mayfair* issue with a splashy photo of the members' enclosure during the Woodbine spring race meet, he spotted a former brothel-keeper. "Hodgins, this is disgraceful!" snapped Maclean. "People of questionable reputation must be kept out of our pages; we don't want their pictures or their names." The staff was increased to include a society editor knowledgeable in the local Who's Who and Why.

In 1928, what was to become the most enduring and profitable of Maclean's female-oriented trio of magazines was founded. Whereas *Canadian Homes and Gardens* and *Mayfair* were attempts to cordon off segments of the female audience, *Chatelaine* would embrace all. This was to be a magazine that would neither change nor mould its audience, but dog each step its mistress took.

Even the name was selected after a national contest, which offered a $1,000 prize and drew over 75,000 entries. Hundreds of women arrived at the title—"it has the same distinctive gracious meaning in both the French and English languages," said one entry—beating out *Canadian Woman, Canadian Womanhood, Woman's Realm* and *Eve's Sphere*. But Hilda Pain, an Eburne, British Columbia rancher's wife, had been the first off the postmark with *The Chatelaine* ("The" was dropped in 1930).

The cover of the March 1928 first issue showed a seated, russet-haired young woman in a red flowing robe decorated with what looked like

THE **Chatelaine**

A Magazine for Canad~~ian~~ ~~Wom~~en

March 1928

10¢

In this Issue:
"How I Thought of the $1,000.⁰⁰ Title" — by the Winner

Children, a lovely gown — and in milady's hand a brand new magazine. Chatelaine's *first issue.*

giant fried eggs. The journal was subtitled "A Magazine for Canadian Women," but the woman's head blocked the last three syllables in "Canadian and the first one in "Women," so that it read "A Magazine for Can men", perhaps a prescient allusion to the recipes that would follow. Mrs. Pain, however, said that she pictured "a gracious figure of a chatelaine standing at the head of a flight of steps, inviting with outstretched hands the women of Canada to enter and enjoy the restful charm of her home."

The restful charm depended on getting good, inexpensive help, and Maude Petitt Hill's article "What's the Matter with Housework?" ("In one city...we found the actual cost of having a worker come in every day till five o'clock for a month of thirty days was $97.50, without laundry! This is very well for emergencies, but manifestly it is not going to meet the need of the average Canadian home.") sounded a chord that would be repeated many times in the future. *Chatelaine* was resolutely middle class.

Edited by Anne Elizabeth Wilson, the three-column, seventy-eight-page magazine alternated fiction with articles and included poetry by Dorothy Livesay and Ron Everson, the latter contributed "The Little Dressmaker." The first verse ran:

Poor Amy's dress was drab and grey
  When at her old machine
She stitched the steady years away,
  But now her gown is green.

The mix would become familiar to Canadian women. There were token articles on social problems—"What Are We Doing to Keep Children From the Reformatory" by "A Juvenile Court Probation Officer"—and the changing structure of family relations—"Where a child can be a child," concerning McGill's and the University of Toronto's "schools for very little children and training for their parents." Trends in decorating and fashion were explicated in Wilson's "What Is This Modernist Movement?" ("An explanation of the new and somewhat bewildering note in decoration") and "Paris Favours a Feminine Mode" ("The Boyish Figure Fades From the Picture.") There was a successful-woman profile on the pianist Gertrude Huntley, and fiction was encapsulated in the title of one story: "The Love Rainbow." But the magazine's centre was the departments or columns on crafts, food, budgeting, cosmetics, gardening and dressmaking: "Variations on a Wool Flower Theme," "A Spring Tonic in Every Meal" (about "Vitamines" [sic]), "The Domestic Workshop" (new appliances), "The Family Purse," "Varying the Lenten Menu," "Meals of the Month" and Vogue patterns.

Byrne Hope Sanders, who became editor in 1929, ran *Chatelaine* until 1942, then from 1946 until 1951. Born in Port Alfred, South Africa, she had come to Canada at the age of eleven and had attended St. Mildred's College. A newspaper reporter at age seventeen with the *Woodstock Sentinel Record*, she spent three years as an advertising copywriter for the T. Eaton Company, then three years as editor of *Business Woman*. In 1932, she married Frank Sperry, but retained her professional name. Under her regime *Chatelaine*'s circulation was nearly 122,000 by 1930, closing in on the *Canadian Home Journal*'s 132,000 and well ahead of the *Western Home Monthly*'s 103,000.

Founded in 1889, Winnipeg's *Western Home Monthly* was in the process of becoming a national magazine. In October 1932, it became the *National Home Monthly* (1900-50) and acquired 100,000 subscribers west of the Great Lakes. Less specifically directed to women than *Chatelaine*, the *Home Monthly* in 1934 was still bound in Winnipeg, but was edited in Toronto.

Most of these magazines prospered, at least temporarily. Between 1928 and 1933, the circulations of *Canadian Home Journal, National Home Monthly* and *Chatelaine* had all roughly doubled. That the increase and onset of the Depression were simultaneous was one signal that a strongly supportive mass audience was in place.

The Depression itself invaded the genteel pages of the magazines. In the January 1933 *Chatelaine*, the General Motors "Body by Fisher" ads ("Harry, please close that window...there's a terrible draft on my neck.") shared space with Sanders' "Editor's page," which noted that the National Council of Women had required more women to work on administering relief. An anonymous open letter, "I am a Canadian Mother," stated that "I am provided with groceries. No milk...no butter at all...no meat but fat pork for beans." (The only other protein in the month's ration for a family of nine was six pounds of broken codfish.)

In the next few months, the magazine reported, "All types of experience, opinions and suggestions" flooded in. "Another Canadian Mother" was indignant: "No couple has a right to get married without some means of livelihood, and certainly have no right to bring children into the world without means of supporting them." *Her* children need carrots, tomatoes, fruit. "So do mine, but they cannot have them because the money must go to buy the despised pork and beans and flour for my less fortunate sister and her family." And in the next issue, Mederic Martin, member of the Quebec Legislative Council, urged that women stay home as a means of alleviating the Depression: "The full dinner pail for thousands and thousands of women has made the depression worse for all of us—men, women and children."

In March 1934, the *Home Journal,* typically 104 pages, boasted about its Home Service Bureau: "in a quiet street in a residential section stands a red-brick house with broad white veranda and a tall green hedge— just a pleasant home-y sort of house." Directed by University of Toronto graduate Katherine M. Caldwell, later Bayley, it provided "genuine home-testing for the good products (which are also given extensive laboratory tests), for the household management equipment and the recipes which must win approval if they are to be recommended to you—and second, it provides a background of actual experience against which every word that appears in the housekeeping section of Canadian Home Journal is written." The magazine also had another long-enduring feature, the "Well-Baby Centre," begun in 1929, and conducted by Dr. Helen MacMurchy, and was dispensing Eleanor Dare's advice. A Dare column in November 1934 decreed: "Write it in letters of fire that you will NEVER live with your daughter-in-law, even if you love each other. No home is big enough for two mistresses."

Whatever title they went by—"Centre," "Clinic," "Workshop," "Bureau"—such departments were in some sense services. Yet they were also ways of institutionalizing audience surveys and market research. Readers' material problems, at least, could inevitably be solved with freshly bought consumer goods.

Women still aimed to please. In *Chatelaine,* Dr. Anne B. Fisher's "Live with a Man and Love It" ("If it's glamour he wants, do something unexpected and gay that will surprise your husband.") in July 1938 perhaps related to Lieutenant-Colonel Fraser Hunter's article on war which observed that "As soldiers, women would excel in the study of strategy." Fiction was the mixture as before. Even Martha Ostenso, author of the powerful novel *Wild Geese,* was reduced to romantic frippery in May 1938 with "The Years Are Shadows": " 'I suppose I had better kiss you,' said Spot Galway as a casual statement of fact."

The war years pinched the length and paper quality of all magazines. The *Canadian Home Journal,* for example, dropped to sixty-four pages by March 1944 and looked dismal: narrow columns, uninventive layouts involving red headlines and coloured blocks of type—all might have reminded the reader that the editors and columnists were aging. A sample tabulation of contents indicates the magazine's emphases: three pieces of fiction and one poem; among the articles, nine were on general topics, six on food and cookery, five on home decoration and maintenance, three on beauty and health, and eleven under the skirt of Needle-Arts-Handicrafts-Fashions. A 1944 "Well-Baby Clinic" discussed the Dominion-Provincial Day Nurseries, where children two to six years old with mothers engaged in direct war work or other essential industries were looked after, with the expenses shared by the federal and provincial governments.

Over at Maclean-Hunter the war was also being unkind to *Mayfair* and *Canadian Homes and Gardens*. Ronald Hambleton, who was an assistant editor on *Mayfair* in 1944, provides a look at J. H. Hodgins, the long-serving editor:

> Hodgins, then in his fifties and running to flab, was the kind of chainsmoker who holds the cigarette in his lips until it has smouldered completely to ash, which then falls off. He was fussy, petulant, and untidy, and bustled about his office as a woman about her kitchen....His staff, before I came, included fashion editor Vivian Wilcox, a stenographer and office girl, and the retained services of various experts like landscape architect Dunington Grubb and the head of the Chatelaine Institute, Helen Campbell, who contributed recipes. Next door, was the office of the advertising man, Richard Huestis, a tall imposing man with a blotchy face, whose philosophy for man was Onward and Upward through Transport. He believed that a man is born to a Ford, and gradually moves upward in life through a Chevy, a Dodge, a Buick, and a Cadillac.

Hambleton reveals an unpleasant side of Hodgins's character. Hodgins, who was looking for a new fashion editor for *Mayfair*,

> knew that I came from Vancouver, asked my opinion of a young woman who had written a letter of application. It so happened that I knew her personally, and had met her father, a well-known professional man. I could therefore say to Hodgins quite truthfully that in my opinion she would be an asset to any magazine; she was well-educated, poised and attractive, and could write well. On that recommendation, Hodgins offered her the job, and sent her a routine Company application form....When I arrived at my desk about a week later, Hodgins came in at once shaking with anger and white with what I think must have been fear. He flung a piece of paper on my desk and shouted, "Why the hell didn't you tell me she was a Jew!"
>
> I was so taken aback that I could say nothing but that I did not think it made any difference. "Well, it does," he shouted again, "now I've got to get her off my back." Later that

Maclean-Hunter stalwart Floyd Chalmers shakes the gloved hand of Chatelaine's editor Byrne Hope Sanders. Is that mistletoe in the background?

morning, I saw both her application and the letter he had just written. Opposite the word Religion, she had written Parents Jewish. His letter stated that, unknown to him, another officer of the Company had already chosen someone for the appointment, and therefore regretfully etcetera.

Upset, Hambleton asked Hodgins if he could work only for *Canadian Homes*, then heard himself saying he'd lost confidence in him. The next day he found a note that said he was fired.

According to Hambleton, Maclean-Hunter wanted to separate *Mayfair* and *Canadian Homes and Gardens*, selling the latter. As a step toward it, the company appointed Samuel McIlwaine, a Simpson's department store advertising man, as *Canadian Homes* editor. McIlwaine, however, was more interested in effective selling layout than in boards and nails. Since the company wanted to cash in on the postwar housing boom that was underway, McIlwaine was shipped to England to represent Maclean-Hunter advertising and his job at *Canadian Homes* was taken by Jean McKinley.

While Byrne Hope Sanders worked in Ottawa between 1942 and 1946 for the Wartime Prices and Trade Board—a Canadian prototype for centralized social planning—*Chatelaine* was run by its managing editor, Mary Etta MacPherson, assisted by Almeda Glassey and, on occasion, Lotta Dempsey. Like the *Home Journal, Chatelaine* was not at its visual best: photos were blurry, the art slapdash—even when done by the thirty-five-year-old, Montreal-born Jack Bush. Bush, who later became a highly regarded abstractionist painter, "loves art," the magazine said, "and the business of making a living, too."

Back from Ottawa, Sanders decided that *Chatelaine* would launch a Department of Consumer Relations to help focus and present women's points of view to the public, government and industries. But romance continued to stroll arm in arm with practicalities. In May 1947, a love story came "from one of the busiest typewriters in Canada. It belongs to Eva-Lis Wuorio...feature writer of the Toronto *Globe and Mail*, fiction-writer extraordinary in her spare time (from 12 midnight to noon next day)." The Finnish-born Wuorio would appear in many postwar magazines. The December cover showed a photograph of a girl about to be kissed under the mistletoe.

SANDWELL'S
SATURDAY NIGHT

Following Frederick Paul's sudden death in 1926, Hector Willoughby Charlesworth was named editor of *Saturday Night*. But his impact on the magazine had begun long before.

Born in Hamilton in 1875, the son of a bootmaker, Charlesworth apprenticed as a bookkeeper until his employer, who had tapped trust funds in his charge, absconded to Buffalo. After stumbling into journalism at *Saturday Night*, and briefly working there, he became a critic of painting, drama and music (and city editor) at the *Toronto Mail & Empire* from 1904 until 1910. Rejoining the magazine, this fluid, indeed garrulous writer took on many tasks there, one of which led him into a celebrated tussle with the young painters who in 1920 would officially form the Group of Seven.

Like some members of the Group, Charlesworth belonged to the Arts and Letters Club, which had been founded in 1908 and until 1920 was located behind the No.1 Police Station, its entrance at times flanked by a manure pile and a stack of firewood. The men who were members of this social club helped form such local institutions as the Toronto Symphony, the Mendelssohn Choir and the Hart House Theatre. Among the regulars were also some commercial artists from Grip Limited, the painters J. E. H. MacDonald, Frederick Varley, Arthur Lismer, Franklin Carmichael and Franz Johnston. They customarily sat at the "Artists' Table" with Lawren Harris and A. Y. Jackson; across from them was the "Knockers' Table," best exemplified by Charlesworth, who, with his carefully trimmed beard, puff and hat, already bore a much remarked resemblance to the late Edward VII. Charlesworth later thought that he was "Saxon and Celt in almost equal proportions, and physically almost always identified by Highland Scotsmen when I come into their company as one of themselves this despite the fact that I bear the pure Saxon-Yorkshire name of Charlesworth."

Whoever he resembled, there was a crossfire of friendly insults between tables. Soon the exchanges would not be so pleasant. Although the new painters got support from some private patrons and the

National Gallery, and received a fair share of favourable critical reception, they took to heart those who were contrary-minded. At first, Charlesworth was mildly appreciative, speaking in the 20 March 1915 *Saturday Night* of their "pigmentary enthusiasm." But almost exactly a year later he attacked them in "Pictures That Can Be Heard": "The chief grudge that one has against these experimental pictures is that they almost destroy the effect of very meritous and sincere pictures which are hung on the same walls. The chief offender seems to be J.E.H. MacDonald who certainly does throw pots of paint in the face of the public." Yet *The Tangled Garden*, the painting in question, "is a masterpiece as compared with *The Elements* or *Rock and Maple*, which for all they really convey might just as well have been called *Hungarian Goulash* and *Drunkard's Stomach*." MacDonald responded in the *Globe* with a somewhat overwrought "Bouquets From a Tangled Garden."

Then in May 1919, when MacDonald, Harris and Johnston mounted an exhibition of Algoma paintings at the Toronto Art Gallery, Charlesworth called it "a display which is at least vital and experimental." Despite or perhaps because of this faint praise there were more confrontations between the respective tables. To the painters, Charlesworth was now "Old Heck." On 9 December 1922, Charlesworth, distressed by the absence of academicians in the National Gallery and the presence, thanks to the curator Eric Brown, of the Group of Seven, called the National gallery "a National Reproach." Charlesworth was counterattacked by Jackson: "After Mr. Charlesworth is through rearranging the National Gallery at Ottawa, might we not lend him to New York to straighten out the Metropolitan Museum? They have a lot of fake stuff by Cezanne, Rockwell Kent, Prendergast and other experimental painters which he could shove down in the cellar for them."

When the Canadians exhibited at the British Empire Exhibition at Wembley in 1924, Charlesworth called the enthusiastic English press reaction

> Flub-dub, every word of it, but no doubt sincere flub-dub,
> based on the conviction that this is the pure-quill Canadian
> stuff: and that other types of landscape painting which
> present the beautiful pastoral phases of this country are false
> and insincere. At least that is the theory which the exponents
> of "emphatic design" have tried to choke down the throats of
> the Canadian public...the areas of primeval rock and jack-pine
> constitute Canada's gravest problem in an economic sense
> and the most serious barrier to her political and social unity.
> We cannot deny them; but they are not all of Canada....

Although there is a certain incorrigible stupidity in these comments, other pieces in *Saturday Night* during 1924—"Freak Pictures at Wem-

bley," "Canada and her Paint Slingers"—made the occasional perti-
nent point. In his editorial of 29 January 1925, "The Group System in
Art, New Canadian 'School,'" he argued that "all groups or schools
which adhere to fixed methods and opinions are a handicap to artistic
progress" and that the Group's paintings were "essentially timid, as
though each member were afraid of violating his fraternal oath."

Perhaps the interesting point about Charlesworth's clashes with the
Group of Seven—which officially disbanded in 1930—is not that they
differed on artistic objectives but that he and most of the painters
belonged to the same small clubby world. If Charlesworth's civil
warfare with the Group of Seven demonstrates an engaging pusillanim-
ity, albeit combined with aesthetic obtuseness, his friction with another
Saturday Night staff member, the more intelligent if not quite so versatile W. A. Deacon, shows a less engaging side to his character.

William Arthur Deacon, later best-known for his long tenure as book
editor of the *Globe and Mail*, made an impact of his own on *Saturday
Night*. A tall thin moustachioed man with spiky hair, a long nose and
receding chin, Deacon was born in 1890 in Pembroke, Ontario. He
rejected Methodism in favour of Theosophy—from 1920 he edited the
Canadian Theosophist and gave up the law to follow journalism. A gentle and generous man, Deacon in late May 1922 was introduced to Fred
Paul by B. K. Sandwell, already a well-known man of letters. "Deliri-
ous with joy," though only on a six-month trial, he became what he
later termed "the first full-time, professional book reviewer that Canada
had ever seen."

*One hopes that the ideal reader of
W.A. Deacon's* Saturday Night
*literary column will not knock over
Winged Victory with his foot.*

The Book Page logotype that Deacon inherited from Peter Donovan
showed an ideal reader, vaguely like Eustache Tilley in aspect, eye-
glasses on a ribbon, reclining in an easy chair, his polished shoes repos-
ing on a desk that bears a statuette of the *Winged Victory*. A row of books
is in studied disarray upon a shelf, and, judging by the distance from
his eyes that the reader holds the volume, he is obviously longsighted.
In his own way, Deacon was longsighted, too, for he set about becom-

ing the man he had described a year earlier as a "herald—an anonymous figure, existing solely for the purpose of making known the names and deeds of the new arrivals.... [Yet] my enthusiasms far outrun what is seemly in a herald; I have within me something distantly akin to what made Walt Whitman shout: 'to you, endless announcements!'" His first book pages were in place by 1 July. Replacing "P.O.'D." (Peter Donovan had departed to London at the behest of Lord Beaverbrook), Deacon styled himself "Candide."

The weekly that Deacon had joined, in the words of his biographers John Lennox and Clara Thomas—and this might just as accurately be applied to the *Saturday Night* of 1987, "was directed to married, professional and business, 'upwardly mobile' readers, conservative and sedate in their standards and temperately nationalistic in thought and habit, with their values confidently and sometimes defensively centred on their own expanding, middle class opportunities." The paper, between twenty-eight and thirty-six pages, was printed on newspaper-sized (37.5 cm x 50 cm) coated stock and divided into three sections: general, financial and women's. The 1921 circulation of more than 36,000 would dip to about 32,000 by 1927.

Deacon was soon doing his tireless best for his employer; intellectually cosmopolitan but emotionally Canadian, he often wrote long reviews of six books weekly and brief notices of double that number. He sold ads to publishers like Macmillan, fickle and prickly, and Graphic Press of Ottawa, keen to buy lineage, hard-pressed to pay for it. Besides his "Candide" work, he also wrote, under his own name, a syndicated advice column for the financial section called "Law and Common Sense."

Although "The Book Shelf" was at first unremarkable if comprehensive, Deacon got into his stride from the issue of 28 October 1922, in a column called "Saved from the Waste-Basket," a relaxed assemblage of letters, notes, comments and messages. People began writing him. In November, Deacon quoted from Tom McInnes's letters, sent to him from Hong Kong, and printed McInnes's wonderful "Zalinka:"

Last night in a land of triangles
I lay in a cubicle where
A girl in pajamas and bangles
Slept with her hands in my hair.

Impressed by the volume of mail, Paul placed him on staff permanently and gave him a raise.

Thanks to Deacon's efforts and upon his urging, in 1925 *Saturday Night* began publishing a supplement sixteen to twenty-four pages long entitled "The Saturday Night Literary Section." At the start, Deacon assigned reviews, sold advertising and pasted up the pages. Later he had sub-editing help from May Sharples and the use of an advertising salesman; either way, it was an impressive production for one man. Deacon now used a facsimile of his own signature rather than "Candide."

Despite the many ads he had peddled, the first supplement lost money; notwithstanding, Deacon wanted to convert it to a quarterly in the fall of 1927 and to expand into a monthly as soon as he could. None of this happened. Between 28 November 1925 and 17 March 1928 there were only seven supplements, the last three also issued for a second week.

Carefully laid out, the "Section" carried the black-and-white drawings of Charles Comfort, only recently arrived from Winnipeg; poems by E. J. Pratt and Raymond Knister, who had published stories in Paris's *This Quarter* and had edited *The Midland*, an Iowa City monthly that H. L. Mencken called "probably the most important literary magazine ever established in America"; and Deacon's fellow Theosophist Wilson MacDonald, a lyrical egomaniac. Among the reviewers of twenty to thirty-five books in each issue were such lucid academic figures as Pelham Edgar at the University of Toronto, Archibald MacMechan at Dalhousie and B. K. Sandwell (McGill and Queen's), the latter contributing comic verses and sketches, such as "December Afternoon in a Book Store" and "The Disappearance of Aloysius McTurk." Deacon published Madge Macbeth, another sometime novelist, Fred Jacob, the playwright Merrill Denison and Marshall Saunders of *Beautiful Joe* fame. Two other useful reviewers were J. L. Charlesworth (no relation to Hector), who worked for the Canadian Manufacturers' Association, and John H. Creighton, editorial manager of the Oxford Press. The books reviewed were both Canadian and international, tilting somewhat toward the former; Deacon published a special Canada issue on 2 July 1927.

He also set up the continuing feature of letters from expatriates: the luckless, tubercular, but cheerful British Columbia free-lancer Francis Dickie from Paris. A photo of Francis Dickie that *Saturday Night* published in 1926 is especially poignant to a writer: it shows Dickie, hands in pockets, standing between two piles of bundled manuscripts, one up to his knees, the other higher than his head. From London, Sheila Rand (Ruth Cohen), formerly a Winnipeg journalist but now the author of inexpressibly cloying collections of prose poems under the pseudonym "Wilhemina Stitch," wrote of encounters with the English great and near great.

This less than stellar cast produced lively and pleasantly varied results. While Dickie and Rand were keeping him advised of events abroad, Deacon was having trouble at home connected with his hectic free-lancing to the *Literary Digest*, the *Saturday Review of Literature* and many other newspapers and magazines in Canada and the United States. During his six years on the magazine he also published four books: *Peter*

MacArthur, Poteen, Pens and Pirates and the delightfully mocking biographical-critical study *The Four Jameses,* which originated in *Saturday Night* pieces. Deacon had a gift for parody and had already had a go at that tremendous hack, Arthur Stringer. For the day, he was well paid at *Saturday Night;* on the other hand, he also had a family of five to support. Certainly there was no slacking-off at his employer's. He had gotten along with Fred Paul; such was not the case with Hector Charlesworth.

After Harold Gagnier died in 1922, Consolidated Press was run by Mabel R. Sutton, secretary-treasurer, then president, and by some accounts a proper dragon. Morale plummeted and several people resigned abruptly, especially in the company's profitable trade paper division. At *Saturday Night,* Sutton incited Charlesworth to hector—the pun is intentional—Deacon about his work outside the magazine. The latter had to plead that he needed the extra money. And though advertising lineage in the Supplement had grown five times what it was in 1924, it tended to fossilize in the accounts receivable column.

The Canadian patriot Charlesworth thought Deacon showed "too much partiality for Canadian writers." Then, pressured by Sutton, Charlesworth ordered Deacon to cut his external work and in the fall of 1927 to drop the "Saved From the Waste-Basket" column. In January 1928, he wrote (that he would write rather than speak to someone in his own small office is significant): "I have repeatedly spoken to you as to the policy of *Saturday Night* in this matter; which is to publish as many reviews as possible of from half to two-thirds of a column long, and embracing as wide a field of interest as possible....I must ask you to regard these orders as final, otherwise you will compel me, much against my will, to consider a change in the direction of the department." Kind, genial Hector Charlesworth.

The 17 March 1928 "Literary Section" was Deacon's last, and his last "Book Shelf" soon followed. He left the following week, and was replaced by Sutton's nephew Horace.

Charlesworth, who had been milking his journalistic past in readable but formless memoirs like *Candid Chronicles* (1925), *The Canadian Scene* (1927)—most of it had first appeared in the magazine as "Reflections"— and *More Candid Chronicles* (1928), proved to be a caretaker editor who made no substantial alterations to *Saturday Night.* His long-time presence in Canadian letters was perhaps summed up by a Vancouver newspaper columnist who, when the novelist Arthur Stringer proposed an exchange of Canadian and English authors, suggested that Charlesworth be traded for G. K. Chesterton—"with, if England insisted, a minor female poet thrown in." In 1932, Prime Minister R. B. Bennett appointed him the first chairman of the Canadian Radio Broadcasting Commission where he served until 1935, when he and the Conservatives were deposed by Mackenzie King. Back in

The thoughtful
B.K. Sandwell as
seen through
Karsh's lens.

Toronto, he remained an all-purpose critic for newspapers and magazines, including *Saturday Night*, and wrote more memoirs. He died in 1945.

Although born in 1876, in Ipswich, England, only four years later than Charlesworth, Bernard Keble Sandwell was temperamentally better equipped to cope with the fast-accelerating times. He came with his parents to Canada as a child, took classics and, a top boy, edited the school paper at Upper Canada College, where his contemporaries included two future prime ministers, Arthur Meighen and Mackenzie King. At the University of Toronto, like Charles Gordon ("Ralph Connor") and Frank Underhill, he was a pupil of Maurice Hutton. A keen amateur actor, he once appeared on the professional stage as Sarah Bernhardt, "one of a crowd of supers hired at the university to rush on stage and shout *'à bas la courtisane!'*"

Equipped with a B.A., two years' secretarial work on a London, England, daily and a few months as a cub reporter on the *Hastings Observer* in England, Sandwell became managing editor of the *Hamilton Morning Post* in 1901. J. H. Cranston was then a reporter on the paper but later was the *Star Weekly* editor for whom Sandwell wrote humorous sketches. Cranston recalled: "When the *Post* gave up its ghost, B.K.'s salary was over $400 in arrears. He was in a dentist's chair having four of his front teeth pulled out when the bailiffs walked into the *Post* offices and took possession. 'It was four years before I could afford a permanent denture,' he laments."

He reported for the *Toronto News* and, armed with a letter of introduction from Joseph Atkinson, became drama critic of the *Montreal Herald* (1905-11) and, as well, edited the Montreal *Financial Times*. He had taught economics at McGill under his friend Stephen Leacock and English at Queen's. Fired from Queen's in murky circumstances, he was awarded an honorary doctorate seventeen years later and was elected rector. Very much a public, yet self-contained man, he helped found the Canadian Author's Association, which he later called "a group where virgins of sixty write poems of passion," and from late 1918 edited the *Canadian Bookman*. Based in Montreal, from 1925 to 1932, he free-lanced to many magazines. *Saturday Night* was always a good customer for a wide range of material.

If Charlesworth's print persona was that of the amiable clubman, Sandwell's was that of the eighteenth-century essayist, capable of writing gracefully and wittily on anything that chanced across his field of vision. Introducing *The Diversions of Duchesstown*, one of Sandwell's collections of miscellaneous pieces, Robertson Davies said, "The essayist of yesterday was a different creature from the columnist of today; it was not his purpose to exhibit his own personality for laughs; it was, rather, to take the reader by the hand and share some reflections with him." As a public speaker, Sandwell—a regular on the banquet circuit—"drew heavily upon this essay style, and it was an unfailing pleasure to hear him move elegantly through a paragraph, arriving at the end with enviable self-possession, after syntactical adventures which would have destroyed a lesser man." In Davies's view, "His training as an economist was sweetened and enriched by his enthusiasm for literature and particularly for the theatre. To the world of the arts he brought balance and common sense. When he wrote of politics, his character as an economist kept him from partisanship, and his character as a man of letters kept him from expecting miracles from imperfect mankind."

With his shock of white hair and pink complexion, large nose and ears but receding chin, Sandwell became an unthreatening paternal figure to many young writers. Wearing a suit that looked, as one employee said, "as though he had bought it off one rack and hung it on another," he would straggle in late (and sometimes leave town without telling anyone) to a messy office and a desk piled high with newspapers and clippings.

To Madge Macbeth, who was his Ottawa society commentator, he confessed

> that it was virtually impossible for him to refuse material he didn't want when some beaten, shabby, hungry-looking creature, wearing a greenish overcoat when it was warm and no overcoat when it was cold, timidly handed a manuscript across his desk.
>
> "Sometimes," Dr. Sandwell said, "they carry an old cotton umbrella with several ribs sticking through the cloth. I think it's the umbrellas—and maybe the shoes—that get me."

Sandwell was especially susceptible to poets—he was the first editor to pay Earle Birney for a poem: ten dollars, enough for a week's rental of a flat. "They have so few friends—and really, such difficult people!"

Affable, courteous, attentive and tolerant in person and on paper, Sandwell had an editorial manner, Davies says, that was "always that of well-bred controversy. Whatever the weapon his opponent might choose, be it the bludgeon or the firehose, B. K. Sandwell always fought with a rapier....he never raised his voice in print."

Certainly, he gave tongue often. Besides his "Front Page" editorials— he sometimes wrote seven at a sitting—he also reviewed books and plays, the latter sometimes under the pseudonym "Lucy Van Gogh." As an editorialist and the sometime president of the Canadian Civil Liberties Association, his views were certainly more libertarian than those of his magazine's core readership. But he was a fervent royalist, believing that individual freedoms were better protected under a constitutional monarchy than when left to the will of a capricious majority and its self-serving legislators. The abdication crisis of 1936, he wrote in April 1937, demonstrated to Americans "the genuinely democratic character of the British royal system." It followed that he believed Canada would have a more liberated, important place in a world centred on Britain, than in an unequal North American alliance dominated by the United States. Americans were fickle friends, after all; boastful latecomers to the Allied cause both in the First and Second World wars.

Whenever the majority sought to suppress or persecute a small group, Sandwell could generally be counted on to speak out. He protested the firing of Marxist university professors and the brutality with which Doukhoubors and Japanese Canadians were treated. He was sympathetic to Quebec's resistance to wartime conscription. Frequently during the late 1930s, he deplored Canada's inaction in bringing Jewish victims of Naziism to Canada and, closer to home, the reluctance of recruiting officers to accept Jews into their units. He welcomed newcomers: a headline in the 6 March 1936 issue was "Canada's Need is Immigrants: Increase of Population by Immigration would tend to Remedy Many Present Ills—Conditions Favourable."

Yet, card-carrying liberal humanist though he might be, his positions were sometimes inconsistent. He did not, for example, oppose the compulsory sterilization of the mentally handicapped, though he thought there should be safeguards, and he defended capital punishment, writing in the October 1934 *Canadian Home Journal* that the state "cannot afford" to hold "more sacred" the lives of criminals than those of their victims. The rise of kidnapping, he said, had led to "the almost complete stop" of "the whole recently fast-growing movement for the abolition of the death penalty."

Even when most convinced of his own position, he never took himself too seriously. Often compared in his day with John W. Dafoe of the *Winnipeg Free Press* as Canada's pre-eminent editorialist, he would be perhaps best remembered for this simple little squib:

Let the old world, where rank's still vital,
Part those who have and have not title,
Toronto has no social classes,
Only the Masseys and the masses.

In his 1927 preface to *The Privacy Agent,* he was almost wistful. "Careful readers of these pieces will discern that I consider the world to be susceptible of improvement. These pieces are, in fact, intended to improve it. I admit that their publication in the above-mentioned periodicals (including *Saturday Night*) does not seem to have improved it much. In book form they will doubtless be more efficient. Go, little book, and make the world better."

The first number Sandwell was responsible for, 12 November 1932, of the paper that he fully converted from a Toronto sheet to a national magazine, was inauspicious enough. The cover photograph was of the financier J. Pierpont Morgan, and George Gilbert's "Concerning Insurance" column oozed, well, reassurance. Insurance "at once gives freedom from worry, peace of mind and security, which enables a man to keep his mind on his work in the daytime and sleep well at night." Immediately following was the filler "According to a recent survey made public by the Dominion Department of Fisheries, Canadians serve fish at nine meals a month, on the average."

But there was nothing fishy about the quality magazine Sandwell brought Canadians during the 1930s. If the book page was not up to Deacon's standard and the large financial section something of a wasteland for those not playing the markets, there was much else on offer, beginning with the "Front Page" editorial and "The Passing Show" column of brief humorous paragraphs.

There were three main sections in the 38 cm x 53 cm format—huge by later standards. The first dealt with current events, including a large international component. The second was an *omnium gatherum* of "People-Travel-Fashion-Homes-The Arts." Graham McInnes, London-born, Australian-educated, and later High Commissioner to Jamaica and Canadian ambassador to UNESCO, was art critic until 1941; Royal Canadian Academy shows were given a huge amount of coverage; and Bernice Coffey was the society expert. The third section, the financial, was divided into "Business," "Finance," the "Gold & Dross" advice column, "Insurance," "The Market" and "The Mines." Yousuf Karsh, the Armenian-born Ottawa photographer, later to be world famous, frequently did the cover photos, including, in 1941, the celebrated portrait of Winston Churchill, cigarless and glowering. Peter Donovan contributed a London letter and Walter Lippmann did "Across the Line," a column of U.S. commentary.

Not all, or even most of, the prose was weighty. Looking back fifteen years to the issue of 29 October 1938, Hugh Garner commented, "There is something fey and fascinating about the daisy-chain prose of women's-section writers that throws us, holding our sides, into the holly-hock beds....'A gay aftermath of the Onion and Pottery markets is the Meitschimarit, a fair which provides a happy get-together of unmarried workers on Bernese farms...Carrots to the head! Following flower toques come the vegetable ones, amusingly tied up with the theme of the dress.'''

Frothiness is of course preferable to, or at least no more sinful than, solemn owlishness. Two of Sandwell's female contributors never suffered from the latter. One was Mary Lowrey Ross, who often served as cinema reviewer in the 1930s and remained with the magazine well into the 1960s. Widely admired for her wit, she was married to the shy Eustache Ross, who was a University of Toronto astronomer and, as W. W. E. Ross, a fine imagist poet. Another was Madge Macbeth. The Baltimore-born Macbeth, who as a child made her start by revising the Bible, had to support her own two children as a young woman in Ottawa. As she recalled in her memoirs, "Writing had advantages, for it required no financial outlay other than pen and ink and I could dash off material at home between cooking up baby food, changing wet clothes and performing the other jobs contingent upon a nurse." As Sandwell put it in his foreword to *Over My Shoulder:*

> Madge Macbeth has spent a reasonably long lifetime in Ottawa, and most of that time she has devoted to just watching it go by. Occasionally she writes novels, short stories, sketches, satires; but not to the extent of letting them interfere with watching Ottawa go by. And Ottawa is a place which goes by quite a lot, and in which quite a lot gets by— which is another matter. Madge knows all about what goes by in Ottawa also.

Under Sandwell, *Saturday Night* at first prospered. The magazine broadcast a program called *The Voice of the Front Page* on the Toronto radio station CFRB, and in March 1935 boasted that "with favourable atmospheric conditions this broadcast can be heard as far as Saint John, New Brunswick, in the East, and considerably beyond Winnipeg in the West." Reviewed books unavailable to readers could be ordered by mail through the Saturday Night Book Service. In 1937, the magazine claimed to have the third-largest volume of advertising lineage in North America, outranked only by the giant U.S. magazines *Collier's* and *Saturday Evening Post.*

Meanwhile, the entire world was in lockstep toward war. On 27 November 1937, Dora Sanders Carney, the sister of *Chatelaine* editor Byrne Hope Sanders, reported in "Refugee Dawn" how her young family had survived "Bloody Saturday" in the International Settlement in Shanghai: "Three bombs were dropped on our main streets, well within boundary limits, killing altogether about eighteen hundred people." On 3 September 1938, C. B. Pyper, an editorial writer for the

*Robertson Davies
still wrote for*
Saturday Night
*when this photo
was taken in
1961. Two
decades earlier
he'd been B.K.
Sandwell's
Literary Editor.*

Toronto Telegram, piped that "All over the world—in Canada as elsewhere—the responsible statesmen have approved of the policy of appeasement." In this *mêlée, Saturday Night* hardly knew which way to turn, except to the Lord and the British Crown. The second-page lead article on 8 April 1939 of what now called itself "The Canadian Illustrated Weekly," was, "Will the United States Start the Next War?"

In September 1939, the magazine reduced the subscription rate to Great Britain and British Dominions, Colonies and Protectorates from five dollars to three dollars, the same it charged Canadians. "The publishers have lately come to feel, and the outbreak of the war has strengthened them in the feeling, that it is important in the interests of Canada and the Empire" that a magazine like *Saturday Night* "should be more widely known in Great Britain and other countries." This was less commercial opportunism than a sincere contribution to the war effort.

The issue of 30 December 1939, full of war stories, Sandwell's "Two Liberties," reprinted from a Bowmanville, Ontario, weekly, the *Canadian Statesman,* noted with unaccustomed asperity that the American editor of the (U.S.) *Liberty* was "bitterly opposed to the war and is, moreover, distinctly anti-British....Obviously, *Liberty* would not sell many copies in Canada if it published such material here. So the anti-British articles are dropped. In their places are sweet exhortations to the Canadian people to go forward and face their duty; to accept the challenge laid down by Hitler; to join in the struggle to free the world from the bondage of fear." Among those advertising in the magazine was the Canadian government; hence "even the taxpayers' money is used to subsidize a most insidious anti-British campaign in the United States."

Along with prize-winning essays by young British evacuees, the Christmas 1940 issue of *Saturday Night* featured seven pages reviewing gift books. The schoolboy who "conducted" what was termed "The Christmas Bookshelf" was Robertson Davies.

It was the beginning of a long connection with *Saturday Night*. Replacing Hal Sutton, who had died in a boating accident, the twenty-seven-year-old, newly married Davies swelled the permanent staff of the magazine to six, one of whom was Sandwell's secretary. "The Editor," Davies recalled, "dealt with politics and the higher reaches of Art; two men dealt with Finance, which was a very big factor in that paper, itself a long-standing money-loser; there was a woman who did Women's Affairs; and then there was the Literary Editor, who did anything else that turned up, including books. The financial officers of the publishing company that produced the paper harried us unmercifully because *Saturday Night* did not attract enough advertising."

Davies, whose Deptford trilogy would establish him as one of the best Canadian novelists three decades later, had been to Oxford and done a spot of acting at the Old Vic. Before he left in 1942 to become editor of his father's *Peterborough Examiner*, Davies tussled with the paper's assistant business manager and its proofreader, a "demon grammarian"; unwittingly gave the bum's rush to Pelham Edgar, the distinguished University of Toronto professor and long-time contributor; conversed in semaphore with the magazine's deaf-mute compositor; absorbed theatrical legends from Hector Charlesworth; and generally made his mark as a reviewer and miscellaneous writer. In one way or another Davies would contribute to *Saturday Night* for decades to come. He has left a wonderful record of his boss on the job:

> He was a man for whom it was easy to work. He created an
> atmosphere in which good work was warmly appreciated,
> and unsatisfactory work was gently, though unmistakably,
> rebuked....Because his health was uncertain he had mastered
> the art of working with a minimum expenditure of energy; he
> was not one of those bosses who moves through the office
> like a whirlwind, galvanizing his assistants into feverish but
> unfruitful activity. He was a boss who, if he found you with
> your feet on the desk and your eyes closed, was prepared to
> believe that you were thinking. He never nagged and he
> never bustled, but I never knew anybody to fail to produce
> the necessary work for him, on time. He was himself a gen-
> tleman and he treated his assistants as if they also were gen-
> tlemen; if this treatment did not work, the offender was

advised to find a post under a boss more suited to the needs of his personality.

Sandwell, Davies says, "was a prodigious worker" whose duties included

dealing with the many visitors to the *Saturday Night* office, writing his editorials and special articles, and smoking numberless cigarettes of his own making; he worked a great deal at night, reviewing books and preparing the speeches which he delivered with so much grace and wit; even when he was ill he dictated his work into a machine, and astonishing numbers of filled wax cylinders would arrive at the office for transcription by a typist. He was a rapid writer, and long experience had made him a master of the journalist's craft of preparing his material in his head and putting it down quickly and finally on paper.

Sandwell was far from being a sedentary editor. In 1941, while Willson Woodside was writing a weekly analysis of military and political events—his only Canadian counterpart was Matthew Halton on the radio—Sandwell joined a planeload of journalists, including Grattan O'Leary, sent to gather propaganda material about Britain's indomitable spirit. Expecting to return by plane, Sandwell and the others became stranded in Lisbon, finally limping to New York on a slow, neutral Portuguese boat.

Sandwell's patriotism at home was roused by those he regarded as slackers. He was angered by an F. R. Scott article in the *Canadian Forum* that attributed Quebeckers' resistance to possible conscription to their distrust of imperialism, and was indignant that the U.S. novelist Theodore Dreiser had told reporters he admired the Soviet Union and hoped the Nazis would conquer England. Sandwell linked the two in an editorial of 8 August 1942. "The advantage of a man like Mr. Dreiser is that he blurts out frankly what is in his mind, while people like Professor Frank Scott say the same things in subtle and polished phrases which do far more damage and which cannot be dealt with by the Toronto police commissioners or the Minister of Justice."

If this was rhetorical overkill, so was Scott's reply in *Saturday Night* on 17 October: "It may be difficult for you, as an Englishman resident in Canada, to understand how some Canadians can advocate for Canada a policy based on an independent estimate of what is needed to save humanity...I want to eliminate, as the best elements in England want to eliminate, the last relics of economic exploitation and Anglo-Saxon domination from the British Empire." Sandwell had to remind the writer that he had come to Canada at the age of twelve.

Although the war created prosperity for many industries, the same could not be said for the Canadian magazine industry in general and

Saturday Night in particular. As early as September 1939, the magazine's size was substantially reduced. The issue of 2 September 1939 had only twenty six-column pages in two sections; by 1940 the page size had shrunk to 32 cm x 40 cm, and the paper was of inferior quality. The immediate postwar years did not mark a turnaround: after the advertising manager had sold the largest contract in the magazine's history— fifty-two full-page ads for the Simpson's department store chain—he discovered it could not be accepted because of a paper shortage. Nor did the magazine's contents satisfy some. Complaining in 1946 about the lack of poetry markets, Earle Birney noted that the magazine allotted "about one per cent (about half the space for its cooking recipes) to serious verse, some of which is readable, and the rest appears to have been chosen as a kind of decorative cement to fill gaps left by articles which failed to reach the bottom of a column."

But the magazine still had its serendipities. In a January issue in 1946, George Orwell, of all people, appeared in the women's section with a mouth-watering and, at this point, nostalgic piece about English cooking. Certainly his opening sentence must have struck a sonorous chord with the residents of Prohibition-ridden Ontario: "We have heard a good deal of talk in recent years about the desirability of attracting tourists to this country. It is well-known that England's two worst faults, from a foreign visitor's point of view, are the gloom of our Sundays and the difficulty of buying a drink."

By 1947, the magazine, now spread across five columns, had shoddy paper, and its layout was disorganized and crowded. At a typical fifty-six pages, *Saturday Night* had many more pictures and tended to be altogether newsier-looking. It even scored a scoop of sorts with its cover photo in November 1947, which, if a reader looked closely, revealed that the model aircraft a federal minister was holding was in fact a secret all-weather plane, the AVRO XC-100.

But many editors or editorial contributors, such as the managing editor P. M. ("Pat") Richards, Bernice Coffey and Herbert McManus, dated from before the war, though the magazine had a few newcomers like Ottawa correspondent Wilfrid Eggleston, then busy setting up the Carleton College (later University) School of Journalism, art critic Paul Duval and an ex-Air Force officer named John Yocum.

For years *Saturday Night* had been idling along at a 30,000-circulation level. Yocum undertook a survey to determine if readers and advertisers would welcome *Saturday Night* as a newsmagazine. Since the results were favourable, the magazine went ahead with plans to compete with the much larger, wealthier *Time*, aiming for a circulation of 75,000. In keeping with this objective, Consolidated Press's vice-president, Roydon Barbour, who had been with the company since 1925, hired the young Lloyd Hodgkinson as advertising manager.

Though circulation and advertising rose, the magazine was losing as much as $200,000 a year by mid-century.

By now the seventy-four-year-old Sandwell had cut back his contributions to editorials and arts reviews. Appointed managing editor in September 1949, John ("Jack") Yocom reduced the page format yet again, this time to 26 cm x 34 cm, and introduced a news roundup covering more than twenty-five subject areas. The 1951 mastheads listed many correspondents coast to coast, not to mention, complete with titles, some twenty-two editors. Sandwell was promoted to the academic-sounding post of editor emeritus, and continued to come to the office. The new editor was Robert Farquharson, a friend of W.A. Deacon and former managing editor of the *Globe and Mail*. Farquharson was a newsman who very much liked to employ other newsmen.

All this was a considerable departure from the Sandwell man-of-letters tradition, humorous and humane, critical but empathetic. When, in one of his books, Sandwell said that the "skits" in it were "not studies in History, Economics, Relativity, Psycho-Analysis or Farm Management" and that "If the reader wants my views on those subjects he will have to wait until I can do a book on them. I have done the skits first because they seemed to me to be more important"—he might have been speaking about his editorial work. To have grace, wit and, if possible, wisdom was his defense against a barbarous age.

PART THREE

THE WEIGHT COLLAPSES

The glum era was punctuated by death dates on tombstones. One by one, magazines crumbled and collapsed, were merged or absorbed: *New World Illustrated* (1948), *National Home Monthly* (1950), *Canadian Home Journal* (1958), *Canadian Homes and Gardens* (1962), *Mayfair* (1961), the Canadian *Liberty* (1964), the *Family Herald and Weekly Star* (1967), the *Star Weekly* (1969).

The only consumer-magazine publishing company showing real stamina was Maclean-Hunter, the only area of substantial growth was in the weekend newspaper supplements. By 1980, when the last of the supplements, *Weekend* and *The Canadian*, merged to form the hapless *Today*, such mass-circulation hybrids were anachronisms. The troubles of magazines were chronicled by the Royal Commission on Publications (the O'Leary Commission) in 1961, and by the 1970 Report of the Senate Special Committee on the Mass Media (the Davey Committee).

Quite apart from their legislative repercussions, the Commission and the Committee gathered a vast body of information never before assembled about Canadian magazines. What made their similar findings even more impressive was that the chairmen of the groups, Grattan O'Leary and Senator Keith Davey were, respectively, an arch-Tory and an arch-Grit.

Apart from weekend supplements, there were a few other pockets of prosperity. The business press—Southam and Maclean-Hunter bought some old magazines and started a few new ones—successfully plodded on making its small punctual profits. In quantity if not quality, government and crown corporations were also busy. Trans Canada Airlines' *Between Ourselves* of the late 1940s (later Air Canada's *En Route*) was one example. By 1971, the federal government was producing twenty-seven nontechnical magazines—none with advertising—for national distribution, twenty-one of them free. Circulations ranged from 350 copies to 3,000,000, the largest being the Canadian Government Travel Bureau's *Current Events*.

The causes for the consumer disasters were many, starting with the material shortages and distortions that inevitably followed the Second

World War. That impetuous medium, television, was widely blamed, especially in the 1960s. TV advertising began in just 1952, yet by 1956 Canada was second only to the United States in the number of broadcasting stations. In 1953, only ten percent of Canadian households had TV sets; in 1961, the year eight private TV stations linked to form the CTV network, eighty-four percent had them. Magazines' share of total advertising revenues declined from 4.2 percent in 1954 to 2.4 percent in 1969.

And of course there were those ancient villains, U.S. magazines flowing across the border; and some more recent ones, the Canadian editions of *Time* and *Reader's Digest*, a pair that sopped up national brand advertising like enormous sponges. In 1950, Canadian magazines accounted for 28.8 percent of the total circulation; by 1959, the figure dropped to 23.3 percent. In 1958, *Maclean's* led in advertising dollars spent that year; in 1963, the leader was *Reader's Digest* and, in 1968, *Time*. Without the expense of circulation drives, U.S. overflow magazines dominated Canadian newsstands through U.S.-owned distribution systems.

All was not a united front against the interlopers. Organizationally, magazines were balkanized. The Periodical Press Association and the Magazine Publishers Association excluded U.S.-owned magazines from membership. On the other hand, the Magazine Advertising Bureau, formed in the mid-1960s, included *Time* and *Reader's Digest* but excluded weekend supplements and controlled-circulation magazines, which were just becoming important. The MAB's total circulation, as measured by the Audit Bureau, came to include eighty-five percent of all consumer circulation for a total slightly less than that of *Weekend/Perspectives* and *The Canadian* combined.

Nationalists might have been encouraged that Canadians bought 147 million copies of U.S. magazines in 1959, and ten years later only 130.5 million. But this only reflected a decline in magazine reading. The decline for Canadian magazines in the same period went down from 45 million copies to 33.8 million. Lowered magazine readership was global: by the early 1970s such long-established, U.S. mass-circulation magazines as *Woman's Home Companion, Collier's, Literary Digest, American Magazine, Liberty, Life, Look* and the *Saturday Evening Post* had all perished.

The O'Leary Commission discovered that between 1950 and 1959 *Time* raised its circulation from 6,182,000 to 10,946,000 and *Reader's Digest* from 7,843,000 to 11,625,000. At the same time as Canadian general-interest magazines decreased from five to two, *Time* and *Reader's Digest* were taking forty percent of every dollar spent on magazine advertising.

Of course, if *Time* and *Reader's Digest* were really Canadian, as they claimed, then there was no problem. As B. K. Sandwell said in 1951,

The plain truth is that most Canadian readers have no consciousness that these foreign periodicals are foreign; they seem
like the natural reading-matter for Canadians, and if every
now and then they discuss something about which the Canadian can do nothing himself, such as who shall be President
of the United States or how much shall be advanced to
Europe under Marshall Aid, he still feels a lively interest in
these questions.

Along with this attitude, which argued well for Canadians' cosmopolitanism, was a disinclination to consider that the health of
national magazines was jeopardized. A study prepared for Vincent Massey's 1951 Royal Commission on National Development in the Arts,
Letters and Sciences was able to say complacently that "We are
informed that the important Canadian magazines...manage to survive
and even to flourish although American periodicals outsell them by
more than two to one."

By the mid-1950s it was obvious that the only magazines flourishing
were the imported ones: almost four-fifths of magazines read were of
U.S. origin. Apart from *Time* and *Reader's Digest*, U.S. women's magazines like *Family Circle* and *Woman's Day* were absorbing Canadian
advertising through special editions. And, if *Time* was here, could
Newsweek be far behind?

A Commission

In 1956, Finance Minister Walter Harris, introduced a twenty percent
tax on advertising in magazines containing 25 percent or more editorial
material identical to that found in their non-Canadian editions and carrying advertising not in the parent publication. Nine magazines were
directly affected, including *Time* and *Reader's Digest*. The Conservative opposition argued vehemently against the budget measure and was
joined by newspaper editorialists. In various forms, their arguments,
adapted to circumstances and sometimes contradictory, would be reiterated for the next two decades.

Tariff protection, they said, was unnecessary: Canadian magazines
could compete if they were more efficient and of better quality. Canadian magazines were just plain incompetent and couldn't meet the
demands advertisers made. If the tax forced *Time* and *Reader's Digest*
out of the country, there would be a heavy economic loss in jobs;
moreover the two magazines helped maintain a strong industry because
they encouraged advertisers to choose periodicals instead of TV. Magazines were not badly off, anyway—this argument was based on the
prosperity of weekend supplements. The tax was arbitrary and led to
unfair competition; in any event, *Time* and *Reader's Digest* could simply raise their ad rates to make up for the increased levy. The tax was
a form of censorship and interfered with Canadians' reading habits.

The tax would disturb the faith of investors. The tax was a creation of Liberals.

Time noisily protested; the *Digest* launched a court case, claiming the legislation was outside Parliament's jurisdiction, and was in turn sued by the federal government. The government had only collected just under $500,000 when the Conservatives won the federal election and promptly repealed the tax. Six months later, *Family Circle*, which had discontinued its Canadian edition, resumed publication; *Argosy* and *True* began publishing here, and *TV Guide* started an Ontario edition. Other magazines, like *Life* and the *Saturday Evening Post*, offered split-run advertising. As for U.S. advertisers, there was no compelling reason for them to buy space in Canadian magazines when their own publications could serve them just as well.

U.S. publications gained Canadian advertising dollars by several cunning methods. The oldest, simplest form was overflow circulation: part of the U.S. magazine's press run designated for Canadian distribution but identical in content to that read at home. Then there was the split run or regional edition, by which a magazine could insert specifically directed advertising. In some types of editions—like *TV Guide*—there might be an inserted editorial section of Canadian content.

The "Canadian editions"—notably *Time* and *Reader's Digest*—were produced as separate, self-contained press runs. The Canadian editorial content consisted of four pages in the case of *Time*, while *Reader's Digest* confined it to explanatory boxes and footnotes. With material mostly borrowed from the parent edition, but with much flexibility in laying out ads, this was the profitable best of both worlds.

In the matter of newsstand distribution, two U.S. companies, Curtis Publishing and Select Magazines, controlled about forty percent of newsstand magazine distribution. Canadian magazines obtained only about ten to twenty-five percent of their sales through newsstands, compared to fifty percent for U.S. magazines sold in Canada. As for postal rates, the U.S. Post Office had recently reduced the postal rates of magazines mailed to foreign country, making some consider that the immense volume coming into the country overloaded the Canadian postal system. One estimate attributed $6 million of a $22-million deficit on second-class-mail operations in 1960 to U.S. publications mailed from outside. Whether Canada was subsidizing U.S. magazines would be another question for years to come.

Faced with these dilemmas, John Diefenbaker took the favourite course of Canadian politicians: he appointed a Royal Commission. The chairman was the editor of the *Ottawa Journal*, a spunky little Irishman named Grattan O'Leary. (Although Diefenbaker may have shared the Conservative antipathy to interfering with the marketplace, he was personally no fan of *Time* and positively loathed the new U.S. President, John F. Kennedy.) Formed in late 1960, the Royal Commission

*An old news-
paperman used to
pounding out
copy, Grattan
O'Leary headed
the Royal Com-
mission on
Publications.*

on Publications held eight months of hearings across Canada, accumulating 4,500 pages of testimony. Its secretary was the young Michael Pitfield, later a powerful civil servant during the Trudeau years.

Realities of the Canadian magazine market were reflected in the physical substance of submissions. The Canadian submissions were sometimes crude, Gestetnered documents; those of *Time* were impressive in typography and design, and came with maps, diagrams of layers and echelons of editing, as well as capsule biographies of Canadians who had made good inside Time Inc.

Among these was Robert T. Elson, who had been *Time*'s first editor in Canada in 1943, a deputy managing editor and general manager of *Life* and chief of *Time*'s London bureau. The credentials of *Time* editors and correspondents, past and present, were lauded. Edwin Copps, who was now a contributing editor of *Saturday Night*, was quoted thus: "it is a tribute to TIME that when mistakes are made they are particularly annoying because the reputation, the background of the magazine, the obvious effort that goes into it make the error all the more aggravating when it is found. It is rather like finding a flaw in a diamond." Through *Time*, Canadians got to see the world, the world got to see Canada.

In backing *Time*, Stuart Keate, a former correspondent who had become publisher of the *Victoria Daily News*, got in a gentle dig by pointing out that Grattan O'Leary had once been the Canadian editor of the defunct U.S. magazine *Collier's*. *Time* itself testified that although it had ceased looking for a Canadian printer while the excise tax on advertising revenues was enforced, it expected to find one soon, at which point its edition would be entirely printed, mailed and distributed within Canada. Already it bought its paper here. *Time* paid twenty-nine full-time Canadian employees and as many as seventy-five part-timers. According to the managing director, Lawrence E. Laybourne, "so much

Canadian news is carried in *Time* that it may be said confidently that no other journal provides as much information about Canada to as many readers throughout the world." This, Floyd Chalmers later admitted, "came appallingly close to being the truth."

The comic high point of the hearings occurred after Time Canada repeatedly touted the magazine's Canadian credentials. When Henry Luce, hailed northward from New York, was asked by O'Leary whether *Time* Canada was a Canadian magazine, the great imperialist sturdily replied, "I may be in some disagreement with my colleagues, but you said, sir, that you want me to be very plain. I do *not* consider *Time* a Canadian magazine." On the other hand, Lila Wallace, who had ventured up from Pleasantville, New York, with her husband, DeWitt, observed that *she* was the daughter of a Winnipeg clergyman. It was Canadian content of a sort.

In June 1961, the O'Leary Commission presented a far more forcible report than anyone might have imagined. It forthrightly stated that "a nation's domestic advertising expenditures should be devoted to the support of its own media of communications" and that "there can be no excuse for the republication in Canada of periodicals which are not much more than facsimiles of those abroad."

The Report dismissed the freedom-of-speech arguments by observing that all countries assisted and protected their periodicals in one way or another. It defined a Canadian periodical as "one published in Canada, owned either by Canadian citizens or, if a corporation, by a company incorporated under the laws of Canada or one of its provinces and which is controlled and directed by Canadian citizens and is not a licensee of or otherwise substantially the same as a periodical owned or controlled outside Canada." Such a magazine was located and edited in Canada by Canadian residents, and typeset and printed here.

According to the Report, "but for the profitable existence of business papers, there would be no Canadian general consumer mags today. Almost without exception, they have been heavily subsidized from the business paper profits of their publishers." The Canadian predicament was worsened by overflow circulation and split runs. The Report urged that periodicals with domestic advertising entering from abroad be excluded under the Customs Tariff, including postcards, coupons and inserts letting the consumer know a service or product was available in Canada.

What proved to be the most controversial recommendation concerned what the Report regarded as the unfair competition of Canadian editions of magazines like *Time* and *Reader's Digest*.

> The simplest and most direct method of dealing with the diversion of Canadian domestic advertising to foreign periodicals printed in Canada is to deny to the taxpayer the deduction as a business expense that he now enjoys for domestic

advertising expenditures in a foreign periodical. Such a step may be easily administered because the advertiser must claim the deduction.

The result of non-deductibility would be approximately to double the cost of domestic advertising in a foreign periodical wherever printed.

What the U.S. magazines lost in advertising, the "purely" Canadian ones would pick up, it was hoped. As for the potential loss of *Time*'s Canadian coverage, the Report perhaps too optimistically believed that "the parent magazine would still have to maintain some staff in Canada to provide that part of the world-wide news coverage required for the domestic edition." As for postal rates, the Report recommended that the delivery rates on second-class mail be repealed, and almost equally optimistically suggested that the United States be asked for compensation. Concerning "quality" and literary magazines, the Commission recommended that such magazines "carrying less than one-third advertising content be granted free mailing privileges for their first 5,000 copies per issue and for authorized sample copies."

U.S. lobbying, busy since 1957, now became frenetic. Subtle and not-so-subtle threats became commonplace. If the Report was implemented, a Montreal aircraft-components company just might lose a major U.S. contract, the White House advised the government. At home, reaction was mixed. The weekend magazines were predictably enthusiastic. Jack Kent Cooke and Arnold Edinborough of *Saturday Night* praised the Report, Cooke saying that the sick Canadian patient "should enjoy a healthy, lusty and successful future." But the Thomson newspapers and the *Globe and Mail* opposed its supposed suppression of press freedom, and Michael Wardell, publisher of the *Atlantic Advocate*, termed it "wicked and foolish."

After cabinet brawls, the Diefenbaker government proposed in January 1962 that part of the forthcoming budget would enforce some O'Leary recommendations: foreign periodicals with Canada-only advertising would be barred, and the tax write-off for advertising would be disallowed (a fifty percent write-off would still apply for ads in *Time* and *Reader's Digest*). But then, because the government was pressured, or was just nervous about the impending election, the measure went missing from the budget. The Conservatives returned to power with a minority on 18 June 1962, and did nothing more. Then in April 1963 it was the Liberals' turn to form a minority government. In February 1964, Lester Pearson's finance minister, Walter Gordon, proposed that essentially the measures of two years earlier be enacted.

Time and *Reader's Digest*, with their allies, organized a lobbying blitz. The U.S. State Department warned that quotas on Canadian oil exports might be reviewed, that a major U.S. aircraft-components contract to a Canadian firm might be cancelled and Congressional approval of the

Canada-U.S. Auto Pact might be denied. Montreal MPs and cabinet ministers were besieged by protests. Douglas Fisher, then a New Democratic Party MP for Port Arthur, Ontario, was barraged with plaintive or angry letters and telephone calls from employees and their wives dependent on the paper mill in his riding, which supplied the *Reader's Digest*. Such powerful, Yankee-loving cabinet ministers as Bud Drury and Paul Martin pulled their weight to exempt *Time* and *Reader's Digest* from protectionism.

Meanwhile, changes in the magazine industry were weakening the cause of those who, like Mark Farrell of *Weekend*, thought that if the two magazines were exempted, "We might as well attempt to fight an outbreak of typhoid fever by making an exception of Typhoid Mary." Advertisers were switching in droves to other media and most of the largest magazines—*Time* and *Reader's Digest* included—suffered lost revenue. Maclean-Hunter, worried about the consumer market shrinking more, decided that *Time* and *Reader's Digest* were helping to keep it intact. That was the official stand, though some suspected that the company's increasing presence in the United States made it fear retaliation.

In 1965, the Pearson government passed a law that disallowed the deduction of advertising expenses for business purposes except for magazines "edited in whole or in part in Canada and printed and published in Canada," but exempting *Time* and *Reader's Digest*. As far as the proprietors of the *Star Weekly* and *Weekend* were concerned, this meant that the foxes were securely locked in with the chickens.

On Weekends

In 1946, the circulation of *Weekend*'s predecessor was still stagnant at about 300,000. Like the *Star Weekly*, the Montreal *Standard* carried a photo-news section, a condensed novel, colour comics, short stories, feature articles and columns. But big changes were coming.

Lord Atholstan's newspapers, including the *Standard* and *Montreal Star*, now belonged to John Wilson McConnell, an Irish immigrant's son who made a fortune with St. Lawrence Sugar and other interests. One of his sons, John Griffith, had studied newspapers in London and New York and in 1948, with the help of A. Davidson Dunton, Mark Farrell and others, revamped the magazine, greatly expanding its photojournalism.

In the wake of the successful U.S. newspaper supplement *This Week*, the *Standard* signed contracts with several Canadian dailies to carry a shorter version in their weekend papers. The innovation—the papers raised weekend prices and shared advertising profits—was instantly successful and led to the appearance of the first *Weekend* on 8 September 1951. The Audit Bureau circulation for the eight newspapers carrying it was 900,000, compared to the *Star Weekly*'s 800,000. It would

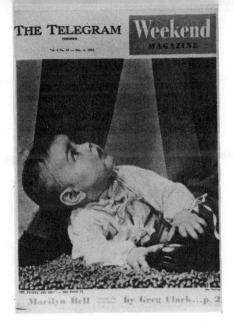

Greg Clark, a baby and marathon swimmer Marilyn Bell — it all added up to the homey Weekend *of the 1950s.*

rise to almost 1.5 million within five years. At its peak, *Weekend* appeared in the Saturday edition of forty-one papers with a total circulation of more than two million.

Designed as light entertainment with no editorial policy at all—early issues didn't even have a masthead—the supplement allowed advertisers to run four-colour ads inside the newspaper package at a cost half that of the traditional bound magazine. At first, *Weekend*'s member newspapers, such as the *Vancouver Sun*, paid 1.3 cents per copy, but as the supplement's circulation and advertising soared *Weekend* began to pay them.

One man vital to *Weekend*'s early success was Mark Farrell, a man of unusually mixed qualities. Born in 1913, the son of a well-to-do stockbroker who died when Mark was six, Farrell went to a Catholic boy's school in England and later to McGill University. There he was influenced by F. R. Scott and Eugene Forsey of the League for Social Reconstruction, even while studying for a commerce degree. He attended the American Institute in Moscow and, while taking courses in Toronto to become a certified accountant, was the unpaid business manager of the *Canadian Forum*, as well as secretary of the Ontario CCF. He also played the stock market.

Hired as a promotion manager by the *Standard*, Farrell was turned down by the RCAF at the outbreak of World War II because of a stammer, and instead became an accountant with the British Air Command in New York and signing officer for the Bank of England. After the war he rose to become the *Standard*'s general manager, overseeing the construction of a $2-million rotogravure plant completed in 1949. With the help of Farrell's extensive publishing contacts, what had seemed like an expensive folly began producing extensive profits. Farrell did not define his supplement's content: he once told its editors that "the range of *Weekend* varies from the dull and competent to the dull and incompetent.''

Consistently better-written than *Weekend*, the *Globe Magazine* was launched on 4 May 1957 as part of a new eight-page section of the Saturday *Globe and Mail* (Before the *Globe* and *Mail* combined in 1936, the former had published a turn-of-the century illustrated weekend supplement, and an Edwardian one edited by M. O. Hammond achieved a substantial reputation). Its lead story was a long exposé on Canada's "Strange Divorce Laws." Started on the initiative of a *Globe* editor, Richard ("Dic") Doyle, the *Magazine's* editors included Oliver Clausen, a Dane who had been a *Time* writer, and Kenneth Bagnell, a former minister who had edited *United Church Observer* and would later edit the *Imperial Oil Review*. But the supplement lost money. When the *Toronto Telegram* died, *Weekend* was cut off from the Toronto market, and in 1971 the *Globe*, now part of the FP chain, was able to replace at little cost its own supplement with the larger, blander national one.

Meanwhile, in 1959, *Weekend* had started a French version, *Perspectives*, with some changes in content. *Weekend's* cross-Canada success led the Southam newspaper chain to seek part ownership, but it was turned down by John G. McConnell. Southam then went partners with the *Toronto Star*, whose *Star Weekly*, overshadowed by its Montreal rival even after it switched to tabloid format in 1953, had been losing advertising.

To organize the new supplement, Southstar commissioned Ross Munro, who had been a famous wartime newsman and now published the *Winnipeg Tribune*. Munro in turn hired Harry Bruce as editor. Bruce, the son of the novelist and Canadian Press general manager, Charles Bruce, had worked for newspapers, the *Star Weekly* and *Maclean's*, among other publications. Within a few months he hired a team and put together the first issue of *The Canadian* on 12 November 1965. Its lead article was entitled "The Day Canada Turned the Moon Blue...and 99 Other bizarre and significant Canadian accomplishments." *The Canadian* found its way into Southam newspapers that had carried *Weekend*, and the latter was picked up by some in the Free Press chain.

Ironically, *The Canadian* was entering the supplement field just as *Weekend*—and the idea of such mass supplements was beginning to wane. By the late 1960s, *Weekend's* contents had less "filler about Hollywood starlets and dancing mice," in the words of Paul Rush, the supplement's managing editor from 1968 to 1973, and later publisher of the *Financial Post's* Moneywise Magazine. But it was also becoming physically thinner and less profitable.

It was worse for the *Star Weekly*. In 1967, the *Toronto Star* hired Peter Gzowski to edit the *Star Weekly*, by now a chronic money-loser, and implored him to acquire a large audience of young adults. Although Gzowski was proud of the editorial changes wrought by a staff which included Jack Batten, Walter Stewart and Bill Cameron, the magazine lost $2 million on a circulation of 646,000 and ceased as a distinct entity by 1968. Although *The Canadian* temporarily jumped ahead of *Weekend* in circulation, it never made the big money the Montreal publication had in the early 1950s. Now it formed an odd *mésalliance* with the former *Star Weekly*. Sold on newsstands, a new *Canadian Star Weekly* included colour comics, a condensed novel and the "Panorama" picture section—in effect the cover and part of *The Canadian*. To make life even more complicated for the reader, a separate roto supplement— the husk of *Canadian Homes and Gardens*—was tucked into what resembled a bundle of throwaways.

Home on the Range

Troubled in the late 1960s, the company that turned out *Weekend* killed one of its oldest and much loved publications, the *Family Herald and Weekly Star*. From its headquarters on St. James Street—"one of the strangest places in the world to edit a farm magazine," in the words of the *Herald's* last editor—the *Montreal Star* for some years had attempted to convert the old rural fireside favourite into a businesslike, scientifically alert farming magazine. Although its circulation, more than 400,000, exceeded such chief competitors as the Prairie-based *Country Guide*, *Free Press Weekly*, *Prairie Farmer's Advocate* and *Western Producer*, it was handicapped by the high costs of rotogravure production dictated by its *Weekend*-producing parent.

With its homey fiction and columns by H. Gordon Green and James Eayrs, whose world affairs column attracted a large volume of mail, and with an Ottawa correspondent, the *Family Herald* attempted to remain a general interest magazine, a kind of newsweekly, while tracking the rise of agribusiness. It was an uneasy compromise, and one perhaps doomed to fail, given that the farm population was continuing to decline even as the agricultural industry was spending more money.

The *Family Herald* tried various strategies: it purchased the circulation lists of the defunct *Farm and Ranch Review*; in 1962 it reduced the number of its issues from fifty-two to twenty-six, then in 1967 to twenty-one. All in vain: just short of its hundredth birthday, the *Family Herald* was closed down. The editor, Peter Hendry, learned of the fact while on vacation.

Although the *Herald's* subscription lists were acquired by the *Free Press Weekly*, it would be Winnipeg's *Country Guide*, slanted toward the businessman-farmer, that emerged emerged as the principal Canadian farm magazine.

Family Herald
Canada's National Farm Magazine
July 18, 1968—80th Year. No. 11—TEN CENTS

Liberty
HOW WE CAN G
MONEY FOR EV
WHO WILL SUCCE
10 NEW FEAT

The Nation and its Provinces

Among regional magazines, the *Atlantic Advocate* of Fredericton, edited by Brigadier Michael Wardell, in 1956 replaced C. C. Avard's *Maritime Advocate and Busy East*, previously named the *Busy East*. The editor said the Maritimes' depressed state no longer justified "Busy." The next year the *Advocate* absorbed the *Atlantic Guardian* of St. John's, Newfoundland, a small monthly that three expatriate Newfoundlanders had begun in Montreal in 1945. Brigadier Wardell, a protégé of Lord Beaverbrook who sported an eyepatch and had been a member of England's pre-jet Jet Set, was considerably more vivid than his magazine.

The absorptions did not result in profits for its publisher, the University Press of New Brunswick, whose interests included the *Daily Gleaner* newspaper. On the West coast, Mitchell Press began *Western Homes and Living* (1950-66, when it was incorporated into *Vancouver Life*). Vancouver-based, and with most of its circulation in British Columbia, it made its profits from commercial printing and a few business publications.

A few brave people attempted to start general interest national magazines. The pallid *Canadian Life*, commencing in 1949 and issued by Advance Publishing, lasted all of three years. Its first number led off with Vincent Massey's "On Being Canadian."

The *Canadian Commentator* (1957-71,) "An independent journal of Canadian opinion, called itself simply *Commentator* after October 1962. Published by the business-magazine publisher W. H. Baxter, the monthly specialized in politics and social coverage of the Canadian and world scene. Its editors included Marcus Long, Paul Fox, John

Gellner—who later founded the *Canadian Defence Quarterly*—and Gordon Donaldson.

Then there was *Canada Month* (1961-72), edited by Daniel Woodward and funded entirely by its fourteen-member staff, including as assistant publisher the future fine-art-press publisher and financier Christopher Ondaatje. According to the American-born editor, a former owner of an industrial marketing company, *Canada Month* was started because "I felt no expression was being given on a national basis to traditional and still viable ideas of personal freedom, such as freedom to engage in an enterprise of one's own choice."

With a circulation of 7,500, the glossy Montreal news-oriented magazine had the benefit of advice—and an advertisement in the opening issue—from *Time*, which no doubt considered *Canada Month* a useful ideological ally. In helping it, *Time* was also attempting to show the public it was a good Canadian citizen. The art curator Alan Jarvis suggested that "with all those black lines the magazine should be called Obit." After a "forerunner" issue in July and its first official issue in October, the magazine lost a reported $200,000 in its second year. To stay alive, it received help from Paul Desmarais's Power Corporation. By 1972 it had dwindled to newsprint and emaciation.

Cooke's Tour

If Jack Kent Cooke's experience proves anything, it's that even a sensational moneymaker can run aground when it comes to publishing Canadian magazines.

In November 1936, Cooke, a cocky, nattily dressed, twenty-two-year-old, was a traveling salesman for a soap company when he got a job running a radio station in Stratford, Ontario. The man who paid his salary—twenty-five dollars a week if funds were available—was Roy Thomson: stingy, gauche and ungainly, but disarmingly candid and oddly likeable.

Thomson had become expert at getting good men to work for next to nothing, and Cooke soon showed he was a super salesman, first in Stratford and then in Toronto, where he represented Thomson's embryonic empire: three small radio stations and one small newspaper. Thomson and Cooke became great pals, sharing pranks and little outings to the burlesque theatre. Thomson bought more radio stations, and Cooke managed them, and in 1941 they agreed to share future profits. When three Quebec stations were sold, Cooke took his proceeds and bought a Toronto station he renamed CKEY. Although invited in, Thomson declined because it seemed too expensive.

It was an error. Cooke made CKEY pay hugely. But although Cooke now had his own office in a separate building from Thomson's, they were still buddies. In 1946 they acquired— along with a chain of drive-in movie theatres—*Canadian Liberty*. A photo exists of a grinning jut-jawed

BABY IS SURRENDERED

The Alberta government urges unmarried mothers to give up their babies for adoption, providing they are reasonably attractive and healthy. The mother is asked to sign away her rights to the child—not later than six days after the birth—to a representative of the Child Welfare Commission. The transfer to guardianship is without court procedure or outside counsel or advice. There is no provision made for mothers after surrender of their children to the provincial Commission.

CHILD IS FARMED OUT

As the child grows older, the government finds it cheaper to place him in a farm home or in some other place where he can work for a living. In other provinces, there is a probationary period before adoption, out whether the child and parents are suited other. But Alberta law does not require the investigators have found that the whole welfare of the province is based on cheapness, and health and best care of the children.

In Alberta babies were surrendered, then farmed out, Liberty *shrieked in late December 1947.*

Cooke pointing out something in the magazine to a deceptively benevolent double-breasted Thomson, who has a sheath of pens in the chest pocket of his double-breasted, wide-striped suit.

The source of amusement could not have been a fat ad. *Canadian Liberty*, renamed *New Liberty*, lost money every month. This of course was anathema to Thomson who once said, "What is editorial content? The stuff you separate the ads with." What kept the ads few and far between was the fact that liquor advertising was then illegal in Ontario.

Cooke and Thomson soon had problems with the stuff between the ads. On 27 December 1947, Dr. Charlotte Whitton, a feisty little Ottawa woman, provided the facts that informed Harold Dingman's ghostwritten "Babies for Export." The piece charged that loose adoption laws in Alberta effectively led to babies being sold to U.S. couples. Published in defiance of an Alberta request that the story not be printed while a royal commission was still in progress, the piece incited the Alberta attorney-general to charge Cooke, Dingman and Whitton with "conspiring to publish a defamatory libel." This was an unusual formulation that required the trio to appear in Edmonton not Toronto, the place of publication. This occasioned a future article about press freedom, especially because the RCMP had seized *New Liberty* files as evidence and—in a tactical error—even raided the homes of Whitton's allies, several Imperial Daughters of the Empire. In any event, the crown dropped twelve of the thirteen charges, and in April 1948 the court acquitted Cooke—the sole defendant left—on a charge of "counselling the publication of a defamatory libel."

Although the outcome was important to Canadian press law— legislation was soon passed stating that a person charged with defamatory libel or conspiracy to publish such must be tried in the province

That New World *imitated* Life *is shown in this December 1945 photo sequence of a German boy quarrying bread from a dump.*

where a publication is issued—and Thomson had stood loyally by his partner, it was not the kind of thing he liked to be involved in.

New Liberty was becoming a sensationalist rag, with Dingman doing most of the ragging. A 16 August 1947 Dingman story was headlined "Canada Is Curing Cancer!" It read: "At the Kingston clinic eighty percent of the cases that can be seen and treated are cured—a rate that compares favourably with appendectomies!" And on 20 December he tangled with another provincial government: "Canada's first CCF government bluffs crippled and aged by diverting Dominion payments." The subheading read, "Saskatchewan treasury monthly deprives 17,000 old and blind of $3.75 each." The five-cent *Liberty* now cost ten cents and by 1952 was a monthly not a fortnightly. The next year it achieved a circulation of 223,000, but it still lost heavily.

In March 1948, Cooke saw a chance to make two losers into a winner. In Montreal, where liquor ads could run with impunity, E. P. Taylor's Anglo-Canadian Corporation had founded *New World Illustrated* eight years earlier, followed by its French counterpart *Nouveau Monde*. Although *New World*'s circulation had risen from 70,000 newsstand copies to about 200,000, including some 145,000 subscriptions, it had so far lost a total of $400,000. On the other hand, the beer baron was able to advertise his beer. "It's later than you think," the magazine said in its February/March issue in 1948, in a scare story about "Canada: No Man's Land of World War III." So it was, at least for the magazine. By 1948, Taylor had other things than beer and magazines on his mind: his gigantic Argus Corporation was only three years old. All things considered, Eddy Taylor was glad to sell his magazine for a paltry $100,000 to a Cooke bent on mass circulation.

In the course of these transactions, a relieved Roy Thomson sold his half share in the magazine to Cooke. He did not realize, however, that he was about to lose his blue-eyed boy, as well. After Cooke landed a profitable "personal deal" to manage an Ottawa radio station from Southam Press, cutting Thomson out of it, the pair split. Cooke later regretted taking on the Ottawa contract alone, calling it "one of the great mistakes of my life."

Both men became multimillionaires, but neither did it through magazine publishing. Cooke at least tried. In 1952 Cooke—by then the owner of the Toronto Maple Leafs baseball club, among many other things—saw an opening in Consolidated Press. Following the departure of several key executives during 1950-51, Consolidated had been foundering under the ancient Mabel Sutton. Cooke bought it and, with it, *Saturday Night, Canadian Home Journal, Farmer's Magazine* and eight trade journals.

This was all very well, but Cooke was pinning his big circulation hopes on *New Liberty*. High Garner, in a ten-year period, free-lanced almost 200 magazine pieces to *Liberty* under his own name and a variety of pseudonyms, such as "Jarvis Warwick" and "Dr. E. Jackson Francis," a kindly advisor on martial problems. In the Christmas 1957 issue, he published a short story and four articles; a year later he published *six* articles in another issue, among them "I'm Sorry I Married an Older Woman" by "Trevor Gamble" and "I'm Glad I Married an Older Woman" by "Peter Thurston."

> For years it [*Liberty*] had the biggest circulation in the country, and by far the largest single-copy newsstand sale of any Canadian magazine. Its circulation was a miracle, for hardly anyone ever admitted buying it, but claimed they'd just happened to pick up a copy in their barbershop or dentist's waiting room....It was a strident, vulgar, thumb-to-nose little periodical, just the right size and heft to be read in a bus or train. It became popular by ignoring such negative intangibles as prestige, while offering escapist reading for a time....In the days when some holier-than-thou periodicals still refused to advertise the demon rum, *Liberty* ran enough beer and liquor ads to give the members of the WCTU the vapors [liquor advertising had become legal in Ontario], which it often did.

Certainly, *Liberty* was an odd magazine, saving money on fiction rights by running ancient stories by Edgar Allen Poe, Ambrose Bierce and Algernon Blackwood, an "I Am a Canadian" series suffixed with "Negro" or some other appellation, and covers showing Hollywood stars. Among its features were the "Vox Pop" letters to the editor and "Taking Liberties," a scrapbook of malapropisms and misnomers, some even supplied by *Liberty* itself: one 1947 cover was headlined

CANADA'S GREAT IMMIGRATION SCANDAL, A GREAT SHORT
STORY BY JOHN STEINBECK.

Even when it sold as many as 540,000 newsstand copies, which it
did in 1959, the magazine had no more than five editorial staffers, pad-
ding out its masthead with secretaries and free lancers under impos-
ing titles. As editor, Joseph Lister Rutledge was succeeded by Jim Harris,
Herbert C. Manning and Keith Knowlton. One managing editor was,
briefly, Ken Lefolii.

In 1954, Cooke brought in Frank Rasky, the Toronto-born son of an
immigrant Russian Jewish cantor and provisioner, who had been busy
in New York writing about movies and Broadway shows. As Garner
remembers,

> Rasky took over a desk alongside that of Keith Knowlton. For
> a couple of weeks I wasn't sure which of them was the edi-
> tor. Cooke hadn't fired Knowlton, but was anxious to put
> Rasky in the editor's job; I thought the way he did was pretty
> dirty pool. Knowlton and I talked about it, and I told him
> that as long as Cooke was still paying his salary to sit it out,
> let Rasky do the work, and wait for a formal dismissal. I
> would have sat there until Doomsday, but poor Knowlton
> was not like me.

After a few weeks, Knowlton quit and went to *Chatelaine* as managing
editor, then was a copy editor for *Maclean's*.

Rasky's Broadway Boogie-Woogie was signaled in an October piece
called "I Joined Canada's Red Party." The contents were somewhat
tamer than its title. Stunt-minded, Rasky ran a "Mr. Hercules of
Canada" strong-man contest, as well as cover stories about starlets like
Marilyn Monroe ("Why I Love My Highbrow Husband,") playwright
Arthur Miller—and Brigitte Bardot ("The Secret of Her Pouting
Appeal"). He also liked nudists and disasters—"The Vancouver Bridge
That Tumbled Down"—Tom Alderman on sports and the cartoons of
Peter Whalley. By 1959, *Liberty* was calling itself "Canada's Young
Family Magazine."

Cooke, meanwhile, was getting a sour reception in the close-knit
Toronto business community. Garner, who also worked for a while
as Cooke's public relations man, said that he tried to "destroy the attitude then prevalent among members of the press—as well as among
the business community and the Toronto Establishment—that Cooke
was a ruthless person who paid low wages to his employees, fired them
on whim and a person who flaunted his new-found wealth wherever
he went."

Garner's efforts were in vain, as far as Ralph Allen was concerned,
for Allen would caricature Cooke in his novel *The Chartered Libertine*
as "Garfield Smith, sole owner and president of radio station CNOTE,

part owner and business manager of the Toronto *Daily Guardian*, chief debentures holder and Editor Emeritus of *True Blue Revelations Magazine* and non-stockholding past chairman of the board of the rather disappointing Drive-in Dentistry Inc...."

Despite Garner's disapproval of the way Cooke got rid of Knowlton, he found his employer immensely likeable and often generous.

> Cooke signed notes for bank loans for many of his employees, sent the family of one of his CKEY announcers to Arizona to live because one of the children suffered from a severe asthmatic condition, and did many anonymous acts of kindness. He kept anonymous drunks on his payroll (including me) despite many phone calls he received from people.... He always told me about the calls, and laughed as he mentioned them.

To Garner, Cooke was "a tough, intelligent, intuitive, perspicacious man who, having begun with nothing, made a fortune the hard way through his natural ability and salesmanship." Garner "learned a lot from him about millionaires, style and taste, and how the Establishment (of which he was never accepted as a member) lived and acted. I used a lot of this to describe the character 'Alex Hurd' in *A Nice Place to Visit*, a novel I wrote fifteen years after last seeing Jack Cooke."

If Cooke was a larger-than-life character, the same could not be said of his magazines. He "brought nothing but money to magazine publishing," snorted Floyd Chalmers. But among his consumer magazines, only *Liberty* consistently made money in the 1950s. The rest were heavy losers: Cooke's company had lost, in fact, more than $500,000 on its magazines since 1952. In May, Cooke dismantled most of his publishing structure: *Canadian Home Journal* merged with *Chatelaine, Farmer's Magazine* was absorbed into *Canadian Countryman*, Maclean-Hunter bought four trade magazines and Southam picked up the commercial printing business.

Then came the shocker. On 4 May 1960, Congressman Francis Walter (Democrat, Pennsylvania) introduced into the U.S. House of Representatives an unprecedented "private bill for the relief of Jack Kent Cooke," waiving normal citizenship requirements of permanent and physical residency. It was passed in September, and Cooke became a U.S. citizen.

Liberty was sold to Fengate Publishing Company. Its new publisher was the magazine's former advertising director, E. H. (Ted) Prince. The magazine dwindled badly in circulation, and Rasky left in 1962. Between December and 19 February 1964, it did not appear at all, and afterward only twice monthly. In July 1964, thirty-six pages long, it whimpered to a close.

In the United States, Cooke went on to acquire the Los Angeles Kings hockey team, Los Angeles Lakers basketball team and, most successfully, the Washington Redskins football team, besides other less sporting enterprises. He took up residence in the Virginia hunt country and did, in fact, very well in his spiritual home.

Free lancers

As disastrous as the period was in terms of magazine closures, it was still a time when a novelist could, if needed and without undue compromise, make a satisfactory if hard-won living by writing for the monthlies. One such was Morley Callaghan, outlasting a long drought between novels, who was a fixture in the 1940s *New World Illustrated*.

What made it relatively easy in the first postwar years was that the communications business was expanding, as free lancers like Max Braithwaite discovered. "These were the halcyon days in Canada. Plenty of work for everyone, reasonable prices, loads of opportunity, so that even a free-lance writer could make a good living, raise a family and have a lot of fun." In the 1950s, Hugh MacLennan wrote some of his finest essays for *The Montrealer* and contributed a Montreal letter to Cooke's *Saturday Night*, as well as work for *Maclean's* and *Mayfair* and the U.S. *Holiday*. Elections were doubtless a help: for *Maclean's* in 1953 and 1957, he did pieces with the identical title "Why I'm Voting Liberal." During the 1950s, he averaged almost thirty articles a year, including a weekly letter to *Saturday Night*, along with editorials and monthly articles for the *Montrealer*.

But MacLennan augmented his free-lance work with teaching English part-time from the mid-fifties until he joined the McGill faculty full-time in 1964. An even better example is Hugh Garner. Between September 1949 and February 1971, he produced 436 magazine articles and essays. He was a fast writer. One weekend he wrote four "think pieces." Two went to *Liberty*, one each to *Maclean's* and *Saturday Night*. In 1957, he sold *fifty-six* articles.

Moreover, Garner drew on his magazine work for fictional material. Walter Fowler, the unhappy would-be novelist in *The Silence on the Shore* who edits the trade journal *Real Estate News*, one of "Matheson-Corbett"'s ten or twelve trade rags, covets an editor's job on *Living*, "the company's prestige consumer magazine." But he is bested first by the editor of *Motel and Motor Court Magazine*, then by a rival from *Narcissus*. In *A Nice Place to Visit*, his free-lance hero, Ben Lawlor, deals not just with Alex Hurd but with Frank Ronnick, the "young, deliberately scruffy" editor of *Controversy*, "The Magazine for Thinking Adults." This was a

> wheeler-dealer hybrid, put together on the skeleton of a dying arty "Art" magazine that had featured the no-talent daubings of a bunch of corduroys-with-beards, and the alleged sculptural erections of mad pipe-fitters, frustrated window-dressers and plastic-box mechanics. The magazine's other bisexual parent had been a sleazy stock tip-sheet disguised as a legitimate

brokerage brochure, the phony good taste of its cover
exceeded only by its inside necromancy predicated on the
sure rise in value of already dead mining properties. Both of
these literary lemons had been acquired by Mr. Morgan
Crayshaw, a *nouveau riche* ex-bucketshop operator....Out of
these two outrageous journalistic parents, whose marriage
was like the post-parturient nuptials of a bar-bell salesman
and a spangled drum-majorette, had sprung the new magazine
for the current in-crowd. It had been baptised *Controversy* in
rye-and-ginger ale, the favorite tipple or sip of the kind of
editorial staff whose controversial stand, like that of a service
mess, stopped short of women, politics and religion. This left,
to justify the misnomer, such minor debates as the use of the
steel animal trap, use of the grade-school strap and articles
titled, "Should Johnny's Tonsils Come Out?"

If these details resonate with those of contemporary magazines, the
connections were probably intended. In a November 1975 *Saturday
Night*, Garner and others were asked, "Do you use real people in your
fiction?" Amid cant and disingenuousness from others, Garner said,
"I have never consciously copped out of using as a character in a novel
or short story somebody I knew and on whom the character was
based....I used a former acquaintance in one of my novels, and drew
him as a stupid, opportunistic clot. I have seen him once or twice since,
but he failed to recognize himself in the book. Not so strangely; he actually *is* a stupid, opportunistic clot...."

Starting his free-lance career, Garner was "wagering the feeding,
clothing and housing of my young family against literary and money-
earning acceptance and success. God takes care of fools and drunks,
they say, and I was both." Yet for him there was "no other job for which
I was so fitted psychologically and temperamentally, and no other career
which would have interfered less with my drinking."

The two categories of magazine editors, Garner said, were "those who
liked an editor's job as some people like being ledger-keepers or life
insurance underwriters, and failed writers who take editing jobs to stay
as close to the writing business as they can while drawing a regular
weekly or monthly salary." Failed writers made bad editors, he claimed.
For him the halcyon period of willing writers and good, or at least compatible editors did not outlast the 1950s. According to him,

You didn't need the gifts of prophecy or foresight by 1956 to
know that a great number of North American magazines were
about to fold up. Of those that were still in operation fewer
and fewer were publishing short stories or fiction of any
kind. The publishers and editors of these magazines blamed
the public, whom they claimed preferred factual articles

rather than fiction. The truth was, in Canada at least, that it was the fault of a new breed of semi-literate magazine editors, graduates of schools of journalism who didn't know a short story from a sonnet.

As for the magazines themselves, most succumbed, he thought,

not by unfair American competition and the seduction of the Canadian advertiser, but by inept management, sales unaggressiveness, editorial stupidity, dull editorial content, and an unwillingness to cater to the tastes of the average Canadian reader....In the past the totally false belief of Canadian editors that their readers preferred facts to fiction wiped out the best training ground for the beginning Canadian creative writer, and the lack of literary taste or knowledge on the part of our editors made them prefer the imported junk, the formula short story that killed the short story medium in this country.

A somewhat different tack was taken by *Maclean's* editor Ralph Allen—himself a novelist—who told a 1955 conference on writing that non-fiction was a creative art form, especially as practised by those like Bruce Hutchison, Blair Fraser and Pierre Berton. Neither "the poet nor the novelist has any monopoly," he said, "of the fresh and meaningful talents in Canadian letters today."

Little and Literary

There were always poets and fiction writers who, though they might have envied the fees the largest consumer magazines paid, did not wish to compromise their artistic standards. For them, there could only be one meaningful print outlet, the literary or "little" magazine.

Of course, these were not the only outlets. University reviews like the *Dalhousie Review* and *Queen's Quarterly*, particularly when Queen's English professor Malcolm Ross was literary editor during 1953-55, published new writers. But these, like the bilingual Quebec review, *Culture* (1940-71) and the *University of Toronto Quarterly*, for whom Northrop Frye wrote the elegant, influential section on Canadian poetry for its annual "Letters in Canada" from 1950 to 1960, were primarily scholarly journals of the humanities. The unscholarly but influential *Explorations: Studies in Culture and Communication* (1953-59), edited by Edmund Carpenter and Marshall McLuhan, launched "probes" into society and media.

The *Canadian Forum*, weak and unpersuasive politically during the early 1950s—it had become much less determinedly socialist—made up for it later in the decade with belles-lettristic contents under literary editor, Milton Wilson. It was also the arena of literary sparring between the poet Irving Layton and those he called "white-livered recreants"—Wilson, Northrop Frye, A. J. M. Smith and Millar MacLure. By the 1960s, the *Forum* regained its political verve, and indeed some of its key editors and contributors, such as the historians Ramsay Cook and William Kilbourn, helped rouse academic support for the Liberal leadership candidacy of Pierre Trudeau, a sometime *Forum* contributor.

A writer cannot exist in a vacuum: he or she needs an intelligent audience. To help prepare that readership, a few critical magazines evolved. CBC radio producer Allan Anderson's *Reading* (1946), co-edited by Lister Sinclair and Ronald Hambleton, was an early worthwhile attempt at a magazine of arts criticism, as was Nathan Cohen's *The Critic* (1950-54), later crudely lampooned as *The Genius* in Mordecai Richler's novel *The Incredible Atuk*. The most important magazine for literary criticism was George Woodcock's *Canadian Literature* (1959—) at the University of British Columbia. In the magazine's early years, Woodcock, a philosophical anarchist and self-educated polymath, open-mindedly kept *Canadian Literature* from becoming a narrowly academic journal.

The prototype of the university-based, strictly literary magazine so prevalent in the 1960s and 1970s was *The Fiddlehead* (1945—), although for its first seven years it was merely a privately circulated mimeographed compilation of poems by members of Fredericton's Bliss Carman Society. But after Fred Cogswell, a University of New Brunswick poet and translator, became editor in 1952 it grew into an artistically thriving quarterly and the focus for an energetic group of University of New Brunswick writer-professors. Editorially ecumenical, the magazine drew contributions from across Canada and the United States. Two other magazines, *Quarry* (1952—) in Kingston, Ontario, and *Prism International* (1959—) in Vancouver, developed in the same way. At first student-oriented, or linked with a university department, they evolved into worthy general literary magazines.

But the energy for the new writers who emerged during and after the war was concentrated in the "little magazines" that were often associated with small presses and were part of a network that bypassed consumer magazines and trade publishers. Their first centre was Montreal where, within a few months of each other, the poetry magazines *Preview* and *First Statement* began in late 1942 and early 1943. Although the editors of both magazines differed in their socialist alliances and forms of nationalism, they had alert social consciences and a sense of renewing Canadian literature. Among those who helped edit *Preview* were Frank Scott, A. M. Klein, P. K. Page and Patrick Anderson, the last influenced by W. H. Auden's work. The writers in *First Statement* —John Sutherland, Louis Dudek and Irving Layton—inclined toward U.S. modernists like Ezra Pound and William Carlos Williams.

After bickering about aesthetic ends and means, the two magazines

Tamarack Review's *first covers depicted the magazine's namesake conifer.*

ISSUE TWO WINTER 1957 $1.00

The Tamarack Review

MORDECAI RICHLER — RODERICK HAIG-BROWN
ALICE MUNRO — A. J. M. SMITH
DOUGLAS GRANT — CARLYLE KING
JAMES REANEY — DARYL HINE
PHYLLIS GOTLIEB — GERALD SCOTT
GEORGE JOHNSTON — ROBERT WEAVER

merged in January 1946 as the *Northern Review*, edited by Sutherland, a gifted Nova Scotian poet and critic whose forthrightness soon led Scott, Page and Klein to withdraw from the editorial board. A dynamic editor, Sutherland's bias shifted from Marxism to conservative Catholicism, but his prescient taste remained consistent. He died of cancer complicated by tuberculosis in 1956, and with him died the magazine.

The 1940s and 1950s marked the time when writers took magazines out of the hands of editors and into their own. *Preview* and *First Statement* were examples, as was Vancouver's *Contemporary Verse* (1941-52), edited by Alan Crawley, assisted by the poets Anne Marriott, Dorothy Livesay and Floris McLaren. Others were Raymond Souster's *Contact* (1952-54) and *Combustion* (1957-60) in Toronto, and in Montreal, Aileen Collins's *CIV/N* (1954-56) and Louis Dudek's *Yes* (1954-70) and *Delta* (1957-66) in Montreal. In pre-Confederation Newfoundland, the 1940s saw, as Patrick O'Flaherty notes, a literary awakening that embraced such St. John's magazines as the *Courier* (1941-46) and *Protocol* (1945-51), begun by the brothers Charles and Harold Horwood.

Many of these periodicals were writer-centred "little" magazines. But there were also tries at establishing popular, general literary magazines, such as Paul Arthur's handsomely designed *Here and Now* (1947-49) and the ambitious Montreal magazine *Exchange* (1961-62), a glossy cultural journal backed by a clothing manufacturer and edited by Stephen Vizinczey, later famous for his novel *In Praise of Older Women*. *Exchange* aimed for a minimum circulation of 20,000 but became absorbed into *Canadian Commentator*. Both lost considerable money.

By far the most important and enduring of these magazines was the *Tamarack Review* (1956-82). If magazines of the period either catered to, in Louis Dudek's words, "meticulous moderns" or "lumpen intellectuals," there was no doubt as to which camp the *Tamarack* belonged. Eclectic as the magazine was—and often exemplary in its balance of fiction, poetry and essays—*Tamarack*'s editors seemed to regard themselves as meticulous arbiters of taste. As Robert Weaver noted in his first editorial, "We're committed, as all editors should be, to the proposition that saying something well is the basis of civilization."

Born in Niagara Falls in 1921 and educated at the University of Toronto, Weaver joined the Canadian Broadcasting Corporation in 1948 and became the CBC's man-about-culture, producing numerous showcases for literature and the arts.

All the arts were reviving in Canada. Apart from a surge in radio and TV dramatic programming, there was a new interest in the visual arts. This was recorded by *Canadian Art* (1940-87) which started as *Maritime Art: the Journal of the Maritime Art Association* and was renamed in 1943 when it moved to Ottawa. Becoming *Artscanada* in 1967, it was, with its Quebec equivalent, *Vie des Arts*, founded in 1958, the most important magazine of painting and sculpture for many years. Between 1958 and 1965, *Jazz Canada*, the *Canadian Composer, Opera Canada* and *Performing Arts in Canada* were all started.

It was in this climate that Weaver began his literary magazine, partly intended to succeed his friend John Sutherland's *Northern Review*. A contributor to many magazines, Weaver banded with a few others who had unbounded confidence in their own impeccable taste for "excellence" together with "standards," a much employed word in the magazine. These included two Oxford University Press editors, Ivon Owen and William Toye, the University of Toronto professor Millar MacLure, who was later editor of the *University of Toronto Quarterly*, the immigrant writer Kildare Dobbs and the poet Anne Wilkinson, who gave vital financial support until her death in 1961. As well, there was a nebulously defined editorial board of well-known writers, but it disappeared from the masthead in 1960. In 1960, Weaver and his friends were joined by the poet, editor and anthologist John Robert Colombo. For the year 1964, he acted as the magazine's first and only paid editor.

In its first decade, the *Tamarack* undoubtedly was the best Canadian literary magazine, and its editors were aware of the fact, pompously entitling an anthology of work from it *The First Five Years*. Introducing the book, Robert Fulford claimed that "One piece I wrote for the *Tamarack* four years ago has been mentioned to me more often, and discussed more widely, than many pieces I have written for publications which have a thousand times as many readers." Fulford approvingly quoted from a 1957 *Tamarack* editorial which observed that

> The dream of a distinctively Canadian culture still possesses
> us. It is an idle dream. In the first place, the fact of our
> sovereign independence doesn't make us a distinct nation, it
> only makes us a political unit. In the second place, we do not
> become more distinctively ourselves by pursuing singularity,
> by countering the Daughters of the Revolution with the
> Daughters of the Empire, or Davy Crockett with Pierre Radis-

son. Such gestures, like the beaver-and-maple-leaf school of writing, are evidences of a provincialism, not nationalism.

Tamarack, a champion of Canadian literature, was in fact run by a cabal of anti-nationalists whose editorial stance might be summed up in Kildare Dobbs's Summer 1958 review article when he said, "It would have been a disaster for Western culture if the sages of Alexandria, instead of commenting upon and annotating the ancient Greeks, had gone combing the desert for an indigenous literature. The invention of Canadian letters, as a distinct study for academic study, has been a blessing only to those scholars who are paid to investigate it." There was often an attitude to Canadian writers in the *Tamarack* that might have been put: "Very *good*, little boy, you keep filling up those scribblers now and some day you'll grow up and be a big strong man like your British and American cousins."

Writing about the O'Leary Report in 1961, Weaver deplored the nationalist slurs against the good names of *Time* and *Reader's Digest*, and opposed any protectionist action against them. He did suggest that a small tax be applied against all magazines published in Canada, the proceeds to be given to the Canada Council. "This fund should then be used to assist magazines that need support to stay alive, but the bulk of it should be used to establish and subsidize indefinitely one national monthly of the type of *Harper's* or the *Atlantic Monthly*."

The *Tamarack* itself would become dependent on the Canada Council, the federal arts body set up in 1956 with Peter Dwyer, a former spy, as its first director. By the early 1970s, the magazine, an emblem of the mandarin internationalism of the 1950s, seemed isolated by the cultural nationalism that was a phenomenon of the 1960s, although it published many writers associated with it.

Identified with the Toronto establishment, *Tamarack* had also lost the privileged position of being one of the few outlets for new work. Suddenly there were many new small presses and little magazines, including a swarm of irregular, experimental mimeographed magazines generated by the poets Bill Bissett and B. P. Nichol. There were university-based literary magazines like the *University of Windsor Review* (1965–), the *Far Point* (University of Manitoba, 1968-73), *Ellipse* (Université de Sherbrooke and devoted to English and French poetry in parallel translation, 1969–), *West Coast Review* (Simon Fraser University, 1966–) and *Malahat Review* (University of Victoria, 1967–), founded by John Peter and the poet and critic Robin Skelton. The West Coast was especially active. *Tish* (1961-65) promoted the poetics of the U.S. Black Mountain school and two of *Tish's* editors, George Bowering and Frank Davey, went on to found, respectively, *Imago* (1965-73) and *Open Letter* (1965-69, 1971–), "A journal of writing and sources." Then, too, there were such general literary magazines—sometimes with political and cultural admixtures—as *Evidence* (1960-67), Henry Beis-

sel's *Edge* (1961-69) in Edmonton and Montreal, and James Reaney's *Alphabet* (1960-71), originating in London, Ontario, and focussing on the "iconography of the imagination."
(1960-71), originating in London, Ontario, and focussing on the "iconography of the imagination."

There seemed, in short, no lack of imagination. By the early 1970s, *Tamarack* editors had their own thriving careers and less volunteer time to devote to putting out the magazine. *Tamarack* stopped publishing entirely between 1972 and 1974, and by the late 1970s seemed to possess neither the energy to persevere nor the courage to quit. At last it ended, having survived such friends and contributors as Anne Wilkinson, Alan Crawley, Hugh Garner, Ethel Wilson, A. J. M. Smith, John Glassco and Peter Dwyer.

Maclean-Hunter

The one magazine publishing company that, though encountering problems, remained fairly stable in the fifties and sixties was Maclean-Hunter.

In 1950 Donald Hunter, heir to the aging Horace Hunter and to Maclean-Hunter itself, became vice-president and managing director, Floyd Chalmers moving up to president. The Maclean-Hunter fifties were marked by overall profits fed by the business papers, but losses in virtually all the consumer magazines.

To stem these losses, Maclean-Hunter sold *Mayfair* and attempted to revamp *Canadian Homes and Gardens* before selling it, too. It also acquired the *Canadian Home Journal*'s subscription list and merged it with *Chatelaine*, to *Chatelaine*'s great advantage. In 1960 and 1961 it founded French editions of *Chatelaine* and *Maclean's* respectively. Entering the 1960s, Maclean-Hunter owned forty-five publications in Canada, three in the United States and three in Britain, and had moved into a new $6-million building, a squat green architectural frog situated at University and Dundas—Chalmers thought that with its limestone façade the building "had the look of a very expensive bird coop."

Meanwhile, Maclean-Hunter had bought into CTV's Halifax outlet. The old guard was changing. Napier Moore had retired from the company in 1954, and Horace Hunter died in 1962. Although Chalmers was past retirement age in 1965, he still took part in board meetings. But when he dropped into Donald Hunter's office, "I was annoyed to be treated as if I were already out of the picture...."

Not surprising, because the company had recently promoted a packsack of new executives, one of whom, Donald Campbell, had not even risen through the ranks but had been recruited from the Atomic Energy Commission. Chalmers was not much involved in Maclean-Hunter's entry into the new growth area of communications, cable TV. A board-sitting benefactor of orchestras, the Stratford Shakespearean Festival—

Tom Patterson, Stratford's founder, had been an associate editor of the Maclean-Hunter's trade magazine *Civic Administration*—and other cultural causes, Chalmers used some of the proceeds from the sale of his stock to start the Chalmers Foundation in support of the performing arts.

In 1964, Hunter became president and the company went public on the Toronto Stock Exchange. By now Maclean-Hunter had, besides its consumer magazines and sixty-two trade papers, a commercial printing plant, trade shows, annuals, and chunks of radio and TV stations in Ontario and Nova Scotia, as well as other interests in the United States, Britain, France and Italy. Having reached a status quo accommodation with *Time* and *Reader's Digest*, Maclean-Hunter saw its net profits soar to more than $2.1 million, and in 1967 established a wholly-owned subsidiary, Maclean-Hunter Cable TV. Early in 1968, Donald Hunter, whose family owned fifty-one percent of the shares, and Chalmers agreed that the latter should retire as chairman of the board at age seventy. Although Chalmers remained a director, Hunter told him he would have to vacate his office. The banishment was only temporary, but it was shabby treatment for one of Maclean-Hunter's most faithful soldiers.

A Committee

Plus ça change.... In 1967, Henry Luce asserted, in case anyone didn't know, that "I am a Protestant, a Republican and a free-enterpriser, which means I am biased in favour of God, Eisenhower and the stockholders of Time Inc. and if anybody who objects doesn't know this by now, why the hell are they still spending 35 cents for the magazine?"

In 1969, *Time*, together with DeWitt Wallace's *Reader's Digest*, accounted for fifty-six percent of domestic magazine advertising, a thirteen-percent increase since 1958. Although Canadians were reading fewer magazines of all types and nationalities, and advertisers were spending less of their budgets on magazines, *Time's* circulation since 1960 had risen from 215,000 in 1960 to about 440,000 in 1969, and the *Digest's* from 1,448,000 to 1,968,000.

Reader's Digest and *Time* were still getting a break on their postage bill, although the subsidy was reduced in 1968, when at least the Post Office Act had been amended to define the two magazines as non-Canadian. Through its mailing list based on *Digest* subscribers, the Reader's Digest Association sold books, records and other things to forty percent of Canada's five million families.

Although the Senate Special Committee on the Mass Media did not concern itself just with magazines, it certainly considered such fundamental facts about the industry. The man who chaired it, Keith Davey, was a sales manager of a Toronto radio station when in 1961 Lester Pearson appointed him executive director of the Liberal Party. He served until 1966, at which point he was named a senator. For a year he was also commissioner of the Canadian Football League. The most die-hard loyalist among Liberals, and a tireless coach of federal electoral campaigns, Davey was also a nationalist. The staff he hired might be expected to share at least nationalist sympathies: his executive consultant was Borden Spears and a ghostwriter of the final report was Alexander Ross.

Commencing in December 1969, the committee, made up of fifteen senators, heard about 500 briefs from 100 witnesses before it closed hearings the following April. The parade included E. P. Zimmerman, president of the Reader's Digest Association (Canada) who pointed out that thirty percent of the *Digest's* common stock was held by Canadians, and that more than ninety cents of every revenue dollar remained in Canada. He recited statistics about Canadians employed, Canadian material published and the *Digest's* export of the last. The *Digest's* editorial staff was almost as large as *Maclean's* and it paid writers as much as five times what *Maclean's* or *Chatelaine* could offer. Most of the *Digest's* famous condensed books were being edited, set, printed and bound in Canada. The *Digest* gave bursaries to "the burgeoning writer...."

Timen, too, were good boys. Stephen LaRue, *Time's* managing director, noted that the magazine now ran up to six pages in its Canadian section; had four bureaus—and, he didn't immediately add, twelve regional editions across the country, and seven staff correspondents. Canadians were getting the same magazine everyone else in the world got, *plus* Canada!

The Canadians who happened to own magazines were more equally divided in opinion than had been the case with the O'Leary Commission. Most of those who did not belong to the Magazine Advertising Bureau, whether associated with Southam or the *Toronto Star* or *Weekend,* wanted *Time* and *Reader's Digest* stripped of advantages. But those in the bureau—the French and English editions of *Maclean's*, the three *Chatelaines, Saturday Night, Actualité*, the *United Church Observer* and *TV Hebdo*—as well as a few others, wanted or expected nothing better than the status quo. *Toronto Calendar* even recommended that *TV Guide* get tax-exempt-advertising status. In contrast to Floyd Chalmers, Maclean-Hunter's R. A. MacEachern and Lloyd Hodgkinson had kind words to say about their rivals. In Hodgkinson's words:

> We don't retract anything we have ever said about the desirability of Canadian media being run by Canadians.
>
> Sure, we can wish our magazines got more advertising revenue. We can look enviously at the $11 million per year which *Time* and *Reader's Digest* may be regarded as taking out of the Canadian pot. The other side of that is that if the Canadian consumer magazine industry was mainly represented by *Maclean's* and *Chatelaine*, those magazines might not get as much advertising revenue as they do now,

because of the buying habits of the industry—buying by category of the media....For us in the consumer magazine league, the motto is, Live and let live.

Compared to other media, magazines were presented as an endangered species. "I would regard television generally as the chief competitor," said William Nobleman of *Saturday Night*. In this context it was inconceivable to the Magazine Advertising Bureau, whose job was to promote overall industry sales, that diminishing the status of *Time* and *Reader's Digest* would result in more, not fewer magazines. Nobleman went so far as to declare that "without the *Reader's Digest* and *Time* magazine there wouldn't be a magazine industry in Canada." *Time* spent $12,000 a year advertising in *Saturday Night*.

Even Grattan O'Leary, now a Senator himself, was not so keen about changing things. Mainly, the old warrior was disgusted. Were Canadian magazines these days even worth preserving? He had seen recent issues of *Maclean's*, he said, that "might just as well have been published in San Francisco or Timbuktu...." When he had made his report, *Maclean's* "was, within its ability and financial capacity, trying hard to explain and to interpret Canadian life to Canadians. That is not true today." Blaming both Liberals and Conservatives for not enforcing his report's recommendations, O'Leary told the Committee: "...if Moses had been a Royal Commission, the Israelites would still be in Egypt."

The Committee published its report in December 1970. Among the findings in its four volumes was the fact that the U.S. men's magazine *Playboy* "collects about as much money selling its magazine in Canada as do the seventeen largest English-language consumer magazines combined." The biggest reason for "the industry's palsied state" was the invasion of *Playboy* and all the other overflow magazines.

But the Report's recommendations emphasized that the U.S. birds were laying their eggs in the wrong nests. If the ownership provisions of Section 12A of the Income Tax Act—the legislation that followed the O'Leary Report—hadn't been applied, "we are certain that Canadian magazines would be a lot sicker than they are." How much better medicine it would be to repeal the exemptions for *Time* and *Reader's Digest*! A majority on the committee decided to recommend

> that if events warrant it, *Time* and *Reader's Digest*, as a condition of publishing their magazines in Canada, be required to sell seventy-five percent of the stock in their Canadian subsidiaries to Canadian residents, and that three-quarters of their officers and directors be Canadian residents. (*Reader's Digest* is almost halfway there already; thirty percent of the Canadian subsidiary's stock is held by Canadian residents, and four of its six directors are Canadian.)

Although it took its time, the Liberal government introduced Bill C-58 in 1975. Not only would *Time* and *Reader's Digest* have to have seventy-five percent Canadian ownership, their editorial content must be "substantially" the same proportion.

Since 1970, the binge of lobbying for and against the Davey recommendations had caused Maclean-Hunter to reverse its position yet again. It now sensed a chance to replace *Time* with a newsmagazine of its own and generated some novel ideas from commentators. In the *Canadian Forum* Abraham Rotstein and Morris Wolfe separately proposed that a "Publishing Development Corporation" be set up with powers to, in Wolfe's words, "place limits on the number and kind of holdings any one owner would be permitted; appoint salaried public directors to the boards of large media corporations; provide subsidies for essential but uneconomic publications; establish quotas for the newsstand distribution of Canadian books and magazines and a crown corporation to handle that distribution; establish a crown corporation to produce a national newsweekly."

By 1975, the *Digest* admitted that it was taking more than twenty percent of the roughly $39 million that members of the Magazine Advertising Bureau had in gross advertising revenue. But this, its spokesman said, was only part of the picture: the newspaper weekend supplements grossed $27 million, controlled circulation magazines $5.5 million and business publications netted $37 million. *Time* preferred public relations to statistics: it sponsored a touring exhibition of contemporary Canadian painting.

The lobbying reached a climax in December 1975 when opposing groups of magazine writers sent letters to the House of Commons Committee on Broadcasting, Films and Assistance to the Arts. Kenneth Bagnell, Fred Bodsworth, Bruce Hutchison, Gordon Green, Harold Horwood, Sidney Katz, Adrian Waller and David MacDonald noted that "Over the years, *Digest* editors in Canada have been consistently fair and professional in their dealings with us. The *Digest's* superior rates of payment help many writers and artists to survive in the precarious field of magazine journalism. Those fees also enable Canadian contributors to apply to Canadian subjects the time, depth of research and creativity that they deserve." June Callwood, Jack Batten, Dick Brown and Alan Edmonds agreed that the two magazines, although "excellent," were "not now and are not likely to be" ones "that contribute to our national cultural life by providing a forum or meaningful source of income to Canadians."

Perhaps the strongest arguments against allowing deduction of advertising in *Time* and *Reader's Digest* as a business expense was ethical, not economic. If income tax legislation was the best way to encourage Canadian magazines, and the point was debatable, then those it encouraged should be Canadian. Despite all their claims to the contrary, *Time* and *Reader's Digest* were not.

Bill C-58 passed.

SATURDAY NIGHT
UNDER SEVERAL MASTERS

The moment in the fall of 1952 that B. K. Sandwell learned Jack Kent Cooke had acquired Consolidated Press, and with it *Saturday Night*, he is said to have removed his bag lunch from a desk drawer and headed on home. Certainly, the two men were very different people.

Neither Sandwell, nor the editor, Robert Farquharson, wanted much to do with the brash young capitalist who had become synonymous with money uncouthly made. The war had not been kind to the magazine, and Cooke seemed the final blow. Certainly, his management style contrasted with that of Mabel Sutton who, Robertson Davies later recalled, had been served by "a group of palace eunuchs" and presided over Consolidated Press like the Empress of "a sort of Byzantine Empire." Cooke would, it was assumed, either drastically alter its character in order to make it profitable, or kill it off if it wasn't. Either alternative appeared equally dire.

At first Cooke said that he wanted "to develop a news magazine which will look at world news through Canadian eyes rather than American eyes. The sooner this is changed the better." He also went to some pains to prove he was not the evil genie. Following Farquharson's resignation—he joined the Canadian diplomatic corps in Washington and afterward became director of information at NATO headquarters in Paris—Cooke announced an editorial board to include Robertson Davies, University of Toronto philosophy professor John Irving and E. J. Pratt. He also embarked on a wide-ranging talent hunt to fill the post of editor. Cooke spoke to novelists, such as Hugh MacLennan, Morley Callaghan and Davies, to journalists, such as Edwin Copps, then an editor in the New York office of *Time* and a future Ottawa correspondent for *Saturday Night*, even to the magazine's contributor Anthony West, the son of H. G. Wells and Rebecca West, who wrote for the *New Yorker*. The only taker was the Welsh-born Gwyn Kinsey, editor of the Thomson-owned *Woodstock Sentinel-Review*, whom Cooke had met when he was working for another Thomson paper in Timmins. Cooke ran soothing advertisements proclaiming that "It is high time that thinking, mature Canadians should have an intellectually stimulating journal of opinion," and expressing the hope that *Saturday Night* would be it. Although some of the staff veterans had departed—like P.M. Richards, who went into public relations—another signal was sent out with the restoration of old *Saturday Night* standbys like "The Front Page," "Society" and "Gold & Dross" sections.

Printed on coated stock and about the size of *Maclean's*, the magazine had Davies as book editor and added letters from correspondents. MacLennan wrote a letter from Montreal, as did the swishy British man-of-letters, Beverley Nichols, from London. Kinsey himself was expected to go on the public-speaking circuit, a role both Sandwell and Arnold Edinborough, his successor, were superbly equipped for. But Kinsey remained the archetypal competent and conscientious small-town editor, putting his paper to bed.

One of the unsteady props of the staff was Hugh Garner, whom Cooke had moved to the magazine. Garner told about office life at the time. Termed "an Associate Editor, with capital letters,"

> In reality I was a staff writer, whose job it was to write a weekly piece, plus the fabrication of a department I had begun called "The Backward Glance." It was a dream job, for I was given *carte blanche* as to subject matter, wrote my own heads, did no other editorial work, and was left severely alone by the editor, who had troubles enough without having to ride herd on me.
>
> I occupied a small office redolent of ancient journalistic history and the musty smell that clings to the pews in abandoned churches. On one side of me was the editor's office, and on the other side was an office the same size as mine, occupied by another associate editor, Willson Woodside, the foreign affairs man. Woodside had taken a dim view of me from the beginning, and I in turn largely ignored him, leaving him to his crusades for a retrogressive but orderly capitalist world. I broke all the journalistic tenets at one time or another, whistling loudly when I had no hangover, and driving the rest of the staff into the far reaches of the building in order to concentrate on their work.

The *Saturday Night* building was kitty-corner from a government liquor store and an employment office. For Garner, "Gazing at these symbolic and prophetic edifices filled most of my mornings." At noon he would join his cronies at a hotel for more than one beer.

> Occasionally, on the first four mornings of the week, I would drag my bloodshot gaze away from the window and write a batch of several weeks' "Backward Glance" columns for future use. I quickly developed a formula for writing these pieces about former issues of the magazine, and once when I got sick of writing them, Jack Kent Cooke...threatened to beat

my brains out if I so much as mentioned giving them up.

Friday afternoon was our editorial deadline on the magazine, and after procrastinating for the first four days of the week, I would realize that I still had my weekly piece to write. I missed the deadline once. Usually I would sit down shakily at the typewriter, hoping for some inspiration, or better still, hoping the old building would collapse and give me a legitimate excuse for not writing anything at all.

At first I researched some of the pieces, but stopped this nonsense when a three-part piece on cemeteries and funeral customs resulted in all the undertakers taking their ads out of the mag. They were replaced by beer and liquor ads eventually, which were not only more aesthetic and eye-pleasing but far more profitable....

In his collection *Author! Author!*, Garner adds another delicious tidbit.

Some Friday mornings, as the clock hands bore on inexorably toward deadline time, I would search my desk or look into the outer office for an idea that would give me two thousand words. Something invariably turned up...."The Office Drone" came from catching a glimpse of a fellow editor sitting doing nothing at his desk. This man, who had worked on the magazine for many years, had made a life's work out of doing nothing. When the piece was printed he failed to see himself in it, which says a great deal about the vacuum he had built around himself over the years.

Garner "learned in those days that a known lush can't afford to suffer such normal indispositions as the flu or a heavy cold." Debilitated as he often was, Garner did an amazing amount of work. Besides the amusing and well-turned "Backward Glance," he was also involved with the magazine departments "Television" and "The Literary Life." He wrote short stories, recollections of the navy and the Spanish Civil War, and a diatribe against pipe-smokers. He did a series of articles on undertakers, called "The Sweetest Racket This Side of Heaven." Even after Cooke's departure he was busily engaged: on a trip to the Maritimes he found pieces in interviews with Lord Beaverbrook and Premier Louis Robichaud, with the general manager of a Sydney, Nova Scotia steel mill and with Robert Stanfield, the newly elected Nova Scotian Premier. From his experience on the magazine, he also produced the succinct judgement: "an article is what *Maclean's* publishes; an essay is what *Maclean's* turns down and you later read in *Saturday Night*."

Under Cooke and Kinsey, the magazine still maddeningly lost money and, increasingly, prestige. It was now more a magazine of comment and less news-oriented than it had been in Farquharson's day. One of Kinsey's comments, the leading editorial of 13 November 1954,

prompted a flood of protesting letters. Referring to Vincent Massey, Kinsey said, "One more Governor-General as grey and remote as Mr. Massey will finish the job of making Canadians forget that there is such a thing as a royal dynasty in Canada." Among the protesters was the Ottawa mayor and sometime *Saturday Night* contributor Charlotte Whitton.

The new page size of 20 cm x 28 cm, about *Time*'s dimensions, didn't help the magazine's fortunes. The next move was to turn the weekly into a bimonthly. This was fine with Garner, since it allowed him more time to drink beer and daydream, but not for most of the other staffers. In protest, Willson Woodside, Mary Lowrey Ross (the movie critic and humour columnist), W. P. Snead (the stock analyst), Margaret Ness (the women's editor) and Paul Duval (the art critic), in addition to some assistant editors, all walked out. One of those resigning quipped that if *Saturday Night* came out every two weeks, "it wouldn't be Saturday Night any more...it might as well be 'Bath Night.'"

Snead's "Gold & Dross" question-and-answer column might have referred to *Saturday Night* when, shortly before the walkout, it produced the following exchange:

"Is there a chance that Nicola Mines can stage a recovery?
—C.S., Montreal
"No."

Cooke must have had doubts himself. But he put a brave face on the matter by announcing on 14 May 1955, the first fortnightly issue, that editorially "The format and character of SATURDAY NIGHT will not be changed, but the reduced frequency of publication will permit a stronger, healthier growth. Financially fixed costs have become too heavy a penalty for producing a weekly magazine of this kind—postal charges alone, for example, are three times as large for a weekly as for a bi-weekly publication."

Riding Saturday
Night*'s ups and
downs was the
chipper Arnold
Edinborough.*

Kinsey remained on the magazine, which now suggested a newer, more populist touch: through 1955 the front page portraits were often of new actresses like Shirley Douglas. But he, too, gave way in 1957, when Robert Marjoribanks succeeded him. Born in Scotland, Marjoribanks was at age thirty-five a veteran of the *Financial Post* and the Canadian Press wire service, and had been a public relations man, editor of *Farmer's Magazine* and managing editor of *Canadian Home Journal*. Kinsey remained as an editorial page contributor.

By now Mary Lowrey Ross and Paul Duval, at least, had adjusted themselves to the new schedule of publication, and the magazine still featured Davies, MacLennan, Garner and Anthony West, with Maxwell Cohen the new foreign affairs specialist. Marjoribanks made few changes and the magazine remained visually dull, with uninspiring little boxed headings to introduce departments. In any case, Marjoribanks lasted only a year. The man who succeeded him as editor of "Canada's Magazine of Business and Contemporary Affairs," Arnold Edinborough, would have much greater impact.

The Cambridge-educated Edinborough had been a Queen's University English professor and editor of the *Kingston Whig-Standard*. A cultivated man, he won a Military Cross in World War II and had an ongoing interest in the performing arts. He had been a contributing editor to the magazine, specializing in economics, and at the time of his appointment had just completed a series of articles on education. A joiner and board member of many societies, with his smooth speaking style and neatly groomed beard, he bore a superficial resemblance to, respectively, B. K. Sandwell and Hector Charlesworth.

About this time, Cooke sold Saturday Night Press, the magazine's printing arm, to Southam and disposed of some of his publishing interests. Then in August 1961, he shocked the Canadian business world—not to mention his own family—by jettisoning all his Canadian investments, including *Liberty* and *Saturday Night*, and emigrating to the United States. The buyer Cooke found for the consumer magazines was the Fengate Publishing Company, owned by Percy W. Bishop, a Toronto promoter of oil and gas stocks who had recently ventured into real-estate dealings. With *Saturday Night's* circulation about 70,000, Bishop aimed for 100,000.

Edinborough, who had enlivened the magazine, reduced the editorial staff and for the first time provided a coated paper cover detached from the magazine's main body, remained as editor—he also became the first editor of *Performing Arts in Canada*—and even briefly acquired the title "publisher." With him were the longtime managing editor, Herbert McManus; two newcomers as associate editors: John Gellner—the Czech-born defence expert who later edited *Canadian Commentator*—and *Canadian Defence Quarterly*—and Kildare Dobbs, later *Saturday Night's* mangaging editor; as well as the Ottawa editor, Peter Stursberg.

Bishop soon ushered in a silly season that would have no rival until the summer of 1987. In November 1961, with the help of Western oil money, the stock promoter bankrolled a consumer magazine called, with great originality, *The Canadian*, edited by the English-born Arthur Lowe, sixty-four, a sometime Social Credit candidate and former editor of *Apartment Owners and Builders Magazine*. In July 1962, Bishop announced he would merge *The Canadian* and *Saturday Night* to form a monthly.

For Edinborough and some of his staff, this would not do; despite, or because of the fact that Social Credit was then a significant force in national political life, it stood for much that the liberal-minded Edinborough could not countenance. He and several editors resigned. The new *Canadian Saturday Night*, which boasted the magazine's first colour cover in August, illustrated their wisdom.

Although Lowe had disclaimed that the magazine was a Social Credit party organ—in *The Canadian* he had said, "What I see good in Social Credit will appear in the magazine, and what I see good in the NDP, if there is any good in the NDP, will also appear in the magazine"—it certainly had a point of view, perfervid patriotism, delivered in August 1962. The new management wanted "to provide a magazine for Canadians which will help to bring about a revival of Canadian nationalism." For Arthur Lowe,

> The chief reason for the collapse of our morale has been the overwhelming effect during the past twenty years of U.S. preponderance in two areas of communication—TV and the periodical press. This preponderance has resulted in Canada being brain-washed as no nation before it in history—brainwashed by the full range of TV productions and periodical reading matter turned out by the United States, and glorifying—quite naturally—their own country and way of

life. Small wonder that we have developed an inferiority complex.

This oratory was familiar stuff, but might have led to renewed editorial purpose. Instead, there was an ongoing clumsy satire called "The Chronicles" by "Zadok" involving "John the Preacher" and "Lester the Learned," the federal political rivals John Diefenbaker and Lester Pearson. In March 1963, Lowe was urging that a new government be set up, "a Confederation Alliance made up of right-wing Liberals, Conservatives and Socreds, with the one purpose of forming a strong government to meet the present emergency."

Past the opinion pages, the magazine was a disorganized jumble of colour and black-and- white. The only steadying factor was those long-timers who continued to write for it: Stursberg, John A. Irving on books and Mary Lowrey Ross. There were riveting headlines, such as "Why the Big Rush to the Ski Slopes?"—Shirley Venning, "a Toronto woman, has been skiing since she was 18 years old."

Predictably, the amalgam was a financial disaster—indeed, all Bishop's publishing enterprises ended in a shambles of debt in 1964—and in June 1963 Edinborough formed a company, Saturday Night Publications, to reassemble the pieces of his old kingdom. He bought *Saturday Night* for the price of its printing bill, and had a neat revenge in the August issue: "As I was saying, before I was rudely interrupted by *The Canadian*, this country needs a forum where the issues of the day can be debated with wit, intelligence and responsibility. *Saturday Night*, true to its old and proud name, intends to provide that forum."

Edinborough hired MacLaren Advertising as public relations counsel, with Edgar Cowan, a future publisher of the magazine, one of those assigned to the account. In two years, Edinborough increased circulation from 82,000 to 90,000 and doubled advertising revenue. Maclean-Hunter, anxious that it not be perilously isolated in its struggles against the Canadian editions of *Time* and *Reader's Digest*, agreed to keep printing *Saturday Night* and to defer payment of its troublesome bill. Maclean-Hunter's reprieve was vital, but not a universal panacea. The magazine continued to lose money, and was kept afloat in part through large loans provided by the stockbroker David Fry.

Editorially, Edinborough continued the shift he had set in motion prior to the Bishop acquisition: a greater emphasis on popular culture epitomized as early as the 1962 series "Anatomy of Newsstands" written by himself, Fulford and Kildare Dobbs. Fulford's contribution in March 1962 was "Dream world of the sex magazines" and in 1965, at the suggestion of the managing editor, Harry Bruce, began writing a column of movie reviews, taking the pseudonym "Marshall Delaney" to avoid conflicts with the *Toronto Star*, where his own by-line was prominent.

Edinborough was sensitive to a new audience. As William Nobleman, the future publisher of the magazine who had left *Chatelaine* to become advertising director, later told the Davey Committee: "...those who were responsible for taking *Saturday Night* over in the summer of 1963 had for the most part a background in education, because the thing which has struck us was that the tremendous expansion in the number of persons being exposed to a post-secondary education would for the first time create in Canada the kind of market which has long existed in the United States for specialized journals of comment and opinion."

At least that was to be the tantalizing hope. In the attempt to fulfil it, Edinborough made increasing use of Kenneth McNaught, hired energetic young writers and editors like Harry Bruce, Jack Batten, Peter Gzowski and Wendy Michener, ran fiction—and a short story contest—and in May 1965 devoted an entire issue to the controversial subject of Medicare.

As Edinborough said later,

> I was convinced when I bought *Saturday Night* that a magazine with a coherent concept of what it was doing to create an audience could, in fact, create that audience. *Saturday Evening Post* and *Maclean's* had both lost that idea of the audience they were trying to create.
>
> I wanted it well-written, to cover a wide range of topics that could be made to seem of immediate interest to people the magazine was aimed at, with bitchy hard writing that stirs things up.

In 1968, perhaps to stir things up, Edinborough replaced himself as editor.

EVERYBODY AT *MACLEAN'S*

I
Irwin and Allen

For many, the *Maclean's* of the late 1950s is the best magazine to have appeared in Canada and Ralph Allen the best editor. In Allen's pilgrimage toward sainthood or even divinity, Arthur Irwin functions as John the Baptist.

Irwin, who was a clergyman's son and whose first wife was a clergyman's daughter, was born in Ayr, Ontario. He attended two universities and was a gunner in the First World War. Discharged in 1919, he filled castor oil bottles in a drugstore, picked fruit, was a rodman on a railway construction crew, sold books in rural Manitoba and, most presciently, delivered newspapers. (Late in life he was publisher of the *Victoria Times*.) From 1920 until 1925, he reported and wrote editorials for the *Toronto Mail and Empire*. Bruce Hutchison remembered him as "a lean, silent, superbly tailored fellow...his opinions sunk in a deep well to spill out with sudden vehemence, at unexpected moments."

Coming to *Maclean's* in 1925 as associate editor, he had many other interests, including figure skating—he co-authored and produced an ice ballet—and international affairs. When Irwin was appointed editor of *Maclean's* in 1945, not only had he been there for two decades, but he'd been managing editor for the previous three years.

In his own way, Irwin was a nationalist and he was determined to make the magazine more identifiably Canadian. He might have endorsed the 15 June 1948 piece "If We Join the U.S.A.," by the historian A. R. M. Lower. "Every few years old satan comes around to us Canadians, displaying the glittering rewards he has for a little easy submission: these invariably wear such labels as 'Commercial Union,' 'Unrestricted Reciprocity' or simply 'Reciprocity.' He has been back again recently and this time his package is marked 'Customs Union.'" Lower thought that "One of the first demands that would follow a Customs Union would be a demand for common citizenship."

Irwin didn't waste time expanding his staff. His greatest influence on *Maclean's*, in fact, would be as personnel officer. By the end of the year he had added, as assistant editors, Hal W. Masson, a former Air Force man and RCMP warrant officer, and a young newspaperman named Scott Young. Many of the significant editors and contributors were from Winnipeg or farther west: Ralph Allen, his most important acquisition; Allen's buddy, Trent ("Bill") Frayne; and W. O. Mitchell, fiction editor from 1948-1951—he had sold his first "Jake and the Kid" story to *Maclean's* in 1943. Another Westerner, John Clare, was from 1946 successively assistant, fiction, articles and associate editor, as well as features writer.

In 1947, Scott Young in turn hired a tall, ungainly twenty-five-year-old Vancouver newspaperman named Pierre Berton. Berton soon proved his worth. His "They're Only Japs" on 1 February 1948 was an outstanding piece on the plight of the Japanese Canadians expelled from the West Coast during the war.

These, along with Gerald Anglin, the cartoonist Len Norris and Eva-Lis Wuorio, as well as the men hired not long before he officially became editor—Blair Fraser and Lionel Shapiro—Irwin would pass on to his successor. This cast, and the people *that* successor commissioned or hired—Peter Newman, Christina McCall, Peter Gzowski, Robert Fulford, Barbara Moon, Robert Collins—would come to dominate Canadian print journalism.

Soon it became obvious that, under Irwin, *Maclean's* would become very much an editor's magazine, one characteristic of which is the sheer hardship of getting an idea past an editor. Jock Carroll's misadventure in 1947 illustrates not just this, but what was topical in Canadian magazine publishing just before mid-century. Carroll had suggested that he "be assigned to do stories on Yousuf Karsh, the famous Canadian photographer, or Guy Lombardo and his Royal Canadians. Failing that, I wondered whether they would care to send me out West to examine the farm mechanization, or to the North Pole to see if the Russians were getting too close." He "also suggested a story on Greg Clark and Jimmie Frise. It had just been announced that they were ending long careers at the *Star Weekly* and were going to work for the Montreal *Standard*." Replied Ralph Allen, then assistant editor:

> I'm sorry to say that your affinity for unfortunate coincidence is still downright sensational.
>
> We have carried profiles on Lombardo and Karsh within the last two years, and don't think either of them warrants a repeat.
>
> We consider Clark and Frise direct competitors, and can't afford to publicize them.
>
> You probably saw that *Life* is just out with a preview of your "Who Owns The Top of The World?" piece.
>
> And we have a story on farm mechanization on assignment right now.

A few new writers got past the roadblock. The Nova Scotian novelist Ernest Buckler regularly wrote for the magazine between 1948 and

1951. Edna Staebler, a neophyte writer who sold her first magazine piece—about going swordfishing in a Cape Breton snapper boat—to Scott Young, then articles editor, was published in July 1948. She became adept in the late 1940s and early fifties at gentle, sympathetic but sturdily constructed pieces about out-of-the-way ethnic minorities like the Old Order Mennonites, Amish and Hutterites. Staebler did not react unkindly to having her fishing article cut in half; others were more abrasive about the editing gauntlet writers had to endure.

In 1949, one of Hugh Garner's articles, a piece about Toronto's Jarvis Street, had been assigned to Berton, who was about to complete his first book, *The Royal Family*, based on articles he'd done for the magazine. Berton was managing editor. According to Garner, Berton

> ...knew a hell of a lot less about Jarvis Street or any street in Toronto for that matter, than I did....Berton had been conditioned by the *Maclean's* editors to think that a magazine article had to be researched to death. Though an excellent non-fiction writer and assiduous researcher himself, he, like all of the literary Lochinvars who had invaded Toronto from the West, knew nothing of the city at that time. I wrote the Jarvis Street piece, beginning at its upper end at Bloor Street, where it faced the facade of a chronic-case hospital cruelly named The Home for Incurable Children....I described its denizens also: the rich, not-so-rich, poverty-stricken, the whores, junkies and criminals who had made Jarvis and Dundas streets *their* corner.
>
> When I handed the piece to Pierre Berton he told me to go back and interview the unfortunates in the Crippled Civilians workshop. It was embarrassing to me and to them but I did it. Not that it mattered a goddam to the story....
>
> There was a block of cheap rooming houses situated where the Moss Park armories now stands, which I described from a viewpoint on the opposite sidewalk after nightfall. I saw a young man in one of the upper rooms practising his violin and a girl ironing some clothing on a dresser top. Berton, who had a blind, prejudiced eye for a semi-fictional vignette in a factual article, asked me, "What was the violinist's name?" Christ, that was the last straw! "I didn't find out his name, but it sure as hell wasn't Jascha Heifetz!" Berton rewrote the piece himself, something like writing about Vancouver's Stanley Park, and it became a piece of *Maclean's* pap called "The Stately Street of Sin" over the magazine's by-line "Gratton Gray."

Garner, who already was annoyed that Irwin had rejected his short story "One, Two, Three Little Indians," in spite of its being approved by the rest of the staff, didn't write anything more for *Maclean's* for five years. In Garner's words

> many magazine journalists were constantly being put off by the insane desire on the part of the editors of *Maclean's* to write only the truth, the whole truth, and nothing but the truth, as if they were bloody court reporters. I once met Trent Frayne on Yonge Street, and he was quite distraught, having just had an article turned down by the magazine after spending a month on it. Mackenzie Porter, for years one of the stable of salaried *Maclean's* writers, once had six or seven articles turned down in a row.

An Englishman, Porter—later known for blimpishly affected writing—produced the tautly written "Slaughter on Saturday" in the 15 September 1949 issue, concerning a man who had killed three people and wounded four others with a hunting rifle before killing himself. But it was Berton, as Ronald Hambleton says, "who became identified with the article format in which he was a master...."

> The format was simple: an opening which telegraphed the total content or message; a series of paragraphs, each of which, at best, carried an anecdote involving a named person, preferably with a quote; and a last clinching anecdote for a curtain. Such a format required a topic big enough in news terms to survive the rather mechanical treatment; and a reservoir of factual and anecdotal material so large that there could be no suggestion of padding. I contributed to the magazine only two or three articles in 1948 and 1949, and it was the hardest money I ever earned....

"Only Berton," Hambleton said, "was apt to take it as a personal affront, an outrage, if people came in with stuff that was not exactly what he would have done in their place. *Better* than he could have done was impossible.

> He was also master of the instant judgement. One day, shortly after the discovery of the Chubb crater in Ungava, formed by the impact of a mass of rock from space, I suggested an article on it, to be called "The Biggest Hole in the World." Berton pondered over that for all of three seconds, then said, "The article's in the title. What else is there to say?"

Maclean's titles during the late 1940s tended to be on the stark side. First-person accounts had titles like "I Married a Jew" and "I Married an ex-Convict." Significantly, Irwin's editorials bore the title: "In the Editors' [note the plural] Confidence."

As Maclean's
*editor, W.A.
Irwin prepared
the way for the
better-known
Ralph Allen.*

Irwin, whose first wife had died in 1948—he would later marry the poet P.K. Page—left the magazine in 1950 to join the National Film Board, and eventually became an ambassador with postings in Australia, Brazil and Mexico. During the twenty-five years he was with the magazine, the circulation had more than doubled, and now stood at about 411,000.

The 1 January 1950 "Mid-Century Review" was a kind of *l'envoi* for him. Among the nine pages of special articles and stories was one by playwright and CBC arts critic Lister Sinclair entitled "Mankind in the Age of Science." Fred Bodsworth did a survey piece on the year 1900, and John Largo one on 1950. The cover, a decorative calendar, was by Oscar Cahen, and the cartoons were by Len Norris, a contributor since 1947, who, before becoming staff cartoonist for the *Vancouver Sun*, was art editor of *Canadian Homes and Gardens*. Robert M. Hutchins, chancellor of the University of Chicago picked the "Greatest Ten of Our Time"—Gandhi, Einstein, Freud, Schweitzer, Eleanor Roosevelt, Churchill, Lenin, F.D.R., Sun Yat-Sen, Henry Ford—and Gilbert Seldes thought "TV could absorb virtually all other entertainment."

Announced as the new editor on 1 February 1950, Ralph Allen had been born in Winnipeg in 1913. One of four children, he grew up in prairie towns like Oxbow, Saskatchewan, where his father was a CPR station agent and an insatiable writer of letters to the editor. At sixteen, Allen went to Winnipeg to become a sports writer for the *Winnipeg Tribune*. Jim Coleman, a teenage reporter in the same Winnipeg period who later became a well-known sportswriter, has said, "Before Ralph Allen, sports writing in Canada was pretty pocky stuff. He brought English to the sports pages." In Winnipeg he shot craps, drank at a bootlegger's and shared a house with Trent Frayne, and met the nurse who would be his future wife, Birdeen Lawrence of Regina. He married her in 1939, the year after he'd moved to Toronto to become a *Globe and Mail* sports columnist. Three years later he joined the army

An abstract painter when he wasn't illustrating Maclean's *covers, Oscar Cahen might have been mocking himself on 15 October 1951.*

as a gunner in the Royal Canadian Artillery and in 1942 went overseas as a gun-crew sergeant with the 30th Anti-Aircraft Brigade. While an N.C.O. he contributed "The Sarge," a comic column on army life, to the *Globe*. Then, on the newspaper's initiative, he was discharged in 1943 to become its war correspondent. He landed with Canadian troops in Italy and on D-Day, and witnessed the liberation of Paris, the crossing of the Rhine and the war trials at Nuremberg.

Among his fellow correspondents were Greg Clark, Ross Munro, Lionel Shapiro and Peter Stursberg. Trent Frayne wrote in *Liberty* that Allen was reputed to be "next to General Montgomery, the most unusual dresser in the entire Allied forces." His uniform consisted of "a pair of yellow corduroy breeches...a stretched and faded turtle-neck sweater, covered by a rumpled battle dress blouse...a beret...and scuffed Oxfords instead of boots." He won an Order of the British Empire for his war coverage.

After the war he went back to the *Globe* briefly and published his war novel, *Homemade Banners*. Then at *Maclean's* he became in turn assistant, associate and managing editor. Irwin said that Allen couldn't make up his mind whether he wanted "to be the conductor of the orchestra or the first violin." In 1949, thinking he would have more time to write novels, he worked briefly as a sports columnist on the *Toronto Telegram*. Then, upon Irwin's urging, *Maclean's* rehired him. Allen would remain as editor until 1960. Until 1964, he spent half the year as contributing editor of *Maclean's*, the other half writing his own books. By the time Beland Honderich hired him as managing editor of the *Toronto Star* in 1964, he had added three books to his published total, which now included five novels—*Homemade Banners, The Chartered Libertine, Peace River Country, Ask the Name of the Lion* and *The High White Forest*—and a history of Canada called *Ordeal by Fire*.

Allen regarded his books as his most important writing. He seems to have had a vocational conflict. As far as his wife, Birdeen, was concerned, "There isn't any doubt in my mind that what Ralph wanted was to be a full-time writer, a novelist, but he had a family to support and he didn't want us to go through the kind of financial hardship he'd experienced as a child." This comment, and those of others who knew him, suggest a sense of wasted gifts. However, he was a better journalist than he was a novelist or historian.

The reverence with which this freckled, red-haired, pudgy, pipe-smoking man is regarded is probably unique in the history of Canadian journalism. To the adoring Christina McCall, he was "an editor of such compelling strength and honesty that nearly everybody who ever worked for him trusted him completely." Gregarious—he was a panelist on the CBC radio program "Now I Ask You"—and a gifted story-teller, he loved to eat, drink and gamble. An omnivorous reader and enthusiastic quoter of his reading, he was, McCall said, "never sleek or smug or sophisticated. He hated pretension of any kind and always refused to own property."

Romantically devoted to his wife, though in conflict with his son Glen—a future journalist—he was a man's man, frequently going fishing on weekends with newspaper and wire service chums like Greg Clark and Gilles Purcell. To McCall, "he was burdened with the most Presbyterian of consciences, that he felt *responsible* to every human being he met...."

Certainly, this demanding and complicated man who, said the Montreal novelist Colin McDougall (*Maclean's* serialized McDougall), "stood in sunlight and brought warmth to those around him," was not unflawed as a journalist. He was capable of stupid errors in his own work. His story in February 1950, "Was Kurt Meyer Guilty?" concerning Canada's "only war criminal," said that Meyer was "serving his life sentence in Dorchester penitentiary in Nova Scotia"—Dorchester is in New Brunswick. He could also badly misjudge tone, as in "Fourteen days in Cyprus" (20 June 1964), when he said in his lyrical opening about the Cyprian spring: "Even the Mediterranean smells of North Africa and Sicily—the wog and Ay-rab smells of Tunis, Algiers and Catania—are miraculously missing."

Allen has often been praised for a courageous opinion piece he'd written called "What if Herbert Norman *had* been a communist?" in which he admitted that during the Depression he had once voted Communist. But he was not impervious to a spot of J. B. Maclean-style Red-baiting. On 15 Nov. 1950 he published—shades of Whittaker Chambers—T. G. McManus's "The Reds Are Ready to Wage War Inside Canada," introducing it thus: "Until he broke with the party four years ago, T. G. McManus, a member of the Communist Central Committee for Canada, had already been shown his underground hide-out, been issued his code name and his orders for sabotaging industry—all part of the Communist

A hands-on editor, Ralph Allen uncharacteristically addresses a black-tie dinner.

blueprint for treason if war should come between Canada and Russia.''

He excelled at pleasing his masters. Except for minor clashes, he got along well with Floyd Chalmers, who was vice-president and president of Maclean-Hunter during Allen's term. Allen's editorial tribute to John Bayne Maclean is just a shade *too* eloquent:

> It is our feeling...that the magazine to which he gave his name cannot, in simple reality, concede the death of John Bayne Maclean. For as we mourn him, the parts of him that lived were as close and challenging as tomorrow's deadline or the next stack of proofs....Over the long haul he sought to prove or disprove nothing except that understanding comes with knowledge. That is why, as we honour him and mourn him, we cannot quite bring ourselves to believe that he is dead. Perhaps somewhere in this issue of the magazine there will be a sentence or phrase that will cause some young man or woman to believe that Canada is a better or more interesting place than he or she had realized, or that something is amiss in Canada that he or she must try to fix. Perhaps in time some new better thing will come of that small new stirring of awareness. And John Bayne Maclean...will be embarked on the 89th year of a valiant and fruitful life.

Yet when due compensation is made for the sometimes excessive praise he has received, Allen was obviously a remarkable editor. Although he satirized the CBC in his novel *The Chartered Libertine* and opposed government support for individual writers, he was a nationalist who shared with Blair Fraser and Hugh MacLennan the liberal (and at times Liberal) vision of an independent bicultural Canada. Because he was a novelist himself, he had a great sympathy for fiction writers, continuing the short story competition that had started in 1948 and establishing one for novels. One of Allen's favourite words was "balance" and he introduced such new features as the historical "Flashback" articles and the yellow-hued pages first called "Preview," and then "Maclean's Reports" to add timeliness to the magazine. "For The Sake of Argument" was also one of his innovations. Managing to escape the opprobrium that accrued to his junior editors, he guided his staff with judicious authority. In his era, *Maclean's*, as Pierre Berton said, started "a school of writing with Ralph Allen as the faculty."

With his new managing editor, John Clare, Allen conducted business in cramped offices on the fourth floor of the ramshackle Maclean-Hunter building. From the summer of 1952, when she started as a clerk-typist at the age of seventeen, Christina McCall worked part- and full-time for seven years. As she remembered later:

> What really happened was that I fell in love—with magazines in general, and with *Maclean's* in particular. With the smell of glue and the sight of page proofs, with the layouts on the art department wall, with the cover paintings hung in offices and the schedule sheets clipped to beaver-boards. But most of all with the kind of people who were running that magazine, with the ideas they projected and with the *élan* with which they lived.
>
> ...I do not suppose that I will ever regard with anything but affectionate respect the people who worked for Ralph Allen in those days; that I will ever again think of anyone as having as exciting and as germinal a journalistic mind as Pierre Berton displayed; or as much personal grace as Blair Fraser possessed; or as much professional know-how as Leslie Hannon, the copy editor, and Gene Aliman, the art director; or as much daring as Sidney Katz who talked to criminals and call girls, and swallowed LSD, a drug nobody had ever heard of, all in the name of *Maclean's*; or as much glamour as Barbara Moon who wrote all night and was said to own a Balenciaga; or as much caustic civility as Mackenzie Porter who knew about wines and wore suede shoes in an era when Canadians drank in beer parlours and were addicted to Sunday suits.

McCall, who later married another *Maclean's* staffer, Peter Newman— she left the magazine when Newman was Ottawa correspondent—has supplied an insider's look at the editing process, in fact, an excellent summary of the process at many large general magazines.

> Very few usable articles ever came into the magazine over the transom. Most of the ideas for articles originated from memos or brainstorming sessions, held first in the editor's office and later at editorial luncheons. These ideas were then

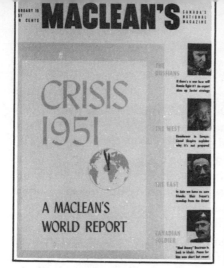
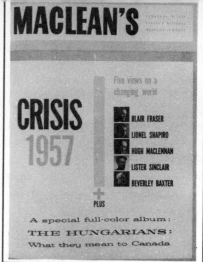

Maclean's *loved the word "crisis": representative covers from 1951 and 1957.*

assigned to staff writers or a select group of free lancers (a group that other writers bitterly—and not unjustifiably—complained it was almost impossible to join), researched extensively, often for as long as a month or more, written and submitted to the articles editor, who would comment at length on the manuscript and then pass it "up the line" to Berton and Allen. ("Where's my piece?" writers would be heard asking, neurotically. "Up the line," secretaries would answer.)

The article would then, more often than not, come back to the writer to be re-written. Three re-writes were not uncommon; one staff writer later claimed his first article was done eleven times; and it was sufficiently remarkable when Barbara Moon wrote a profile of Nathan Cohen, the drama critic, that required only one word change, for the other writers to buy her champagne.

The editors rewrote as much as they edited. The free-lancer Max Braithwaite, who often contributed to the "Flashbacks" section, quotes Allen as once telling an assistant, "This will have to be rewritten before we can reject it." Yet some pieces did get approved and, as McCall explains, were

> sent on to the copy department to be titled, copy-edited and then checked by young college grads in cashmere sweaters who looked on themselves and their duties with serious, superior eyes. The checking system was based roughly on what was known of the *New Yorker* method and many a writer cursed when he was told that par on a golf course in South Carolina was one stroke less than he had written or that the number of sacred cows in India was a hundred thousand more than he claimed. (One girl was renowned in this

small circle, for sending out a checker's letter—under the usual imperious statement that these facts, unless challenged, would appear in an upcoming *Maclean's*—addressed to a man called something like Nicholas Papaladopolous and containing two facts: "1. You are a Greek *restauranteur*" and "2. You are the owner of Nick's Grill."

Two of the men who gave *Maclean's* its character in the 1950s worked from bases outside the Toronto office. Before his death from cancer in 1958, the Montrealer Lionel Shapiro, a *Maclean's* foreign correspondent since the late 1930s, had published nearly one hundred articles for the magazine and was, besides, a best-selling novelist, as well as a successful broadcaster and TV and motion picture screenwriter in the United States. In a 19 October 1950 *Maclean's* piece called "The Myth That's Muffling Canada's Voice," he claimed that a "Canadian literary tradition" should best "become a tradition in the outside world first and belatedly in Canada." In a moving tribute published on 5 July 1958—and notable for its sincerity and post-Freudian unembarrassment —Allen observed that Shapiro had shared an apartment with his mother:

> The person to whom he had been closest throughout his life, the person whose sympathy and comfort would have meant the most to him in his last weeks, was the one person he felt he must not confide in. His mother, with whom he had shared a great and tender devotion throughout his life, was seriously ill too under the care of nurses in the Montreal apartment which was her home. Shapiro was convinced that if he told her of his own condition she might find the shock too difficult to bear.

Shapiro, Allen said, was "egotistical, neurotic, melancholy, obstinate and generally difficult." One of his friends had a favourite and no doubt made-up story about him that he used to tell in Lionel's presence. "'But John,' Shapiro would say, 'here I've been talking about myself for two hours. How about you talking about me for a while?'" When healthy and prosperous, Shapiro "was one of the most notorious and chronic worriers who ever set foot on earth. A hangnail, a cold in the head, a lukewarm letter from an editor, or a drop of fifty cents in the stock of Imperial Oil or Royal Bank could set him off on a lament of several days and positively Biblical gloom. But he was much too proud to let himself be frightened by anything really dangerous."

Even more important to Allen's *Maclean's* was his Ottawa editor— meaning correspondent—Blair Fraser.

Tall, thin, lantern-jawed, Fraser was born and raised in Sydney, where his father rose from steelworker to the management ranks of the Dominion Steel and Coal Corporation. A sickly, asthmatic youth, Fraser eventually worked summers in the steel plant and attended Acadia University. After a year's unhappy private schoolmastering at Stanstead College, south of Montreal, he reported for the *Montreal Herald* and the *Montreal Star*, marrying Jean Macleod, a social worker and fellow Maritimer.

A responsible married man, he quit newspapering to take the job of associate editor of the Montreal Heat, Light and Power Corporation's house organ, but lost it with the onset of the Depression. After getting a job through his father hosing Dosco coal on the docks, he worked as a proofreader on the *Montreal Gazette*, and successively became reporter, assistant city editor, city editor, news editor, editorial writer and book editor, establishing a weekly book page. In 1943, he was appointed associate editor. But as his successor Edgar Collard told Fraser's sons after his death, "The *Gazette* at that time was a Conservative paper, with a large C and your father was never a large C conservative." He joined *Maclean's*, writing his columns two or three weeks prior to publication and researching hard to make sure they remained timely.

To Collard, Fraser "was a total Canadian. Most Canadians are haunted with echoes of other lands...and become almost ghosts, haunted by ancient whispers. They cannot identify themselves, let alone be identified. Blair Fraser had no ghosts." Yet this substantial man, who in 1945 called Mackenzie King "our greatest Prime Minister," later scooped the country with the story of King's astonishing involvement with spiritualists and crystal balls. But Fraser, as his sons noted, "took pains to avoid a sensationalist treatment of the news."

Though no one doubted his integrity, he may have been a little too much at home in a world of discreet dinners, buried files and close-mouthed establishments. His companions on the last canoe trip he took in his life included the chancellor of the University of Toronto, a vice-president of a chemical company, the chairman of the Manitoba Liquor Commission and a vice-president of the Brazilian Light and Power Company. One person who almost joined them was Pierre Trudeau.

Although it was sometimes claimed that Fraser was a closet Liberal, he seems to have been almost universally regarded as a decent and honourable man. Sometimes that scrupulosity got him into trouble. In his 15 February 1952 "Backstage at Ottawa" column, called "B.C. Coalition Commits Suicide," he discussed the crumbling of the Liberal-Conservative provincial government and implied that its attorney general, Gordon Wismer, had been involved in a suspect real estate transaction and had used favouritism in granting liquor licences. When Wismer sued him and Maclean-Hunter, Fraser refused to reveal his sources in court. Although the case did Fraser credit among his colleagues, it ended badly for him and them, setting as it did a Canadian precedent in giving a journalist no legal protection of his sources. Later

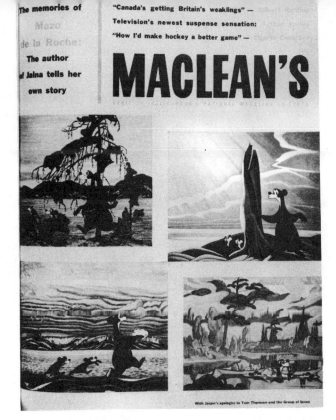

Simpkin's Jasper invades the Group of Seven's terrain on 27 April 1957.

in the year, *Maclean's* published an apology and made a cash settlement. Legal trouble even pursued him after his death. In 1970, *Maclean's* paid Igor Gouzenko the relatively small sum of $750 in an out-of-court settlement of a libel suit launched in connection with Fraser's 1964 article that had allegedly belittled the Soviet's role as a valuable defector.

Intelligent and courteous, a graceful stylist, Fraser was a strong federalist who personally admired Lester Pearson and deplored John Diefenbaker, but took care not to let it show in his copy. He wrote on 1 August 1953, during a federal election which saw the Liberal government back with a reduced majority, "Liberals are in a kind of Indian summer period and they know it all too well. They are quite certain they are coming back for one more term. But their certainty that it's the last term is so prevalent, so generally taken for granted, that it looks like a Freudian 'death wish'—a half-conscious desire to be defeated."

As a foreign correspondent in the period 1962-63, he was an equally shrewd observer, writing on 19 October 1963 in "The Tragic Strength of Apartheid" that "there is only one thing in sight that could weaken South Africa's position, by destroying the intellectual and moral pretensions of apartheid beyond repair, and that is the unqualified success of some other African nation in establishing a multi-racial state with a black majority."

But he was happiest in Ottawa, and writing about the nation. In his last article for *Maclean's*, "René Lévesque and the Separatists," he said

in July 1968 that separatists "cannot be deterred or defeated by economic arguments alone. Nothing can defeat them but proof that the
French identity can survive in Quebec and anywhere else in Canada,
whether backed by a majority or not."

The Canada of the 1950s, and *Maclean's* itself, was distinctly different from that of 1968. This was the *Maclean's* of whimsical covers by
Oscar Cahen (a mainstay also of *Chatelaine* and *New Liberty*, Cahen was
also a well-known abstract painter) and homey ones by Franklin
Arbuckle and Rex Woods. An Arbuckle cover for 29 October 1955 was
a sign of the times: an old man is puttering with a broom outside his
brick, gabled house; next door a high rise is going up. And, beginning
in 1948, the magazine ran cartoons by "Simpkin" (James Simpkin)
featuring Jasper the bear—a connection that would last until 1972. It
was also the magazine that included the majestic tedium of Bruce
Hutchison's work, and such departments as "In the Editor's [singular
this time] Confidence" editorials; "Backstage at Ottawa"; a "Letter,"
like Beverley Baxter's from London; followed by the feature articles
and fiction, a review column, for example, Clyde Gilmour on movies;
"Quiz"; "Cananecdotes"; "Mailbag"; "Wit and Wisdom"; and
"Parade." From March 1955 the magazine came out every two weeks
instead of twice a month that is, twenty-six issues a year instead of
twenty-four.

A favourite Allen contributor throughout the decade was June Callwood, Trent Frayne's wife, who was also a staple in *Chatelaine*. Her
"Not So Happy Gang" on 1 February 1950, about a bonhomous singing group on radio, was masterful reportage. In 1958, she had three
separate articles on diverse scientific topics published within five
months: the engine that was being built for the Avro Arrow, Canada's
innovative supersonic jet interceptor; the birth control pill; and, least
modestly of all, the universe.

Farley Mowat was now a regular, and there was still a good deal of
fiction in the magazine—the results of the annual competitions for short
stories and novels. The preface to the 1955 results for short stories
mocked such Canadian conventions as the "Small-Boy-Growing-Up-
On-the-Prairies Story; the Brave-Farmer-Battling-the-Frontier Story; the
Heroic-Bush-Pilot-Saving-the-Pretty-Girl Story." The 1955 winner for
novels was Morley Callaghan for "The Man With the Coat"—renamed
in book form *The Many-Coloured Coat*—which was illustrated with nine
pages of Cahen colour sketches. An 11 June piece that year featured
Herbert Manning's "What Virtue has done to Montreal." Wrote Manning: "The reformers are still chasing 'the girls' out of town and forc-
ing the bars to close on time." Allen himself was still doing a lot of
writing, including a multipart series on the boxer Jimmy McLarnin entitled "Don't Call Me Baby Face."

It was Allen who had to abase himself two years later. In the edition of 22 June 1957, Allen's "The Election and Democracy," which had to go to press before the federal election results were known, solemnly stated: "For better or for worse, we Canadians have once more elected one of the most powerful governments ever created by the free will of a free electorate. We have given that [Liberal] government an almost unexampled vote of confidence, considering the length of its term in office." The issue hit the newsstands a day after John Diefenbaker formed a new Conservative government. The next issue's "We Were Dead Wrong on Your Vote" accurately remarked that its predecessor was "worthy of a place in our trade's chamber of horrors beside the newspaper headlines and magazine covers which in November 1948 greeted Thomas E. Dewey as the new President of the United States some hours and days after he had been liquidated by Harry Truman."

In 1959, the year after Peter Newman went to Ottawa as its correspondent, *Maclean's* lost Pierre Berton. By now Berton had published several books and was a panelist on the CBC TV show *Front Page Challenge*. All this extracurricular activity, especially in a competing medium, did not sit well with the Maclean-Hunter executives, including Floyd Chalmers. Irked at any suggestion of curtailing his television work, Berton quit to become a *Toronto Star* columnist.

By 1960, the magazine's format encompassed the tinted paper "Preview"—"A Look at Tomorrow in Terms of Today"—with interwoven unsigned cartoons and caricatures, and "Backstage at Ottawa," "With Firewater," "In Diplomacy," and "In Education." There was also a "Background" of very brief items. By now Peter Gzowski, Ken Lefolii and Hal Tennant were assistant editors. The favoured feature writers were John Gray, Alan Phillips, a former jazz musician and ranchhand who began to contribute to *Maclean's* in 1956, and Robert Thomas Allen, prolific Toronto free lancer who specialized in light comic pieces.

It had been, by and large, a decade of external growth and internal stability. If, upon leaving, Ralph Allen had cried, *"Après moi...tout le monde!"*, he might have been justified.

II
Here Comes Everybody

The last issue to list Ralph Allen as editor was that of 23 April 1960. The May 7 issue had Blair Fraser at the top of the masthead. Much preferring to report to *Maclean's* readers, not Maclean-Hunter management, Fraser accepted reluctantly and gave himself two years to do the hated job. Later he would comment, "You know, whenever we got a really good article, I'd think, 'Gosh, what a first-rate writer Alan Phillips is!', and when we got a bad piece, I'd think 'What a lousy editor I am!' You can't keep going with an attitude like that!"

Neither was the administration happy. In Chalmers's view, Fraser relied too much on his managing editor, the Vancouver-born Ken Lefolii, whose penchant for exposés invited libel suits. Certainly, Lefolii's irreverence was signalled early. The 7 May issue with his piece "Is Air Travel Obsolete?" contained the statement, "Where there is a conflict between saving money and saving lives, money wins...." And on 13 August, in "I Sold My Vote—Twenty Times," the Montreal journalist Cathie Breslin told how the Union Nationale had taught her how to stuff five ballots into a box at once during the recent Quebec election. Her candidate *still* lost to René Lévesque. Said Breslin's instructor: "Well, they got their boys out too."

Under Fraser, the New Zealand-born Leslie Hannon, formerly in charge of the copy desk, opened a new London bureau, and the Maritimer Ian Sclanders went to Washington as U.S. correspondent. Marika Robert became a frequent contributor and there were cartoons and covers by George Feyer, Peter Whalley and Ed McNally. Perhaps swayed by the visual impact of television, the magazine under art director Alan Fleming began to have more imaginative layouts and picture spreads.

By 1962, Fraser wanted out. He was sent to London as overseas correspondent, and then returned to Ottawa, with Chalmers grumbling about the expense of shunting his family and him around the world. Fraser's self-educated sucessor, Ken Lefolii, a peripatetic traveller of Icelandic ancestry who once had worked in the Far East and Australia, was someone Chalmers "didn't like or trust."

The lack of trust may have had something to do with money. A factual error in a Lefolii piece called "Is Air travel Obsolete?" published shortly before his appointment had, his friend Peter Gzowski later noted, cost the magazine about $50,000 in cancelled advertising. As well, Lefolii's aggressive editing drew libel suits amounting to nearly nine million dollars. Although the suits spooked Maclean-Hunter management, none—except for a derisory $1 in damages awarded a Mafia don after an Alan Philips article appeared—were successfully prosecuted. They did, however, cost money to fight.

For the then huge sum of $1,000 a column, Pierre Berton had returned to express his opinions at the end of the magazine—thought to be a coup since his daily column in the *Toronto Star* had been tremendously successful. On 18 May 1963 Berton's piece was headlined "It's Time We Stopped Hoaxing the Kids About Sex." If, said Berton, his own daughters should "find themselves bedded with a youth (and I trust it will be a bed and not a car seat) I do not really believe the experience will scar their psyche or destroy their future marriages. Indeed I would rather have them indulge in some good honest, satisfying sex than be condemned to a decade of whimpering frustration brought on by the appalling North American practice called 'petting.' "

After the predictable outcry from *Maclean's* readers and a concerned memo from Chalmers, who feared lost advertising revenue, Berton wrote a second column replying to his critics. This never saw print in *Maclean's*—but did in the *Toronto Telegram* as "the column *Maclean's* wouldn't run." The publisher, Gerald Brander, who had that job since 1960, discreetly said he had "experimented with Mr. Berton on a series of magazine columns called the Pierre Berton page. After a period of six months [or 12 articles] we have decided to discontinue this feature." An incidental irony was the fact, according to Fulford in his memoir *The Best Seat in the House*, that although the editors resented what they regarded as managerial interference in this matter, Berton's column generally had been disappointing.

Maclean's was now in the news as much as it was reporting it. A 1964 Gzowski piece, "The Maple Leafs Money Machine," sinned against the advertising gods by doubting a claim by the Schick razor company that the entire hockey team had shaved with one blade. Even worse, Gzowski had copiously quoted coach Punch Imlach's favourite expletive, spelled in *Maclean's* as "----ing." When Chalmers saw the article, he ordered that copies already printed be destroyed, and "----" be substitued for "----ing." Gzowski would think of the incident as "The day the Schick hit the fan," Lefolii as a "----ing fuck-up."

If Gzowski and Lefolii upset management, they had admirers among his staff, including Fulford, whom they had hired in 1962 and who became articles editor, roughly third from the editorial top. The pair, Fulford recalled in *The Best Seat in the House*, "created a working atmosphere as good as any I've ever known.'' A master of the judicious silence, ''Lefolii was sympathetic and yet demanding, funny but also, in his way, stern.''

The Lefolii regime ended when Ronald McEachern, who had been shifted from publisher of the *Financial Post* to head Maclean-Hunter's magazine division, killed a Harry Bruce story about a Toronto newspaper strike, claiming it was unfair to both sides and a Toronto story, not a national one. Lefolii and Gzowski quit. Chalmers was pleased, at least about Lefolii, but was discomfited when staff writers Barbara Moon and Robert Fulford, reports and reviews editor Harry Bruce and assistant editor David Lewis Stein all resigned. They celebrated by drinking champagne and smashing glasses. For some, the best epitaph was provided by the U.S. critic Edmund Wilson, who in his book *O Canada: An American's Notes on Canadian Culture* commented that the editors had ''succeeded in transforming *Maclean's* from a rather inferior version of the kind of thing that we get in *McCall's* or the *Saturday Evening Post* into an outstanding journalistic achievement'' and called it ''regrettable that a change of management which involved putting a curb on the free expression of the findings and views of these writers should have resulted in the resignation of almost the whole staff and converted the magazine back again from a serious venture in reporting to an exploit in the higher pulp.'' As for Floyd Chalmers, he would later ask, ''Who won that battle?'' and then answered his own question: ''Nobody.''

Given what was happening at *Maclean's*, two of the magazine's 1964 features were especially symbolic: a 1 July 1964 Rex Woods cover showed a group squabbling over the design of the Canadian flag; the 19 September issue renamed the ''For the Sake of Argument'' column to simple ''Argument.''

By now many of the old *Maclean's* staffers, along with some new ones, had departed. Ralph Allen, Peter Newman, John Clare and Leslie Hannon had gone to the *Star* or *Star Weekly*. Mackenzie Porter had moved to the *Toronto Telegram*. In August there were new, or fairly new, arrivals: Keith Knowlton, who had been managing editor of *Chatelaine*; Hal Tennant, who had worked at *Maclean's* before becoming managing editor of *Canadian Homes and Gardens*; Alexander Ross and Jack Batten. In charge of these editors and staff writers was Borden Spears.

At first named executive editor, later editor, Spears had been managing editor at the *Toronto Star* and executive editor at the *Financial Post*. Not in good health—he had lost a lung to cancer in 1961—he was a tactful, fatherly and selfless man, a good choice to rebuild the staff and restore morale. He capably performed the former; the latter was probably beyond repair.

Under Spears, *Maclean's* cut back to monthly publication. By January 1967 it had a circulation of 575,000. Moreover, it made a profit.

Then, in January 1969, it switched to a page size closer to *Time*'s—it was now 20.5 cm by 28.5 cm—with more articles and features beginning and ending in one sequence of pages, rather than being "jumped."

But the impact of this diplomatic man was perhaps best expressed in the people he hired or rehired. German-born photographer Horst Ehricht, who became photography director in 1965, and art directors Imants Abolins and Jon Eby gave the magazine a new look that by 1968 included giant type in the table of contents, and a front-of-the-book "Maclean's Reports" on yellow newsprint. Alexander Ross and Philip Sykes served as managing editors; there were now "Maclean's Interviews"; the by-lines of Jon Ruddy and Douglas Marshall appeared often.

It was Marshall who movingly described the death of Blair Fraser on 12 May 1968, a month after Pierre Trudeau had been elected Liberal leader and two weeks after a federal election had been called. A keen canoeist who journeyed with a group of friends calling themselves the Voyageurs, Fraser drowned while on a weekend trip.

If Fraser represented an older, more dignified order, the feistiness of the young contributors, their unwillingness to respect their elders, was amply illustrated in Peter Gzowski's September 1968 review of Hugh MacLennan's novel *Return of the Sphinx*. MacLennan, who had been one of Ralph Allen's favourite contributors, was dispensed rough justice by Gzowski. Under the title "Yes, But Can Our Major Authors Write?" Gzowski compared MacLennan's work to that of the unspeakable best-seller Jacqueline Susann: "I can see little reason to treat MacLennan's newest work...with any more respect than *Valley of the Dolls*." Attacking the novel from several angles, he concluded that MacLennan had "written a very dull, impossible-to-believe book, falling far, far short of his pretensions"...that was "stilted, joyless and without insight....The only misconceptions *Return of the Sphinx* casts any light on are those about whether our so-called major writers are, in fact, able to write." MacLennan's Macmillan publisher, John Gray, wrote the reviewer: "My protest simply takes the form of a suggestion: that you paste a copy of your review in a scrapbook and read it once or twice a year, every year."

Another spot of irreverence might have been detectable in January 1969, when the cover depicted a papier-mâché caricature of "Our Pop-up Man," the recently elected Prime Minister, Pierre Trudeau. "I bought him sight unseen. Now what?" And the February editorial was "Let This Be Our Last Year in NATO." But lest readers be alarmed, there appeared in April one of Robert Thomas Allen's humorous, life's-little-vicissitudes pieces, "Hands Off My Door Knobs!"

It was as if the Maclean-Hunter management could not abide Spears's relatively pacific regime. In 1969, storm clouds rolled in, most of them swirling about the figure of R. A. McEachern.

In an earlier incarnation, Charles Templeton was a Bible-thumping revivalist.

Ronald McEachern, who had been with Maclean-Hunter since 1937, had a Ph.D., played the organ and had lectured in history at the University of Toronto. For many years he had been editor of the *Financial Post*, though he had never learned to type. He seems to have been disliked by almost everyone, including Floyd Chalmers, who would describe him as "a tense, brittle, somewhat unsocial work addict" who at the *Post* "wrote insulting comments" on his staff's copy and "rarely sent a kind note."

Brought in by Chalmers to sort out the libel suits Lefolii's staff had accumulated, he proceeded to prove himself a walking disaster as a publisher. Apparently deciding that *Maclean's* needed a high-profile editor, he took it into his head to hire Charles Templeton in 1969.

By this time Templeton, a high school dropout, had been: a newspaper sports cartoonist; a Youth for Christ evangelist and colleague of Billy Graham; a TV playwright, panelist and interviewer, producer and director of News and Public Affairs for the fledgling CTV network; managing editor of the *Toronto Star;* a candidate for the Ontario Liberal leadership; president of an advertising display company; and a partridge in a pear tree.

In debt from his last political campaign, Templeton welcomed McEachern's offer of a hefty salary, leased luxury automobile with free gas, oil, parking and washes at the company garage, paid-up pension, two weeks' paid vacation before starting and, if he wished, a five-year contract—not to mention a replica of McEachern's own rosewood drop-leaf table.

As Templeton describes him, McEachern was "a short, skinny man, stooped from a chronically bad back. He was in his late sixties, had thinning hair, a cadaverous face and an abrupt manner of speaking. When he wished to be, he was warm and companionable." The companionability worked, and Templeton prepared to move in, having gotten, on the advice of his friend and radio-show colleague Pierre Berton, assurances that he would be allowed to develop the magazine as he wished. There was a week's delay, however, when it was discovered that Templeton's new office was six inches larger than that of Maclean-Hunter's president, Donald Hunter (by now Chalmers was chairman). Naturally the floor space had to be reduced.

Upon arriving, Templeton got a taste of that old, warm *Maclean's* feeling: a group of feminists protesting a current issue that had run an excerpt from the anthropologist Lionel Tiger's supposedly misogynistic *Men in Groups*. Feminists weren't the only problem. Templeton was soon assaulted by a barrage of memos and scrawled-upon galley proofs from McEachern, many of them portraying *Maclean's* staff, the editor later remembered, "as lazy, untalented, pseudo-sophisticated and guilty of moonlighting on company time."

Spears, meanwhile, had been renamed executive editor. It was all very awkward. Templeton knew and respected Spears, and at McEachern's request, asked him to stay on at the magazine. But less than three months later McEachern sent Templeton a memo telling him to fire Spears. It was quickly retracted lest it cause more unfavorable publicity for the magazine.

McEachern certainly had a right to fear such. Resentful of Templeton who had never edited a magazine before replacing Spears, the key staff at *Maclean's* were ready to resign. But Spears calmed tempers. Given extended severance, he went back to the *Star*, where, among other things, he became the ombudsman columnist. By then he certainly had the qualifications to arbitrate disputes.

The chief of the magazine division was still on Templeton's back. He harassed him at weekly meetings, he asked a New York magazine consultant and Doris Anderson, *Chatelaine*'s editor, to suggest changes to the magazine, he vetoed changes Templeton made. According to Templeton, some of McEachern's suggestions included beginning a monthly, reader-contributed feature on " 'The Best Joke I've Heard on TV' " and doing "an article on a man in South Carolina who imports dragonflies to combat a mosquito problem...."

Templeton initiated a few changes. There was a new masthead design in June 1969, and the introduction of "Platform," a "Department of lively comment on national affairs." The first platformers were Dalton Camp, Laurier LaPierre and Keith Davey, a Templeton favourite for the department. August brought an odd two-page spread, on the left page was "Three Poets on the Moon," poems by Margaret Atwood,

Barry Charles and Al Purdy, barely legible against a dark background; on the right was a colour ad for the Bulova Oceanographer watch. Among the review columnists were Philip Sykes on books, Douglas Marshall on TV, Larry Zolf on films and Mavor Moore on ''The Lively Arts.''

When Templeton planned an entire issue devoted to analyzing the media, with the lead article by Peter Gzowski, McEachern ordered Templeton to cancel Gzowski and pay off the author, despite the fact that McEachern had not only not seen the article, but that the piece had not even been *written*. Next, Templeton's boss decided that the money losing *le Magazine Maclean, Maclean's* Quebec counterpart, should be stripped down to its editor Mario Cardinal, move to Toronto and become a mere translation of the English magazine.

Templeton objected to this politically insane suggestion. By then he was barely speaking to McEachern and his Toronto staff was prepared to walk out. Failing to get a definitive answer from Donald Hunter, Templeton quit and was joined by Cardinal. For its part, the staff sent out a press release: ''In the considered judgement of the undersigned *Maclean's* staff, Mr. Templeton and Mr. Cardinal are justified in their resignations. Mr. Templeton has been subjected to destructive harassment for several weeks. Mr. Cardinal, editor-in-chief of *le Magazine Maclean*, was misled into believing that the company would retain a measure of French-Canadian expression. Both men handled an impossible situation with dignity and principle and stand high in the esteem of their colleagues. In the interests of the magazine, Mr. Templeton has asked his staff to remain at their posts. Members of the staff will make their individual decisions on his request; those decisions will depend largely on the degree of editorial independence accorded by management to Mr. Templeton's successor.'' It was signed by the managing editor, Philip Sykes, as well as Alan Edmonds, Walter Stewart, Doug Marshall, Marjorie Harris, Jon Ruddy, Courtney Tower and others.

Nor was this the only missive that flew about. In a blistering letter to McEachern, Templeton accused him of harassment, interference, subterfuge and ''language that is intemperate, peremptory and arbitrary. Your attitude is akin to that of a master and a scholar and is often insulting in tone and content.''

While Templeton went on to other careers, the question naturally arose as to who would succeed him at *Maclean's*. Amazingly, on 6 October 1969, it was announced that it would be one-time staff member and rejected contributor, none other than Peter Gzowski. During Senate Committee hearings, Keith Davey asked McEachern, ''Now, who changed their mind? Did Gzowski change his mind about you or did you change your mind about Gzowski?'' McEachern replied, ''He asked for the job.''

Gzowski was certainly qualified. He had first joined *Maclean's* in 1958, a youthful veteran of three Thomson newspapers and at one point the youngest managing editor in the country. He had written cover stories, worked on the copy desk and edited the yellow pages, been Quebec correspondent in 1961, and was managing editor when he had quit in 1964. Since then he had gradually returned to the pages of *Maclean's*, at first camouflaged as the television reviewer "Strabo," then under his own name.

According to a friend, Harry Bruce, Gzowski did not then have the cuddly persona cross-country listeners would later come to love on his CBC-radio programs *This Country in the Morning* and *Morningside*. No, even before he returned to *Maclean's* as editor, Gzowski was fiercely ambitious.

> There was a look that came over his face in the magazine days. Perhaps some staff writer was urging on him a bad story idea. Perhaps a bunch of us had been sitting around his office for a solid hour, trying to think up the Perfect Article for an upcoming issue, but everything was stale. You could catch no change in the shape of Peter's mouth, or the expression in the red-rimmed eyes. He'd just push his hand back through the messy hair, look sideways at nobody, and there'd be this shadow of *distaste* all across his face, as though a welling of heartburn had just hit him. It wasn't deliberate. He couldn't help it. It said, *"I haven't the time for this, I just haven't the time."*

He certainly did not have much time at *Maclean's*. In February 1970, Gzowski ("Yes, once more, we're making some changes at *Maclean's*") set up a department called "In Our View—And Yours," to include Harry Bruce's column, readers' letters, a cartoon and "odd pronouncements, reports and wisecracks that strike us as weirdly typical of the times." But then, after less than seven months at the magazine, he resigned in April 1970. He'd had conflicts with both Hunter and McEachern, whose inimitable memos termed Bruce's column "ego ramblings." The management had suggested he take an extended leave of absence— *anything* to avoid another resignation. For Gzowski, the flashpoint appeared to have been a somewhat raunchy piece on the Montreal police morality squad by the novelist Mordecai Richler that, although toned down on request, still got vetoed by management. Ironically, only the week before his resignation Gzowski had announced a staff shake-up. Philip Sykes, the managing editor, would be transferred to Montreal; Courtney Tower, editor of the "Reports" section, and Imants Abolins would leave, with Abolins replaced by Ralph Tibbles of the *Toronto Star*; Keith Knowlton would go to the *Financial Post*.

When the dust settled, Sykes was appointed a senior editor and Gzowski was busy trying to raise money to launch a new Toronto magazine to be called *This City*. Had *Maclean's* readers only known much about it, the ruckus inside the magazine rivaled in entertainment value anything it had cause to report. As it was, the masthead during 1969-71 must have bewildered them. Often no editor was given, with only Philip Sykes listed at the top as managing editor. The magazine's length ranged from a high of 132 pages in April 1969 to a low of sixty-four pages in August 1970. In April 1971, there was no editor *or* managing editor listed, merely the designer, Ralph Tibbles.

Under these unsettled conditions, no editor could be expected to make much lasting impression on the magazine's pages, not even one so dynamic as Gzowski. The highlight during his tenure, for example, may have been Alan Edmonds's and photographer Don Newlands's May 1970 piece on the "S.S. Typhoid," about a typhoid fever outbreak in Vancouver. (The English-born Edmonds, who came to Canada in 1960, later became known for publicly enjoying himself on the CTV program *Live it Up!*) Figuratively speaking, the magazine was something like that ship.

Yet, despite all the turmoil, *Maclean's* circulation continued to grow. When Ralph Allen left in 1960, it was about 516,000; in 1970, it was 749,000. The next editor to be appointed was Peter C. Newman. He was the sixth—or was he the seventh?—editor in ten years.

WOMEN'S MAGAZINES
SHAKEOUTS AND BREAKOUTS

The magazines hardest hit in the postwar period came under the category of home, family and women's. The first to go was the *National Home Monthly*. With tight budgets and uncertain editorial direction, it had attempted to be both a general and a women's magazine. This was a formula for failure.

In 1946, E. P. Taylor hadn't thought so. On his way back from buying the British Columbia forestry portions of his Argus Corporation, Taylor stopped off in Winnipeg "to see," as Floyd Chalmers drily recalled, "if anything interesting was for sale in Manitoba." All that seemed on offer was the Stovel family firm that produced the *Home Monthly*. With the help of a public issue of bonds and preferred stock, Taylor bought control.

Apart from the debt financing, one enterprising thing Taylor did about the firm was to offer Chalmers the presidency and a stock option that would let him own it in a few years and would, incidentally, double Taylor's investment. The cagey Maclean-Hunter executive declined, and Lloyd Stovel remained president.

The *Home Monthly* was a losing cause. The number of its pages dropped from ninety-six in October 1946 to sixty-four in December 1947. A heavy cut-rate selling drive—including pretty women selling the magazine in beer parlours—instilled little confidence in advertisers, especially after a 1949 Canadian Advertising Research Foundation survey found that more than half the magazine's readers lived in rural areas and tended to have low incomes. And there were few readers per copy.

It was a beatable combination. Although it had made a profit for most of its sixty-one years of existence, the magazine lost severely after 1947, sinking to a circulation of 318,000. After a desperate three-month shift to a vest-pocket format, the *Home Monthly* collapsed, leaving the company with about $200,000 worth of useless printing equipment and costing fifty-four staff members their jobs. Rather than blaming itself, the company—which also published eight business publications—blamed both the depredations of *Time* and *Reader's Digest* and the hypocrisy of Manitoba legislation that forbid beer and liquor advertising, yet condoned its presence in magazines coming from outside the province.

Proof of the magazine's dismal performance came when *Canadian Home Journal, Maclean's* and *Chatelaine* absorbed the unfulfilled subscriptions. The trio added only an extra 12,000 copies to their circulations.

Elsewhere the postwar housing boom at first helped the circulation of *Canadian Homes and Gardens*, which had absorbed the smaller *Your House and Garden* in 1951, to shoot toward 100,000. But it was Maclean-Hunter's flagship women's magazine, *Chatelaine*, whose 1951 circulation was about 374,000, on which most of the profits or losses would ride.

In 1951, *Chatelaine*'s long-serving editor Byrne Hope Sanders, named a Companion of the British Empire for her war work, became partners with her brother Wilfrid Sanders, who for the previous ten years had been director of the Gallop-polling organization in Canada. This was a natural move because, under Sanders, *Chatelaine* had been keen on questionnaires—one of which had revealed that Canadian women did not realize wartime taxes on luxury were still in effect.

Lotta Dempsey, the new editor, had begun as a newspaper reporter in Edmonton, then had moved to Toronto in 1935, where her first freelance assignment—for the *Star Weekly*—had been to interview secretaries about their relationship with their bosses. Between free-lancing for *Chatelaine* and various editorial appointments there, she had written 316 articles, features and special columns in fifteen years—some of them under the names Carolyn Damon (fashion), Annabel Lee (beauty) and John Alexander (features)—taking time out only to have a baby and to do public relations work for the Wartime Prices and Trade Board.

A chirpy, energetic woman, Dempsey was, Sanders said in her farewell editorial, "what most of you are—a Canadian wife and mother." Upon being named editor, she "began dropping in at the office, apologetically but enthusiastically, a week ahead of time, bristling with ideas tapped out on her typewriter 'at four a.m. when I couldn't sleep.'" Dempsey displayed her editorial style in June 1952:

> There was literary feasting along with the salads when
> Associate Editor Almeda Glassey entertained a group of dis
> tinguished *Chatelaine* writers—all *Chatelaine* contributors—in
> honor of gold medal novelist Germaine Guevremont of Que
> bec, during her Toronto visit recently.
>   The guests—Canadian Authors Ass'n [sic] executives—
> included (right to left) Isabelle Hughes, Marjorie Campbell,
> Maud Parlow French and Isabel LeBourdais....[Guevremont
> was the] only woman and only Canadian on *Saturday Review
> of Literature's* list of the world's ten most promising authors

COMPLETE — A NEW NOVEL BY MAZO DE LA ROCHE

Chatelaine
FOR THE CANADIAN WOMAN
NOVEMBER 1952 30 CENTS

THE MUCH MISUNDERSTOOD
DUKE OF EDINBURGH

LMOST LOST MY HUSBAND"
See page 7

CANADIAN TALENT & BEAUTY SERIES
June Callwood — Writer

To belong in Chatelaine's "Canadian Talent and Beauty Series" in 1952, the talented June Callwood needed beauty — and a child.

last year. We charged her to hurry back to Sorel and concentrate on her first story in the English language which is to be for *Chatelaine*.

Dempsey's *Chatelaine* concentrated on young parents—there was a postwar boom in *them*. There were other sorts of articles. In June 1952, "Canada's greatest gadabout," Kate Aitken, whose radio broadcasts were immensely popular, contributed "Tells You How to Travel Without Trouble." She "wrote travel tips for you while flying around the world in 308 hours—103 flying, 201 working, 4 in bed." The magazine had not tired of royalty. An article posing the question "Can the Duchess of Windsor Ever Live in England" prompted many letters in August 1952, saying "Let the Windsors Wander."

The November 1952 cover was of a mother and baby, June Callwood and her daughter, Jennifer. Earlier, Callwood had informed the magazine she "would be producing no more stories for a few months because she had a most vital project on the way...." This Madonna and Child cover would have been more to the liking of E. G. Reid, who in this issue wrote to protest a September cover: "With all the beautiful flowers, fruits, and other subjects to choose from, all you have to offer is another leg show, on a scantily clad young woman."

In August 1952, Dempsey left to become a columnist on the *Globe and Mail* (and later on the *Toronto Star*), and John Clare was named editor. In retrospect, Floyd Chalmers was unable to account for why a man had been named editor. Probably because he was handy. With

Maclean-Hunter since 1946, the New Brunswick-born, Saskatchewan-reared Clare had until recently been managing editor of *Maclean's.*

While Clare was editor, an underling made considerable headway. Doris McCubbin first appeared on the masthead in February 1952 in charge of "editorial promotion." Her job was to get the magazine noticed on radio and TV. She also wrote articles, managed the service department and became managing editor at the time of Clare's appointment. Like Lotta Dempsey, she was an Albertan: she had been raised in Calgary and had free-lanced for the local *Herald.* Like Byrne Hope Sanders, she had worked in the Eaton's advertising department.

Although as Doris Anderson she later made her reputation as the feminist editor of *Chatelaine,* the influence of the women's movement was not conspicuous while she was managing editor. A January 1957 feature, "How to Cook for a Man," revealed the secrets of Corporal Arthur Finnegan, the cook at the RCAF base at Goose Bay, Labrador. "'Women make one big mistake cooking for men. They get too fancy.' He reports that air-force men generally pass up highly spiced foods, lima beans, prune whips and most salads and fish." The male-tempting picture layout showed three boxes that read, left to right: "First, tempt him with that delicious smell... And if he's a man who likes his food hearty then... You can't miss if you serve him Veal Scallopine." The recipe was on page fifty-two.

The fiction that *Chatelaine* published still conformed to the formulaic romantic conventions hilariously summarized by Joyce Marshall in June 1950—oddly enough in—*Chatelaine* in '"Ten Plots I Could Do Without.'' Excerpts follow:

> Plot Number One: Mother Takes a Holiday:
> Harassed wife and mother, burdened to the teeth with
> domesticity goes for a holiday alone and meets the Oh-so-
> fascinating man. He doesn't know she's married. (She intends
> to tell him but doesn't get around to it.) She reminds him of a
> candle or a lily and in no time at all she consents to walk
> along the shore with him after dark. Then, while the lost
> dreams of girlhood begin to flutter in her heart, he Shows
> Himself in His True Colours. Furthermore he considers that
> by walking alone with him at night she has shown herself in
> hers. Aghast and scandalized, she flees to her hotel and
> catches the first train home. (There is always a train leaving
> almost at once, though it necessitates rapid packing.) And
> back she goes to the dear dull husband who has no True
> Colours to show himself in and who, she now realizes, makes
> the Whole Thing Worth While After All.

> Plot Number Eight: The Boss Comes to Dinner.
> Husband doesn't let his wife know till half past four. It's

"But What About Love?" runs the headline for Ann Gibbons's story in November 1952. "Stacey had a dream — all about a big house, a rich husband . . . and love."

Wednesday. The store are closed and there's nothing to eat in the house. And there's Promotion in the Wind. So our heroine opens cans, talks her neighbour into lending her the spare roast she chances to have about the house, whips up a meal somehow. But her troubles aren't over. One of the children spills soup in the boss's lap, while the other crawls under the table to play choo-choo. Promotion recedes as sadly the wife ladles soup out of the boss's lap. But it seems that he is Human After All. He's tired of perfect meals which is all he ever gets at home. He enjoys the novelty of a lapful of soup, and he loves the way the shine is working through the powder on the little wife's nose. It reminds him of his own wife's nose in the happy day when they were poor and had no maid to serve them perfect meals. And he offers the young man a promotion twice as good as anything he had dared to expect.

Plot Number Nine: Old Flames Last Flicker
Heroine meets her old beau who has been a blazing success while her husband, dear dull fellow that he is, has been a plodding half-success. They meet for a drink in one of those discreet little places off the Avenue. (She feels very daring as she sips hers and hopes it won't go to her head.) Disillusionment may come in either of two ways. He's changed so much that his new hardness and ruthlessness frighten her. Or he's changed so little that he's now a pathetic would-be Playboy with a Paunch. With a little sigh she puts the image she has half-cherished all her married life out of her mind and hurries home to the happy apartment or bungalow where Love Lives.

Yet *Chatelaine* also blended in more challenging fiction. Alice Munro's work appeared in the magazine, and the story that won *Chatelaine*'s fiction contest in 1957, by the playwright Elda Cadogan of Durham, Ontario, was a sympathetic tale of teenage sexual confusion. A boy is charged with rape; as for the alleged victim, "Her parents had told her just what to say in court. But why couldn't she tell the real story of that soft September night?"

Not all *Chatelaine*'s literary content was so authentic. Hugh Garner recalled that, after he'd gotten a poem from a woman in a Kingston penitentiary and promised to try to get it published, he'd sent it to John Clare, who ran it in *Chatelaine*. Then he got a phone call from Clare: "Listen, Garner, don't give me any more stuff from your jailbird friends! That poem was stolen holus-bolus from *Ladies Home Journal* and they're threatening to sue!"

In 1958, the magazine lost a longtime columnist on marital and medical problems when Dr. Marion Hilliard, the chief of obstetrics and gynecology at Women's College Hospital in Toronto, died. Hilliard had written a best-selling book based on her *Chatelaine* work. In other departments, though, the menu was as before. In November, the magazine noted that "Women on their toes look for the Chatelaine Seal of Approval whether for spices or corsets, doors or baby carriages. The square Seal sign means the product is on the level. We know!" The magazine recommended Blue Ribbon spices.

The only problem was, *Chatelaine* gave no reasons *why*.

The next few years were to be fatal for some Canadian home and women's magazines. Which would not have been so disheartening had new ones started. But few had or would in the three decades after the war, and those that did were small, like *Newfoundlander: Newfoundland Home Monthly* (1949-53) and Cassie Brown's *Newfoundland Woman Magazine* (1961-64).

Mayfair, handmaid to the affluent, was reduced to beggary. Dispatched from *Maclean's* to edit it, the self-confessed hack Eric Hutton—a survivor of the defunct *Magazine Digest* and *National Home Monthly*—gave Robert Fulford, its assistant editor, his first chance to write about painters.

In 1955, Maclean-Hunter sold its money-losing *Mayfair* and its semi-annual *Canadian Bride* to Montrealer David B. Crombie, an advertising and promotion man who had once started *Nassau* magazine for the Bahamas government and most recently had been with *Reader's Digest*. *Mayfair*, which had earlier competed with newspaper women's pages and the society pages of *Saturday Night*, reaching a peak circulation of 20,000, had by now attempted to become a leisure and travel magazine. Pierre Berton said in 1958 that "this magazine stands foursquare for those eternal values which have helped us to build this new, raw nation of ours—*money*." Renamed *Mayfair International*, the magazine had little success and capitulated in 1961.

Elsewhere the postwar housing boom at first helped the circulation of *Canadian Homes and Gardens*, which had absorbed the smaller *Your House and Garden* in 1951, to shoot toward 100,000. By 1954, when Robert Fulford joined as a copy editor, it was struggling. Jean McKinley, an editor deeply steeped in the current theories of industrial psychology, "ran her thin and unsuccessful service magazine in a style that wouldn't have been inappropriate for some lush American publication like *Vogue* or *House and Garden*." Under McKinley and her successor Gerald Anglin *Canadian Homes and Gardens* was a cosy, attractive twenty-five-cent magazine—Jeanne Mehinnick on antiques, Peter Varley in charge of photography—and had given Floyd Chalmer's daughter Joan a job after her graduation from the Ontario College of Art. The magazine tried a new format and title, *Canadian Homes*—"The New Magazine of Canadian Living"—in 1961 to small effect. The next year it was sold to Southam Press and became a flimsy newspaper rotogravure insert.

Throughout the 1950s the circulation of the only magazine to pose a direct threat to *Chatelaine, Canadian Home Journal*, ranged in tandem with it between 400,000 and 500,000 copies. Selling at ten cents to *Chatelaine*'s fifteen, it was edited by Mary Etta MacPherson, a former *Chatelaine* person and the wife of Herbert McManus, who edited *Mayfair* and now worked for *Saturday Night*. True to the inbred nature of Canadian magazine publishing, the author of the "How to Stay Married" column in the *Home Journal* was J. K. Thomas, former publisher of the *National Home Monthly*; a typical title was January 1955's "The Belittling Wife: a Message for Mrs. Dagwood."

Given that Jack Kent Cooke, owner of its publisher, Consolidated Press, wanted to get out of magazine publishing, *Canadian Home Journal* was probably doomed, even apart from the fact that it was losing money. In 1958, Cooke sold it to Maclean-Hunter for $250,000, $10,000 of which was for the name and $240,000 tax-deductible for the subscription list. Losing money in the 1950s, *Chatelaine*, after a merger with the *Home Journal*, suddenly became profitable. The cover price was a compromise fifteen cents, and for a while the magazine bore the compendium title *Chatelaine, the Canadian Home Journal*.

The results were impressive. The merger gave *Chatelaine* the largest paid circulation of a Canadian magazine up until then, and record amounts of advertising lineage and dollar volume. By 1959, *Chatelaine*'s circulation was nearly 746,000—it had doubled in eight years.

After John Clare left *Chatelaine* in 1957, Maclean-Hunter procrastinated about naming the obvious candidate, Doris Anderson, as editor, and throughout 1957 and 1958 anomalously listed her at the top of the masthead as managing editor. Anderson's bitterness at the delay later came through in interviews and in her novel *Rough Layout*. As Ander-

Plucked eyebrows and upswept perm notwithstanding, the capable Doris Anderson led Chatelaine *into the feminist revolution.*

son tells it, neither her fiancé nor Maclean-Hunter management wanted her to be editor.

Floyd Chalmers won't admit it happened, but it happened all right. He dropped into my office one day with the news that he was going to make Gerry Anglin the editor. "Well, I'll resign," I told him. He was stunned. "But you're getting married and you're going to be a hostess"—I loved the priority— "and a mother!" My future husband didn't want me to take the job either. He thought it fine being married to a managing editor but he didn't want to marry the editor—which was *the* big job. Damn it all, I'd worked for it.

Anderson respected Anglin, but "really didn't think he knew as much about women and women's magazines as I did. So I gave my husband a choice: either I'd stay at home and write short stories and he could support me, or I would take the editor's job. Reluctantly, everyone agreed; they decided to give me a chance, though I didn't get the title for a year or so. As 'managing editor,' I completely redesigned *Chatelaine* and had a baby while I was doing it. *Then* they made me editor."

In his memoirs, Chalmers disputed this version. "Doris thinks her job was in jeopardy when she married, but this isn't true. I thought it was good for the magazine for her to marry and have children, which she did. I must say that Doris managed the births of her three sons with great thoughtfulness. She usually had them about five hours after finishing the last editorial and sending the issue off to the printer."

For all its unpersuasive romantic trappings and its pervasive air of special pleading, *Rough Layout* is fascinating both as a *roman à clef* and an insider's look at the mechanics and politics of producing a magazine.

Judith Pemberton, the heroine, is the managing editor of the magazine *Young Living*, housed in "Meridian Corp'."'s high rise on University Avenue in Toronto. Meridian also publishes *Canada's Own*

Magazine, "a hybrid of *Time* and a general magazine" that "combined news and short articles." Married with two children, Judith believes in the "present-day carefully worked-out equations for coupling: Equality, Sharing, Respect and Communication equals home."

Balancing home and work is not easy, nor is work itself.

At the turn of the century, women's magazine had been filled with etiquette, crafts and cooking as middle-class women strove to master the niceties of moving upward in North American society. The thirties and forties had found magazines instructing women in how to cope with a depression [sic] and then the war. Post World War Two brought another change. The stress was on families and "togetherness." But since the mid-sixties, women had been seeking other lifestyles and freedoms In the mid-seventies, most Canadian women did not consider themselves feminists. Her readers expected to be instructed and entertained in a general magazine like *Young Living*. The management of Meridian expected her to attract readers, but she must not get too sensational (which would scare away advertisers) or get into any law suits. She had to convince management that she could provide the right "mix" of personality profiles, how-to pieces, and "think" pieces to satisfy all potential readers.

The editor of *Young Living* is an alcoholic former newsman who was Pemberton's mentor when they both worked at a newspaper. Also on staff is the art director, who "constantly pushed for innovation, and he considered fashion photography the ideal place to experiment with avant-garde photographers." The fashion editor, however, "was dedicated to showing women the cut of the garment and the detailing." Pemberton's copy editor, ally and colleague on a transition house for battered women, is the capable Gretchen, who is described doing a typical magazine task: "She had black-pencilled half a dozen sentences and all superfluous words. The lead, which had been overwritten and vague, was now compact and punchy, and it exactly fitted the space that Greg had blocked out on the layout—the big, blue-squared sheet they used to show precisely where pictures and copy would fit."

Driving her and Gretchen crazy is the publisher, the insanely grinning Gordon Bradbury, "Crazy Horse", who pesters Jude with "unworkable ideas, fussed about colour reproduction, and wasted precious time. He called *Young Living* 'the Product.' He spoke of circulation as '750,000 units a month,' the cover was the 'packaging.' Readers were 'potential consumers.'" He had a "degree in commerce from the Zenith Academy for executives, an obscure correspondence school in Iowa. Three secretaries had been fired because they simply could not translate into any kind of logical prose the lengthy monologues he spent hours dictating every day." Because Crazy Horse can't make up his mind about the size of the issues, the editors can't plan "the back-of-the-book-turns" and the magazine is late to the printer.

Judith's husband tells her that one day "They'll move him into some spot where he can't do any harm. Like Corporate planning—that's a good catch-all for corporate duds." In the meantime, Crazy Horse plagues her with ideas like doing fashion photographs on 8 × 8 film, which she knows isn't fast or flexible, and is expensive. But it does show skin tones. "Crazy Horse's vision. Battalions of trend-setters filled the streets; jumped into cabs wearing ultrasuede; wore shoes by Charles Jourdan, nail colour by Revlon, mascara by Elizabeth Arden, blusher by Dubarry and five different shades of eye makeup."

Judith tangles with obtuse Meridian executives, is courted by a *Canada's Own* features writer and poet and despises that magazine's editor, "Roy Baxter":

> During his association with *Canada's Own Magazine* legions of young women had either been broken before his big black pencil and his mocking caustic tongue or broken into his bed....Other young women were brought along as "researchers". They collected the facts, sweated in libraries, made the phone calls and then offered up all this information on neatly typed pages to the writers—all male—who got the bylines. Researchers were being trained, Roy said, to become writers. In good time.
>
> But in the last few years, the women on the magazine had rebelled. Now there was a woman copy editor. Another woman ran one of the minor departments. Another woman wrote a regular column, a caustic pan of her own sex on most occasions. Roy moved with the times.

But Baxter is only a minor problem. When Judith discovers her husband is having an affair, she retaliates by sleeping with a nice old millionaire. Back at the office she learns that Crazy Horse wants to replace the editor, about to retire, with a brainless but photogenic TV hostess. She confronts Meridian's boss and gets the job—on a trial basis.

The magazine that Doris Anderson began to command was to be, as the final issue of *Canadian Home Journal* said, "a newly planned, freshly edited women's magazine, combining the best of both publications and adding many new features." But in the event, *Chatelaine* greatly predominated.

According to Anderson, Maclean-Hunter "didn't want me to push articles on feminism or inequality or anything like that, but I was already doing it before they realized what was going on and the magazine was *very* successful.'" As she told her interviewer, "We redesigned the whole magazine, giving it a more mod look with lots of white space and contemporary graphics and layout. I started columns on mental health, on activities for women in their communities and on politics."

Anderson may give herself too much credit. She was marching in step with a new audience that no self-respecting publisher would choose to ignore. That she did sometimes lead the battalion is unquestionable. The headline for an April 1962 editorial asked: "What's become of the dreaded 'women's vote'?" The subheading was "We're not taken seriously."

In promoting her views, Anderson was assisted by writers and editors who would become highly visible in Canadian writing and broadcasting. Though it would be a 1973 *Globe Magazine* article that led to her best-selling book *Some Men Are More Perfect Than Others*, Merle Shain, a Toronto social worker who had turned to free-lancing, did a lot of work for *Chatelaine*, including a rapturous cover story, "Pierre Trudeau: His Own Man," in September 1968. Shain had been a Trudeau worker during his campaign for the Liberal leadership. A frequent contributor was Sondra Gotlieb, wife of Allan Gotlieb, later Canadian ambassador to the United States. She later wrote the humourous *Wife Of....* (satirizing sentences like the preceding). Barbara Frum, later a stellar interviewer on radio and TV, wrote features, the first being a piece about why lawyers didn't want women on juries. Adrienne Clarkson, the television host, diplomat and publisher, was books editor for a time. Michele Landsberg, who returned to work after her husband, Stephen Lewis, became Ontario NDP leader, was given office space to write a guaranteed eight articles a year.

Landsberg told Susan Crean:

My feminism was there but it was not the burning issue for me that children were. Doris fought me every step of the way on that. When I wanted to write a piece on breast-feeding, she would insist that I balance it and not overemphasize the importance, in case I made other women feel guilty that they had to wean their babies and return to work. I didn't understand their point of view then; I had contempt for it. But Doris was sensitive and was always on the side of choice for women.

"Landsberg," says Crean, "soon joined with the other *Chatelaine* women who would gather around at editorial meetings once a month to complain that yet another nameless model was being put on the cover. It wasn't feminist. 'It sells copies,' Anderson would growl. End of the monthly debate."

Anderson did not in fact lose sight of the vast majority of her readers, who were far from being doctrinaire feminists. Lily McQueen's "Why You Can't Get Domestic Help" in November 1967 was an age-old topic for women's magazines. *Chatelaine* ran "Are You Mrs. *Chatelaine*?"

Carole Anne Soong is what Mrs. Chatelaine is all about
BY MOLLIE GILLEN

She's a person in all her roles: ardent supporter of the
rights of the individual, full partner in marriage and
parenthood, project director of an LIP grant, active
member of the B.C. Status of Women Council, elected
alumni senator of the University of British Columbia,
and the unanimous choice as our 1973 winner

*By 1973,
Chatelaine had
totally revised
what it was all
about.*

contests—prize: $1,000 and a dishwasher, china set, wristwatch and
Corningware—and articles with titles like "Omar Sharif—Lonely Man"
and "Steve McQueen—A Family Kind of Man." But along with the
inevitable coverage of the Royal Family ("A Visit to Princess Margaret's
Dressmaker"), she could use humour to make a serious point, as in
Sonja Sinclair's October 1968 article: "Chatelaine's secret agent, Bozena
Svobodova, set out in a fright disguise and jawbreaking accent to expose
discrimination of Canadian bureaucrats against new immigrants."

The combination worked. In 1957, 10.7 percent of the adult Canadian reading public read *Chatelaine*. In 1962, the figure was an astonishing 22.1 percent. By 1970, *Chatelaine*'s monthly circulation was 979,000.

The late 1960s marked two determined bids to reach women through
controlled circulation magazines. In 1966, *Homemaker's Digest*, owned
by Gordon Badger and Randall Muner, made such inroads that it was
launching versions of itself in the United States, Britain and Germany.
Eventually, though, they had to sell off their U.S. interests and lost control of the Canadian edition. Maclean-Hunter produced a controlled-
circulation magazine of its own, the 800,000-circulation *Hostess*, initially profitable but one that succumbed as a result of a steep increase
in postal rates. The company, however, succeeded in 1966 when it
hived off *Miss Chatelaine*. It was soon selling 120,000 copies.

Doris Anderson, named to Maclean-Hunter's board of directors in
1972, was at or near the top—not just of the company, but of changing
social mores.

A March 1963 article suggesting that abortion might at times be per-
missible almost got her fired. By January 1973, she was able to say confidently that "...Dr. [Henry] Morgentaler is on trial for the fourth
time—a miscarriage of justice, a personal victimization, and a mock-
ery of our jury system." Abortion, she said, "should be taken out of
the criminal code and become a matter between a woman and her doctor."

The 1973 "Mrs. *Chatelaine*" was the new ideal: "Carole Ann Soong is what Mrs. Chatelaine is all about." The magazine described her as "a person in all her roles: ardent supporter of the rights of the individual, a full partner in marriage and parenthood, project director of a LIP [Local Initiatives Project] grant, active member of the B.C. Status of Women Council, an elected alumni senator of the University of British Columbia and the unanimous choice as our 1973 winner."

Summing up her two decades in charge of *Chatelaine*, Anderson used what could easily be interpreted as the Royal Imperative in September 1977:

> When I took over in 1959 as editor, women in politics, medicine, law and business were as rare as whooping cranes. Less than one percent of the House of Commons, two percent of the legal profession, five percent of doctors were women. Hardly any women were enrolled in business schools, nor did any woman sit on any stock exchange, and very few appeared on boards of most corporations. When we wrote our first article on battered babies in October 1960, the public and social agencies were appalled. We were accused of being sensational—until two years later the issue of battered babies became a high-priority topic, and laws were passed to try and protect these tiny helpless victims.
>
> The first time we ran an article on reform of our abortion laws in March 1963, threats that the magazine would be closed down and that I personally would be fired resulted. (And we still get the same virulent letters every time we return to that controversial topic.)..."We've encouraged women to get into politics at every level and there are more women in politics today than at any time in Canadian history. We've argued that Canadian children in Canadian schools should learn about their country from Canadian schoolbooks—and not from imports. We've forwarded the idea that Canadians should be able to see films about Canada in Canadian theatres. We've labored long and hard to keep the magazine industry in this country alive and flourishing against pretty tough odds at times....

That *Chatelaine* was alive and flourishing was due to several factors: the shakeout in the industry that put *Chatelaine* alone among mass-circulation Canadian women's magazines; the dynamic leadership of Doris Anderson; and a society that was changing so fast it was hard to tell whether Anderson was a product or an instrument of the revolution—or both.

PART FOUR

THE UNCOMMON MARKET

Sometimes it seemed as if every magazine in Canada was in pell-mell pursuit of the same ideal consumer. This vision of upward mobility had two cars, two homes and one large disposable income.

"Consumer," not "reader," was the operative noun. Magazines were bought not so much because of their editorial contents but because they and, even more so, their advertisements, complemented the consumer's lifestyle. Of course, advertisements had long been a mainstay of magazines, and one function of magazines had always been their totemic social significance: how they looked on the coffee table, how well they blended with the reader's status. But never before had these qualities been so overpowering.

And never before had the line between selling and information been fudgier, especially in the form of "advertorials" in which advertising and editorial content were virtually indistinguishable. Controlled-circulation magazines, distributed on "postal walks" through affluent neighbourhoods, were another example. The *reductum ad absurdum* was probably the "magalogue," which promoted its consumer goods by means of a unifying editorial theme. In late summer 1987, it was reported that six new consumer publications chiefly peddling clothing and cosmetics—including two magalogues—would be launched within the next nine months.

Another kind of blurring occurred in the method of magazine distribution. Some controlled-circulation magazines displayed their wares on newstands; some paid-circulation magazines selectively gave themselves away in order to guarantee advertisers a specific number of readers.

Magazines aimed "vertically" at increasingly specialized audiences, yet more often than not were part of multi-media corporations. No matter how different their subject matter, the magazines of the 1970s and 1980s often seemed published for the same consumer, the red logos of their covers beckoning the shopper to buy, buy, buy. Marketers took their vocabulary or mental habits from sociologists. They talked of "taste cultures," "lifestyles" and "market segments," and sought their buyers in extroverted belongers, emulators and achievers. As William Leiss has said, publishers had come to regard their magazines as "vehicles which organized audiences into clearly identifiable target groups that could be sold to advertisers; the audiences themselves became the 'products' generated by the media industry."

To that end, magazines endlessly engaged in "restructuring" and "repositioning," emphasizing "service" articles—often uncritical surveys of buyable goods. Magazines often resembled trade shows: a subscription was like the admission charged for the privilege of spending *more* money. If there was any trend away from narrowly defined blocks of consumers in the late 1980s, it was probably toward "psychographic" magazines, which emphasized their readers' mind-set, not lifestyle.

Whatever their specialty, often the magazines seemed edited and written by the same person. So formulaic was the visual design and writing of many magazines that the annual awards ceremony of the National Magazine Awards Foundation sometimes seemed intended to publicize the presentation of a gold medal from a tuxedoed Tweedledee to a corduroyed Tweedledum.

Some trends had critics within the magazine community. Val Clery commented that

> The success of an original magazine format (*New York* magazine is a pertinent example) prompts a proliferation of similar magazines or supplements here, scrabbling with each other over every ignominious scrap of information on city living and over every fragment of available advertising, to the ultimate intellectual and financial impoverishment of all. Financial gossip magazines become briefly popular with affluent readers and inevitably the formula is reproduced by competitors; every general-interest sprouts a financial gossip section, with inevitably diminishing returns.

One journalist quoted by Peter Hendry, the last editor of the *Family Herald and Weekly Star*, trenchantly called one intrinsic weakness of readership surveys—which often led to a magazine's radically changing format and emphasis—the "Apple Pie Theory of Journalism." A survey discovers that readers like recipes:

> On that basis, the entire magazine switches to recipes. Further research reveals that, among all the recipes, those which

are most popular with readers are pie recipes and once more the magazine is changed to specialize completely in pie recipes. One more batch of research discovers that the most popular kind of pie recipe is apple pie. You end up with a magazine which publishes nothing but apple pie recipes.

Overlapping editorial and advertising functions worried some, like Don Obe, a former editor of *The Canadian* and *Toronto Life*. "It's understood that advertisers want to reach upscale readers, the people who spend the most," said Obe. "Now there is tremendous pressure on editors to do stories that supposedly appeal to these people, and editorial formats are reshaped to fit that market."

Those who edited paid-circulation magazines sometimes had a class prejudice against controlled-circulation magazines, claiming that the latter practiced pseudo-journalism. Yet the better controlled-circulation magazines, like *Quest*, often shared writers with periodicals like *Saturday Night*. And the editors of both sometimes perceived the calculations of the Print Measurement Bureau as unreliable and tyrannical. The PMB, which was founded as an industry-wide nonprofit organization in 1973 and, ten years later, influenced the purchase of about $200-million in national advertising annually, surveyed the readership of consumer magazines and provided information on the customer's age, education, income, marital status, occupation and product usage. It was the PMB's report on *Quest* that led to that magazine's demise.

The Aftermath of Bill C-58

The mid-1980s were economically buoyant, and many new magazines came bobbing in on the tide. This prosperity—perhaps more apparent than real—was one reason for growth. Television, too, proved not to be the murderous bogie that had been feared in the early 1960s. Just as the uncommon market emphasized "targeting" among magazines, something similar was happening in radio and TV, which had its specialized Pay-TV channels and cable systems. In 1967, 42.2 percent of Canadian households had cable television. In 1981, the figure was 70.7. Then, of course, there was Bill C-58.

The impact of Bill C-58 was pervasive, and its ownership provisions were not even substantially undermined by the Canada-U.S. Free Trade Agreement enacted in 1988, which called for the abolition of those sections of the Income Tax Act stating that magazines must be printed or typeset in Canada before advertisers could claim a business expense deduction. The other provisions of Bill C-58 were left intact, as was the customs tariff, introduced in 1966, which forbid the entry into Canada of periodicals which had split runs or which carried more than five percent of advertising referring to "specific sources of availability in Canada"—though the government proposed that the tariff would be altered to permit the entry of Canadian-owned but American-printed magazines. Defenders of the Free Trade Agreement—such as Maclean Hunter, which had been the main beneficiary of Bill C-58—also pointed out that the Canadian government was committed to ensuring that Canadians must have a chance to buy a Canadian subsidiary of a company involved in a cultural activity if it underwent a change of foreign owners.

Opponents of the Free Trade Agreement, such as most members of the Canadian Magazine Publishers Association, not only resisted any further trend towards one big continental market but noted that the agreement had a "notwithstanding" clause which allowed the United States to retaliate with actions of "equivalent commercial value" against any future cultural policies that might harm its interests. As well, the United States considered that the Canadian second-class postal rate—vital to the magazine industry's welfare—amounted to a subsidy. Nationalists feared that this measure—like many other "Canadian subsidies"—might eventually vanish.

Whatever the outcome of the Free Trade Agreement, there is no doubt that Bill C-58 had given an important psychological boost to many smaller magazines. Certainly it was difficult to see that anyone lost from it.

Reader's Digest remained the largest-circulation magazine in Canada, reaching about 1,344,000 subscribers. The Reader's Digest Association (Canada) Ltd., having been given softer treatment than *Time* on its content requirements—and indeed adding more material of Canadian origin and authorship—solved the problem of Canadian ownership for the French and English *Digests* in October 1976 by putting them under the umbrella of a tax-free foundation, some of whose proceeds were supposed to advance Canadian journalism. The remaining, highly profitable part of the company—the mail-order business in books, records and educational materials—remained largely owned by Reader's Digest Inc. of New York.

Time chose a different method. Although still printed in Canada, it published its last Canadian editorial pages on 2 March 1976. With a circulation of 550,000 in 1976, it cut its advertising rates in half and dispensed with special rates or subscription bonuses. Although a year later its circulation was down to 300,000, by 1986 it had recovered to about 350,000, in the interim dramatically increasing its ad and subscription rates.

Since both *Time* and *Reader's Digest* were still printed in Canada, they got more attractive rates than if they were mailed from the United States, although higher than those enjoyed by Canadian-owned magazines. And both remained profitable. Even *Newsweek* began to be printed in Canada and put on a direct-mail drive that raised its Canadian circulation form 59,000 to 116,000.

No losers there.

This 1989 cover of the repatriated TV Guide *offered untypical Canadian content.*

TV GUIDE
April 22-28 $1.00

WHY I QUIT MAN ALIVE by ROY BONISTEEL

DANA DELANY
China Beach may be a losing battle—but she'll survive

Plus: On the set of The Jim Henson Hour

Money Matters
Canada Business Week

Although U.S. magazines accounted for more than seventy-five percent of newstand sales, the U.S.-owned *TV Guide*, for many years a circulation-leader among Canadian magazines, was taken over by Télémedia, a Montreal-based company that owned a string of radio stations and community newspapers, *Canadian Living* and, since 1986, two success stories of the preceding decade, *Harrowsmith* and *Equinox*.

In the case of *TV Guide*, whose 1988 circulation was 816,000, the acquisition did not necessarily mean steeply increased Canadian content. The television critic Joan Irwin, who had been an associate editor on the magazine, pointed out in August 1986 that her U.S. bosses had been "monumentally bored by just about everything Canadian. Trying to get a Canadian feature into the magazine could take weeks of strenuous argument, first getting past the yawns and then beating down the hostility." Then, too, it was "cheaper to rejig a U.S. story or insert a few paragraphs of Canadian content than it was to commission an original Canadian story." Native born though they might be, the new owners, in Irwin's view, didn't show any "evidence of real dedication to Canadian television."

Dedicated or not, Télémedia—whose principal officers included chairman Philippe de Gaspé Beaubien, and his wife Nan-b [sic] de Gaspé Beaubien—was plainly a contender, one that by 1988 had become the largest publisher of Canadian consumer magazines.

Télémedia's magazines were printed by Southam Inc., which also had a minority ownership in the company. (Best known for its chain of newspapers and trade journals, Southam itself had little success in bringing forth consumer magazines.) Télémedia's amazing growth—in 1988 alone it bought seven magazines and launched the fashion-and-beauty magazine *Expression*, not to mention a Quebec edition of the weekly *Paris Match*—was partly at the expense of Comac Communications. Formed in the mid-1960s, Comac Communications—at different points owned by Bell Canada Enterprises and Torstar, publisher of the *Toronto Star*—became the dominant producer of controlled-circulation magazines. At its height, Comac's holdings included *Quest, Homemaker's, Ontario Living, Western Living* and *City Woman* (later *Career Woman*) and city magazines in Calgary, Edmonton and Vancouver.

Comac, like Torstar, had a fatal touch when it came to publishing profitable magazines. *Quest* and *City Woman* were shut down, and in 1988 it sold *Ontario Living* to the *London Free Press*. That same year it sold *Western Living* and the western city magazines to Télémedia (ironically, Jeffrey Shearer, president of Télémedia Publishing, once had bought the same four magazines when he was an executive with Comac), as well as *Homemaker's/Madame au foyer*. Télémedia then merged *Homemakers/Madame au foyer* with *Recipes Only/Bien manger*, and turned its newly acquired city magazines into local editions of *Western Living*.

One trend of the 1970s, however, was the *rise* of city magazines—city and entertainment magazines jumped from seventeen to fifty-six in the ten years after 1975—and the great success among these was *Toronto Life*, published by Michael de Pencier's Key Publishers. The flexible and versatile Key, from its stake in the rejuvenated *Canadian Business* to trade magazines (*Quill & Quire*) to book publishing (Key Porter Books), was inserted in many doors. As a creative entrepreneur, de Pencier not only engineered highly successful magazine spinoffs like *Toronto Life Fashion* and expanded into the United States and Great Britain, but at times demonstrated what could even be termed disinterested goodness. He joined in resurrecting *Canadian Art*, and formed a nonprofit foundation to publish the children's magazines *Owl* and *Chickadee*.

Key's partner in publishing *Canadian Art*, and in a few other ventures, was Maclean Hunter—hyphenless since the early 1980s. During the 1970s Maclean Hunter had gotten in and out of money-losing, or at least unpalatable, attempts at both magazine distributing (Metro Toronto News) and book publishing (new press and Macmillan of Canada). When Donald Hunter learned that he was dying, he sold most of his family's stock holdings to a company controlled by management and other "friendly" hands. After Hunter had died in 1976—the year Maclean Hunter purchased the big Quebec monthly *l'Actualité* and merged it with *le Magazine Maclean*—Donald Campbell took over as chairman.

Campbell embodied one trend the Davey Report had isolated: the transition from owner-operators to professional managers. As Floyd Chalmers said, "...he had never sold a page of advertising; he professed no expertise in the production end of publishing. But he was a brilliant executive and more than anyone else gave the company its high rating with investment analysts." *Maclean's* replaced *Time* as the largest news-magazine in Canada, and *Chatelaine* was highly profitable. Under Campbell and his successor as president, Ronald Osborne, Maclean Hunter had a lot more going than magazines. In 1982, when the company was the fourth-largest cable TV operator in Canada, it bought control of the *Toronto Sun*, a sensationally successful tabloid daily with "Sunshine Girl" pinups and the type of editorials best labelled as "Nuke the Pandas." In 1987, in a cross-ownership move, it sold the *Financial Post* to the *Sun*, which announced plans to start a daily version to compete with the *Globe and Mail*'s "Report on Business" section. That periodical publishing that year would account for only 28 percent of its $1,126 million corporate revenue was a measure of just how large, and multifaceted, Maclean Hunter had become.

Perched on Maclean Hunter's multi-media octopus during the 1970s was Donald G. Campbell.

More, Sometimes Merrier

Although there were significant topical gaps—for example, no successful general magazines about arts and entertainment, or on science or sports—now as never before Canadian magazines covered the range of human concerns. Between 1971 and 1986, forty-five percent of the more than 5,000 magazines circulating in Canada were launched, and Canadian magazines in general rose from thirty percent of total circulation to about forty per cent. Despite several sharp increases in postal rates during the 1970s and 1980s, subscription sales trampolined from thirty-seven percent of the market in 1971 to sixty percent fifteen years later.

The sheer abundance was overwhelming. One survey calculated there were 2,150 periodicals—including newsletters serving trade, professional, technical, agricultural and business interests; 1,150 consumer periodicals—including TV/radio and public association/advocacy; 500 scholarly and educational; 650 artistic and literary; 600 religious.

Although these figures are deceiving in that most of these periodicals only remotely resembled ones like *Maclean's* or *Saturday Night*, some of the special interest magazines had large circulations. In 1986, *Leisureways* (the main inflight, travel, and tourism magazines had increased from fourteen to twenty-five in the previous ten years)—reached a peak readership of more than half a million, as did *Legion*, the Royal Canadian Legion's publication, *Canadian Churchman* (Anglican) and *United Church Observer* had circulations of 273,000 and 261,000 respectively. Far behind were the once-prevalent farming magazines. The leader here was Public Press's *Country Guide* in Winnipeg, with about 72,000 subscribers.

Infrastructures

A mature industry of any kind builds up infrastructures, ranging from group associations to training programmes. The Magazine Advertising Bureau, so audible at the Davey Commission, was now mute, more or less replaced as by Magazines Canada, and balanced by another industry group to promote advertising, the Council of Canadian Magazines. The Canadian Business Press spoke for about thirty publishers and more than 250 publications. The Canadian Periodical Publishers' Association, with more than 270 members—mostly in Ontario—represented magazines with interests as diverse as *Acadiensis* and *Worker Co-ops*, and in 1988 decided to change its name to the Magazine Publishers of Canada.

The CPPA, founded in the early 1970s, was partly funded by the Canada Council and other arts bodies. Besides lobbying governments, educating its own members and doing general promotion, the CPPA acted as a subscription clearinghouse and a small-scale distributor.

Free-lance writers, too, made their input through groups that created standard contracts, listed markets and provided advice on dealing with editors and publishers. Both the Writers' Union of Canada and the Periodical Writers' Association of Canada made their starts in 1973 and 1976 respectively.

Another sign of sophistication was the National Magazine Awards Foundation, which annually publicized achievements in editing, writing, illustration, photography and design. To train future achievers, there were now diploma or degree programs in magazine work at the Banff School of Fine Arts and Ryerson Polytechnical Institute in Toronto. The latter published an annual *Review of Journalism*, and the hint of intelligent self-criticism to be found there were reinforced by the socially conscious *Content* (1970—), founded by Dick MacDonald and published after his death by the Carleton University School of Journalism, and the useful, breezy and brightly designed trade journal *Masthead: The Magazine about Magazines* (1987—).

Some general facts about the industry had not changed. Ontario still dominated magazine publishing: in 1988 about fifty-five percent of Canadian periodicals, producing sixty-four percent of the total revenue, were published in that province. And U.S. magazines still outnumbered Canadian ones in total circulation volume. Statistics Canada reported that only $20-million worth of Canadian magazines were exported, but $800 million came into the country. One was lucky, or possibly drunk, to find more than two or three Canadian magazines in the serried ranks of the average convenience store newsstand.

Weekend Casualties

Apart from *Quest*, the most conspicuous death since the 1970s was that of *Today*, the last of the mass-circulation newspaper weekend supplements.

By 1979, *Weekend*—its company, the Montreal Standard Ltd., had merged with FP Publications in 1973—and *The Canadian* were more relics of the preceding era than viable concerns. The net advertising revenue of all weekend supplements peaked during 1971-72 and had been sliding since. As if huddling together for comfort, they were printed on the same presses and were managed by the same advertising agency.

Newsprint prices were going up; the rotogravure printing process was expensive. With rising costs, a merger seemed the best solution to some. Following a polling firm's market survey, *Weekend* and *The Canadian* became a peculiar hybrid called *Canadian Weekend* in October 1979, the same year the *Toronto Star* ended its experiment with its Sunday *City* supplement. Disputing dire fiscal predictions for his supplement and disliking the new format, *Weekend*'s editor, John Macfarlane, resigned, and Gordon Pape, *The Canadian*'s publisher, took charge of the new venture.

Carried by eight Southam newspapers, three Thomson newspapers and seven others, including the *Toronto Star*, *Canadian Weekend* fumbled and faltered. On 15 March 1980, *Today* was born, with yet another updating in format and orientation, and delivered as part of eighteen newspapers. In combination with the French-language supplement *Perspectives*, *Today* was supposed to reach half of all Canadian households. The cost of a full-page advertisement was almost $40,000.

The strange *ménage à trois* that became partners in *Today* were Thomson Newspapers, Southam and Torstar Corporation—which knew a good executive when it saw one: its president was Paul Zimmerman, formerly a *Reader's Digest* executive, and an effective lobbyist. It was

Although Today's *penultimate cover proclaimed that Down syndrome babies were worth keeping, advertisers did not share the same opinion about the weekend supplement.*

Torstar, dismayed by a drastic drop in advertising lineage, that signed *Today's* death sentence by withdrawing from the partnership in mid-1982. The last issue appeared on 28 August.

In 1984, a novelty appeared in the long, problematic association of newspapers and magazines. The nation's second-largest English newspaper—and the only one nationally distributed—the *Globe and Mail,* began its *Report on Business Magazine.* This signalled something new on the Canadian scene: the publication of glossy magazines that, four to twelve times a year, were bundled with the parent daily. Following *Report on Business,* the most editorially impressive of the trio, the *Globe* also launched the travel magazine *Destinations,* and a would-be rival to *Toronto Life* in the urban lifestyle sweepstakes which bore the unremarkable title *Toronto.* In 1988, the *Globe* started *Domino,* an upscale fasion quarterly, and bought Bob Harris's *Montreal Magazine,* announcing plans for a western region lifestyle magazine. Although only *Report on Business Magazine* was immediately profitable, the newspaper benefited from the fact that the magazines boosted newsstand and box copy sales above the *Globe's* average circulation of 326,000. And, with the benefit of their dual status the *Globe's* magazines soon won awards from the National Magazine Awards Foundation and the International Society of Newspaper Design.

Symptoms

Several unrelated incidents convey the mood and texture of the Canadian magazine industry since the late 1970s.

• The January 1978 issue of *Canadian Yachting,* founded in 1976 as a sister publication to the fourteen-year-old *Pacific Yachting* and published by Vancouver's Interpress Publications—later by Maclean

Hunter—was the fattest issue yet of a special interest Canadian magazine but was bettered by *Wedding Bells*, whose third anniversary issue in 1988 had 586 pages and weighed a hernia-inducing 1.42 kilograms.

• The same year, *Harrowsmith*, the magazine for back-to-the-landers, and *Toronto Life*, the magazine for trendy urbanites, arranged an ad exchange. Said *Harrowsmith*'s advertising manager, "Well, our readers don't spend all their time weeding the turnip patch."

• In October 1984, Southam produced preview issues of *Verve*, a bimonthly dealing holistically with health concerns, and sent 75,000 copies to the homes of patients and clinics. Losing money, *Verve* was sold in 1988 to Family Communications and merged with *You*.

• In 1986, the 100,000-circulation *Today's Parent* sued the 25,000-circulation *Toronto Parent* over duplication of its name. But *Today's Parent* was also getting static from the much larger U.S. magazine *Parents*. Although *Today's Parent* lost the court battle, *Toronto Parent* went out of business. The same year, two Hamilton, Ontario lifestyle magazines, both distributed free to 40,000 households, were involved in a court battle. The judge dismissed *Hamilton This Month*'s claim that *Hamilton Cue* had confused readers and advertisers by using a similar design. In 1988, Toronto's Clarco Communications attempted to launch *Sass*, a magazine for teenagers but found the start-up complicated by the fact that the U.S. *Sassy* had been launched the same month. After publishing one issue, *Sass* retreated.

• The B.C. Securities Commission investigated four companies involved in a tax-shelter plan to market a glossy culinary magazine called *Enjoy*. Regulatory authorities also issued cease-trading orders against two other firms who were selling licences to market a magazine called *West Coast Dart Digest*.

• *Executive* magazine changed its name to *Successful Executive*. Southam's *Successful Executive* failed in 1988.

• Direct mail advertising for *Vista*, launched in the fall of 1988, included a quotation from its chairman, Frank Stronach: "If you want to be a winner, read about them."

Perennial Hope

One summer evening in 1986, I was browsing in the Metropolitan Toronto Reference Library near a shelf of books on the media. A stocky, middle-aged, bearded man was scooping up books and ferrying them back to a table where his wife or friend was busy with papers and more books. We began chatting.

The man was starting a magazine.

Out of a briefcase he drew a colour photocopy of the proposed cover for Volume One, Number One of *Mad Money*. Priced at $1.50, it showed a red sports car parked in front of that ersatz Toronto castle, Casa Loma. The cover lines included: "DYING HUSBAND GIVES WIFE WIN-

NING LOTTERY NUMBERS," "$50 MILLION NOBODY WANTS," "JACKPOT WINNER BEATS ODDS OF 17 TRILLION TO 1," "30% OF AMERICANS HAVE MAD MONEY" and "RETIRE A MILLION-AIRE BEFORE 50." I wished him luck.

I have not been able to determine if *Mad Money* ever reached a newsstand. But the man's proposed publication did sum up something about 1980s magazines, just as the desperate hope or delusion in his eyes expressed the emotion any person who wants to start a Canadian magazine must possess—in superabundance.

MACLEAN'S
THE NEWSMAGAZINE

Although Peter Newman had ample credentials to become *Maclean's* editor, he was a novelty in so WASP a bastion as Maclean-Hunter. A Jew of Czech ancestry, moreover born (in 1929) in Vienna, he had at least been schooled in such approved institutions as Upper Canada College and the University of Toronto. The pipe he puffed perpetually was like a badge of establishment respectability.

After a stint as a *Financial Post* editor in Toronto and Montreal from 1951 to 1956, Newman became Ottawa editor of *Maclean's*—his personal and journalistic style a marked contrast to that of his colleague Blair Fraser—and remained there until 1964. In 1959, he published his first book, *Flame of Power*, but the book that made his reputation was *Renegade in Power*, a scathing account of the Diefenbaker administration. Newman's bias might be detected in his titles: Diefenbaker was a "renegade"; the difficulties of the Pearson government, which succeeded the Diefenbaker regime, were due to the *Distemper of Our Times*. In any event, the author's fascination with power was a constant. Moving to the *Toronto Star*, he rose to become editor in chief in 1969.

He was, even then, an unusual man around whom legends clustered about his pre-dawn working habits and addiction to jazz—he belonged to a band named the Bouncing Czechs. Secretive and hypersensitive, he has been called by John Fraser "a solemn and solitary figure who had somehow worked out a professional accommodation to loneliness and hugely profited thereby."

Although Newman returned to *Maclean's* in February 1971, the May issue was the first under his editorship. At first his arrival seemed to presage another instalment in the recent turmoil on the magazine. Philip Sykes, the managing editor who had been acting editor after Peter Gzowski's departure, quit when he was passed over. Gone from the May masthead were staff writers Doug Marshall, Allan Edmonds and Pat Annesley, as well as the photo director Horst Ehricht. Altogether nine people were dismissed. In their places were associate editors John Macfarlane, Christina Newman and Walter Stewart.

What he was doing, Newman said a year later, was to reduce the Toronto office essentially to a production unit in which editing, illustration, but relatively little writing was done. With the same editorial budget he now had assignments farmed out to free-lancers across the country. He even had a map on the wall: every time he used a story from outside Toronto he stuck a pin in it to remind him that the magazine had to deal with the entire country. When there were many staff writers, he said,

> we were listening to ourselves; you can't sit in an air-
> conditioned office, seventh floor of a downtown Toronto
> skyscraper, and decide what you're going to put in a national
> magazine. This way, we're getting suggestions from all over
> the country—people who know they have access to
> Maclean's—and we're publishing not just established writers
> from all over the country, but new writers which before we
> weren't doing.

He used novelists increasingly—and even poets like Alden Nowlan— and aimed to even further decentralize the magazine by appointing five regional editors. Within Newman's first year, fewer than half the Maclean's stories came from Toronto writers.

All this was in keeping with the nationalism that then dominated Canadian public life. In his moves, Newman had the support of Donald G. Campbell, who had succeeded Donald Hunter as Maclean-Hunter president the previous year. Maclean's had been losing money and Campbell even considered killing it. In his view it had become "a second-rate publication for a number of years, too cute, to coy, too smart....I don't think there's any question that there was improper management interference. But I think they had at least four out of six or seven editors who never should have been editors."

Campbell turned for help to Chatelaine's deft publisher, Lloyd Hodgkinson. With Hodgkinson, too, Newman was compatible. Along with the editors of Chatelaine and the Financial Post, Newman joined the board of directors. Just as important, Ronald McEachern, irate that he had been overlooked in favour of Campbell, had quit.

The results in Newman's first year were impressive: renewal rates increased, advertising was more varied—the old Maclean's had a preponderance of ads from tobacco and liquor companies and circulation was up about ten percent, making the combined English and French total around 954,000.

Not a convinced believer in strict objectivity, Newman at the time tended to favour advocacy and interpretative journalism. The journalists he used, such as Harry Bruce and Melinda McCracken, and certainly the poets and novelists, were subjective enough, evidenced in McCracken's hostile 1972 cover story on Adrienne Clarkson. Its title, given that Clarkson had Chinese parents, was in questionable taste: "Scrutinizing the Inscrutable." A newly restrained management did not even intervene in June 1972 when *Maclean's* ran "How the Media Withheld the Message in Kitchener," which noted that one of the with-holders was the Maclean-Hunter-owned radio station CHYM.

But then, having shaped *Maclean's* into a national magazine divorced from Toronto media politics and revolving-door personnel, Newman abruptly changed tack. As early as 1972 he wanted *Maclean's* to once again become a twice-monthly magazine. Interestingly, though, he didn't want to make it a *weekly*, which is what it eventually became. He had told an interviewer:

> I suppose Canada could have its own version of *Time*, but it's
> not *Maclean's*. *Maclean's* is not a newsmagazine. And the
> trouble with starting a truly national newsmagazine in
> Canada is that you would then really be competing with
> *Time*—not Time Canada but Time International—and it'd be
> very difficult to duplicate that kind of news service. I don't
> think it'll work.

What changed Maclean-Hunter's and, it would seem, Newman's mind was the federal Liberal government's impending Bill C-58. Introducing the bill in the House of Commons, Hugh Faulkner said, "I am confident that the enterprise and skill of the Canadian magazine industry will seize this opportunity. It is my hope and expectation that this decision will result in the creation of a Canadian newsmagazine."

This of course was a none-too-subtle reference to *Maclean's*. The company spent $4.5 million on new offset press and binding equipment, made the transformation to photocomposition technology and set up leased wire service and newsphoto lines. The first phase was to move to twice-monthly status. Suddenly *Maclean's* was hiring again, building up to a staff of seventy-two. The senior editor, later foreign editor, was David North, who had come from Britain in 1974. With him was John Macfarlane, now executive editor in charge of feature articles. Mel Morris, who had been with the magazine since 1973, was managing editor and news editor was Jim Peters, who had been city editor at the *Montreal Gazette*. From *Time* itself came its Toronto bureau chief, Robert Lewis, who was sent to Ottawa. Also from *Time* were senior editor Paul Nowack and chief researcher Arlene Arnason. Another *Time* man, Geoffrey James, would later join as an art critic. The business editor was the *Globe and Mail*'s capable financial reporter Terence Belford. The magazine's Ottawa correspondent, Walter Stewart, moved to Washington, and the magazine began signing up thirty-five stringers, or free-lance correspondents, around the world.

All this was in aid of a magazine that would have a planned array of four feature articles on news-related themes, accompanied by sixteen pages of reports, eight pages on Canadian and foreign news and four pages each on sports and business. Each issue would open with a question-and-answer interview and close with a column by Vancouver journalist Allan Fotheringham. At the back of the magazine would be departments covering topics, such as medicine, law, the media and religion, as well as the cultural categories the old *Maclean's* had covered.

Arriving on 6 October 1975, the 122-page newsmagazine *Maclean's* had a cover story on the cabinet shuffle after Finance Minister John Turner's resignation, with the powerful cabinet minister Donald MacDonald on the cover itself. There were signs of strain in the layout department. All the articles were not listed on the contents page, and pages 16 and 80 ran *a* to *d* and page 48 from *a* to *p*. Its fifty-eight percent of advertising, outscored, if one was an ad salesman, *Newsweek* and *Time*, and was erratically intermingled with the editorial matter.

Free-lance journalist Paul Saltzman interviewed the Indian Prime Minister, Indira Gandhi. Apart from India, there were three pages on "The World," an article on the United States and a department on "Canada." Marci McDonald's "Carole Taylor Doesn't Want to Be Perfect" concerned the TV star's marriage to the Vancouver mayor. McDonald, later *Maclean's* correspondent in Paris and Washington, had come from the *Star* where, as it happened, she had written a flattering account of Donald Campbell.

The short departments included "People"; "Business" (the collapse of the Bricklin car manufacturer in New Brunswick); "Sports"; "Medicine" (vasectomies); "Advertising" (advertising accounts lost to U.S. agencies); "Travel" (Cuba); "Press" (on "Aislin"); "Education" (learning French); "Cities" (a place called New York); "Art" (on the painter Miller Britain of Saint John); "Television" (by Ron Base); "Films"; and "Books." The articles were boxed, pictures were bled (extended) to the page's edge, and there was a maple leaf tucked into the logo.

Among the new *Maclean's* people writing about people was Barbara Amiel, who as a CBC script assistant had been written about in "The Way It Is the Way It Is" in a December 1968 issue. Born in 1940 in London, England, she had come to Canada as a twelve-year-old, graduated from the University of Toronto in 1963 and until 1972 fought addictions to 222s and the antidepressant Elavil. Working on Adrienne Clarkson's *Take 30* TV show, she became busy on and off camera in the CBC Public Affairs Department, covering among other things the 1968 Liberal leadership convention. Although her only previous magazine experience had been two guest columns in *Toronto Life* and a piece for the *Maclean's* back pages called "Let's Reinstate Debtors' Prison," she began doing book reviews. Eventually she became a columnist. Before and after that appointment—Newman initially wanted to alternate the "Culture" column between her and Mordecai Richler—she showed her capacity to arouse liberals' ire.

In the 4 April 1977 issue, Amiel's "The Collapse of Great Britain" diagnosed Great Britain's social and economic ills and stated: "The British might work, at least in the sense of pulling together, when they feel the enemy at the gates. But Britons don't seem to feel that at all: the Huns are gone, and nobody really believes in the reality of the Russian Bear." Soon Newman was getting letters of protest from human rights commissions in Manitoba and Ontario, and responding to objections from the trans-Canada Alliance of German-Canadians. All were vigorously rebutted by Amiel, who further resented, as she made clear in her memoir *Confessions*, being gently interrogated over lunch by Rabbi Gunther Plaut, Vice-Chairman [sic] of the Ontario Human Rights Commission. In Amiel's view, Plaut—who had presided at her marriage—was asking her to "explain my opinions. Not my acts, not my misdeeds, but my *opinions*." To her, the Commission had set up its liberal "Thought Police" and "felt confident enough to outlaw, and, if necessary, to prosecute, Error." Amiel's opinions ideally placed her to represent the libertarian right in the magazine's configuration, just as Fotheringham would take up the attitudes of the left behind a façade of wit and acerbity. Newman remained, as always, in the power-obsessed middle.

In the 1976-77 period, the magazine was prone to cuteness. Sometimes the attempt to create a catchy cover had unfortunate repercussions. The 22 August 1977 cover, for example, for the story "Metric Madness" depicted an elderly bewildered tailor holding a hand calculator while measuring the bust of an attractive, bikini-clad woman. This brought on the wrath of Charles Templeton's old nemesis, the feminists. A group representing Women After Rights (WAR) attempted to invade Newman's office, and succeeded in meeting Walter Stewart, now the managing editor. (Stewart took the post in February after Morris quit, claiming that without consultation a political story had been toned down after it had left his and the writer's desks: the old *Maclean's* was not *quite* dead.) The war criers were not the only ones to protest even before the silly cover was printed. Associate editor Joann Webb—the only female editor on the staff—objected, as did the features editor, Michael Enright. "My wife wasn't keen on it," he was quoted as saying," and the wife of the managing editor complained loudly about it. And she's a formidable person."

Nineteen seventy-eight was an important year for Newman. It was then that he acquired a new wife, Camilla Turner. But as usual he kept things in the Maclean-Hunter family: he met her when she was an editor on the *Financial Post*—she had also been managing editor of *Flare* for five years. Nineteen seventy-eight was also the year that *Maclean's* became a weekly with the issue of 11 September.

Although softened by premiums, the fiscal shock was considerable to subscribers: for one thing, the yearly rate went from $4 to $19.50.

Maclean's *devoted its first newsweekly cover to Egyptian President Anwar Sadat and Israeli Prime Minister Menachem Begin.*

For the first issue an unflattering but hardly pornographic caricature of Pierre Trudeau had been planned for the cover, but at the last minute this was vetoed by Lloyd Hodgkinson. Substituted was a photo of Egyptian President Anwar Sadat and Israeli Prime Minister Menachem Begin—neither of whom needed caricaturing. Amid staff grumblings, a disgusted executive editor, John Gault, resigned. But the resignation did not have the usual domino effect. If some staff left, others ascended the ladder, like Roy MacGregor, who was that year appointed chief of the magazine's Ottawa bureau. MacGregor had started out on Maclean-Hunter trade magazines and, apart from two years as associate editor of *The Canadian*, had been successively an associate and assistant editor and senior writer.

The year of the weekly *Maclean's* also marked the start of tangled dealings with Canadian film producer and movie house owner Garth Drabinsky. A January cover story listed Drabinsky on a list of "new wave achievers." Whatever he thought of that, Drabinsky did not like the 6 November 1978 profile that followed and was written by an excellent feature writer, Ian Brown. Drabinsky sued and eventually settled for $70,000 and an apology, drafted by him and his lawyer, which appeared on April Fool's Day 1980 and stated that he had been "referred to in a manner that was mean-spirited and incorrect, misleading and offensive, both in tone and content" and "gives quite the wrong impression of Mr. Drabinsky as a person, as a lawyer and as filmmaker." While negotiations were underway, *Maclean's* ordered its film critic, Lawrence O'Toole, to postpone reviewing Drabinsky's picture *The Changeling*.

Maclean's was not permanently scared away from the litigious Drabinsky. On 28 September 1987, "King of the Silver Screen" was Brian D. Johnson's cover story on "Movie Mogul Garth Drabinsky's Stunning Rise to Wealth and Power." John Bemrose's accompanying review of the Drabinsky-financed *The Glass Menagerie* was tepidly favorable; Johnson was all liquid sweetness. And the editor, Kevin Doyle, noted in "A Man of Extremes" that Drabinsky dealt "head-on with whatever obstacles came his way."

On the masthead page of 29 December 1980, Newman ("Oil and gas are running low but CanLit thrives to keep us warm") was shown with a pensive finger on his chin. He approvingly quoted from a Ron Graham novel, *Noughts and Crosses*, that "One cannot be too paranoid these days." Still, paranoia must have been more applicable outside the *Maclean's* offices, because the staff was firmly in place. Whatever other changes happened, writers and editors, such as Roy MacGregor, David North, Marci McDonald, Brian Johnson, Angela Ferrante and Val Ross, would serve with the magazine in one capacity or another over the next few years. In fact, key columnists Barbara Amiel and Alan Fotheringham, the sports editor Hal Quinn and art director Nick Burnett would have identical positions in 1987. By 1983, the magazine had twenty-three Canadian correspondents. Among these, more women than ever before took on prominent roles. The 15 June 1984 issue, for example, covering John Turner's Liberal leadership victory, had three of four cover stories written by women, including one by Ottawa bureau chief Carol Goar. Appointed to that post in October 1982, she went to the *Toronto Star* in 1985. Perhaps most vital to *Maclean's* pretensions as a credible newsmagazine was David North, who had assembled thirty-three correspondents, most of them free-lance, as well as about one hundred occasional contributors or "stringers."

Nor would the lineup markedly differ, being much like that of 29 December, with the exception of the dropped "Podium" opinion section. That issue included an editorial, a "Backstage" (B.C.); a "Podium"; a "Profile" (Canadian Radio-Television Commission chairman John Meisel); an interview "Q & A" (June Callwood); "Letters"; "Canada"; "World"; "U.S.A."; "People"; "Sports"; a column by managing editor Roderick McQueen, "Business"; the cover story; the Amiel column; "Advertising"; "Art"; "Books"; "Theatre" and Fotheringham's end piece.

In May 1982, Newman announced that, effective in September, he would resign from *Maclean's* to write books. By then he had written seven of them, including such bestsellers as *The Canadian Establishment*, made into a TV series; *The Bronfman Dynasty* and *The Acquisitors*. He would soon undertake a biography of Conrad Black called *The Establishment Man* and a two-volume history of the Hudson's Bay Company (an excerpt from the second, *Caesars of the Wilderness*, ran in *Maclean's*). He would remain a Maclean Hunter director and, under the made-up title of senior contributing editor, write a weekly business column. Ralph Hodgkinson, Newman's running mate, was by now vice-president of Maclean Hunter's magazine division. *Maclean's* new publisher would be James Miller.

Posing in 1982 against a backdrop of magazine covers, Peter C. Newman was about to leave Maclean's.

In an editorial written a week after the announcement, Newman noted that "Sometimes the staff functioned with the cool precision of a crew on an attacking submarine. At other times I wondered how I came to preside over Canadian journalism's most elaborate day care centre." Whether this latter impression was related to the staff's voting to unionize in 1982, he did not say. But as he told the *Globe and Mail's* William French, only five staff members had been fired in the past three years. When he had taken over, the magazine had had an editorial staff of eleven; when he left there were seventy.

Hodgkinson intimated that the new editor might well come from within the magazine. "Newsmagazines don't have to have high-profile editors," he said. "A newsmagazine doesn't project the personality of its editor." Whether Hodgkinson was right or not, Kevin Doyle, like Mildred Istona at *Chatelaine*, was not a journalist in Peter Newman's public mode.

Born in Ottawa, Doyle, who was fourteen years younger than Newman, had acquired a Master of Science degree from the London School of Economics, had reported for the *Windsor Star* and served the Canadian Press in Ottawa, London, Europe, Asia, Africa and the Middle East, as well as Washington. He'd been foreign and national editor at *Maclean's* in 1976-77, an editor at *Newsweek*, returning to *Maclean's* as deputy editor in 1981-82. Newman, busy with his own book projects, had tended to be a *laissez-faire* editor. But he had strong, small "l" liberal political views, a particular brand of nationalism. Doyle was an anti-nationalist. A year after he took over he told a reporter, "North Americans are conditioned in their expectation of newsmagazines by *Time* and *Newsweek*. That's the standard we're judged by, whether we like it or not. We have to establish that credibility with Canadians"—hoped, in fact, that *Maclean's* might one day have a wide sale in the United States.

Maclean's *editor
Kevin Doyle, far
right, and his
staff. Beside him
is managing editor
Robert Lewis.*

Doyle was also an interventionist editor who clearly favoured a wire service style. In 1983, one *Maclean's* writer would comment, "Before, I admit, there had been excesses of rhetoric from us all, epitomized by Newman himself. Everyone remembers Newman writing sentences like 'Joe Clark stole into his office like a wild faun caught eating broccoli.' Now we've gone to the other extreme, and those 'wild fauns' don't look so bad after all." But at least one beneficiary of the Doyle style was Newman's column. It would be relatively free of the hyperbolic excesses typically found in his large untidy books.

Not everyone was happy with Doyle's ascendancy. Managing editor Roderick McQueen resigned. His place was taken by Robert Lewis, a native of Waterloo, Quebec, who was *Time's* Montreal bureau chief between 1967 and 1967 and who spent seven years as head of *Maclean's* Ottawa bureau. Another key person was Robert Miller, a former foreign correspondent for the *Globe and Mail* and parliamentary reporter, foreign editor and political columnist for the *Toronto Star*.

The dissension within the magazine now centred not on personalities or policies, but on the mundane matter of money. In October 1983, the fifty-one staff members who belonged to the Southern Ontario Newspaper Guild staged a two-week walkout—the first in Canadian magazine history—to ask for a nine percent salary increase. While they were away, Doyle and his editors continued to produce the magazine.

The union won, if only by getting a contract signed at all. The next year's salary increases would be kept to an average five percent, and the twenty-nine lowest-paid staffers received a total of $29,000 in recognition of overtime worked in 1983, when several senior positions had not yet been filled. Salary increases in 1984 would range from two percent for the highest-paid employees to seven percent for the others. More than half the magazine's editorial staff would get overtime, although they would be excluded from the company's deferred profit-sharing plan. This was not to be the only labour dispute. On 1 April 1987, seventy editorial and production employees who were members

Columnist Allan Fotheringham opened many a can of worms, said Roy Peterson, his cartoonist companion.

of the Southern Ontario Newspaper Guild went on strike after five months of bargaining, and even organized a boycott of the magazine. But the dispute was settled quickly and the magazine, put out during the strike by Doyle and his senior staff, did not miss an issue.

Despite labour unrest, the magazine was profitable. To put out *Maclean's* and handle other contracts, the company installed a $7.5-million press, the largest in Canada. With a circulation of 645,000 (only three percent of it sold at the $1.75 newsstand price; the rest was subscriptions) in 1984, it published its first issue with $1 million in advertising. The advertising was needed because subscription copies grossed a mere 75 cents an issue, less postage expenses, the cost of premiums to lure in purchasers and the administrative costs entailed in serving the subscription. In 1985, Lloyd Hodgkinson retired: seeing *Maclean's* through from monthly to weekly newsmagazine had been his biggest achievement at the magazine.

On the editorial side, Allan Fotheringham's column tended to attract a lot of legal attention. A reference to wife swapping in his June 1984 column resulted in the B.C. Supreme Court's ordering him, Doyle and managing editor Robert Lewis, in January 1986, to pay $10,000 to each of two Vancouver lawyers. The satirist's is a high-risk profession. Another problem derived from a 24 March 1986 column on the life of John Magee, a World War II Canadian airman who before dying young in 1941 wrote the famous lines beginning "I have slipped the surly bonds of earth..." lines misattributed by U.S. President Reagan in his comments on the explosion of the space shuttle *Challenger*. In writing about Magee, Fotheringham had plagiarized a 1982 article in the British publication *This England*, the latter's managing director claimed. According to Doyle, "what may have happened is what's happened to many of us. If you've got a pile of clips and you're lifting information from a whole lot of them, you may at times lift a phrase word for word without even thinking about it." And Fotheringham noted that he had received a mass of letters and documentation about Magee after Reagan had quoted him, "So I used all of them and put them together." The matter was settled out of court.

Sometimes Fotheringham's ready colloquialism led him into syntactic absurdity. In the 21 December 1987 issue, below a glowering photograph, he wrote: "England, the birthplace of soccer, a game it sent around the world, now has its major clubs banned from appearing in Europe proper. So terrified are the continentals of these descendants of Shakespeare who are so enamored of Maggie Thatcher's brand of capitalism that they killed 39 spectators in Brussels in a fun-filled match." The *continentals* killed the spectators? If at times the prolific Fotheringham appeared rushed in his writing or careless about splicing his research, his column—beautifully mated with Roy Peterson's excellent cartoons—was often the best-written one in the magazine and funny with a rare consistency.

One example among many will suffice: in a 5 October 1987 column noting that "Three Canadians made the Filthy Top List" [lists of world's richest men recently run by *Forbes* and *Fortune*] because they wouldn't give you a Kleenex if you wanted to sneeze," he had good sport at the expense of K. C. Irving, Ken Thomson and the Reichmann brothers. The Reichmanns, he said, "toss tips around like manhole covers."

A newsmagazine exposes itself to the perils of public opinion every week. When in December 1986 *Maclean's* ran a cover story about the proliferation of war toys, its good intentions backfired. About 200 British Columbian stores took *Maclean's* off their shelves because, to dramatize the piece, the magazine had run a cover depicting a gun-toting Santa. A newsmagazine trifles with icons at its risk. In late 1987, the Canadian Olympics Association filed a lawsuit seeking a publication ban and damages in connection with a special Olympics issue scheduled for January 1988 that it alleged violated its trademarks. Time, Inc., one of the Olympics' corporate sponsors, had complained, and in any event, the Olympics organization had become notorious for zealously guarding its territory. *Maclean's* went ahead with the issue.

Throughout 1987, *Maclean's* championed the Canada-U.S. Free Trade Agreement. On 20 April 1987, for example, Barbara Amiel commented, "Myself, I like popular American culture for my lowbrow times, European ideas for cerebral exercise and the joy of living in a politically independent Canada for peace of mind. But one thing I know, and no

Canadian nationalist can persuade otherwise: in the 20th century, when it comes to pop culture, *Dallas* wins." On 19 October 1987, a "Redrawing the Nation" cover showed Mulroney flanked by U.S. and Canadian flags. Inside was a Doyle editorial, "A Continental market," endorsing the agreement, and a Diane Francis column entitled "Nothing to Fear but the Fearful." And during late 1987, as if in visual support of the free trade agreement, *Maclean's* (it should be remembered that by now Maclean Hunter had extensive holdings in the United States) covers often had a colour scheme that was red, white, and blue.

By the end of 1987 it was possible to assess how well *Maclean's* had succeeded in its objectives. Its format aped that of *Time*, even to the extent of a "People" department full of meaningless trivia, with "Passages" (births, deaths, appointments and the like) a parallel to "Milestones." Yet in other respects, the magazine succeeded more than might have been hoped. For a newsmagazine that lacked the global resources of *Time* and *Newsweek*, *Maclean's* had done a creditable job with its international reportage, skilfully covering the deposition of Ferdinand Marcos in the Philippines and the U.S. invasion of Grenada. One example of a correspondent in action was associate editor Tom Fennell and his 17 August 1987 cover story on the Hong Kong billionaire Li Kashing. After being spurned by Li's aides, Fennel was about to board a plane home, when he encountered Li at the airport, seeing friends off. Introducing himself, he got a ride back into the city in Li's limousine and a magazine piece. With capable writers like Rae Corelli, the magazine's Canadian coverage was seldom less than adequate, and certainly more abundant than *Time* ever offered. The columnists were well balanced, and included, besides Newman, Fotheringham and Amiel, such regulars as George Bain, Diane Francis, Charles Gordon, Stewart MacLeod and Fred Bruning of the Long Island, New York *Newsday*.

Oddly enough, *Maclean's*-the-newsmagazine was weakest in its U.S. coverage, providing readers with no good reason to turn away from its U.S. rivals. Marci McDonald's 20 July 1987 cover story, "Lt. Col. Oliver North Hero or Outlaw"—"A tale of deceit, intrigue and espionage"—on the arms-to-Iran scandal, could just as easily have been written by a newspaper re-write man with one eye on the newswire and the other on a U.S. TV channel. The accompanying story, "The Women in the Colonel's Life," teased but did not deliver. In fact, the only illumination shed was an essay the magazine commissioned from *Harper's* editor Lewis Lapham.

In 1988, *Maclean's* published a 700,000-circulation special Olympics issue, redesigned itself and celebrated its tenth anniversary as a newsmagazine.

Whatever J. B. Maclean would think of *Maclean's* the newsmagazine is imponderable, but he might have felt at home with one set of advertisements his namesake was running in 1987 and which recalled the

Colonel's early ventures in selling reproductions of paintings. "The Maclean's Collection" had full-page ads touting reproduced Victorian "masterpieces" by Cornelius Kreighoff and Paul Peel—the latter represented by "Before the Bath." ("Now also available 'After the Bath'").

Fresh from its editorial bath, a 649,000-circulation weekly newsmagazine, *Maclean's* had become what *Time* and *Newsweek* always were: a five-minute dentist's-waiting room read.

VARIETY PACK

If Bill C-58 had simply resulted in swapping a monthly *Maclean's* and five weekly pages of Canadian coverage in *Time* for a weekly *Maclean's*, it might have been accounted a poor bargain. But the fact was—and for a combination of reasons—that Canadians were now offered a greater range and variety of magazines than ever before.

City and Country

Some city or regional magazines predated the Davey Report, but that might have been because the particularities of their chosen area offered them some protection against U.S. magazines: one would not turn to *Time* to find the best new restaurant in one's neighbourhood, or details about the cottage industry that had just set up five miles down the secondary highway.

Many of these magazines, given away at conventions and in hotel rooms, were made up merely of ephemeral listings, and bore names like *What's Up, What's Happening* and *Key to*....Almost every city of any size had at least one.

Some publishers set a tiny island of features in a sea of listings and advertising and called the result a city or regional magazine. A few dealt with hitherto ignored heritage, folkways and contemporary life, and their territory ranged from Nova Scotia to the far North. Among them were *Cape Breton's Magazine* (1972—); *Them Days* (1975—), Doris Saunders's quarterly in Happy Valley, Goose Bay, Labrador; and *Up Here* (1985—), the 14,000-circulation, Yellowknife-based magazine of the Yukon and Northwest territories.

Among many regional magazines, perhaps the most interesting were *Atlantic Insight* (1979—) and *Alberta Report*. In Halifax, *Atlantic Insight* sought to overcome the moribund *Atlantic Advocate*, whose only conspicuous virtue in recent years had been the gruff, wholly individualistic column of the poet Alden Nowlan in the early 1970s, and the recent failure of the bimonthly *Axiom* (1974-78). Founded by Pat Murphy, *Axiom* had achieved a circulation of 40,000, but also suffered a 100 percent staff turnover and a court battle regarding ownership.

Variety Pack 283

Bruce Curtis: still trying to come home

A stylish regional magazine, Atlantic Insight *in August 1987 took up the cause of Bruce Curtis, a Nova Scotian youth convicted of a U.S. murder.*

Before *Atlantic Insight* even started, its publisher, Bill Belliveau commissioned a $20,000 market research study that went so far as to cover the question of the right title. With purchased mailing lists, the magazine had 12,000 subscriptions before the first issue was produced. Under editors Harry Bruce and Marilyn MacDonald it was a handsomely produced, comprehensive monthly, and had a talented humorous columnist in the Newfoundlander Ray Guy, a former *Axiom* contributor. But the magazine lost money and MacDonald clashed with a new publisher, Jack Daley, who took over in late 1982 after a bailout arranged by the magazine's biggest suppliers. In 1985, Daley sold the magazine—its circulation was about 36,000, some 10,000 more than the *Advocate*—to James Lorimer, a Toronto book publisher who had relocated in Halifax. *Atlantic Insight* became a slimmer magazine focussing on small business and community development.

In Edmonton, *Alberta Report* (1973—) resolved to be a weekly newsmagazine, and in 1978 adopted a red border. Jealous of its cover design, *Time* threatened legal action in 1985, alleging violation of its copyright. Called at first the *Saint John's Edmonton Report*, the magazine had been started in October 1973 by a schoolmaster, Ted Byfield, as an offshoot of the Company of the Cross, an Anglican lay order. Keen to combat "secularist and liberal humanist bias," the *Report* drew its workers from among those who answered a 1971 newspaper ad calling on "men and women to join Anglican religious order and run printing plant and newsmagazine. Salary: $1 a day plus necessities."

With communal assistance and some paid help, the magazine saw its circulation rise to 20,000 by 1976. The next year it started a Calgary

The omnipresent
Barbara Amiel,
"a stunning
brunette with a
matching I.Q.",
leaped across
Toronto Life's
first cover.

version, then merged it with Edmonton's in September 1979. Spurning the Milquetoast nature of most newsmagazines, *Alberta Report* had jingoistic pro-West editorials by Byfield and regularly listed lawsuits under the heading "Who's Suing Whom." In 1986, Link Byfield, who succeeded his father as editor, announced plans for a *Western Report*, intended to cover the four western provinces as well as the Yukon and Northwest Territories. By 1987, the magazines' circulation was more than 53,000; the next year the Print Measurement Bureau reported that *Alberta Report* had nearly six readers per copy.

The *Reports* competed editorially with *Maclean's, Time, Newsweek* and the daily papers. For advertising, it also battled a slough of western magazines. Among these were *Edmonton Magazine* and *Calgary Magazine*, both founded by the Vancouver lawyer and enterpreneur Ron Stern in 1978, who at the time also owned *Vancouver*, the successor to *Vancouver Leisure*. Stern sold his three magazines in 1984 to Comac Communications, whose principal Prairies masthead was *Western Living*. In 1989, *Western Living*, now Télémedia's, absorbed the two Alberta magazines and added them to its array of local editions. *Vancouver*, meanwhile, found its local competition in the form of *V Magazine*, distributed with the *Vancouver Sun*.

Those who jostled for market share in Vancouver or Montreal might have envied the blooming good health of *Toronto Life* (1966—). From the late 1960s, Toronto was a place of rapidly made fortunes and skyrocketing real estate values: the old moneyed, white Anglo-Saxon class moved over to share some of its wealth with the city's Italian and Chinese communities. At the same time a renewed interest in urban centres and a new pride in neighbourhood identities appeared. City magazines were in fact starting up all across North America. All these factors worked in *Toronto Life's* favour.

With a cover showing Barbara Amiel leaping for joy—or something— *Toronto Life* began in November 1966, having acquired the subscription list of *Ontario Homes*. It was published by Donald Cromie, who

With his striped tie and laid-back style, Michael de Pencier was the entrepreneurial force behind Key Publishers.

also owned *Vancouver Life*, founded the previous year and which would grow from a listings-type periodical to one with a 70,000 print-run. Not so fortunate in Toronto, Cromie's company sold the money-losing *Toronto Life* to Michael Sifton in May 1967. The Sifton firm owned daily newspapers and had radio and TV interests, chiefly on the Prairies.

Late in 1970, having consistently lost money on a 30,000-circulation, Sifton's company sold *Toronto Life* to Michael de Pencier. As it happened, de Pencier and Peter Gzowski, at loose ends after leaving the *Star Weekly*, once had attempted to raise money to start a city magazine along the lines of Clay Felker's hugely successful *New York*—though to no avail. Now, with the help of Gzowski and other backers, a ready-made city magazine had landed in de Pencier's lap. All that remained was to make it pay.

Like Michael Sifton, de Pencier came from a wealthy family. His sixth-generation Canadian, prep school, Anglican background—he'd married Honor Bonnycastle, a member of another old and rich family—was typical of many publishers who had preceded him. Yet in his relaxed attitude and casual but effective management style, de Pencier was an entirely different kind of entrepreneur.

Having studied and taught philosophy, in 1962 de Pencier joined a Trinity College schoolmate, Phillip Greey, in starting a trade magazine called *Building and Management*—later *Building Development*—for real estate developers. Over the years, Greey de Pencier, later Key Publishers, commenced, acquired, or took shares in such other magazines as *Architecture Canada*—the organ of the Royal Architectural Institute of Canada—*The Curler, Canadian Real Estate Annual* and *Quill & Quire*.

While making money, de Pencier helped found the Canadian Periodical Publishers' Association and gave indirect financial aid to nonprofit magazines like the *Canadian Forum* and *This Magazine is About Schools*.

Among de Pencier's fellow shareholders in Key Publishers were Julian Porter, a useful libel lawyer, and Gzowski, who also functioned in *Toronto Life's* early years as, he said, "a sort of editorial godfather" and later joined de Pencier in a failed attempt to publish a downtown Toronto weekly. In 1972, de Pencier's company bought *Key to Toronto*, a 30,000-circulation listings-type magazine found in hotels. Within six years, de Pencier was expanding into book publishing (Key Porter Books), other magazine enterprises like *Canadian Business* (with CB Media) and *Owl* magazine for children, along with numerous spinoff directories and supplements. De Pencier had the right touch, or hired the right touchers, to make *Toronto Life* grow.

While Tom Hedley was editor, *Toronto Life* produced in October 1977 what was billed as "the fattest consumer magazine in Canadian history." Such consumerism led someone to ask a later editor, Marq de Villiers, "what it was like to edit a magazine for people who bought lucite bidets." To this, de Villiers replied, "My answer to that was 'just because people have money doesn't mean they don't have ideas.'"

Toronto Life grew and grew. In 1981, the magazine bought *Toronto Calendar*, which had been founded in 1969 and had sister publications in Montreal, Vancouver and Washington, D.C., and its holding company CUC Ltd., which also had Ontario cable TV interests. Few of *Calendar's* employees went to *Toronto Life*, but the magazine added 10,000 paid subscriptions from 200,000 controlled-circulation readers. In 1981, with Alexander Ross ("Our whole secret is that we publish phone numbers") as editor, the staff hand-delivered 25,000 downtown copies during a mail strike that debilitated many other magazines.

The most caustic critic of the *Toronto Life* that had emerged since 1971 was *Toronto Calendar's* former editor, Barbara Moon, who wrote in 1984:

> There was no gainsaying: their magazine was fatter, handsomer, slicker [than *Calendar*]. They had name writers I couldn't afford, space for articles that ran up to 7,000 words, an art department with a dizzying budget, and an editorial cast of thousands: researchers, co-ordinators, copy editors, features editors, contributing editors, consulting editors, executive editors, business editors, systems editors, you name it. At the best of times I had two overworked editorial assistants and an associate editor borrowed from other duties for one week of every month. Nonetheless, month after month I reached their back cover with the same inner grunt of relief.
>
> Their preoccupation with "the scene," meaning that mythical downtown arena where fashion leaders and opinion

molders dispense insights and promote causes, had the effect of separating Torontonians into a core of chic, knowing insiders and everybody else, eat your heart out. This struck me as wide of the reality, as well as bad manners. More than that, their appetite for the kinky and the saucy left under-reported a wealth of genuine city lore—cultural, behavioral, explanatory—that I thought a different magazine might explore, given resources.

Commenting on the magazine's March 1984 salute to the city's birthday, Moon noted that "no expense has been spared: silver on the cover; full colour on every other page of editorial; no end of commissioned artwork [conceived by the magazine's art director, Ken Rodmell.]" But the "overall concept is nothing more original than that hardy reader-tease, Who's really Who in the city, a mischievous, arbitrary catalogue of names. As the cover-lines put it, '150 PORTRAITS. The most influential, powerful, glamorous, opinionated, innovative, useful and creative PEOPLE IN THE CITY.'" Unmentioned by Moon, the same issue also hilariously offered a "directory to more than 350 of Toronto's top restaurants."

In 1983, when CBC executive Peter Herrndorf became publisher, and 1984, the magazine made record profits for itself. So attuned to advertisements was *Toronto Life* by this time that a June 1984 issue bisected the two-page spread of an Alberto Manguel article with a full-page card insert for a clothing store.

The September 1984 issue inaugurated features like "Toronto Lifesavers" (city services), expanded its "Epicure" section (recipes and stingless restaurant reviews), redesigned its "Toronto Calendar" what's-on listings and introduced an "Urban Spaces" feature to "celebrate" a favorite *Toronto Life* word—advances in urban design.

Throughout the magazine's career, there were often annoyances in the magazine's fat issues: the grandiloquence of Barry Callaghan—and quieter overwriting (Harry Bruce's "Toronto Islands in Winter" in February 1973: "The islands in winter are also a fine place for lovers, a place to stun a beautiful and sympathetic woman....People touch one another on the cold days over there, and amazing relationships become more possible than they were before"); the soppy "Relationships" columns; the cosy, self-satisfied tone—even when the magazine was being most rueful about itself. The twentieth anniversary issue, which called the "triumph of feminism" the "most significant social change of the last 20 years," had sections called "Our Wheelers and Dealers," "The Books We Read," "The Joints We Hung Out In," "Our Society Unmentionables."

At the same time, *Toronto Life* did occasionally publish fiction and even poetry when there were no obvious commercial reasons for doing so, and the largesse coming its way helped pay for long investigative

Canadian

Special 1986 Annual
$3.50

Bu$iness

500

CANADA'S TOP 500 COMPANIES
WHO'S WINNING, WHO'S LOSING
WHO'S IN HOCK, WHO'S IN SHOCK
WHO'S HIRING, WHO'S FIRING,
and why!

Canadian Busi-
ness *was one of
several magazines
which added
pizazz to brute
numbers.*

pieces like those by Carsten Stroud. In editorial quality—much less in
advertising lineage—it would get little competition from *T.O.* magazine,
launched by Carey Diamond and Bobby Rotenberg and directed at
younger readers, or from *Toronto*, the *Globe and Mail*'s supplement.

Perhaps the magazine's costliest initiative, and most staggering in
scale, was Elaine Dewar's 40,000-word, November 1987 piece on the
rise of the immensely wealthy Reichmann family. Three of the Reichmann brothers and their mother promptly filed a libel suit against her,
Toronto Life and two editors for $102 million—a sum to daunt even the
most affluent magazine. Banned from the National Business Writing
Awards—an action which led to a boycott of the awards by several
newspapers and magazines—the article won Dewar two Magazine
Awards. All the controversy, and the magazine community's loyalty,
obscured the fact that the Dewar article was inconclusive and self-
indulgent.

All Business

In the 1980s, business was the glamorous subject to write about, and
business magazines the glamorous publications. The fascination with
the rich and powerful—whether muckraking or frankly adulatory—
was pandemic, the pace set by journalists like Peter Newman and Alexander Ross. Under Ross and an owner of CB Media, Roy MacLaren—
at one point the federal Revenue Minister—the staid, long-established
Canadian Business became rejuvenated. Taking over *Canadian Business*
in 1978, CB Media published the largest investment newsletter, *The*

Moneyletter, and in 1985 expensively launched a slick magazine of personal finance called *Your Money* that by the next year had a circulation of about 106,000. But a familiar merge-purge occurred in 1988, when the *Financial Post*, taking on a minority stake in CB Media, bought *Your Money* and merged it into *Moneywise*, at the same time as Maclean Hunter sold its *Small Business* magazine to CB. *Moneywise* (formerly *Impetus*), distributed to *Financial Post* and *Medical Post* readers, now aimed for a circulation of up to 300,000.

There were now even regional magazines like *Alberta Inc.* and the controlled-circulation *Atlantic Business*—acquired by *Atlantic Insight's* James Lorimer in 1988—and Vancouver's *Equity*. In 1988 alone Montreal saw the launch of three magazines: *This Week in Business*, *Montreal Business Magazine* and *Quebec Business*. Winnipeg was the base for *Business People Magazine* (formerly *Microsense* and *Business in the Information Age*), *Greater Winnipeg Business*, *Mid-Canada Commerce* and *Manitoba Business*.

At one end of the spectrum was the Conference Board of Canada's *Canadian Business Review* (1974—), which published influential economic forecasts, at the other were magazines which bridged the gap between a special-interest and a general magazine. One of the latter was the neo-conservative monthly *Influence* (1981-88), edited by Peter Worthington, a former editor of the *Toronto Sun* and foreign correspondent. Another was *Vista* launched in 1988 and bankrolled with $10 million by Magna International, the automative parts manufacturer founded by Frank Stronach. According to its consulting editor, Nick Steed, *Vista* would "articulate dreams, provide stepping stones to the future and—most of all—show its readers how to define aspirations and achieve goals at work and play and in personal relationships, style and leisure." Amid this competition, the *Globe and Mail's* handsome *Report on Business Magazine* could afford to be complacent. It had made money practically from its inception.

The generation of the 1960s, revolutionaries or dropouts, now found their righteous causes and psychedelica in the best mortgage or mutual fund.

Controlled Circulations

Anyone fortunate enough to own a house in an affluent urban neighbourhood could count on one thing during the 1970s and 1980s: glossy, ad-filled magazines would come shooting through the mail slot. Moreover, they were free. Among them were magazines like *Success* ("for the minority of men who make it to the top"); the insufferably bland *Goodlife*, launched in 1982 with affiliates in several U.S. cities; and the less disgusting *Avenue*.

How saturated the market became was pointed out in 1982 by Michael de Pencier, one of the controlled-circulation magazines' harshest critics.

At the beginning of this year, you had seven free magazines
going into the same sort of upmarket Vancouver households.
Homemaker's, Quest and *City Women* were going into all the
same homes, with *Vancouver Magazine, Vancouver Calendar,
WestWorld* and *Western Living*. None of those are paid for,
and all of these publishers go around to the beverage alcohol
retailers and say, "Our magazine is reaching the biggest
households in Vancouver."

It was *Quest* that would become not only the best edited and best
written of national, general-interest controlled-circulation magazines,
but their *cause célèbre*. Oddly claiming to be "Canada's first magazine
for men," *Quest's* first number, May 1972, made a faintly plausible
cause for its type of publication.

Quest is paid for the same way most radio and television is
paid for—by the advertiser. No salesman will ever call on you
to sell you a subscription. You will continue to get *Quest* free,
at your home, for as long as you live where you do now.
Quest is distributed only to people like you who live in
selected areas of major Canadian cities.
    This benefits both you as the reader and us as editors and
publishers. And it explains why the old-fashioned mass circulation magazines are ailing while new controlled-circulation
publications, such as *Quest*, are rapidly growing.
    The reason's simple. The old type of magazine had to
appeal to everybody. Controlled circulation doesn't. It is
specialized—and sponsored.
    This means that *Quest* can do a much better editorial job.
Because we know who our readers are, we can concentrate
on creating a new excitement and involvement that the old
type of magazines haven't had since the days before television.

Initially, a quarterly published by Quest Publishing and edited by
Nicholas Steed, *Quest*—with the symbol for maleness dangling from
the Q—was sent to 400,000 homes in six cities in Ontario and Quebec.
When, with the second issue, the magazine came under the control of
Comac Communications, it was delivered to 590,000 homes in the
twelve largest Canadian cities, and was promising six issues in 1973.
After several changes in ownership, Comac was purchased by Torstar
in 1974.
    In 1977, *Quest* recorded a fifty-two per cent increase in advertising
revenue from the previous year. By 1978, *Quest* was delivered to
700,000 Canadian households in twenty-three cities under Hugh J.
Rosser, its publisher, and Jeffrey Shearer, its director of editorial and
marketing. It was now "Canada's Urban magazine." A February 1977

article was Alexander Ross's "How to March to the New Politics": "The new alternative to being pushed around: Small is beautiful." In 1982, an advertorial, "A Quest Special Travel Supplement," attempted to camouflage itself by saying: "Each writer is a professional journalist. Most of them specialize in travel writing."

But under its editor, Michael Enright, a journalistic *wunderkind* in the Peter Gzowski mould, the magazine was more intellectually responsible and visually appealing. Enright, seemed, in fact, to be producing what for some was a contradiction: a quality controlled-circulation magazine. The evidence was in the May 1982 issue with "Piano Forte" by Jay Teitel, a beautifully assembled, nine-page "Ode" to a piano-maker that came complete with Debra Freedman's brown-tinted photographs.

In June 1983, the first bad news came after the Print Measurement Bureau released a report showing that *Quest*'s readership had dropped more than thirty percent since 1980, from 1.6 million to slightly more than a million. Since controlled-circulation magazines depend entirely on advertisers, and advertisers had Pavlovian responses to readership figures, this boded a lot of ill. Moreover, controlled-circulation magazines like *Quest* did not get the same favoured postal rates as those with paid circulations.

The next year, with the same basic staff—Enright, managing editor D. B. Scott and art director Art Niemi—the magazine attempted to recover. In the summer of 1984, the magazine lowered its ad rates and sent itself to fewer households: some 480,000 of them.

Comac asked Enright to tailor the magazine more to managers, owners and professionals. Although he had helped to redesign the magazine, Jeffrey Shearer, who had been a Comac vice-president, left the company to join *TV Guide*. Disputing the PMB figures, Enright seemed bitter: "When we did three $1-million-grossing issues in a row, nobody jumped up and down about what a great editorial product we had," he told an interviewer. "But when we *weren't* selling so many ads, suddenly the quality of the editing was questioned."

The new-look September cover had a different logo and Paul Orenstein's photograph of Barbara Amiel in high heels, hiked-up tweed trousers and ruffled blouse. The story to go with it was "The Business of Being Barbara Amiel." Perhaps of equal interest to the MOPs—Managers, Owners, Professionals—*Quest* was now cultivating articles like Matt Cohen's "My Love Is Young." Wrote Cohen: "Since the nights when King David lay with a nubile young girl to warm his aging flesh, older men have dreamed of younger women."

In his September editorial, Enright made obeisance to "service." "We are not going to preach on politics, morality or religion....What the magazine will provide is road-map information on how to get there." There was a new column called "Working World"—"to examine the latest trends in businesses large and small"; "Staying Alive"—"will speak to men and women in their thirties through fifties who want to redress years of bodily abuse and strive for fitness"; and "Great Escapes"— "will take you out of your urban environment and transport you to other worlds."

Before the transition, Enright had told an interviewer,

> "In a sense, I really feel it's more my magazine than the publisher's. So I value this clear understanding I have with him, and with the company: I edit the book; no one else does. If the owners aren't happy with that, I'll go away. If they don't like me, there will be a brief meeting in the boardroom, we'll all shake hands like gentlemen, and I'll walk out with a wall-hanging."

This was not precisely how Enright went. *Quest*'s revenue dropped from $5.7 million in 1983 to $3 million in 1984, giving a likely net loss for the year of $1 million. Comac was now owned by Tele-Direct, a subsidiary of Bell Canada Enterprises, which had bought it from Torstar for $5 million in 1982. Comac also published *City Woman* and *Homemaker's*, and the previous year had paid $2 million for controlled-circulation magazines in Vancouver, Calgary and Edmonton. But now they weren't swallowing losses.

A diary Enright kept during October, the magazine's last month, reveals the combination of panic and bitterness which typically accompanies news of a publication's impending doom. As rumours of *Quest*'s collapse circulated among staff, the magazine's advertising manager and associate publisher, John Dunlop—later publisher of *Vista*—wondered aloud to Enright whether "he and I could buy the magazine from Comac and try to make a go of it." Within days, *Quest*'s publisher, Hugh Rosser, told Enright that he would likely be replaced as publisher by Glenn Rogers, a Comac vice-president and *Quest*-hater now in charge of *Western Living*.

On 23 October, Enright talked to the managing editor, D.B. Scott, the former editor of the *Toronto Star*'s short-lived foray into magazines, *The City*, and later started *Avenue Magazine*. Although Scott "is exceedingly calm and logical as he always is," Enright detected "a burning anger, quietly underlining his voice." On 29 October, Enright, a vice-president of the National Magazine Awards Foundation, took part in a committee "to design the format for next year's awards and seminars. In 1984, *Quest* won more gold medals for any magazine in the country except *Saturday Night*, with which we tied."

On 5 November, Enright was told *Quest* was closing. Two days later the staff arrived at work and found "an interior decorator going over floor plans for our offices to redesign them." A wake for the staff had been planned, but the company "has refused to pick up the tab. Rosser

THE AGELESS
POWER OF
MOTHER
GOOSE

says he will pay for the food." On the last day of work, Friday, 9 November, the staff arrived to find a man in the lobby scraping the name of the magazine off the glass doors with a razor blade. *Quest*'s last cover story was "The Ageless Power of Mother Goose."

Comac would soon find itself with a shortage of golden eggs. By the end of 1985, a group of partners, which included John Barrington, Tim Murray, and Charles Peterson, purchased Comac for about $5.5 million. Before three years had ended, Comac closed *City Woman* and sold the rest of its major closed-circulation magazines.

Women's Magazines: Having It All

Although women continued to argue for social reform—freedom of choice in abortion, equal pay for work of equal value, the banning of violent pornography—editors of Doris Anderson's vigour and determination went missing from their magazines in the 1980s. Dawn MacDonald, who was *Miss Chatelaine*'s first editor and founded Comac's *City Woman* (1978-85), appeared to have Anderson's energy and initiative. Although *City Woman* had won awards for fashion and religious journalism and gained a 300,000-circulation, MacDonald was dismissed in November 1982, and in 1986 the magazine was transmogrified into the innocuous and smaller-circulation *Career Woman*. MacDonald went on to found, in 1988, *Villagers*, "Canada's journal of the global village," a quarterly dealing with foreign aid and international co-operation.

Largely, though, social reform was out, high-fashion frippery was in. In 1987, Maclean Hunter spent $1 million on new stock and binding for its *Flare*, and Key Publishers invested heavily in boosting frequency and building a national circulation base for *Toronto Life Fashion* (1977—). In 1988, Télémedia launched *Expression*, a fashion and beauty magazine aimed, like most of these magazines, at Canadian women between the ages of 25 and 49, and shooting for the unlikely target of 190,000 in paid circulation. It was not alone: the *Globe and Mail* sank at least

Editorial co-ops often cooked up small magazines like the feminist Hysteria *in Kitchener, Ontario.*

$1 million on its new fashion quarterly, *Domino*. Other newspapers also dabbled in producing similar glossy effusions—such as the *Toronto Star*'s *Elegance*, which inelegantly folded in 1988. The same year, Southam's *Verve* was sold to Family Communications and merged with the latter's *You*. Such failures and mergers were inevitable. The quest for conspicuous consumers required vast expenditures in coated stock and colour photography.

Rebelling against the trend towards lifestyle and fashion-and-beauty magazines were such small feminist journals, often quarterly and published outside Toronto, as *HERizons* in Winnipeg, *Breaking the Silence* in Ottawa, *Kinesis* in Vancouver and *Hysteria* in Kitchener.

For feminists, some statistics of the 1980s must have seemed like the bad old days of the 1950s. In 1986, for example, the most widely circulated magazines in the country—both controlled-circulation—were *Recipes Only* (a top-circulated French version was *Bien Manger*) at 1,677,000, and Comac's *Homemaker's* (*Madame au Foyer* in Quebec) at 1,040,000. In the paid-circulation category, Télémedia's *Canadian Living* (1975—) was second only to *Chatelaine*. All were more absorbed in extolling domestic life than they were in seeing women forge ahead on the job.

For the affluent, the gracious-living ghosts of *Canadian Homes and Gardens* and *Mayfair* survived in the 122,000-circulation *Select Homes*— sold by Southam to Télémedia in 1988—*Canadian House & Home, Century Home* and Maclean Hunter's *City and Country Home*.

Women were far from being solo and self-sufficient, if the Calgary-based *Singles Today* was any gauge. In 1987, the 60,000-circulation magazine had more than sixty pages in personal ads. The twice-yearly *Wedding Bells* and *Bride* took over once the singles problem was resolved, followed by parenting magazines like the bi-monthly *Today's*

Parent, edited in Toronto but with headquarters in Millbrook, Ontario. In 1988, Family Communications played the field; its women's magazines included *Best Wishes* (Quebec version: *Mon Bébé*) *Expecting* (*C'est pour quand*), *Today's Bride* and *You/Verve*. A new interest in children's reading tastes resulted in Key Publishers' *Owl* (1976–) and *Chickadee* (1979–), founded by Annabel Slaight and Mary Ann Brinckman. As far as the lifestyle magazine titles were concerned, the *Living* was *Canadian, Western, Ontario,* or *Easy.*

There were now even several regional women's magazines, like *Woman to Woman* in British Columbia and *Every Woman* in Manitoba. Nationally, though, the field was dominated by *Chatelaine* and *Canadian Living.*

From the start, *Canadian Living*, edited by Judy Brandow since 1977, had half its circulation in southern Ontario and—a rarity among Canadian magazines—achieved more than fifty percent of its sales from newsstands, chiefly in supermarkets, where it often beat out such huge-circulation U.S. rivals as *Family Circle* and *Woman's Day.* With short, practical articles on food, decorating, beauty, fashions, crafts (an annual Design-a-Doll contest) and fitness, *Canadian Living* was a quick read, and a French version, *Coup de Pouce*, was likewise popular. The 539,000-circulation *Canadian Living* also spun off Christmas-craft books and a 120,000-circulation cookbook-style food magazine. In 1988, Brandow, *Canadian Living's* editor in chief, who was also in charge of *Expression* and *Food* magazines, quit—or was fired, depending on the version one heard—after she unsuccessfully ran as a New Democratic Party candidate in that year's federal election.

Jane Gale, the editor of the digest-sized, controlled-circulation *Homemaker's* (1964–, at first quaintly called *Market Maid*), in 1986 also made a troubled departure from her magazine. *Homemaker's* went out ten times a year to households in twenty-eight cities. Yet the magazine was only marginally profitable in the mid-1980s. In 1988, *Homemaker's* new owner, Télémedia, merged it with another editorially slight, big-circulation magazine with sliding revenues, *Recipes Only*, whose French version was *Bien Manger.*

Magazines like *Canadian Living* and *Homemaker's* primarily were intended to ride the kitchen counter and to remind the housewife she needed to stock up on margarine.

At Maclean-Hunter, the prissily named *Miss Chatelaine*, founded in 1969—*New Mother* in 1979 was another *Chatelaine* spinoff—changed its name to *Flare* and became "Canada's Fashion Magazine." Fashionably fat (for magazines), it was dedicated to "What's Hot, What's Not."

At *Chatelaine* itself, the Sudbury-born Mildred Istona had become editor in 1978, having serving as free-lance writer, teen editor and managing editor there, and editor of *Miss Chatelaine* for seven years. A much less public person than Doris Anderson, Istona, along with publisher

Celebrating celeb-rities, in March 1988 Chatelaine *called itself youth-ful, dynamic — and 60 years young.*

Bruce Drane, "repositioned" *Chatelaine* so, Drane said in 1987, it would "not get caught in any one particular demographic segment. *Chatelaine* had been moving toward that with the women's movement under Doris Anderson [*sic*]."

To Istona, *Chatelaine* was "the journal of record of where women have been." Anderson would doubtless have put it, "where they *should* be." By reputation, Istona was not a delegator. Judith Timson, a former columnist and contributing editor, was quoted as saying, "You don't work for Mildred unless you're prepared to be a bridesmaid all your life."

Although *Chatelaine* occasionally took controversial editorial stands—Istona opposed censorship of pornography, and wrote an editorial about Brian Mulroney before the 1980 federal election called "The Politics of Baloney" and hired Maureen McTeer, wife of the former Conserva-tive Prime Minister, to write Ottawa reports—she kept the magazine on a thoroughly 1980s level. Departments included "Me Tarzan, You Jane," with male and female contributors, and "Feeling Good About Yourself."

Istona ran once-over-lightly surveys of cities, and a stingless annual "Best and Worst Dressed Canadians" listing. In May 1987, along with the usual insipid, quickly prepared recipes, the magazine balanced "Mother Knows Best: 17 Celebrated Canadians Share Their Mother's Best Advice," with Charlotte Gray's tough "Will the Real Geills Turner [wife of Liberal leader John Turner] Please Stand Up." In the same issue was an old reliable topic, "Stalking the Perfect Housekeeper," this time by biographer Elspeth Cameron. "Mrs. *Chatelaine*" was now "Woman of the Year." In 1986, she was the Vancouver film maker Sandy Wilson; in 1987, the Edmonton country and western singer, K. D. Lang.

All of it worked commercially. *Chatelaine* was still a highly profitable part of the Maclean Hunter operation, managing a 1986 circulation of 1,089,000 and returning net revenue of $30 million as opposed to, say, a 1974 circulation of 980,000 and a 1981 profit of $20 million. *Chatelaine* might not have been having it all, but at least it was having a large chunk.

Weeding the Turnip Patch

The story of *Harrowsmith* is one of feedbags to (relative) riches. In 1976, a *Kingston Whig-Standard* reporter named James Lawrence, who had arrived from the United States two years earlier, took a leave of absence from the newspaper and got a bank loan of $3,500. With it and a Chargex card, he and his Canadian wife, Elinor, printed 25,000 copies of *Harrowsmith*, named for a village north of Kingston, and mailed 15,000 of them gratis to Canadian subscribers culled from the subscription list of the U.S. magazine *Organic Gardening*. Headquarters was a farmhouse in Camden East, Ontario, across from the Texaco gas station.

The staff, of what Lawrence a few months later called "bleary-eyed moonlights and unpaid volunteers," was also helped by Denis T. Patrick Sears, the Kingston novelist who gave the magazine three pieces—one on barn raising—for the price of a subscription. Sears died later that year and was the subject of a grateful editorial. Aiming for six issues a year—the magazine was conspicuously numbered on the cover so as not to date it on the shelves—Lawrence made much editorial play on the fact that he split firewood to keep the office stoves going and that the telephone was on a nine-family party line. So immediately popular was it that within eight weeks Lawrence had to increase the press run to 40,000 copies.

The magazine was on its way, making contact with an audience composed partly of homesteading organic gardeners and small-is-beautiful idealists, but also many who simply liked the idea, whether or not it was realized, of country living. A surprising percentage of *Harrowsmith*'s subscribers lived in cities, and in 1978 the magazine's business manager reported that more than half were college-educated and had a family income of more than $20,000.

Popular as the magazine quickly became, this probably would not have been enough to keep it going had it not also launched a book-publishing firm that, starting with *Terrific Tomatoes*, produced such best-sellers as the *Harrowsmith Reader*.

The magazine attempted to be down to earth, but it was also slick, leaning to clever puns and inventive titles. For example: "This is a ewe. The ram's name is Dougal McKenzie"—"A look at small-scale sheep

Harrowsmith

Pond Culture•Baconmaking Without Guilt•Sauna Architecture
The Rites of Autumn•Grand Manan Dulsing•Backyard Buckwheat

·WOOD·HEAT·

RENAISSANCE

Harrowsmith *combined back-to-the-land virtuousness with yuppie panache.*

husbandry in Cape Breton.'' Soon it began winning National Magazine Awards, including ''Magazine of the Year'' in 1977. By 1981, *Harrowsmith* had moved to a three-storey gabled mansion, and the circulation was nudging 160,000. But there was trouble down on the farm. James and Elinor Lawrence, who had once been Peace Corps volunteers in Colombia, now began to engage in something like marital guerrilla warfare.

In the breakup of the Lawrences' marriage, the battleground was *Harrowsmith* and *Equinox*, ''The Magazine of Canadian Discovery,'' launched in January 1982. Elinor Lawrence owned half the shares of Camden House Publishing, the parent company, and she was its titular director. She locked her husband and his allies out, and they decamped to run *Equinox*. After messy suits and countersuits, Lawrence acquired all shares of *Harrowsmith* in an out-of-court settlement and fired several whom his wife had hired—two later sued him for wrongful dismissal. James Lawrence remarried in 1984, to *Harrowsmith*'s American production manager, and in 1986 made some momentous changes.

First he sold his Canadian company to Télémedia Publishing Corporation, whose president was now Jeffrey Shearer, formerly with Comac. Remaining editor—and assuring his readers that Télémedia would let the magazines remain in Camden East—Lawrence also announced that he was setting up a U.S. version of *Harrowsmith* in Charlotte, Vermont. About half the new magazine would have overlapping content, and it would still be printed in Owen Sound, Ontario, where *Harrowsmith* had been rolling off the presses since 1976. Since there was no import duty for printed matter going to the United States, this might mean that the company could be paid in U.S. dollars, and pay in cheaper Canadian currency.

At the time of the sale, *Harrowsmith* and *Equinox* had a combined staff of fifty, and were the seventh and eighth largest paid-circulation Canadian consumer magazines, taking in more than $8 million in revenue. That wasn't chicken feed.

Without undervaluing *Harrowsmith*'s achievement, it should be noted that the magazine, like its near contemporaries in the United States, *Country Journal* and *Mother Earth News*, emerged from the back-to-nature and small-is-beautiful movements that were 1960s phenomena. All through *Harrowsmith*'s career, the magazine had walked an editorial tightrope between the pragmatic and the purist. It was never consistently a Pollyanna about rural life: in 1981, it ran a long series on the "Rural Malaise," about back-to-the-land disenchantment. To its credit, it could run ads for Havahart humane traps and in March/April 1986 publish John Goddard's "Out for Blood," a sympathetic account of native Canadians' trapping, then run a more critical account of the virulence trapping aroused in Europe.

If its ecological niche extended to highly expensive home-renovation projects, until March 1981 it banned beer and wine advertisements for ethical reasons and continued to refuse ads for cigarettes, guns, snowmobiles and political parties—all equally dangerous in *Harrowsmith's* thinking. Whether or not Télémedia would be equally virtuous remained to be seen. Some of the new ads, such as a two-page spread of Suzuki all-terrain vehicles roaring along a woodland trail in the March/April 1988 issue, indicated that the answer would be negative.

By 1988 *Harrowsmith*'s glossy, photogenic sister *Equinox* had run to a 163,000-circulation, and was giving the U.S. *National Geographic*—next to *Reader's Digest*, the largest-circulating U.S. magazine in Canada—at least some competition. Although there were popular magazines whose audiences relished the outdoors—*Outdoor Canada, Ontario Out of Doors, B.C. Outdoors, Western Sportsman* and *Eastern Woods & Waters*—the magazine that tapped an audience keen on science, travel and geography was the six-times-a-year *Canadian Geographic*, formerly the *Canadian Geographic Journal*. From 1975 to 1981 it shot from 20,000 to 100,000 copies. Attractive but less polished than *Equinox*, its coverage extended into Canadian history and heritage and—with a per-copy readership of more than five—the *Geographic* achieved a circulation only slightly behind its Camden East competitor.

What Was Left

The rebellious or reformist zeal that had led to the founding of so many 1960s periodicals of social or political comment—many of them existing in a smudgy limbo between newspapers and magazines, "tabloid sporadicals" to use one term for them—had dissipated by the late 1970s. By then, some of their writers were looking into the question of incorporating themselves.

Whether promoting participatory democracy or libertarian socialism, magazines like the monthly *Canadian Dimension* or quarterly *Our Generation* belonged to the social and cultural mood of the 1960s. The magazines of social commentary or criticism that succeeded them did not make much impact on the increasingly materialist society around them. The ones that had some effect were founded no later than the early 1970s. There were, for example, Silver Donald Cameron's *Mysterious East* (1969-72) in Fredericton and Reshard Gool's *Square Deal* (1971-73) in Charlottetown.

Most of these magazines were put together by an editorial collective and were cheaply printed on newsprint. Few exceeded 10,000 in circulation. The oldest of them—apart from the *Canadian Forum*—was Winnipeg's *Canadian Dimension* (1963—) funded through the charitable Manitoba Foundation for Canadian Studies, and supporting the more radical elements of the New Democratic Party. Although sometimes academically leaden, it could be more barbed. After former Manitoba Premier Ed Schreyer was appointed Governor General, the magazine ran a back-cover photograph of Schreyer with the caption "The working class can kiss my ass. I've got the governor-generalship at last."

The *Last Post* (1969-85), founded by journalist Patrick MacFadden and others, came out of Montreal but moved to Toronto in 1972. Livelier than *Canadian Dimension*, its most abrasive contributor was probably the cartoonist Terry Mosher ("Aislin"). During the October Crisis of 1970, it rushed out a broadside of protest.

The monthly *Our Times* (1981—) started out as an ethnic community tabloid, then became an independent magazine covering labour issues and was printed by a worker-owned co-operative. The magazine appealed to unions for advertising, and half its 4,500 subscriptions were bulk orders from unions. Other union periodicals, like the glossy quarterlies of the Canadian Union of Public Employees (the *Public Quarterly*) and the Ontario Federation of Labour's *Ontario Labor*, were in effect house organs.

Some magazines emerged to affirm the identities and represent the interests of their communities, particularly those frequently subject to various forms of persecution or harassment. *Sweetgrass*, founded by Juanita Remi and formerly a magazine called *Ontario Indian*, edited by Dennis Martel, was a short-lived but professionally edited magazine of Canadian native peoples. The *Body Politic* (1971-87), a lively, wide-ranging and often controversial tabloid mainly directed to Canadian homosexuals, sometimes had to defend itself against charges of obscenity and achieved a 7,000-circulation. When it died, only *Rites* (1983—) was left to represent the political interests of the gay communities.

Other magazines attempted to correct what they regarded as a dearth of investigative reporting or thoughtful political analysis. In Ottawa, Tim Creery's inadequately financed and short-lived *Report on Confederation* aimed for a national circulation of 12,000, but only achieved about 4,500. Another Ottawa magazine, *Goodwin's* (1983-85), named for Albert "Ginger" Goodwin, a British Columbia labour activist shot by police in 1918, saw itself as a national "investigative magazine with a social conscience."

This Magazine (1967—) began as *This Magazine Is About Schools*. A proponent of the North American free-schools movement, it achieved early success in the United States. Shortening its name in 1973, it became a nationalist and Marxist-oriented magazine run by an editorial board, because, said an editor, Daniel Drache, "the schools question, curriculum, and teacher organizing needed to be dealt with in the wider context of Canada's political and economic structures."

In 1976, the magazine, with a paid circulation of about 6,000 and an annual $100,000 budget, aimed to make itself a larger, newsier, more investigative publication. It took on board Nick Fillmore, a former president of the Centre for Investigative Journalism, who had attempted to rescue *Goodman's*, and Robert Chodos, a former *Last Post* editor. They were added to the columnists who had given *This Magazine* its reputation: playwright Rick Salutin (the "Culture Vulture" column), the political scientist Mel Watkins and the Vancouver journalist Stan Persky.

This Magazine made headlines in 1987 when reports claimed it was being investigated by the Canadian Security Intelligence Service. Although the federal solicitor general did not deny that *some* magazine was being looked at, he denied *this* magazine was, leading Mavor Moore to say in the *Globe and Mail*,

> Personally, I consider it infinitely more preposterous and outrageous to be told that *This Magazine* is not sufficiently threatening to be the target of an investigation. You have sold me a subscription under false pretenses.
>
> Like many others, I read *This Magazine* to stay abreast of the apocalyptic left just as I keep up with the apoplectic right in the Fraser Institute's papers and the apathetic centre in *Maclean's*.

The relationship of these avidly political journals with governments was bound to be stressful, especially when, in order to elicit tax-free donations, the former claimed charitable status from the latter. *New Maritimes*, the leftwing magazine based in Enfield, N.S., fought with the federal Department of Communications to retain second-class postal registration, with the Canada Council over grants and with Revenue Canada over charitable status. The Regina-based *Briarpatch* also struggled to preserve its charitable status; in 1977 *Canadian Dimension* lost its status and never got it back.

This Magazine received financial support from the Ontario Arts Council and the Canada Council, as did the long-established *Canadian Forum*. Looking forward to its sixtieth anniversary in 1988, the *Forum* was now published by the nonprofit Survival Foundation, and was even able to modestly pay contributors. It seemed a permanent fixture in the Toronto intellectual establishment. Periodically refreshing its layout with redesigns, the *Forum*'s greatest news coup in recent years had been in November 1971, when it boosted its pressrun from 5,000 to 8,000 to publish a leaked copy of the federal Gray Report on Foreign Ownership. But the only social cause that the *Forum*, with its mixed literary and social contents, embraced with anything like its 1930s fervour was that of feminism, a subject to which it had paid scant attention prior to 1970. In any event, there was relatively little outcry when the magazine suspended publication with its February/March 1988 issue.

A year later, though, the debt-ridden *Forum* was back in business. The Halifax publisher James Lorimer teamed with Toronto lawyer Aubrey Golden to rescue the magazine, transferring all its business functions to Halifax and its editorial side to Ottawa under the political scientist Duncan Cameron, John Hutcheson's successor as editor.

The *Forum*, like *This Magazine* or a more recent leftist magazine of culture and social comment, *Fuse*, was caught in a curious dilemma. Among the majority of the population, English-Canadian nationalism and leftist politics had not made significant gains during the late 1970s, leaving Drache to say in a collection of *This Magazine* pieces, "The real choice is always between being strategic or being irrelevant." On the other hand, so dominated by nationalism and liberal or leftist inclinations were the artistic or intellectual minorities that many of these magazines seemed to be preaching to the converted.

Comedy

In the 1970s and 1980s the consumerist antics of the Yuppie generation offered much for the humorist to aim at, but few archers knew the difference between a barn door and a bull's-eye. One who did was Thomas Hagey, a young man with a dairy-and-hog farming operation in Breslau. Hagey's parodies were not just funny in themselves, but a commentary on contemporary magazine publishing.

Playboar *editor Thomas Hagey un-provocatively poses beside Ursowla Hamdress, his magazine's 1981 "Litter-mate of the Year".*

Hagey's first initiative was *Playboar* in 1977, complete with a sow wallowing on the centrefold as "Littermate of the Month"—much to the annoyance of the sensitive Hugh Hefner's *Playboy* magazine. As a *Best of Playboar*, the magazine sold 310,000 copies. Sales were aided by a 1986 promotional tour in which Hagey drove his Pigmobile with a PIGS licence plate across the United States under a "Hams Across America" banner.

But, although celebrated, *Playboar* made more money for Hagey's partners than for himself. Under the auspices of Daydream Publishing, Hagey in 1987 launched a seventy-six-page glossy magazine called *Cowsmopolitan*. According to Hagey, "Pigs have had their day. Cows are becoming extremely popular in the U.S. for some reason. I think it's really neat, all milk and motherhood. There's something really nice about these docile beasts that don't hurt anybody and, good heavens, they have four stomachs."

Among the fodder that *Cowsmo* offered its readers was a "Bachelor of the Month," the magazines "all-bull, no-bull Mr. Avail A. Bull." The diet and beauty features included such indispensable articles as "How to Lose 600 pounds in Just 3 Weeks" and "How to Correct That Gummy Smile." There was also a "before-and-after" photo about tanning: on the left a cow, on the right a set of leather luggage. The editorial by Ellen Guernsey Brown could not be missed, nor the cosmetic ads for Clover Girl and Oil of Old Hay. The publisher was expecting to sell 500,000 copies, most of them in the United States.

Another comedy-minded Canadian who made an impact in the United States was E. Graydon Carter. This former Ottawan had edited the *Canadian Review*, a failed 1970s magazine of political and literary commentary, before taking up journalism in New York. There in 1985 he co-founded *Spy*, a cleverly designed monthly of satire and scandal reportage. Soon some members of the Manhattan glitterati were competing to appear in its pages.

Literature and the Arts

The nationalism and cultural energy of the 1960s in the arts flowed over into the early 1970s. At the same time, small magazines—whether in the arts, humanities, social sciences or "pure" sciences—became increasingly dependent on the limited resources and occasionally incestuous juries of public funding bodies like the Canada Council, the Humanities and Social Sciences Research Council, the National Research Council and the National Sciences and Engineering Research Councils. Whether this was the best means to encourage dissidence, innovation and risk-taking in the arts and humanities was only now and then debated.

A critically sophisticated, or at least informed public, is crucial to writers and artists. Certainly there was a dearth of serious magazines dealing with arts and entertainment, although several papers—*Music Express*, the *Toronto Star*'s *Video and Home Entertainment*, and *Video Scene*—had big circulations through newspaper inserts or bulk distribution in retail outlets. During the 1980s, there were several attempts to create regional arts magazines, such as Winnipeg's monthly *Midcontinental* and Calgary's quarterly *Last Issue*. Nationally, though, the last serious venture in arts reviewing and reportage occurred in the late 1960s. In Montreal, Peter Lebensold, who had founded an internationally oriented film magazine called *Take One*—its specifically Canadian equivalent was *Cinema Canada*—went on to found the *Five Cent Review* (1966-69). Edited by Barrie Lord, the well-designed magazine operated on a shaky financial premise. It was distributed free to bookstores, record stores and newsstands, which then charged their customers a nickel.

Short of giving away a magazine free, the record for newsstand price-cutting probably belonged to the later anarchist, four-page literary magazine, Vancouver's *3¢ Pulp*. Until 1985, *Books in Canada* (1970—) was given out free in bookstores. Founded by Val Clery, who had completed a study demonstrating the lack of public information and criticism about Canadian books, the magazine under Clery, Douglas Marshall and Michael Smith was now and then bracingly irreverent, sometimes thin and always financially enfeebled.

With spotty support from Canadian publishers, *Books in Canada* was heavily dependent on grants from arts councils. *Quill & Quire*, which Seccombe House had founded in 1935 and was directed to booksellers, publishers, librarians and teachers, was acquired by Key Publishers in 1971. An otherwise excellent trade magazine, it had an amateurish section of short reviews. One worthwhile regional initiative in book reviewing was the *Atlantic Provinces Book Review* (1973—), a quarterly that ran a book review service for Maritimes papers and enclosed 20,000 of its 35,000 copies in the *Halifax Daily News*. A smaller-scale, but interesting magazine of literary commentary was *Brick* (1978—), first of Ilderton, Ontario, then Toronto. More academic was *Essays in Canadian Literature* (1974—), published by the literary reference-book firm ECW Press.

In 1983, *Queen's Quarterly* celebrated its ninetieth anniversary. Always grey and solid, it was something like poured concrete: weighty essays and particles of poetry, and occupying a middle ground between stolid scholarly journals—there was now a University of Toronto quarterly called *Scholarly Publishing* (1969—) and risk-taking little magazines. Its scholarship unusually intelligible, the *Quarterly's* pages were seldom open to academic ladder-climbers of the publish-or-perish persuasion. In an age of narrow specialization, it took an interdisciplinary overview, deriving strength not so much from the creative arts as from the humanities and social sciences, particularly from what had once been called political economy.

Among magazines dealing with visual arts and artifacts was the Royal Ontario Museum's *Rotunda* (1968—). A readable journal on all aspects of the museum's holdings in arts, ethnography and natural science, it was sometimes sold on newsstands. As far as the contemporary arts were concerned, Eldon Garnet's *Impulse* (1971—) started out as a strictly literary journal but converted itself into a magazine of avant-garde media. *File* (1972—), the outlet for the Toronto artists' group, General Idea, once faced legal action by Time Inc. because of its *Life*-like logo; *Parachute* (1976—) in Montreal and *C Magazine* (1984—) in Toronto became outlets for new art criticism. Among regional magazines, *Arts Atlantic* (1977—) was co-operatively sponsored by Charlottetown's Confederation Centre Art Gallery and other Maritimes showplaces; the Vancouver Art Gallery's *Vanguard* (1972—) achieved a national reputation.

But the most opulent art periodical to appear was *Canadian Art* (1983—), a quarterly co-published by Key Publishers and Maclean Hunter. Edited by Susan Walker, the publisher of *Quill & Quire,* it had an initial press-run of 20,000, and absorbed the subscription lists of two dying journals, *Artsmagazine and Artscanada*. A glossy magazine with a full-colour cover, its pages underscored how much the number of exhibitions and exhibitor had swelled in the past two decades. *Canadian Art* was not without its detractors; it was, said the *Globe and Mail's* art critic, "a package that perks you right up with snazzy design and big names, just to get you ready for the main course of pap." It portrayed, he said, "the Canadian art world as a Halloween drag ball, Santa's workshop full of busy elves, and the bejowled boardroom of the Toronto-Dominion Bank, all rolled into one dumb package." In 1988, *Toronto*

Life's executive editor, Jocelyn Laurence, became editor of the redesigned magazine.

Until the early 1970s, Canadian literary magazines were often forums for spirited debate about the who, where, why, when, what and how of composition, and of native versus cosmopolitan forces, and in the process brought forward in the 1960s a remarkably talented generation of writers. By the mid-1980s, monotony had set in. Especially in magazines publishing poetry, many touted the same writers and schools.

The generation of the late 1970s and 1980s tended to be flaccidly ecumenical careerists who did not react against their immediate predecessors but instead sought their approval. The bitter rivalries were no longer about artistic principles but over who got on a public reading tour. As to what got written and how, anything went, providing the writer abhorred poverty, pollution, male chauvinism and the arms race.

Few new magazines started, and those that did were clustered during the early 1970s. *Canadian Fiction Magazine* (1971—), founded in Prince George, British Columbia, by Wayne Stedingh, transferred to Vancouver and then Toronto. Under Geoff Hancock, a compulsive anthologist and theoretician of "Magic Realism," the magazine became the only place where a sizeable amount of new Canadian fiction could be scrutinized: by 1985, some fifty authors had published portions of more than seventy books in the periodical. A less impressive publication, with some criticism included, was the *Journal of Canadian Fiction* (1972—).

Like the long-enduring *The Fiddlehead* at the University of New Brunswick, *Event* (1970—) at Caledonia College in British Columbia and the *Antigonish Review* (1971—) at St. Francis Xavier University were academically based but accessible, eclectic outlets for new writers. Karen Mulhallen's *Descant* (1970—) often published special issues, sometimes in book form. Most visually distinctive was Karl Jirgens's *Rampike*, about the length and colour of a Yule log and a "forum for post-modern expression within a thematic format." There were general literary magazines like Bernice Lever's *Waves* (1972-87), and more idiosyncratic ones like Barry Callaghan's *Exile* (1972—). Its title was taken from Ezra Pound's little magazine of the same name, which had published his father Morley Callaghan's fiction. Botanical motifs were favoured for titles. Besides the *Fiddlehead*, there was *Fireweed*, Calgary's *Dandelion* (1975—), the Prairies' *Grain* (1973—) and the Maritimes' *Germination* (1976—).

Magazines become more specialized. There was even an electronic literary magazine, *Swift Current* (1984—), founded by Frank Davey and stored on a computer data base at York University. However technologically innovative, in action it resembled an electronic pen-pal club. Some other specialized magazines centred on the northern sensibility, like Douglas Brown's *Copperfield* (1969-76), and John Flood's *Northward*

Roguishly conservative, The Idler *brought a welcome intellectual insouciance to the Canadian scene.*

For JULY & AUGUST 1988

Journal (1975—), or on feminism. The only real growth among literary or little magazines from the late 1970s was in fact among the latter: two were *Fireweed* and *Room of One's Own* (1974—).

Among many of the literary magazines, the cult word was anything with a "post" in it: postmodernism, poststructuralism, postFreudian.

The Idler (1984—) was definitely "pre." Edited by the Johnsonian Tory, cunningly eccentric David Warren, full of pseudonyms and calculated archaisms, it aimed to be a literary magazine in the widest sense. Anti-abortion, anti-Communist, avowedly Christian in its outlook, *The Idler* described its typical reader as "a sprightly, octogenarian spinster, with a drinking problem, and an ability to conceal it." Among its "hints to authors" in the September 1985 issue, it warned that "we are notorious prudes, easily upset by bull-fighting, lavatory humour, or visits to the sausage factory. We entirely lack curiosity about the sexual fantasies of infants. We try hard not to cuss...." Financed at first by Warren, it was rescued from a cash-flow crisis by Manny Drukier, a wealthy businessman who also published the food magazine *À la carte.*

The Idler was also probably the only literary magazine anywhere to give its name to a pub, opened in 1987, above whose premises the magazine practised its highly individual brand of subversive conservatism.

FULFORD'S
SATURDAY NIGHT

"The strong, powerful personalities are the ones most interesting to write about."
　　　　—Robert Fulford in a CBC radio interview, February 1987

After 1968 there was a question many readers of *Saturday Night* tried to answer. Was Robert Fulford a Vicar of Bray, trimming his journalistic sails to the prevailing winds of status and power? Or was he an honourable man keeping alive the spirit of independent enquiry, a representative and defender of that nearly extinct species, the man of letters?

By the time he became editor of *Saturday Night*, the portly, moon-faced Fulford was already a journalistic veteran: for one thing his father was a Canadian Press editor and re-write man; a great-grandfather was the editor of the *London Advertiser*. Born in Ottawa in 1932, Fulford grew up in the Beaches neighbourhood in southeast Toronto, a pal of the pianist Glenn Gould—they would stretch two cans on a string between their houses in the hope of communicating. Bored with Malvern Collegiate, Fulford worked as a newspaper copy boy and stringer, briefly hosted "Teentime," a radio programme on CHUM, then dropped out of high school in order to cover sports, police, city hall and the courts for the *Globe and Mail*. Whether or not he was employed at one of the eight full-time jobs he held between 1950 and 1968, Fulford busily free-lanced. He was an editor at *Canadian Homes and Gardens* and *Mayfair*, where he worked with Barbara Moon, who later become an indispensable colleague on *Saturday Night*. Joining the *Star* in 1958, he became a columnist at the age of twenty-seven, writing on the arts six days a week. During the next ten years he would shuttle between the *Star* and *Maclean's*. When Arnold Edinborough sought to hire him as managing editor of *Saturday Night*, Fulford had a better idea: he would become editor.

The workaholic and self-confessed print addict ("Sometimes a print addict reveals a touch of erudition and someone asks him, 'How do you manage to read so much?' This can only baffle the true print addict.

What else is there to do?") who in March 1968 took over a national institution, was emphatically no nationalist. In Canadian culture, he said in a piece in January 1960 *Canadian Forum,*

> ...we try to live beyond our means.
> Canada has publishers who cannot find novelists to fill their lists. We have theatres without playwrights, little magazines hungry for short stories, art galleries fighting over painters. We have big, slick magazines which not only have trouble finding writers or editors but actually have difficulty finding people to write about. And now we have a critical magazine, [*Canadian Literature*]...which may find itself short of literature to criticize. We have a kind of artistic autonomy, and we have a sort of critical apparatus; but the people who make the apparatus work—the fiction writers, the playwrights, the other creative artists—are often hard to find. From this angle Canada looks like a giant tomato cannery: dozens of canning machines, hundreds of workmen trained to run them, scores of trucks waiting to transport the finished product but no tomatoes.

Amusing in retrospect, these comments were typical of 1950s cosmopolitanism. By the late 1960s, though, the dominant cultural tendency had veered toward a full-fledged cultural nationalism; there were now, it seemed, an abundance of tomatoes. Fulford became a born-again nationalist. Writing in the October 1970 *Saturday Night*, Fulford said "that this country had not been built without sacrifice and that it might indeed take some considerable further sacrifice to keep it alive....People had to plot and scheme and work long hard hours at boring tasks to make it possible for me, in 1970, to be able to say I am not an American." The anti-Americans, he said,

> ...were always terrible people. They hated Ed Sullivan and so blinded themselves to Jackson Pollock and Saul Bellow. They talked and acted like provincial ignoramuses, and some of them still do. Their vulgar sense of moral and cultural superiority simply has no authentic basis in fact, and never has had. They embarrass me.
> Still, when I worry about it late at night I realize there were moments when they were right and I was wrong....

If some comments indicated a significant change in Fulford's attitude, the magazine itself was not markedly different in the early seventies from what it had been under Arnold Edinborough in the 1960s. Given the meagre financial resources at his disposal, Fulford was plainly doing the best he could with who and what he had. Mary Lowrey Ross, a venerable survivor from the Sandwell era, remained on the masthead, and Fulford continued to employ the people Edinborough had brought to the magazine, such as Harry Bruce, Kildare Dobbs and Jack Batten. There was a gradual shift toward the chronicling of "lifestyles"—so much a feature of 1970s journalism and one that would reach epidemic proportions in the 1980s—and the New Journalism's tendency to use fictional techniques and the first-person singular.

These trends were best exemplified in the inventive work of Toronto free lancer Philip Marchand, a Fulford protégé, whose *Saturday Night* pieces like "Just a Little Love Between Two Swinging Singles" and "The Trouble with Communes Is They Don't Work" formed part of his 1976 collection *Just Looking, Thank You*. There he noted that "The more I began to investigate lifestyles as a journalist, the more I found the pattern repeating itself, the perpetual gap particularly in tightly knit or strongly idiosyncratic lifestyles between what people *said* they were feeling and doing, and what they actually *were* feeling and doing."

One of Marchand's reporting interests was homosexuality, and *Saturday Night* was able to track and even anticipate its emergence into the public consciousness. In September 1969, it ran a cover story, "The Homosexual Life in Canada: After the Trudeau Law," the same month as some newspapers refused to accept an issue of *Weekend* that carried a story on a related subject. Nationalism, too, was embodied in pieces like Robin Mathews's "The Americanization of Canada Means Precisely the Takeover of Canadian Culture" (May 1971). The slots into which the magazine channeled its contents were labeled The Front (always including letters and Fulford's "Notebook"), The Middle (lead articles) and The Back (principally reviews, the movies always covered by "Marshall Delaney," Fulford's pseudonym, and the long-standing concluding page of puzzles). Among the favourite contributors were Doug Fetherling on the media, Anne Montagnes on books, the lawyer Harry Malcomson on arts, Peter Reilly on politics, Martin Knelman on theatre, Morris Wolfe on TV and the media generally and John Muggeridge on historical material. Many of them would appear in the magazine throughout the 1970s, and some persist into the 1980s. There was little visual flair. In fact, with its dull photography and crude caricatures, the magazine looked downright ugly. At its most poverty-stricken, the magazine sometimes began and ended with glossy pages—the rest was smudgy newsprint and sometimes slipped to a pamphletlike thirty-six pages.

Much of *Saturday Night*'s drab appearance was attributable to financial struggles. Until the end of 1974, the editorial staff at most consisted of a designer, a secretary, the assistant editor, Anastasia Erland—and Fulford. The magazine had been losing money to a greater or lesser degree since 1948. To stem the bloodletting, William Nobleman, a former teacher and high school principal who had been appointed vice-president and general manager (later publisher and president) of Saturday Night Publications in 1966, made several moves. In 1968, he

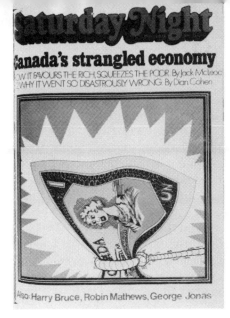

The May 1971
Saturday Night,
embracing born-
again nationalism,
emphasized the
poor not the rich.

acquired the subscription list of Peter Desbarats' *Parallel* (1966-67), a 12,000-circulation Montreal magazine that termed itself "The first magazine ever published in this country which could conceivably interest a non-Canadian" but which Fulford a year earlier had described in the *Toronto Star* as "flat and predictable and rather humorless." For four issues from April 1968 through January 1969, the company published a French-language version of *Saturday Night* called *Parallèle*, and until 1971 Desbarats appeared on *Saturday Night*'s masthead as associate editor. About the same time, the company also published a teachers' magazine called *Monday Morning* and produced educational films. In 1970, Nobleman took over the subscription list of *The Montrealer*, whose publisher, James Collyer, was to receive a share of the hypothetical accrued advertising revenue. The new circulation was optimistically expected to be up to 120,000 from 100,000. This did not occur.

In fact, none of these aggressive moves resulted in profits. The most ambitious undertaking, *Parallèle*, broke even, Nobleman told the Davey committee, but was discontinued because the investment needed to make it profitable would drain the resources of its English parent. The cover stories for May 1971 ("Canada's strangled economy," Jack McLeod's "How It Favours the Rich, Squeezes the Poor" and Dian Cohen's "Why It Went So Disastrously Wrong") might have applied to the magazine itself.

By now *Saturday Night* was drained in several directions. Certainly, there was no single-mindedness at the top. Edinborough and Fulford turned out to be incompatible. As Fulford recalled it in *The Best Seat in the House*, "anything I liked, Edinborough didn't; anything he liked, I didn't." As if this were not enough, Nobleman and Edinborough were warring over business strategy. In 1970, Edinborough left to write a column for the *Financial Post*, by now a peaceful pasture for former

Saturday Night editors, and to become the salaried president of the Canadian Council for Business and the Arts.

Apart from its collegial disturbances, *Saturday Night* owed a $350,000 printing bill to Maclean-Hunter, which the company did not insist on being repaid immediately. And although circulation had jumped about 20,000 between 1968 and 1969, it remained stuck in the 90,000 to 100,000 range. Advertising was actually down. As the Davey Committee report concluded, "If it weren't for a contra [reciprocal] advertising arrangement with a radio station, and the fact that *Time* Magazine chooses to advertise in *Saturday Night*, the magazine and its balance sheet might be even thinner." In fact, just as the magazine was espousing cultural nationalism, Nobleman was defending the nationalists' favorite target, *Time*, before the Davey Committee.

One way or another, *Saturday Night* was spending a lot of time dealing with governments. In mid-1971, the magazine reorganized itself as a nonprofit institution, Second Century Canada Publications, financially controlled by a board headed by Arthur Gelber, a wealthy arts patron and member of a distinguished Toronto Jewish family, and composed of a wavering chorus line of public-spirited businessmen, a few of whom occasionally had to cover the postage bill. It thus became eligible for grants from the Canada Council and the Ontario Arts Council. For the next few years both councils and the federal Secretary of State department contributed money so the magazine could extend its arts and literary content—even poems were run—and the Canada Council gave a publisher $7,500 to produce the *Saturday Night Scrapbook*, edited by Morris Wolfe, to coincide with its eighty-fifth anniversary.

By September 1974, it seemed there might be a book but not a magazine. Nobleman had left; the reorganization hadn't worked: there weren't enough sales or promotional staff; the magazine often was tardy reaching the newsstands. With its September issue in proof but unable to pay its printing bill, *Saturday Night* suspended publication. The private beneficence and government handouts had been unavailing: circulation had dropped sharply and the magazine was losing up to $10,000 a month.

Yet, improbably, and after lachrymose obituaries, the magazine resurrected itself with its issue of May 1975, thanks to a $100,000 donation from Imperial Oil and about three times that amount raised through private investors and a fund-raising campaign aimed at its faithful, long-suffering subscribers. The restructured company was called New Leaf Publications; the publisher was the public relations man and former TV producer Edgar Cowan, backed by a board whose chairman was the dentist-turned-real-estate-developer Murray Frum. Among the directors was one Norman Webster.

"Reborn: Canada's oldest magazine returns with a new style, new writers, new features." In tribute to its literary backers in the govern-

In 1975, editor Robert Fulford and art director Craig Allen oversaw yet another new look for Saturday Night.

ment, it still ran poems and added fiction in each issue, at first segregated from the rest of the magazine by being printed on newsprint. There were sops to consumerism in regular departments on travel (Charles Oberdorf), drinking (George Bain and Christopher Dafoe) and restaurants (Anne Hardy)—restaurant reviews an oddity in a national magazine. The size had doubled to a mostly glossy eighty-eight pages, and the logo leaped out in giant, curlicuelike letters. In Ralph Tibbles's redesign job, the type was larger and the Front, Middle and Back format was abandoned, though it was later revived in the 1980s. Instead, half the contents page was termed "Leisure."

Cowan and Fulford had agreed, Fulford reported in May 1975, that the magazine "should be both more serious and more frivolous...more serious in the sense of containing better researched, more thoughtful and in some cases longer articles; it should also contain serious fiction, bringing to a substantial audience the writers who have developed in English and French Canada...it should be more frivolous, acknowledging and celebrating the pleasures of life."

Among the writers who gained prominence during the late 1970s were Christina McCall Newman, a much more graceful stylist than her husband Peter. Barbara Amiel's first major magazine piece had been a much worked-on exposé on the firing of Dr. Andrew Malcolm from Toronto's Addiction Research Foundation, and the first revamped issue of the magazine had headlined her "The public torment of [Ontario Premier] William Davis." It was a tiny Toronto world: Amiel was married to the *Saturday Night* contributor and *Toronto Life* columnist George Jonas; the same November 1975 issue that carried Fulford's effusive praise of Peter Newman's *The Canadian Establishment* listed his former wife as executive editor.

Women, in fact, generally became more visible in the magazine's pages. The managing editor was Bernadette Sulgit; the Toronto, then

*David Annesley
gave an isolated
visual flair to*
Saturday Night
*in 1976, as in this
caricature of
Mackenzie King.*

Edmonton-based Myrna Kostash, who had first written for the magazine in May 1970, often appeared; Sandra Gwyn became Ottawa editor—later succeeded by Charlotte Gray. Yet though these women were sometimes astute social critics, the overall emphasis of the magazine, as it moved toward the 1980s, shifted from social activism to narcissism, from public to private enterprise. In any case, "elitism" to Fulford had never been a dirty word. The 112-page, ninetieth anniversary issue in December 1977 was chiefly devoted to variations on the theme of "the governing": "ideas" ("identity," "monarchy," "purity"); "elites" (Sandra Gwyn's "The Beautiful People over the decades"); "issues"(French vs. English Canada); and "images" (advertising).

Visually, the magazine was brighter, though still print-dominated. Under art director Craig Allen, the type was larger, odd tiny blobs signalled the end of articles and little arrows marked continuations, and oversized eye-caps introducing sections of articles sometimes made pages look like the board of a Scrabble game in progress. The drawings and caricatures, often a weak point during the Fulford regime, became stronger from the spring of 1975, thanks to the pen of the gifted David Annesley, whose fluid sketches graced the book pages before his premature death in February 1977.

Another of *Saturday Night*'s many changes at the top occurred in 1979. New Leaf was sold to Norman Webster, London correspondent and later editor in chief of the *Globe and Mail* (and nephew of R. Howard Webster, Montreal industrialist and former owner of the *Globe and Mail*). Norman Webster represented Dascon Investments, a family trust for him, his brother Will and sister Margaret Gallagher. Webster, who had gradually become the largest shareholder, now bought out the other participants in the earlier revival. As publisher, Webster appointed an old acquaintance, John Macfarlane, when *Weekend*, the magazine Macfarlane had edited, was absorbed into *Today*.

Macfarlane had an impressive résumé. A former editorial writer and entertainment writer on the *Globe and Mail* and *Toronto Star*, he had edited *Toronto Life* and briefly dabbled in advertising. He had worked twice at *Maclean's*, most recently as executive editor. Tall, enthusiastic, an amateur athlete, he was a perfectionist. So interventionist was he in his new role as publisher that it was problematic to some just how much *Saturday Night* from 1980 on was Fulford's doing and how much Macfarlane's.

Quite apart from Macfarlane's policy initiatives, Fulford was busy in other forms of journalism. He had begun broadcasting in 1955, chiefly on the CBC, and had married CBC radio producer Geraldine Sherman, his second wife, in 1970 (Murray Frum's wife, CBC broadcaster Barbara Frum, was matron of honour). During the seventies he was host of a radio show, *This is Robert Fulford*, and in the mid-eighties co-hosted the TVOntario interview show *Realities*. From 1971 he wrote a weekly column for the *Toronto Star*. Calling Macfarlane his "Christmas present," Fulford was freed from much administrative and editorial minutiae.

As a kind of cash cow to keep the magazine fed, Macfarlane set up Saturday Night Publishing Services, which, on a contract basis, would undertake design, editorial, production and circulation chores for any client who might need a glossy magazine, program or brochure. Soon this spinoff firm was doing business, in one way or another, with the magazine *Public Policy* for the Institute for Research on Public Policy, *Canadian Heritage* for the Heritage Canada Foundation, *Radio Guide* for the CBC, *Royal Bank Reporter* and programs for the Toronto Symphony Orchestra and the Stratford Festival. But perhaps most significant was the fact that, after 1985, Norman Webster's employer, the *Globe and Mail*, farmed out design, editorial and production work to the fledgling company for its three glossy magazines: *Report on Business Magazine, Destinations* and *Toronto*. Indeed, Jack McIver, Publishing Services' editorial director, later became editor of *Destinations*.

Although *Saturday Night* and Publishing Services were separate entities, the latter did typesetting and some circulation work for the former. There was also overlapping personnel. David Macfarlane, a frequent contributor to *Saturday Night*, briefly edited *Radio Guide*. David Frum, son of Murray and Barbara Frum, was hired in the summer of 1980 to do market research for Publishing Services and was often by-lined in the magazine.

Macfarlane also hired at the magazine. He acquired Derek Ungless as art director—later succeeded by Louis Fishauf and Bruce Ramsay— and named Gary Ross senior editor. Both Ungless and Ross were former

Weekend colleagues and both helped shape the magazine's latest incarnation, as did a contributing editor, Ron Graham. He was a former CBC-TV producer who had such useful connections as the Desmarais family of Power Corporation and Liberal cabinet minister and leadership aspirant Jean Chrétien. Uncustomarily flush with cash, *Saturday Night* could afford to let Fulford write long magazine features and longer "Notebook" entries and to groom its own staff. Beginning as secretaries and editorial assistants, Dianne de Fenoyl, Tecca Crosby, Dianna Symonds and Eileen Whitfield eventually became full-fledged editors and writers.

The first "new" *Saturday Night* (September 1980) had for its lead story a 14,000-word profile of Jim Coutts, Prime Minister Pierre Trudeau's cagey advisor. On the cover was a photograph by Nigel Dickson, whose visual work would dominate the magazine. The former was relatively inoffensive, the latter not so, at least to its subject. According to Patrick Gossage, the Prime Minister's press man, "Unbeknownst to Coutts, the photographer used his widest of wide-angle lenses (beware of skinny lenses!), distorting the admittedly short and slightly rotund Principal Secretary into a carnival-mirror caricature. In the two horrible photos that accompanied the resulting article, Coutts looked bloated and self-satisfied."

Certainly, the magazine's subjects often looked strange, as if the photographer had shot upward from the bottom of a manhole or was afflicted with myopia or vertigo. But there was no mistaking the sense of style. That stylishness of design and photography did not extend to the contents of Fulford's contributions and the longer features, which tended to be predictable in form if not always in content. The stories were long, heavily documented, scrupulously checked and expertly spliced, just the stuff to win National Magazine Awards including "Magazine of the Year" in 1984—and to go unread by the general public.

Saturday Night's attempts to cover the "major" issues and appeal to the "important" people sometimes led it into making absurd claims, as in March 1984. "Political clout," headlined a house ad. "When Pierre Trudeau became Prime Minister in 1968, Michael Pitfield set about overhauling the federal bureaucracy. In October 1982, *Saturday Night* published Christina McCall's searing assessment of Pitfield's career. Three weeks later, Pitfield resigned from the most powerful post in the public service."

The magazine was now running cover stories on provincial premiers, cabinet ministers and political fixers, interspersed with the occasional tycoon or cultural icon, such as book publisher McClelland & Stewart's Jack McClelland, and the rare horror story, such as the portrait of the war criminal Helmut Rauca. Seldom did the idea for a cover story show inventiveness. Doug Fetherling's January 1985 story on Eric and Leslie Nielson, brothers who were respectively powerful politician and actor, was an exception. The business historian Michael Bliss joined

In 1985, Saturday Night *featured one celebrity per cover. This is Brian Smale's portrait of comedian Martin Short.*

as contributing editor in 1983; the final-page poem, which had replaced the puzzle page, now became a wry snapshot of public happenings—birthdays, presentations, demonstrations—called "The Spectator."

In September 1985—cover photograph: a giddy portrait of comedian Martin Short—the magazine cut its cover price from an awkward $3.25 to a more manageable $2.75, replaced its logotype with a red but statelier serif face, and added more colour and photography, as well as short, cutesy, Spectator-style photo-illustrated features: "Postcard" (of places) and "Passions" (Murray Frum's art, Sonja Bata's shoes). Fiction vanished. In keeping with this perkier look, the November cover showed Liberal MP Sheila Copps, leader of the so-called parliamentary "Rat Pack," dressed in full leather and astride a motorcycle.

In contrast, the much heralded one-hundredth-anniversary number in January 1987 was a tremendous yawn. Its grey cover had all the vivacity of a trust company's annual report. Edited by Gary Ross, the issue dipped deep into the magazine's well-stocked talent bank, but to little effect. Fulford's "Notebook" was a long tedious account of the Canada of 1887. Jan Morris—before her sex-change operation, James Morris—the British author who had sometimes written powerful and eloquent books, contributed a piece of frippery about Ottawa that was nearly as irrelevant as an earlier one on Toronto the magazine had run. Even normally dependable writers like David Macfarlane and Sandra Gwyn seemed stolid or ineffectual. The liveliest reading in the issue was an extract from Hector Charlesworth's 1925 *Candid Chronicles*, sponsored by the Royal Bank.

The September 1985 refit had not been a radical alteration, but it was an omen. As Fulford had said much earlier of a 1949 change in *Saturday Night* format: "Magazines don't change their formats and designs because the editor is capricious in his tastes; they change because they aren't successful, or anyway aren't successful enough to please their

In 1980, Saturday Night *claimed it was "sneaking up on Conrad Black". But who was sneaking up on whom?*

proprietors, and because they think a new format will attract advertisers or readers, or both."

The sequence of events that led to Conrad Black's acquisition of *Saturday Night*, and the departure of Fulford and Macfarlane, were livelier and funnier than anything that had recently appeared in the magazine—though something similar might have had a spot in the January 1986 issue devoted to "Beautiful Losers."

Saturday Night's circulation now stood at about 130,000, up from 70,000 or so in 1974 but still far from the hoped-for 200,000. As early as the spring of 1985, Norman Webster had learned that the company had lost over a million dollars the previous year, several hundred thousand of it stemming from Publishing Services, the cash cow that now proved to have been a bum steer. Two years later, Webster learned that 1986 had been fiscally disastrous for debt-ridden *Saturday Night* and not encouraging for Publishing Services, especially since the *Globe and Mail* had begun to generate its glossy magazines "in-house." Nor was the prospect brighter for the current year. This solid core of subscribers, about sixty percent of them in Ontario, represented less than a third of the total. Webster nonetheless was presented with a $2-million marketing plan by which losses *might* be recouped: "invest or divest," he was reportedly told by John Macfarlane.

Already concerned in stemming his losses—against Macfarlane's advice, he had declined to purchase *Harrowsmith* and *Equinox* when those magazines were on offer the previous year—Webster wasted no time in putting his magazine up for sale. In the past, Webster had been approached by other interested parties, but one by one, and to a corporation, they had taken a look at the books, shaken their heads sadly and gone away. Rather than endure this again, Webster fell back on a rich and coincidentally erudite man who had already expressed a strong interest in the magazine.

This was the man some regarded as the *bête noire* of Canadian capitalism, Conrad Black. Imagined by some as a corporate orgre who devoured windows and orphans. Black and his brother Montagu had acquired the huge Argus Corporation and dismembered it to their profitable satisfaction. Through their holding company, Hollinger Corporation, the Blacks had, between 1978 and 1985, shucked their holdings in broadcasting, mining and retailing. The author of a massive biography of Maurice Duplessis, Conrad Black now set his sights on becoming a press baron, at first with Sterling Newspapers, a chain of small-town dailies that had out-Thomsoned Thomson in cost-paring. In 1979, he lost to Kenneth Thomson when Thomson outbid him to gain ownership of the *Globe and Mail*. Lately he had followed in the footsteps of Lord Beaverbrook by acquiring a British newspaper, the prestigious *Daily Telegraph* in the process making himself editor in chief while simultaneously taking over Unimédia, a Quebec newspaper chain.

Black and his associate and confidant, Peter White, got together with Webster and a memorandum for the purchase of *Saturday Night* was drawn up, to be refined by lawyers later. It was a satisfactory document from Webster's point of view, though he had hoped to include Publishing Services in the package. The word got out, and it was enough to inspire fear and trembling among some.

It was Black, after all, who had written to the *National Review*'s William F. Buckley in 1973 for advice on how to "at least partially emulate your example" in converting "an existing Canadian magazine [presumably the financially stricken *Saturday Night*] into a conveyance for views at some variance with the tired porridge of ideological normalcy in vogue here as in the U.S.A...."

In 1979, Black and Peter White had been involved in a short-lived free enterprise magazine called *Odyssey*, published partly under the auspices of the Business Council on National Issues.

And it was Black who testified at the Davey Committee in 1969 that "My experience with journalists authorizes me to record that a very large number of them are ignorant, lazy, opinionated, intellectually dishonest, and inadequately supervised. The 'profession' is heavily cluttered with abrasive youngsters who substitute 'commitment' for insight, and, to a lesser extent, with aged hacks toiling through a miasma of mounting decrepitude. Alcoholism is endemic in both groups."

Disraeli-like in texture but decidedly untactful in tone, these were not words to reassure the liberal-minded about the fate of their revered spokesman. According to Peter Gzowski, "Fulford has obviously been the whole magazine for 19 years. If he stays, it should be fine. If he doesn't, I'd be worried. When something happens to an important and fundamental part of the country, you worry." Needless to say, those at the *Saturday Night* were also worried, especially since Black had declined to acquire John Macfarlane along with the magazine. When Fulford met Black and Peter White for lunch, the editor was not reassured, particularly when Black asked him to prepare a list rating his staff. Black, in fact, forcibly reminded Fulford of Orson Welles in *Citizen Kane*. Fulford, the high-school dropout who had received an honorary doctorate from York University only a few days earlier, pondered the problem overnight, then resigned.

The lamentations were copious. Michael Enright, then news director for CBC Radio, said bitterly: "Conrad Black has always reminded me of Richard Nixon; now they've both had their Saturday Night massacres. But if owning his own magazine will keep him out of print, then he'll have done us all a favour. As far as I'm concerned, Bob Fulford was *the* magazine editor of my generation. All *Saturday Night* had going for it was its reputation, and that reputation walked around in the trousers of Bob Fulford."

Now the transfer of ownership entered its slapstick phase. The *Toronto Star's* London correspondent Richard Gwyn, Sandra Gwyn's husband, reported that Webster and Black disagreed about the terms of the sale. Webster thought he'd be getting $250,000 plus absorption of the current debt. Black thought he'd absorb the debt, all right, but that Webster owed *him* $250,000. The *Globe and Mail*, for which Black had been writing a column in *Report on Business*, was reduced to recording a "no comment" from its own editor in chief.

As if matters weren't already complicated enough, Black had offered the editorship of *Saturday Night* to John Fraser, the *Globe's* London correspondent, who was in Toronto on leave to write a book about ballet star Mikhail Baryshnikov. Fraser was no stranger to Black. He had been a boyhood classmate of Black at Upper Canada College and had started as a reporter on the Black-owned *Sherbrooke* (Quebec) *Record*. Fraser, so the rumours went, was requesting a salary starting at $125,000 a year, a five-year, baseball-style no-cut contract and a company car to edit a magazine that was being threatened with Black-patented cuts. One joke going the rounds had a *Saturday Night* staffer noticing a Rolls-Royce parked outside the office. "Gee,"said the staffer, "that Fraser drives a hard bargain."

When the dust—or ink settled, Webster did indeed sell *Saturday Night* to Black, on a straight buyer-absorbs-the-debt basis. Although asked to stay on as head of Publishing Services, Macfarlane's pride did not permit him to pursue this journalistic half-life. He resigned. Peter White became *Saturday Night's* publisher and Fraser was hired at an undisclosed salary, with a contractual clause stipulating that Black would not trifle with the editing; this he'd requested, Fraser said, not for himself but to reassure the staff. Said Webster of his former foreign correspondent, "Someday I hope he forgets this madness and comes back to daily journalism."

Both Macfarlane and Fulford landed solidly on their feet. Macfarlane was parachuted over editor Terrance Corcoran's head to become editor in chief and deputy publisher—later editor and publisher—of Southam's weekly *Financial Times*. Hiring Derek Ungless to revamp the design and Fulford as a columnist, he was soon calling the paper a "business newsmagazine." Macfarlane also joined Jan Walter and his old colleague Gary Ross in setting up a book publishing firm, thus fulfilling a plan that *Saturday Night* had once nursed. Besides continuing his weekly newspaper column and TV interviewing, Fulford was hired to advise a group of cable TV operators seeking a new licence; he and his wife, Geraldine Sherman, went to Japan for two months on twin fellowships from the Asia-Pacific Foundation; and he began a job at the University of Toronto's University College as the "Barker Fairley distinguished visitor in Canadian culture." He also started his memoirs.

It was possible to feel some sympathy for Webster. Even Conrad Black continued to give trouble. He sued the newspaper for an allegedly libelous story on him it had run and was part owner of the *Globe's* rival, the new daily *Financial Post*. Yet, his column remained in the *Globe's Report on Business Magazine* throughout 1987, leading one to speculate that Black would get around to suing himself. (Eventually his column was cut and the *Globe* apologized for portions of the story it had published.)

An outstanding journalist himself and once the *Globe's* London correspondent, Webster had been mocked by Pierre Berton in the *Star* and chastised by George Bain in *Maclean's* for at best hypocrisy and at worst conflict of interest. Bain noted that Webster's Publishing Services had contracts with the *Globe*, and that others of its clients were "institutions on which Webster, as editor in chief of the *Globe*, may be called at any time to comment....the relationship is scarcely one the newspaper, with its fierce interest in appearances of possible conflicts of interest, could be expected to pass over without comment if duplicated in the political realm."

Yet the *Globe's* critical and news coverage of *Saturday Night* never showed favouritism. *Globe* art critic John Bentley Mays reviewed the one-hundredth-anniversary issue as a "tame, blue-rinse walkabout," and the paper's headline called it "A splash of grey." On the same topic, Jim Christy in the *Globe's* "Mermaid Inn" column said that "Suddenly the second biggest, and to my mind, the very best country in the world was reduced to a tiny room atop the Toronto CN Tower with the door locked and the smudged window tightly shut. The writers crowded inside were anxiously rubbing the dirty glass in order to get a glimpse across the lake at the United States to assure themselves that they actually existed." And, after all, Webster's family firm had poured more than $6 million into what must have seemed at times an unpluggable sink. A Paul Orenstein photo ironically published in the *Imperial Oil*

The two-year-old John Fraser, left, a future editor of Saturday Night, first sang for his supper in the December 21 1946 issue.

Review in the summer of 1987 showed a happy Macfarlane, Fulford and Webster, with Webster leaning against a pillar. Up until that point Webster *was* the pillar.

Born in 1944, the new editor of *Saturday Night* was a former award-winning *Globe and Mail* ballet critic and resident correspondent in China, whose book *The Chinese: A Portrait of a People* had been a best-seller. Although he was new to editing a magazine, he had occasionally contributed to *Saturday Night's* pages, making his first appearance in a front page photo on 21 December 1946 as a boy caroler. Taking up his appointment in October, he would, because of the magazine's long lead time, have to wait for several months before making an editorial impact. For the same reason, Conrad Black would have to tolerate a September cover excerpt from the autobiography of United Auto Workers leader Bob White, his personal *bête*.

Fraser could abide the masthead presence of Fulford as editor until the end of the year. After all, he much admired him, as shown in his 1987 collection of vignettes, *Telling Tales*, where the section on Fulford is eerily juxtaposed with an equally friendly one about Black. To Fraser he was "the best journalist in the land," whose "job is to be a witness, nothing more and nothing less."

> Whether he's having a go at a massive, million-dollar cultural report that somehow misses the whole point behind the word "cultural," or the lemminglike way the national media fell into a trap set by a small-town racist and bigot in Alberta who has now got his thesis (that the Holocaust never occurred) admirably disseminated from coast to coast, or how

the nation has abandoned its single most important priority—
the duty to educate its children—to the whims of a tawdry
political agenda: whether it is any of these things, Fulford
struggles to bring the most straightforward, but consistently
bypassed, questions to bear and serves them up in a prose
style as lucid as George Orwell's and as engaging as Arthur
Koestler's.

Claiming that "In an important country he would have been an international titan" and that "In his columns...we learn to take a knight's
move away from events swirling around us and shed the tempting but
illusory comfort of hard-edged ideological positions." Fraser said that
Fulford "has shown his own generation of journalists that their fixa-
tion with other people's actions and intentions, in recording their foibles and their triumphs, the voyeur in all of us can be tempered by
committed concern, intellectual honesty and a crusading love for the
people around you, whether it is manifested by blistering anger or a
just affection for benign follies."

During his long regime Fulford endorsed (at first) Pierre Trudeau,
urged liberalized marijuana laws, decried the lack of government support for the Canada Council, the National Film Board and the CBC,
and questioned Trudeau's repatriation of the Canadian constitution and
Brian Mulroney's Meech Lake accord. But even when he was writing
about his favorite topic, the relationship of politics and the arts, there
is little evidence that his opinions carried any weight among those he
sought to influence. Attempting to lead public opinion, he more often
followed it.

With *Saturday Night*, the influence that Fulford did have was restricted
to his own profession, and in the capacity not so much as editor as educator. He gave many writers like Sandra Gwyn their first exposure in
a substantial magazine. Often the magazine was a stepping-stone to the
writing of books: Gwyn (*The Private Capital: Ambition and Love in the
Age of Macdonald and Laurier*), Christina McCall (*Grits*) and Ron Graham (*One-Eyed Kings*). Gary Ross was a novelist (*Always Tip the Dealer*),
as was Ron Graham (*Noughts and Crosses*). Jack Batten, whose books
on lawyers and judges in a sense derived from an article Fulford had
assigned in 1977, told a reporter in 1987, "I'm still thinking about advice
he gave me, even if I'm writing for someone else." The kind of writer
Fulford tended to cultivate, he told the Davey Committee, was not a
graduate of a journalism school but a "person who breaks out of the
traditional craft of journalism and goes toward some form of personal
expression."

Battering the keys of his 1950s-model Underwood Rhythm Shift Typewriter, Fulford himself did not break out of the traditional craft. He
had the born journalist's great gift of curiosity, and an extraordinary

porousness to popular culture, especially movies. Sometimes the latter enthusiasm led him into writing altogether too much for his own magazine: little in the "Marshall Delaney" column justified running it for two decades. A "compulsive communicator," his chum Peter Gzowski called him, adding that his friends coined the verb "'to fulford', meaning to be so determined to share your own delight in something that you spoil other people's pleasure." Ultimately Fulford was not at his best as an editorialist or even as a critic but at the task he had set for himself at the start: reporting.

The magazine that Fulford had dominated for so long was ultimately too erratic, and from the 1970s too market-conscious, to consistently achieve the stature, translated into Canadian terms, of such U.S. quality magazines as *Harper's* or the *Atlantic Monthly* at their best. Always the most tiresomely self-regarding of Canadian magazines—it published eighty-fifth *and* ninetieth anniversary issues, and one almost expected a ninety-third—it sometimes strained at the seams in attempting to convince the public that its past was illustrious, or at least comic. In the 1980s, rather than focus singly on important but little-known persons and events, the stories usually dwelled at weary length on the rich-and-powerful everyone else was writing about, in the process merely betraying power envy. When it occasionally strayed beyond such obvious candidates for coverage as premiers and prime ministers, the editor's judgement turned out to be skewed or simply crass: the magazine's idea of an important poet, for example—two full-length features in the 1980s—was the moderately talented but very photogenic Susan Musgrave. *Saturday Night* was less a national institution than a Toronto one and the magazine seldom ventured beyond Toronto to seek the writers who might have refreshed its pages.

Yet somehow the Canadian passion for institutions did extend to *Saturday Night* under Robert Fulford. If the regard with which it was held often had less to do with achievement than promise, it had many accomplishments to its credit. Until the 1980s, it was the only large-circulation magazine to publish seriously conceived poetry and fiction. It did cover culture and the media in greater depth than any other Canadian journal. Within its pages it sometimes did present at least the shadowy suggestion of dissent, and of independent enquiry into received ideas. And it did try, with all possible good intentions, to gather the threads of community into that garment of print we have come to comprehend as a national magazine.

SELECT BIBLIOGRAPHY

PRINCIPAL MAGAZINES CONSULTED

Alberta Report (1973—)
Atlantic Insight (1979—)
Canadian Courier (1906-20)
Canadian Forum (1920—)
Canadian Home Journal (1905-59)
Canadian Illustrated News (1869-83)
Canadian Magazine (1893-1939)
Canadian Monthly and National
   Review (1872-82)
Chatelaine (1928—)
Everywoman's World (1914-22)
Grip (1873-94)
Harrowsmith (1976—)
Idler, The (1984—)

Liberty (1932-64)
Maclean's (1905—)
Massey's Illustrated (1882-97)
Mayfair (1927-61)
New Dominion Monthly (1867-79)
New World Illustrated (1940-48)
Queen's Quarterly (1896—)
Quest (1972-84)
Saturday Night (1888—)
Tamarack Review (1956-82)
Toronto Life (1966—)
University Magazine (1901-20)
Willison's Magazine (1925-29)

BOOKS

Adams, John Coldwell. *Sir Charles God Damn: the Life of Sir Charles G. D. Roberts*. Toronto: University of Toronto, 1986.

Allen, Ralph. *The Chartered Libertine*. Toronto: Macmillan, 1954.

Allen, Robert Thomas. Ed. *A Treasury of Canadian Humour*. Toronto: McClelland & Stewart, 1967.

Amiel, Barbara. *Confessions*. Toronto: Macmillan, 1980.

Anderson, Doris. *Rough Layout*. Toronto: McClelland & Stewart, 1981.

Audley, Paul. *Canada's Cultural Industries: Broadcasting, Publishing, Records and Film*. Toronto: James Lorimer/Canadian Institute for Economic Policy, 1983.

Barbour, Noel Robert. *Those Amazing People! The Story of the Canadian Magazine Industry 1778-1967*. Toronto: Crucible, 1982.

Bate, W. Jackson. *Samuel Johnson*. New York and London: Harcourt Brace Jovanovich, 1977.

Bengough, J. W. *A Caricature History of Canadian Politics*. Toronto: Peter Martin, 1974. Ed. with an introduction by Doug Fetherling.

Berger, Carl. *The Sense of Power: Studies in the Ideas of Canadian Imperialism 1867-1914*. Toronto: University of Toronto, 1970.

——————. *The Writing of Canadian History: Aspects of English-Canadian Historical Writing, 1900 to 1970*. Toronto: Oxford, 1976.

Birney, Earle. *Spreading Time: Remarks on Canadian Writing and Writers. Book I:1904-1949*. Montreal: Vehicule, 1980.

Bliss, Michael. *A Living Profit: Studies in the Social History of Canadian Business 1893-1911*. Toronto: McClelland & Stewart, 1974.

Bone, John R., Joseph T. Clark, A. H. U. Colquhoun, and John F. MacKay. *A History of Canadian Journalism in the Several Portions of the Dominion with a Sketch of the Canadian Press Association 1859-1908*. Toronto: Canadian Press Association, 1908.

Bourinot, John George. *Our Intellectual Strength and Weakness*. Marquis, Thomas Guthrie. *English-Canadian Literature*. Roy, Camille. 'French Canadian Literature.' Introduction by Clara Thomas. Toronto: University of Toronto, 1973.

Braddon, Russell. *Roy Thomson of Fleet Street*. London and Toronto: Collins, 1965.

Braithwaite, Max. *The Best of Braithwaite*. Toronto: McClelland & Stewart, 1983.

Bridle, Augustus. *Sons of Canada*. Toronto: Dent, 1916.

——————. *Masques of Ottawa*. Toronto: Macmillan, 1921.

Brown, Robert Craig and Ramsay Cook. *Canada 1896-1921: A Nation Transformed*. Toronto: McClelland & Stewart, 1974.

Bruce, Charles. *News and the Southams*. Toronto: Macmillan, 1968.

Bruce, Harry. *Each Moment As It Flies*. Toronto: Methuen, 1984.

Canada. *The Canada-U.S. Free Trade Agreement*. Ottawa: International Trade Communications Group, Department of External Affairs, 1987.

——————. *Report of the Royal Commission on Publications*. Ottawa: Queen's Printer, 1961.

——————. *Report of the Senate Special Committee on the Mass Media*. 3 vols. 1970.

Carroll, Jock. *The Life and Times of Greg Clark*. Toronto: Doubleday, 1981.

Chalmers, Floyd S. *Both Sides of the Street: One Man's Life in Business and the Arts in Canada*. Toronto: Macmillan, 1983.

——————. *A Gentleman of the Press*. Toronto & New York: Doubleday, 1969.

Charlesworth, Hector. *The Canadian Scene*. Toronto: Macmillan, 1927.

——————. *I'm Telling You*. Toronto: Macmillan, 1937.

——————. *More Candid Chronicles*. Toronto: Macmillan, 1928.

Clery, Val. Ed. *Canada from the Newstands: A Selection from the Best Canadian Journalism of the Past Thirty Years*. Toronto: Macmillan, 1978.

Colgate, William. *Canadian Art: its origin and development*. Toronto: Ryerson, 1943. Foreword by C. W. Jefferys

Collard, Edgar Andrew. *Montreal: The Days That Are No More*. Toronto and New York: Doubleday, 1976.

Colombo, John Robert. *Years of Light: A Celebration of Leslie A. Crouch*. Toronto: Hounslow, 1982.

Cook, Ramsay. *The Regenerators: Social Criticism in Late Victorian English Canada*. Toronto: University of Toronto, 1985.

Cook, Ramsay and Wendy Mitchinson. *The Proper Sphere: Woman's Place in Canadian Society*. Toronto: Oxford, 1976.

Cooper, John Irwin. *Montreal: A Brief History*. Montreal and London, England: McGill-Queen's, 1969.

Craick, W. A. *A History of Canadian Journalism II: Last Years of the Canadian Press Association 1908-1919, with a continuing record of the Canadian Daily Newspaper Publishers Association 1919-1959*. Toronto: Ontario Publishing, 1959.

Cranston, J. H. *Ink on My Fingers*. Toronto: Ryerson, 1953.

Crean, Susan. *News Worthy: The Lives of Media Women*. Toronto: Stoddart, 1985.

Davies, Robertson. *The Well-Tempered Critic*. Toronto: McClelland & Stewart, 1981. Ed. Judith Skelton Grant.

——————. *The Enthusiasms of Robertson Davies*. Toronto: McClelland & Stewart, 1979. Ed. Judith Skelton Grant.

Dempsey, Lotta. *No Life for a Lady*. Don Mills, Ont.: Musson, 1976.

Desbarats, Peter. Ed. *Canadian Illustrated News 1869-1883: Canada's First National Magazine*. Toronto: McClelland & Stewart, 1979.

Djwa, Sandra. *The Politics of the Imagination: A Life of F. R. Scott*. Toronto: McClelland & Stewart, 1987.

Drache, Daniel. Ed. *Debates and Controversies from* This Magazine. Toronto: McClelland & Stewart, 1979.

Dudek, Louis. *Literature and the Press: a History of Printing, Printed Media, and their Relation to Literature*. Toronto: Ryerson and Contact, 1960.

Edmonds, Alan. *The Years of Protest 1960/1970*. Toronto: McClelland & Stewart, 1979.

Edwards, Mary Jane. *The Evolution of Canadian Literature in English: Beginnings to 1867*. Toronto: Holt, Rinehart, 1973.

Eggleston, Wilfrid. *While I Still Remember*. Toronto: Ryerson, 1968.

——————. *Literary Friends*. Ottawa: Borealis, 1980.

Flitton, Marilyn G. *Index to the Canadian Monthly and National Review and the Rose-Belford's Canadian Monthly and National Review 1872-1882*. Bibliographical Society of Canada, 1976.

Fowler, Marian. *Redney: A Life of Sara Jeannette Duncan*. Toronto: Anansi, 1983.

Fraser, John and Graham Fraser. *"Blair Fraser Reports": Selections 1944-1968*. Toronto: Macmillan, 1969.

Fraser, John. *Telling Tales*. Toronto: Collins, 1986.

Fulford, Robert. *The Best Seat in the House: Memoirs of a Lucky Man*. Toronto: Collins, 1988.

——————. *Crisis at the Victory Burlesk: Culture, Politics & Other Diversions*. Toronto: Oxford, 1968.

Garner, Hugh. *Author! Author!* Toronto: Ryerson, 1964.

——————. "Introduction." In *Omnibus*. Toronto: McGraw-Hill Ryerson, 1978.

——————. *A Nice Place to Visit*. Markham, Ont.: Paperjacks, 1983.

——————. *One Damn Thing After Another*. Toronto: McGraw-Hill Ryerson, 1973.

——————. *The Silence on the Shore*. Toronto: McClelland & Stewart, 1962.

Goggio, Emilio, Beatrice Corrigan and Jack H. Parker. *A Bibliography of Canadian Cultural Periodicals English and French from Colonial Times to 1950*. University of Toronto: Department of Italian, Spanish and Portuguese, 1955. Printed by Ryerson Press.

Gossage, Patrick. *Close to the Charisma: My Years Between the Press and Pierre Trudeau*. Toronto: McClelland & Stewart, 1986.

Granatstein, J. L. and Peter Stevens. Ed. *Forum: Canadian Life and Letters 1920-70: Selections from* The Canadian Forum. Toronto: University of Toronto, 1972.

Gwyn, Sandra. *The Private Capital: Ambition and Love in the Age of Macdonald and Laurier*. Toronto: McClelland & Stewart, 1984.

Hambleton, Ronald. *How I Earned $250,000 as a Freelance Writer . . . . even if it did take 30 years!* Toronto: Bartholomew Green, 1977.

Harkness, Ross. *J.E. Atkinson of the Star*. Toronto: University of Toronto, 1963.

Harper, J. Russell. *Historical Directory of New Brunswick Newspapers and Periodicals*. Fredericton: University of New Brunswick, 1961. Foreword by Desmond Pacey.

Hendry, Peter. *Epitaph for Nostalgia, a personal memoir on the death of The Family Herald*. Montreal: Agri-World Press, 1968.

Hulse, Elizabeth. Ed. *A Dictionary of Toronto printers, publishers, booksellers, and the allied trades, 1798-1900*. Toronto: Anson-Cartwright, 1982.

Hutchison, Bruce. *The Far Side of the Street*. Toronto: Macmillan, 1976.

Innis, Mary Quayle. Ed. *The Clear Spirit: Twenty Canadian Women and their Times*. Toronto: University of Toronto for the Canadian Federation of University Women, 1966.

Jowett, Garth S. "The Growth of Mass Media in Canada." In *Communications in Canadian Society*. Ed. Benjamin D. Singer. Don Mills, Ont.: Addison-Wesley, 1983, 158-75.

Kesterton, Wilfred H. *A History of Journalism in Canada*. Toronto: McClelland & Stewart, 1967.

———. *The Law and the Press in Canada*. Toronto: McClelland & Stewart, 1976. With a foreword by Wilfrid Eggleston.

Lefolii, Ken. *The Canadian Look: A Century of Sights and Styles*. Toronto: McClelland & Stewart, 1965.

Leiss, William, Stephen Kline and Sut Jhally. *Social Communication in Advertising: Persons, Products & Images of Well-Being*. Toronto: Methuen, 1986.

Lennox, John and Clara Thomas. *William Arthur Deacon: A Canadian Literary Life*. Toronto: University of Toronto, 1982.

Lennox, John and Michele Lacombe. *Dear Bill: the Correspondence of William Arthur Deacon*. Toronto: University of Toronto, 1988.

L'Esperance, Jeanne. *The Widening Sphere: Women in Canada, 1870-1940, Catalogue of an exhibition held Sept. 27, 1982—Jan.4, 1983*. Ottawa: Public Archives Canada/Dept. of Supply and Services, 1982.

Litvak, Isaiah and Christopher Maule. *Cultural Sovereignty: the Time and Reader's Digest Case in Canada*. New York: Praeger, 1974.

Lower, Arthur R. M. *Canadians in the Making*. Toronto: Longmans, 1958.

Macbeth, Madge. *Over My Shoulder*. Toronto: Ryerson, 1953.

McDayter, Walt. Ed. *A Media Mosaic: Canadian Communications Through a Critical Eye*. Toronto: Holt, Rinehart & Winston, 1971.

MacDonald, Dick. Ed. *Borden Spears: Reporter, Editor, Critic*. Toronto: Fitzhenry & Whiteside and London, Ont.: School of Journalism, University of Western Ontario, 1984.

McDougall, Robert L. *A Study of Canadian Periodical Literature of the Nineteenth Century*. Ph.D. diss., University of Toronto, 1950.

McKenzie, Karen and Mary F. Williamson. *The Art and Pictorial Press in Canada: Two Centuries of Art Magazines*. Toronto: Art Gallery of Ontario, 1979.

McKillop, A. B. *A Disciplined Intelligence: Cultural Inquiry and Canadian Thought in the Victorian Era*. Montreal: McGill-Queen's, 1979.

MacLennan, Hugh. *The Other Side of Hugh MacLennan: Selected Essays Old and New*. Ed. Elspeth Cameron. Toronto: Macmillan, 1978.

McLuhan, Marshall. *The Mechanical Bride: Folklore of Industrial Man*. London: Routledge & Kegan Paul, 1967.

MacTavish, Newton. *Newton MacTavish's Canada*. Toronto: Baxter, 1963. Ed. Ellen Stafford. Illustrated by Richard Taylor.

Mappin, John N. *The Goblin: A Brief History of Canada's Humour Magazine of the 1920s*. Montreal: privately printed, 1988.

Marchand, Philip. *Just Looking, Thank You: An Amused Observer's View of Canadian Lifestyles*. Toronto: Macmillan, 1976.

Mellon, Peter. *The Group of Seven*. Toronto: McClelland & Stewart, 1970.

Moritz, Albert. *Canada Illustrated: the Art of Nineteenth-Century Engraving*. Toronto: Dreadnaught, 1982.

Morton, Ralph Kelly. *Behind the Headlines: Moose River to Shangri-la*. Halifax: Nimbus, 1986.

Mott, Frank Luther. *A History of American Magazines*. 5 vols. Cambridge: Harvard, 1968.

Newman, Christina. Ed. *The Man from Oxbow*. Toronto: McClelland & Stewart, 1967.

Newman, Peter C. *The Distemper of Our Times: Canadian Politics in Transition 1963 1968*. Toronto: McClelland & Stewart, 1968.

———. *The Establishment Man: A Portrait of Power*. Toronto: McClelland & Stewart, 1982.

———. *Renegade in Power: the Diefenbaker Years*. Toronto: McClelland & Stewart, 1963.

Norris, Ken. *The Little Magazine in Canada 1925-80.* Toronto: ECW, 1984.
Nowlan, Alden. *Double Exposure.* Fredericton: Brunswick, 1978.
O'Flaherty, Patrick. *The Rock Observed: Studies in the Literature of Newfoundland.* Toronto: University of Toronto, 1979.
O'Leary, Grattan. *Recollections of People, Press, and Politics.* Toronto: Macmillan, 1977. Foreword by Robert L. Stanfield. Introduction and Personal Postscript by I. Norman Smith.
P. O.'D. [Peter O'Donnell] *Over 'Ere and Back Home: Random Impressions of an Earnest Soul.* Toronto: McClelland & Stewart, 1922.
Paneth, Donald. *The Encyclopedia of American Journalism.* New York: Facts on File, 1983.
Park, Julian. Ed. *The Culture of Contemporary Canada.* Ithaca, N.Y.: Cornell and Toronto: Ryerson, 1957.
Parker, George L. *The Beginnings of the Book Trade in Canada.* Toronto: University of Toronto, 1985.
Peterson, Theodore. *Magazines in the Twentieth Century.* Urbana: University of Illinois, 1964. 2nd ed.
Pitt, David G. *E. J. Pratt: The Master Years 1927-1964.* Toronto: University of Toronto, 1987.
Raddall, Thomas. *In My Time: A Memoir.* Toronto: McClelland & Stewart, 1976.
Reid, W. Stanford. Ed. *The Scottish Tradition in Canada.* Toronto: McClelland & Stewart, 1976.
Richler, Mordecai. *Stick Your Neck Out.* [*The Incredible Atuk*] New York: Simon and Schuster, 1963.
Rohmer, Richard. *E. P. Taylor: the Biography of Edward Plunket Taylor.* Toronto: McClelland & Stewart, 1978.
Rutherford, Paul. *The Making of the Canadian Media.* Toronto: McGraw-Hill Ryerson, 1978.
Sandwell, B. K. *The Diversions of Duchesstown and Other Essays.* Toronto: J. M. Dent, 1955. Introduction by Robertson Davies.
_____. *The Privacy Agent and Other Modest Proposals.* London and Toronto: J. M. Dent, 1928. Illustrated by Arthur Lismer.
Shortt, S. E. D. *The Search for an Ideal: Six Canadian Intellectuals and their Convictions in an Age of Transition, 1890-1930.* Toronto: University of Toronto, 1976.
Siegel, Arthur. Ed. *Politics and the Media in Canada.* Toronto: McGraw-Hill Ryerson, 1983.
Singer, Benjamin, ed. *Communications in Canadian Society.* Don Mills, Ont.: Addison-Wesley, 1983. 2nd ed.
Staebler, Edna. *Whatever Happened to Maggie and other people I've known.* Toronto: McClelland & Stewart, 1983. Foreword by Pierre Berton.
Stephenson, William. *Dawn of the Nation.* Toronto: McClelland & Stewart, 1977.
Stewart, Walter. Ed. *Canadian Newspapers: the Inside Story.* Edmonton: Hurtig, 1980.
Stovel-Advocate Publications. *Submission to the Royal Commission on Publications.* Nov. 25, 1960.
Stuewe, Paul. *The Storms Below: the Turbulent Life and Times of Hugh Garner.* Toronto: Lorimer, 1988.
Swanberg, W. A. *Luce and His Empire.* New York: Dell, 1973.
Taft, William H. *American magazines for the 1980s.* New York: Hastings House, 1982.
Templeton, Charles. *An Anecdotal Memoir.* Toronto: McClelland & Stewart, 1983.
Thompson, John Herd, with Allen Seeger. *Canada 1922-1939: Decades of Discord.* Toronto: McClelland & Stewart, 1985.
Time International of Canada. *Supplementary Submission to the Royal Commission on Publications.* n.d.
_____. *Interim Submission to the Royal Commission on Publications.* n.d.

Vipond, Mary. "The Image of Women in Mass Circulation Magazines in the 1920s." In Alison Prentice and Susan Mann Trofimenkoff, ed. *The Neglected Majority: Essays in Canadian Women's History*. Toronto: McClelland & Stewart, 1977, 116-24.

Waite, P. B. *Canada 1874-96: Arduous Destiny*. Toronto: McClelland & Stewart, 1971.

Wallace, Elisabeth. *Goldwin Smith: Victorian Liberal*. Toronto: University of Toronto, 1957.

Wallace, Frederick William. *Roving Fisherman: An Autobiography*. Gardenvale, Que.: Canadian Fisherman, 1955.

Weaver, Robert. *The First Five Years: A Selection from* The Tamarack Review. Toronto: Oxford, 1962. Introduction by Robert Fulford.

Weber, Ronald. Ed. *The Reporter as Artist: A Look at the New Journalism Controversy*. New York: Hastings House, 1974.

Whalley, George. Ed. *Writing in Canada: Proceedings of the Canadian Writers' Conference, Queen's University, 28-31 July, 1955*. Toronto: Macmillan, 1956. With an Introduction by F. R. Scott.

Wilson, Edmund. *O Canada: An American's Notes on Canadian Culture*. New York: Farrar, Straus and Giroux, 1965.

Wilson, Susannah Jane Foster. *The Relationship Between Mass Media Content and Social Change in Canada: An Examination of the Image of Women in Mass Circulating Canadian Magazines of 1930-1970*. Ph.D. Diss., University of Toronto, 1977.

Wolfe, Morris. *A Saturday Night Scrapbook*. Toronto: new press, 1973. Introduction by Robert Fulford

Writers Club. *Canadian Writer's Market Survey*. Ottawa: Graphic, 1931.

Young, Scott. *Gordon Sinclair: A Life...And Then Some*. Toronto: Macmillan, 1987.

Zwicker, Barry and Dick MacDonald. Ed. *The News: Inside the Canadian Media*. Ottawa: Deneau, 1982. Foreword by June Callwood.

MAGAZINE AND NEWSPAPER ARTICLES

Abley, Mark. "Another Country." *Saturday Night* (February 1986), 9-12.

Bartsch, Werner. "One big roto: more Canadian than Weekend." *Content*, September/October 1979, 3.

———————. "The Rotos: Do They Have A Future?" *Content*, January 1979), 8-13.

Batten, Jack H. "Magazine Chronicle." [Column] *Canadian Forum*, December 1961, April 1962.

Beattie, Earle. "First Issue Of Hybrid Is Healthy If Uneven/ New Maclean's Rewards Reader With Nuggets." *Content*, November 1975, 12-13.

Bennet, Doug. [News stories and features] *Masthead: The Magazine About Magazines*. October 1987-January 1989.

Bissell, C. T. "Literary Taste in Central Canada during the late nineteenth century." *Canadian Historical Review* 31 (September 1971), 237-51.

Bruce, Harry. "Good Old Back Then." *The Canadian*, 15 Nov. 1975.

Butchart, Reuben. "The Earliest Days." *Saturday Night*, 1 Jan. 1938, 12-13, 15.

Callwood, June. "Maclean's." *Canadian Forum*, December 1959, 199-200.

Calvin, D. D. "Queen's Quarterly, 1893-1943". *Queen's Quarterly* 50 (1943),117-129.

Charlesworth, Hector. "Four Decades of *Saturday Night*." *Saturday Night*, 10 Dec. 1927, 4-5.

Cheda, Sherrill. "Magazines in Canada." *Emergency Librarian*, November/December 1980, 4-6.

Chittick, Kathryn. " 'Making Literature Hum': Canadian Literary Journalism in the Twenties." *Studies in Canadian Literature* 6 (1981), 274-85.

Collison, Robert. "Spymaster." *Report on Business Magazine*, February 1969, 64-69.

Colquhoun, Arthur H. U. "After Twenty-One Years: An Appreciation Of What It Has Meant For the Canadian magazine To Attain Its Majority." *Canadian Magazine*, February 1914, 362-64.

_____. "A Century of Canadian Magazines." *Canadian Magazine* , June 1901, 141-49.

_____. "Journalism and the University." *Canadian Magazine*, July 1903, 209-19.

_____. "The Journalistic Field of 1887: Memories of the Background From Which *Saturday Night* Sprang." *Saturday Night*, 10 Dec. 1927, 2,5.

Cook, Ramsay. "A peculiarly Canadian experience." *Canadian Forum* (May-June 1970), 36-37.

Davies, Jeff. "*Axiom* Mag Proved Thesis But Died." *Content*, September-October 1978, 6.

Davies, Robertson. "My Early Literary Life." *Saturday Night*, August 1988, 32-39.

Djwa, Sandra. " *The Canadian Forum*: Literary Catalyst". *Studies in Canadian Literature* 1 (Winter 1976), 7-25.

Doyle, Kevin. ["From the Editor's Desk" editorials] *Maclean's Magazine*, 17 Oct., 24 Oct., 5 Dec., 19 Dec. 1983.

Drummond, Ian M. "Out of the thirties." *Canadian Forum*, April-May 1970, 52-53.

Enright, Michael. ["Editor's Page" editorial] *Quest*, March 1982 and September 1984.

Fetherling, Doug. "At death's door: the struggles of two political magazines." *Quill & Quire*, February 1981, 36-37.

_____.   "Divided   Empire." *Saturday Night*, December 1983, 19-26.

_____. "The end of Fulford's era." *Maclean's Magazine*, 6 July 1987, 53.

Fraser, Blair. "In the Editors' Confidence: Ralph Allen and Maclean's: An Unfinished Story." *Maclean's*, 7 May 1960, 87.

Friedson, A. "Let's pan a magazine." *Canadian Literature* 3 (Winter 1960), 86-89.

Fulford, Robert. "Saturday Night." *Canadian Forum*, June 1959, 52-53.

Gane, Margaret Drury Gane. "Do you use real people in your fiction?" *Saturday Night*, November 1975), 39-43.

Globe and Mail. 23 Oct. 1952; 27 Nov, 1971; 16 March, 26 Oct. 1972; 3 Oct., 9 Oct. 1974 [Geoffrey Stevens column on *Saturday Night* and *Time*],; 23 April 1975; 10 March [David Pyette on *Harrowsmith*], 1 April 1980; 12 May, 13 May, 15 July, 28 Dec. 1982; 13 Dec. 1983; 1 March [Barbara Moon on *Toronto Life*], 18 Aug. [John Bentley Mays on *Canadian Art*], 3 Nov. [William French on *T.O. Magazine*], 3 Nov., 12 Dec. 1984; 29 May [Joan Breckenridge on *Toronto Life* and Marian Stinson on *Canadian Living*], 11 Oct., 19 Oct. 1985 [Fraser Sutherland on small magazines]; 2 April [John Allemang on *Up Here*], 7 April, 10 April, 17 May, 30 May, 11 Nov. 1986; 5 Jan. [John Bentley Mays on *Saturday Night*], 3 Feb., 26 Feb. [Bonnie Hurowitz letter], 13 March, 10 May, 22 May, 2 June [John Partridge on *Cowsmopolitan*], 9 June, 19 June, 25 June, 9 July, 10 July, 11 July [Jim Christy "Mermaid Inn" column], 15 July, 17 July, 18 July [Mavor Moore column on *This Magazine*], 25 July [John Partridge on Conrad Black], 29 July, 10 August, 18 August, 19 August [Ben Fiber on magalogues], 20 Aug. 1987 [Stevie Cameron on Robert Fulford]; 30 Jan. 1989 [H. J. Kirchoff on *Canadian Forum*].

Guglielmin, Donna. "The Overlooked World Of House Magazines: 160-Million-Strong U.S. And Canada Circulation." *Content*, July 1976, 26.

Gzowski, Peter. "The Time the Schick Hit the Fan and Other Adventures at Maclean's." *Canadian Forum*, October 1964, 151-52.

Hawkes, Donald. "New *Maclean's* Graphics Too *Time*like: Critic." *Content*, November 1975, 13.

Hayes, David. "What's Black and White and May or May Not Be Read All Over?" *Toronto Life* (December 1987), 54-60, 108-11.

Horn, Michiel. "The Forum during the 1930's." *Canadian Forum*, May-June 1970, 38-40.

"The Inside Track: The Booming Magazine Business." *Saturday Night,* December 1977, 3-6.

Lawrence, James M. [Editorials] *Harrowsmith* January/ February 1972; May/June, July/August 1976; January/ February 1977; August 1980; March, April/May 1981; November/December 1986; May/June 1987.

Locke, Jeanne. "The Tiger of Canadian Culture is a Pussycat." *Maclean's*, April 1969, 116-18.

MacDonald, Dick. "The National Magazine Called Peter C. Newman." July 1972, *Content*, 6.

McDonald, Marci. "The Tentacles At 481 University Ave." *Content* August 1973, 2-4.

McDougall, Robert L. "The University Quarterlies." *Canadian Forum*, February 1959, 253-55.

Mackintosh, W. A. "Queen's Quarterly, 1893-1954". *Queen's Quarterly* 60 (Winter 1953) 460-61.

McNaught, Carlton. "Volume Thirty: In Retrospect. (Part I.)" *Canadian Forum*, April 1950, 4-6.

McQueen, Rod. "Thoroughly Modern Millie." *Toronto Life*, November 1986, 39,42,46.

Marshall, Doug. "Last Journey of Blair Fraser, Canadian." *Maclean's Magazine*, August 1968), 20, 35-36,39.

Mowat, J. Gordon. "The Purpose of a National Magazine." *Canadian Magazine*, June 1901, 166-67.

Muggeridge, John. "B.K. Sandwell of Saturday Night: a man of his age." *Saturday Night*, December 1972, 27-29.

Mulvihill, James. "The 'Canadian Bookman' and Literary Nationalism." *Canadian Literature* 107 (Winter 1985), 48-59.

Murray, Joan. "Graphics in the Forum 1920-1951." *Canadian Forum*, April-May 1970, 42-44.

Olive, David. "Ads vs. editorial: have new lines been drawn?" *Quill & Quire*, September 1984, 71-73.

"Our Twenty-First Year". *Canadian Forum*, April 1941, 5-7.

Patriarche, Valance. "In Our Early Days." *Saturday Night*, 11 Dec. 1937, 1.

Pelrine, Eleanor Wright. "Jane Gale, editor of *Homemaker's* magazine". *Content* (August-September 1983, 14.

Reid, Robert and Felicity Reid. "Book jackets and covers, book illustration and typography, magazine covers, editorial art, house organs, photography." *Canadian Art* 17 (May 1960,148-65.

Sandwell, B. K. "Magazine Problems." *Saturday Night,* 8 April 1939, 9.

_____."National Periodicals." *Saturday Night* , 5 June, 1951, 7.

_____. "Two Liberties." *Saturday Night* (Dec. 30, 1939), 6

_____. "Two Quarter Centuries and Their Significance." *Saturday Night,* 1 Jan. 1938, 1.

Silburt, Dave. "*Goodwins* just what is this newest alternative magazine an alternative to?" *Content*, August-September 1983, 28.

Stewart, George. "Literary Reminiscences." *Canadian Magazine* , June 1901, 163-66.

Sutherland, Fraser. ["Small Magazines" column] *Quill & Quire*, January, February, March, May, June, July, November, December 1974, January, February, March 1975.

Toronto Star. 21 April 1955; 3 Jan., 6 Nov. 1962; 24 Feb. 1967; 1 Nov. 1969; 29 April 1970, 30 Dec. 1971 [Margaret Daly on Michael de Pencier]; 26 May 1972 [Nicholas Steed letter]; 26 Nov. 1977; 18 June [Frank Jones on *Harrowsmith*]; 16 Sept. 1978; 2 Jan., 10 Jan. 1981; 15 July 1982; 13 Jan., 15 March 1983; 22 Aug. 1984 [Ken Adachi on *Canadian Art*]; 16 Aug. 1986 [Joan Irwin column on Telemedia]; 13 March, 3

July, 5 July 1987 [Leslie Scrivener on Robert Fulford].

Toronto Telegram. 28 Dec. 1961 [Dorothy Howarth on *Exchange, Canada Month,* and *The Canadian*]; 23 July 1965 [Hugh Garner on *Liberty*]; 31 Aug. 1968 [Marq de Villiers' survey of magazines].

Underhill, Frank H. "The first generation." *Canadian Forum,* April-May 1970, 32-33.

Verzuh, Ron. [Magazines column] *Content* May/June 1985; March/April, May/June, July/August, November/December 1986; March/April 1987.

Vipond, Mary. "Canadian Nationalism and the Plight of Canadian Magazines in the 1920s." *Canadian Historical Review,* LVIII (1977), 43-63.

Wallace, W. S. " 'The Bystander' and Canadian Journalism." *Canadian Magazine,* October 1910, 553-58.

Watt, F. W. "Climate of Unrest: Periodicals in the Twenties and Thirties." *Canadian Literature* 12 (Spring 1962) 15-27.

Willison, Lady. "On Adelaide Street." *Saturday Night,* 1 Jan. 1938, 1.

Wilson, Milton. "Anniversary Interval." *Canadian Forum* April 1980, 19.

Winks, Robin W. "Canadian Magazines." *Canadian Literature,* 108 (Spring 1986), 94-102.

Wolfe, Morris. "Empire in print: Maclean-Hunter." *Canadian Forum,* September 1973, 20-26.

INDEX